Revealed sets out to crush any notion that the Bible is a safe, inspirational read. Instead the artwork here, historic and contemporary, takes a warts-and-all approach to even the most troubling passages, trading well-meaning elision for unvarnished truth. If you gaze deeper, *Revealed* springs another surprise, too: it debunks the equally prevalent misconception that a sacred anthology ages in the making can offer no single, unifying message. To see that message, however, might just require a second look at verses that make the pious avert their eyes.

—J. MARK BERTRAND NOVELIST, SPEAKER, AND FOUNDER OF THE BIBLE DESIGN BLOG

Of all the stories the biblical authors could have written down for posterity, *Revealed* homes in on this deleterious collection. These provocative, often-shocking, and relentlessly pervasive stories were not only included in Scripture, but are integral to understanding its message. *Revealed* not only forces us to look again at those stories, but artfully asks us to meditate on them, engaging both our moral and literary imagination.

—ANDREW JOHNSON AUTHOR OF *BIBLICAL KNOWING: A SCRIPTURAL EPISTEMOLOGY OF ERROR*

Revealed reminds us that verbal metaphor does not always translate smoothly into visual form. Awkward or not however, visual form does grab our attention and generates a more graphic sense of what words may be saying. So an illustrated text may come alive for us in fresh ways. What comes to life in *Revealed* is that the Bible is a collection of stories about human foibles and failure rather than triumph. The surprising images in this illustrated Bible remind us once again that we are saved by Grace.

—JOEL SHEESLEY PROFESSOR OF ART AT WHEATON COLLEGE

If your Bible re___ of simply "going through the motions," this is the book for you! Eye-opening woodcuts, lithographs and etchings accompany short Scripture readings, along with evocative blurbs which, for all their brevity, bear much theological and aesthetic wisdom. This one really is for grown-ups.

—JOSEPH W. SMITH III AUTHOR OF *SEX AND VIOLENCE IN THE BIBLE*

Revealed collects a smart range of beautiful printmaking approaches both old and new to illustrate some of the Bible's more unique and uncomfortable moments—opening up a fascinating new way to read a familiar text.

—BRENTON GOOD PROFESSOR OF ART AT MESSIAH COLLEGE

Revealed is a poignant reminder that worldly pessimism isn't dark enough, nor is worldly optimism bright enough. The works of art herein are worthy of thorough, meditative study. You will emerge with a deeper sense of God's willingness to engage the malignancy of the fall.

—WILLIAM EDGAR PROFESSOR OF APOLOGETICS AT WESTMINSTER THEOLOGICAL SEMINARY

In *Revealed: A Storybook Bible for Grownups* difficult passages from scripture—especially the stories "nice" people find offensive—are paired with the art of printmakers and an explanation of what is conveyed by each image. Our imaginations are enlivened as we are led from the shocking murder in the First Family to the terrifying holiness of God. *Revealed* reminds us that God does not blink or evade the true story of human violence and injustice, but neither does he turn from our intimate acts of love.

—MARGIE HAACK AUTHOR OF *THE EXACT PLACE*

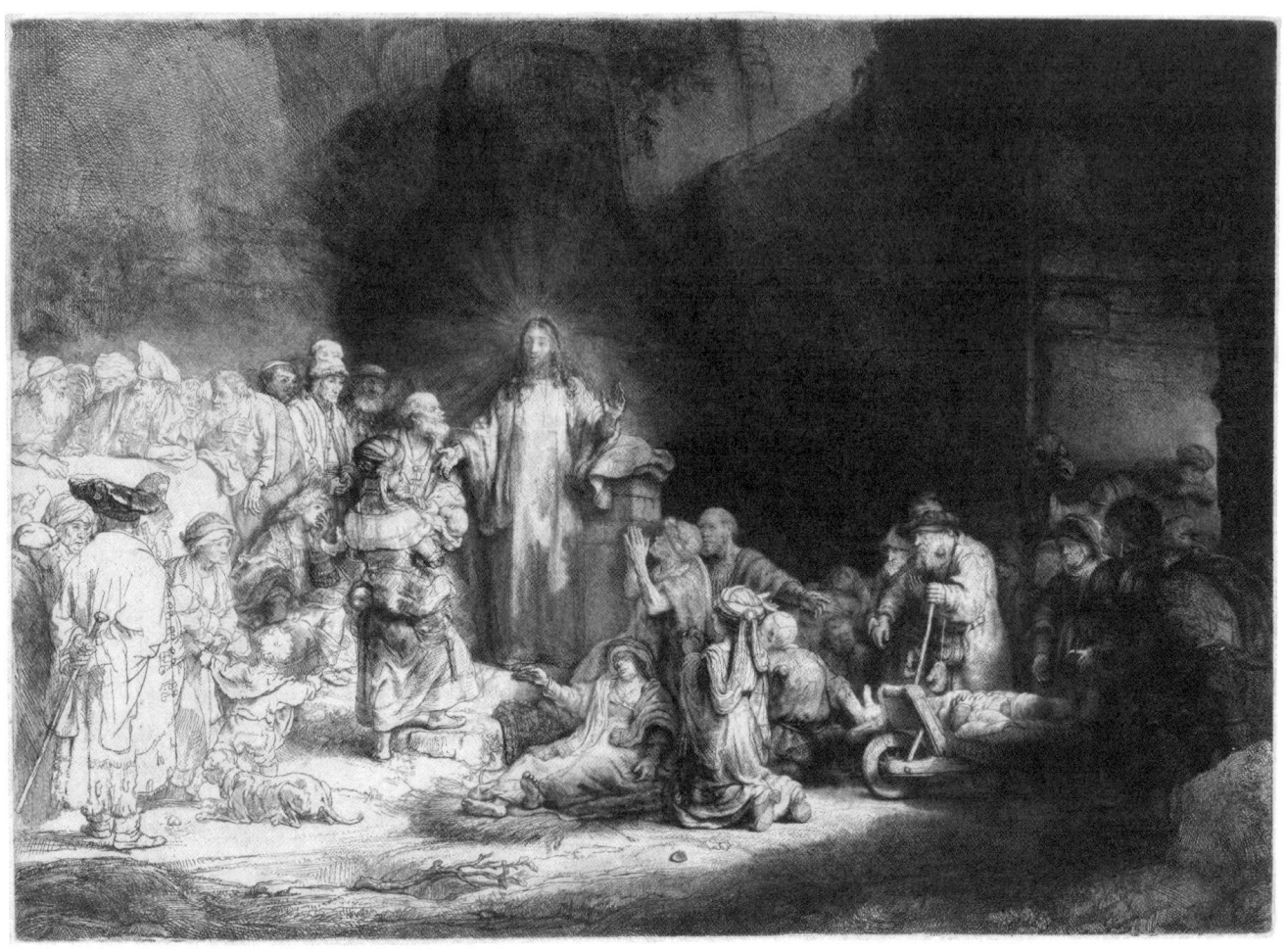

Christ Preaching (The Hundred Guilder Print)
REMBRANDT VAN RIJN | ETCHING

Adam Takes the Fruit/Eve Gives the Fruit (FRONT COVER)
EDWARD KNIPPERS | LINOCUT

The Fall of Man (INSIDE FRONT COVER)
ALBRECHT DÜRER | WOODCUT

Noli Me Tangere (INSIDE BACK COVER)
ALBRECHT DÜRER | WOODCUT

The Babylonian Whore (BACK COVER)
ALBRECHT DÜRER | WOODCUT

REVEALED

A STORYBOOK BIBLE FOR GROWN-UPS

NED BUSTARD

*For Denise —
May this book
encourage you
as you make for
GLORY & for BEAUTY!
—Ned
Bustard*

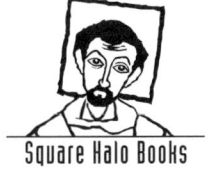

Square Halo Books

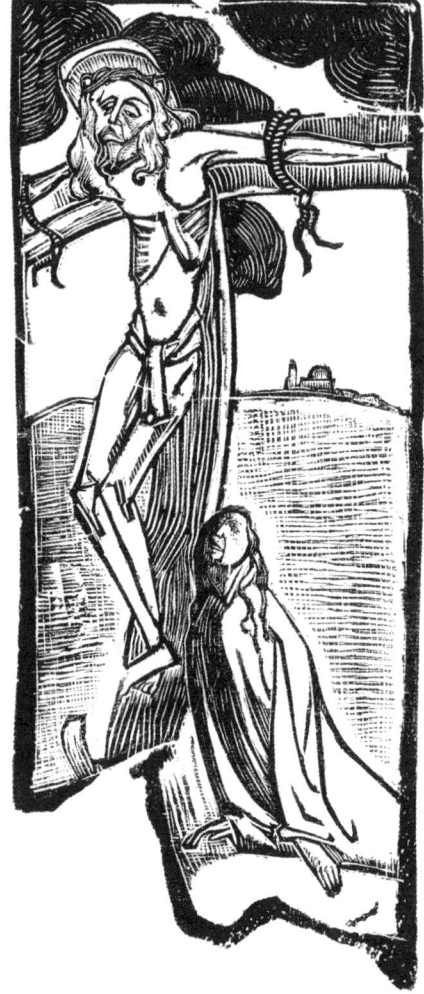

CRUCIFIXION | ÉMILE BERNARD

This book is dedicated to my brothers,
Benjamin James and William David.

Tolle Lege.

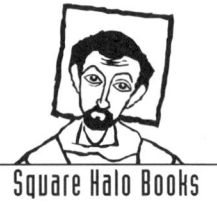

Square Halo Books

©2015 Square Halo Books, Inc.
P.O. Box 18954
Baltimore, MD 21206
www.SquareHaloBooks.com

Scripture quotations are from The Holy Bible, English Standard Version® (ESV ®), copyright ©2001 by Crossway, a publishing ministry of Good News Publishers. Used by permission. All rights reserved.

ISBN 978-1-941106-03-7
Library of Congress Control Number: 2015955596
All rights reserved. No part of this book may be reproduced without permission from the publisher, except by a reviewer who may quote brief passages in a review; nor may any part of this book be reproduced, stored in a retrieval system or transmitted in any form by any means (electronic, mechanical, photocopying, recorded or other), without permission from the publisher.

Contents

Title	Author	Page
NOT SUITABLE FOR CHILDREN	NED BUSTARD	7
THE CREATION OF EVE	ANONYMOUS	16
TWO BECOME ONE FLESH	DUVET	18
THE FALL	KNIPPERS	20
THE PROTOEVANGELIUM	BUTLER	22
THE FIRST MURDER	KNIPPERS	24
ENOCH WALKED WITH GOD	BEERHORST	26
THE FLOOD	CLARK AND BUSTARD	28
THE DRUNKENESS OF NOAH	BUSTARD*	30
GOD'S COVENANT WITH ABRAM	CLARK*	32
SODOM AND GOMORRAH	KNIPPERS	34
THE DAUGHTERS OF LOT	BUTLER*	36
THE BINDING	REMBRANDT	38
THE DECEPTION OF ISAAC	FORTE*	40
THE DREAM AT BETHEL	KNIPPERS	42
POTIPHAR'S WIFE TEMPTS JOSEPH	KNIPPERS	44
INTERPRETATION OF DREAMS	FORTE*	46
MOSES MURDERS	CLARK*	48
THE PLAGUES	ANONYMOUS	50
THE PASSOVER	BRIMBERRY*	52
AN ARMY IS DESTROYED	FORTE*	54
THE MOUNTAIN OF GOD	KNIPPERS	56
THE LORD FEEDS HIS PEOPLE	PRINCE	58
FOR GLORY AND FOR BEAUTY	BUSTARD*	60
THE BRONZE SERPENT	BUTLER*	62
ZIMRI AND COZBI	BUSTARD*	64
RAHAB	BUSTARD*	66
GENOCIDE	HALLA*	68
THE LEFT-HANDED HERO	STANDER*	70
THE DEATH OF SISERA	FORTE*	72
THE MAIL-ORDER BRIDE	BUSTARD*	74
SAMSON AND DELILAH	BUSTARD*	76
THE THRESHING FLOOR	BUSTARD*	78
WHY DO YOU WEEP?	CROSS*	80
THE BATTLE IS THE LORD'S	KNIPPERS	82
DAVID AND BATHSHEBA	BUSTARD*	84
THE LUST OF AMNON	CROSS*	86
THE MOCKERY OF BAAL	JOURDAN*	88
ELIJAH STANDS BEFORE THE LORD	SORENSEN*	90
ELIJAH AND THE WHIRLWIND	KNIPPERS	92
THE DEATH OF JEZEBEL	CROSS*	94
CONFRONTING SIN	BUSTARD*	96
ONE NIGHT WITH THE KING	BUSTARD*	98
BEHEMOTH AND LEVIATHAN	BLAKE	100
SONGS OF DESPAIR	YINGST	102
THE WIFE OF YOUR YOUTH	KNIPPERS	104
MADNESS IN THEIR HEARTS	SMITH*	106
IN THE GARDEN OF LOVE	BUTLER*	108
UNCLEAN LIPS	FORTE*	110
HE HAS BORNE OUR GRIEFS	BUSTARD	112
SEEK THE WELFARE OF THE CITY	BEERHORST	114
THE FAITHFULNESS OF GOD	PRINCE	116
A VISION OF HEAVEN	BUTLER	118
OHOLAH AND OHOLIBAH	VAN STRATEN	120
DRY BONES	JOURDAN*	122
THE FIERY FURNACE	BUSTARD*	124
DANIEL IN THE LIONS' DEN	BUSTARD*	126
THE CRAZY KING	CLARK*	128
THE REDEMPTION OF GOMER	BUSTARD	130
THE LOCUST YEARS	CLARK*	132
IN THE BELLY OF THE FISH	YINGST	134
THE COMING SHEPHERD	BUTLER*	136
YET I WILL REJOICE	BUSTARD*	138
THE DAY OF THE LORD	DÜRER	140
THE BIRTH OF JOHN FORETOLD	CLARK*	142
THE BIRTH OF JOHN FORETOLD	CLARK*	144
THE ANGEL VISITS MARY	MARC	146
THE NATIVITY	OVERVOORDE	148
FLIGHT INTO EGYPT	BUTLER	150
MASSACRE OF THE INNOCENTS	KNIPPERS	152
THE BAPTISM OF CHRIST	BUSTARD*	154
THE TEMPTATION OF CHRIST	CLARK*	156

Contents

THE WEDDING AT CANA CROSS*	158	THE CRUCIFIXION GILL	194	FREEDOM IN CHRIST BUSTARD*	230
THE WOMAN AT THE WELL JOURDAN*	160	THE DESCENT FROM THE CROSS REMBRANDT	196	THE FRUIT OF THE SPIRIT YINGST	232
FROM DEATH TO LIFE REMBRANDT	162	THE ENTOMBMENT OF CHRIST REMBRANDT	198	BUT GOD ANONYMOUS	234
THE SOWER BUSTARD	164	THE RESURRECTION OF CHRIST KNIPPERS	200	THE HUMILITY OF CHRIST BUSTARD*	236
SALOME BUSTARD*	166	JESUS APPEARS TO MARY BUSTARD*	202	LIFE IN CHRIST GASTON	238
FEEDING THE MULTITUDE HAWKINS*	168	ROAD TO EMMAUS ADAMS	204	THE MAN OF LAWLESSNESS SMITH*	240
THE FIRES OF HELL ANONYMOUS	170	THOMAS BELIEVES DÜRER	206	PRAYER ... AND THE FALL BUTLER	242
THE GOOD SAMARITAN KNIPPERS	172	THE RESTORATION OF PETER HALLA*	208	THE BLOOD OF CHRIST VAN STRATEN	244
THE PRODIGAL SON KOELLE	174	THE ASCENSION OF CHRIST FORTE*	210	LIVE HOLY LIVES FORTE	246
THE RAISING OF LAZARUS LINDHOLM*	176	PENTECOST OVERVOORDE	212	SALVATION REVEALED KNIPPERS	248
THE TRIUMPHAL ENTRY JOURDAN*	178	PETER'S SERMON STANDER*	214	THE THREE WHO TESTIFY GILL	250
CLEANSING THE TEMPLE DÜRER	180	ANANIAS AND SAPPHIRA BLOOM*	216	DESTRUCTION OF UNBELIEVERS BUTLER*	252
KILLING THE MASTER'S SON ANONYMOUS	182	THE CHURCH'S FIRST MARTYR KNIPPERS	218	PLAGUES AND UNREPENTANCE DÜRER	254
THE LAST SUPPER BUTLER*	184	DEAD TO SIN, ALIVE TO GOD JOHNSON	220	THE FALL OF BABYLON GILL	256
THE GARDEN OF GETHSEMANE BARLACH	186	NO CONDEMNATION BUSTARD	222	NEW JERUSALEM BUSTARD*	258
JUDAS' KISS DÜRER	188	THE BODY IS FOR THE LORD BUSTARD*	224	ARTIST BIOS	260
PILATE AND CHRIST KNIPPERS	190	GLORIFY GOD IN YOUR BODY PRINCE	226		
SIMON OF CYRENE CORINTH	192	RESURRECTION OF THE BODY CLARK	228	*WORKS MADE SPECIFICALLY FOR THIS BOOK	

Not Suitable for Children

NED BUSTARD

"Is that really in the Bible?"

With the proofs of this book on his lap, my friend stared at me, incredulous. Then he glanced down at the image again, the body of a woman cut into twelve pieces. He shook his head. There was no way that this could be in the Bible. It was too horrific, too real, more like a story from today's headlines than an event from an ancient volume of inspirational literature. And yet there was the whole harrowing episode from the book of Judges, recounted in black and white. This scene was from God's sacred book—and it was not the only one of its kind.

You can grow up in church, like my friend did, in churches that claim fidelity to the full counsel of Scripture, and never discover what is really in the Bible. We skip over and skirt around the shocking bits or we explain them away. And we tell ourselves this whitewashing is for the best, all in a good cause. We keep the difficult passages secret to prevent others from stumbling. We keep them hidden because they are not suitable for children.

This book exists so that those secrets can be revealed.

Some of the worst choices are made with the best of intentions. Many of the stories illustrated in *Revealed* are typically suppressed by people who think they're doing God a favor. This content reflects poorly, they feel, on Holy Writ. To bring them up at all—let alone to call attention to them and represent them artistically—opens you up to charges of impiety and disrespect.

The human authors of Scripture had no such qualms. They told the unvarnished, unexpurgated story of God's dealing with humanity. And their choices are born out by the way this book has been received by readers. Far from diminishing their respect for the Bible, the book has enhanced it. Paradoxically, the people we have been concealing the hard passages from—creating the false impression that the Bible doesn't speak to the world as it really is—come away impressed with the searing honesty of revealed Scripture.

STORYBOOK SCRIPTURE

Sometimes the shocks are hidden in plain sight. Every child knows the story of Noah's Ark, that floating zoo whose two-by-two menagerie was curated by the bearded, smiling saint. But the roly-poly old man on his plump wooden boat is only part of the

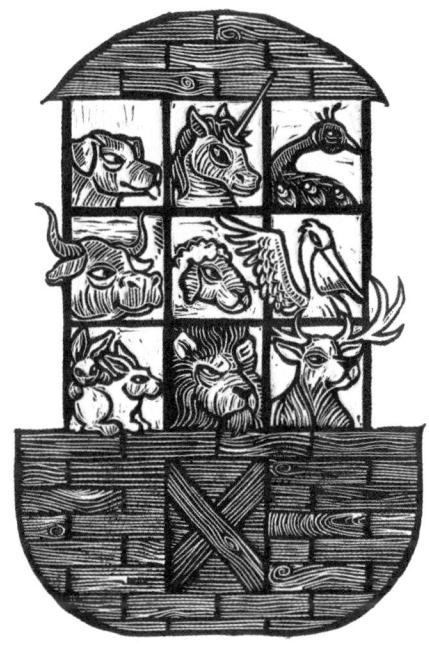

IN CHRIST
NED BUSTARD

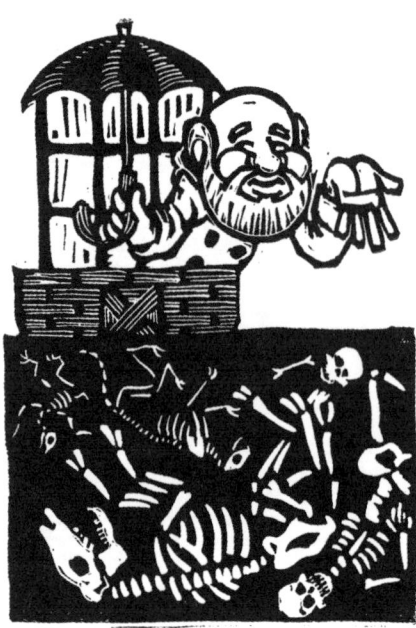

DAY 41
NED BUSTARD

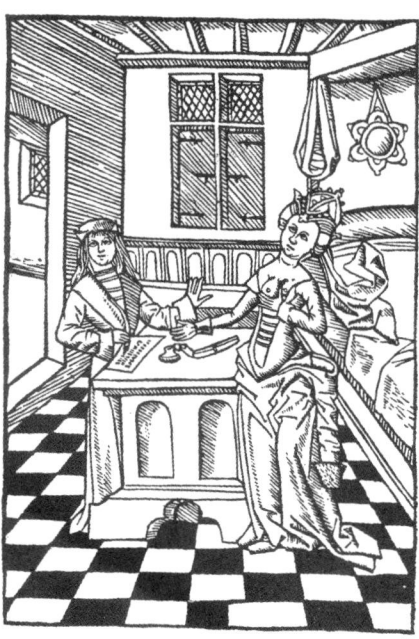

POTIPHAR'S WIFE
UNKNOWN

story. The biblical account of the Flood paints a horrific picture of drowning and destruction. What is lost when we race too quickly to the rainbow, ignoring the millions swept away in a tidal wave of wrath?

Or what is lost when we skip from the parting of the Red Sea straight into Sinai without a thought for the myriad Egyptians swallowed by death?

What is lost when we omit the story of Korah in Numbers 16, buried alive with his whole family, or ignore the fact that, to secure the Promised Land, God's people undertake at his command what would today be classified as genocide?

In an earlier age, children's stories were surprisingly dark (for example, the Grimms' fairytales come to mind). However, that is no longer the fashion. When we tell our children stories from the Bible, we slant them toward our more wholesome tastes.

If we do not elide the violence, we certainly steer clear of the sex. In the Bible, Lot is raped by his daughters. Tamar turns a trick with her father-in-law. Joseph runs from the boss's wife's attempts at seduction. Samson trades his strength for Delilah's bed, and David—the "man after God's own heart"—fathers a child with another man's wife, then murders the husband to cover up his adultery. And yet a surprising number of people who consider themselves familiar with the Bible have no idea about any of this. Or if they do, they try to keep quiet about it.

Parts of the Bible seem unsuitable for children, so we tell them versions of the story more appropriate to their age. *The Children's Bible* (Philadelphia, 1763) was the first Bible for children printed in America, a collection of simplified stories aimed at entertaining readers and giving them a basic familiarity with the popular tales of Scripture. Most Bibles for young readers follow this format, and serve a useful purpose. After all, no one would read *Moby-Dick* in the nursery when there's *Make Way for Ducklings*. By introducing children to the events and people found in Scripture, these story Bibles plant seeds of understanding that can be later watered—and they provide a geographical and historical context for biblical events. The story Bible is like a tricycle: first master this, and then move on to greater things.

The rub with storybook Bibles is that many do not move beyond them. Their understanding of Christianity remains a simplistic, scandal-free, childish religion. Such people are the metaphorical equivalent of a three-hundred-pound, tattooed biker cruising the highways on the same tricycle he rode in kindergarten. These adults, confronting the harshness of a world that pulls no punches, and remembering the soft, uplifting Bible of their youth, imagine that the ancient book has nothing to say to the mature. The reality is quite different.

Revealed is intended to provoke surprise, even shock—not for their own sake, but to awaken readers to the depth and breadth of the Bible. The contemporary belief that the Bible is outdated and irrelevant is best challenged by the Bible itself. Yes, this is an ancient book full of alien cultures, customs, and histories. But it is also a book about people. Ordinary people who are not only spiritual beings, but also greedy, needy, hateful, hopeful, selfish, and sexual.

By reading only the "safe" parts of the Bible, we limit the imagination and remove the mystery of following God. What we are left with is an irrelevant, felt-board faith full of superficial spirituality and bathrobed disciples following a blue-eyed, blond savior. The unexpurgated Bible is an earthy, disturbing, and gloriously impossible account of all of life that must be embraced in its fullness, never filtered down to safe, pretty quotes worthy of a Hallmark greeting card. As printmaker Barry Moser writes, "The Bible . . . is full of sound and fury, not saccharine fluff.

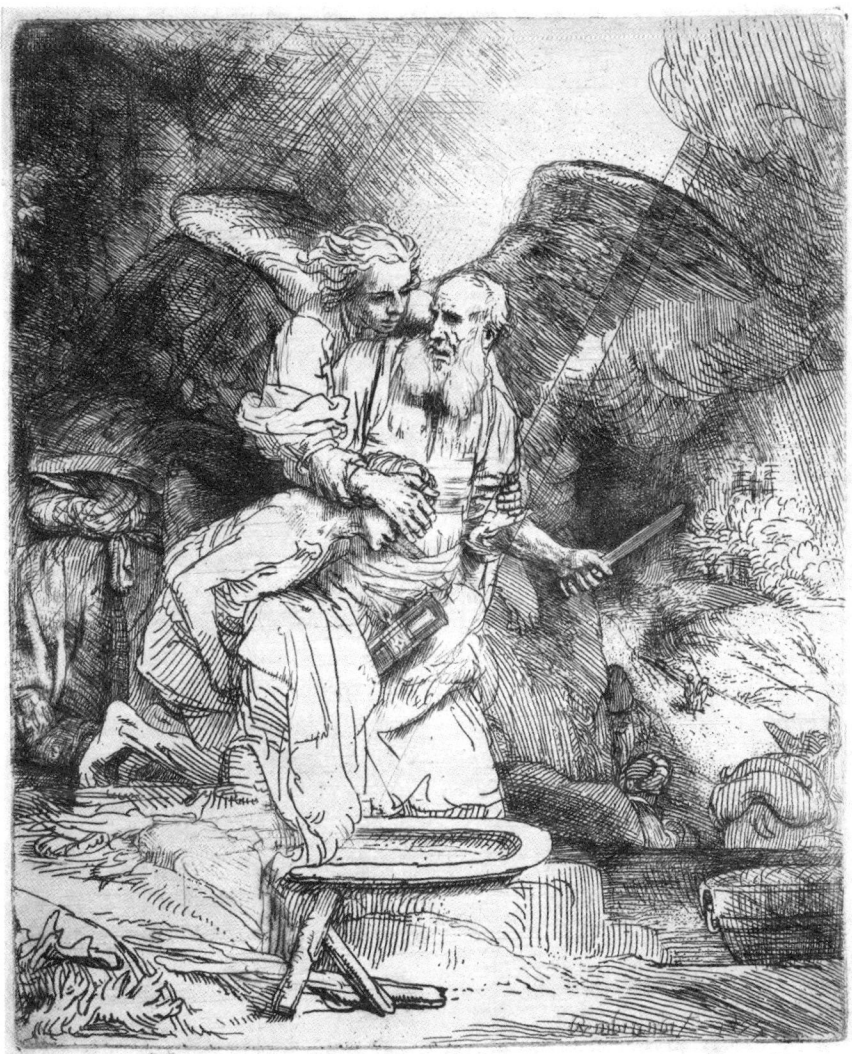

SACRIFICE OF ISAAC
REMBRANDT HARMENSZOON VAN RIJN

Full of a fire and ferocity that share at least equal time with love and redemption. And reading it we ought not avert our eyes, because by not averting our eyes we come more painfully face to face with the truth and goodness that thrives amidst the fierceness."

Let's face it. The world is full of the good and the beautiful —but also the evil and the ugly.

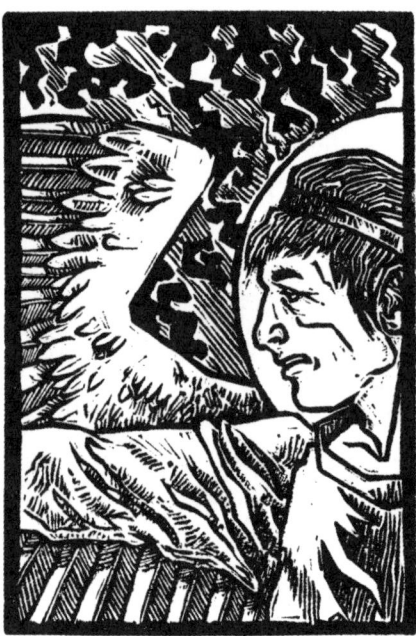
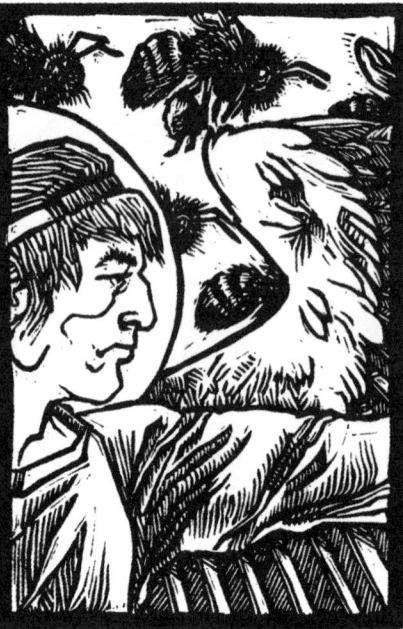

THE INTERTESTAMENTAL ANGEL
MATTHEW L. CLARK

Most people who consider the Bible irrelevant are simply unaware that it depicts the entire spectrum of human existence, and speaks to it. To take the Bible on its own terms, we must view it as a unified story, without omitting the disturbing parts. Otherwise we lose the richness of this interwoven tapestry, where every strand (whether we realize it or not) is integral to the other.

THE SHAPE OF THE STORY
Because the Bible as we know it is actually a library of texts, a collection of sixty-six different books written over the course of a thousand years or more by a wide range of human authors, containing genres of literature as diverse as law, history, wisdom, poetry, letters, and end-of-the-world prophecies, it may sound surprising that this book of books contains a single, overarching narrative.

But it does. And understanding the shape of that overarching story helps illuminate why an understanding of all Scripture—including the awkward or even offensive parts—good for us.

The Bible tells one epic story, most of it taken up with evil, conflict, and sorrow. This drama is what makes it such a good story. The story is filled with hope and despair, heroes and villains—and like the best stories, the good guys win in the end. That victory is what makes the happy ending so . . . happy.

Steve Garber describes the Bible as "the Story that makes sense of all stories," meaning that its historical narrative of Creation, Fall, Redemption, and Consummation encompasses everything that has been, everything that is, and everything still to come:

CREATION In the beginning everything that is was made, and everything was made good. At Creation, the earth was a place of peace where humans could flourish and enjoy both the Creator and one another forever.

FALL Then there was the Fall, where Adam, acting as the head of the human race, broke our relationship with God. The repercussions of that failure rippled out though all of time and space. Death—physical and spiritual—became the norm.

REDEMPTION But God did not give up on the broken world. In his goodness and mercy, he sent Christ to restore what was lost. In the birth, life, death, and resurrection of Jesus Christ rests the salvation of the world.

CONSUMMATION The story climaxes when the whole world is renewed, Jesus returns to Earth, and evil is purged from the universe once and for all.

"To read the Bible the way it is written," Calvin Seerveld says, "you have to give up your own agenda, you have to dwell in the text and see the whole woven tapestry of the bible from Genesis to Revelation. When you do, you will find that God speaks to you and with you." It is reading the Bible in this fashion, as one unified whole, that the beauty and power of God's Word begins to be revealed.

ART SHAPES FAITH

God himself calls for the making of art, as when, in the book of Exodus, he gives elaborate instructions concerning the artwork for the Tabernacle and the Temple. It should come as no surprise, then, that from the beginning Christianity has been a rooted, earthy, and representational religion. From drawings of the Good Shepherd in the catacombs to the Sistine Chapel's magnificent *Last Judgement,* Christianity has offered up to the hungry eyes of the faithful a visual feast.

Art bears witness to the faith, and makes it more accessible. With this power comes responsibility. The art of sculpting the Golden Calf shaped the faith of the Israelites in a negative way

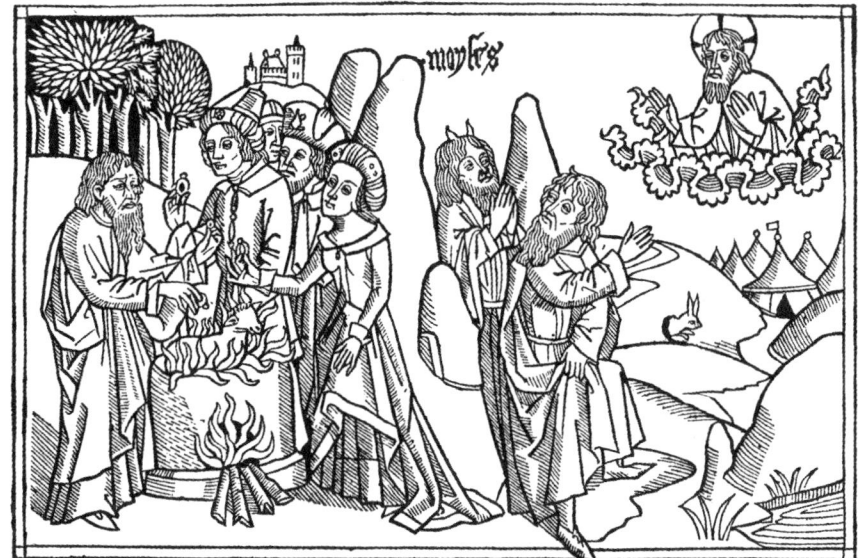

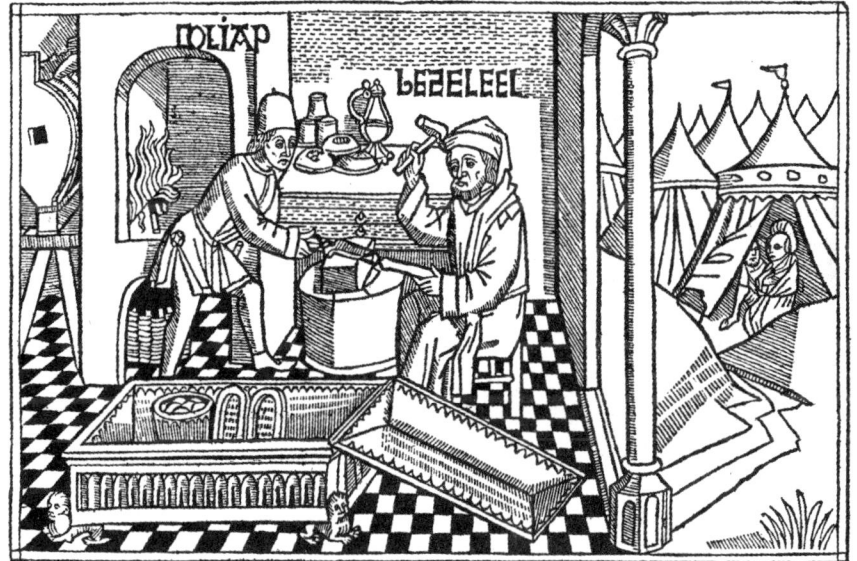

MAKING THE GOLDEN CALF
MAKING THE ARK OF THE COVENANT
UNKNOWN

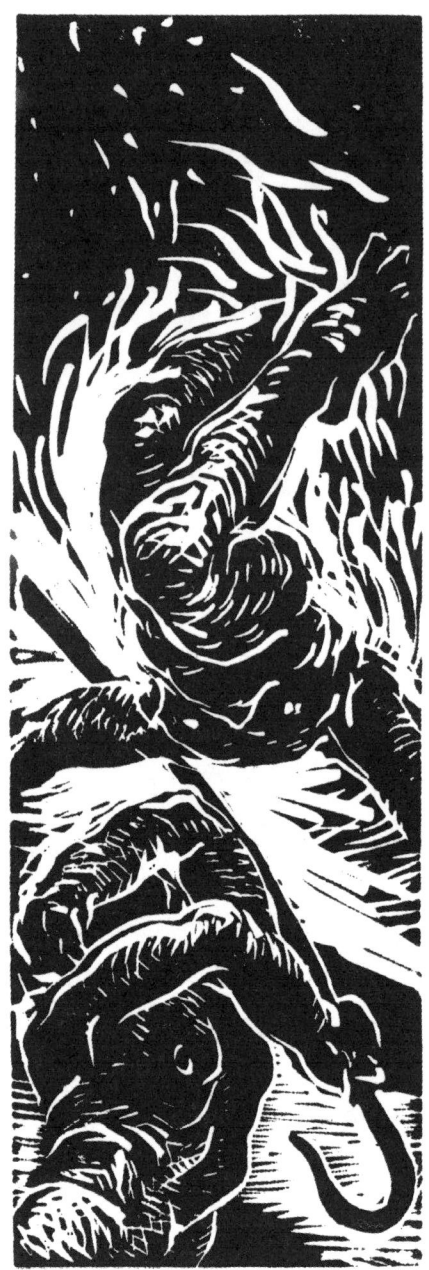

ANGEL AND SHEPHERD
EDWARD KNIPPERS

while the sculpting of the cherubim for the Ark of the Covenant shaped the faith of the Israelites in a positive way. The church needs to make good, theologically rich art, because—for good or for ill—art teaches people how to interpret the Bible. Was Adam with Eve when the Serpent deceived her? Was David a young boy or a grown man when he fought Goliath? How many wise men visited Jesus? All of these questions have been impacted by art over the centuries, and the answers have colored our readings of the texts.

QUESTIONABLE ART

Revealed visually interprets stories from the entirety of the Bible, beginning with Creation as imagined by a fifteenth-century German artist. The work that follows, both historic and contemporary, falls under the general heading of printmaking, an art form particularly well suited to accompany the printed word.

The history of printmaking in Western art includes depictions of the Trinity from the very beginning as demostrated by the woodcut on page 21. Some Christians (particularly in the Reformed tradition) may take issue with this book for that reason. As the Heidelberg Catechism says in reference to the Second Commandment, "God neither can nor may be visibly represented in any way. As for creatures, though they may be visibly represented, yet God forbids us to make or have any likeness of them in order to worship them or serve God by them." The Israelites who first received the Law from Moses at Sinai had been immersed in idol worship of deities who took all manner of animal and hybrid human forms. Reducing God to the form of, say, a golden calf, was not an unimaginable potential pitfall for the people. But in *Knowing God* J. I. Packer writes that, for Christians, the commandment means "that we are not to make use of visual or pictorial representation of the triune God, or of any person of the Trinity, for the purpose of Christian worship." It is the improper use of art in worship not art itself that God is addressing. As Francis Schaeffer reminds his readers in *Art and the Bible*, "It is important to note that on Mount Sinai God *simultaneously* gave the Ten Commandments and commanded Moses to fashion a tabernacle in a way which would involve almost every form of representational art."

Theologian, hymn-writer, and priest John of Damascus (c. 675—750) saw the strongest case for art depicting God in the Incarnation. In Bethlehem the invisible God took on form and became visible. John wrote, "Therefore, I am emboldened to depict the invisible God, not as invisible, but as he became visible for our sake, by participation in flesh and blood. I do not depict the invisible divinity, but I depict God made visible in the flesh."

Most people will see the advantages of making the faith accessible through art, and applaud the beautiful engravings of Rembrandt and the theologically dense woodcuts of Overvoorde. They may question, however, this volume's emphasis on the more R-rated parts of the Bible, suspecting a violation of the principle articulated in Philippians 4:8: "[w]hatever is true, whatever is honorable, whatever is just, whatever is pure, whatever is lovely, whatever is commendable, if there is any excellence, if there is anything worthy of praise, think about these things." Don't the shockingly sexy and violent parts of the Bible fall short of this standard? How can we justify such salacious reading material?

The answer is that, not only are Christians allowed to focus on the unmentionables of the Bible, but to be truly faithful to God's Word, the violence and sex must not be glossed over. Scripture does not flinch when confronted with evil or beauty. Every sphere of life is addressed by God's Word, including the unpresentable parts. God is God over mountains and valleys, joys and sorrows, beautiful births and violent deaths, the marriage bed and the dark alley. If we don't depict the "naughty bits," the great Story of the Bible becomes bland and weak. It loses not only its power but also its veracity, forced to abide in a half life of half truths.

Christ came to save the lost . . . not the misplaced. A book that does not address the deep depravities and gut-wrenching sorrows of the human condition is no good to any of us, believer or unbeliever alike.

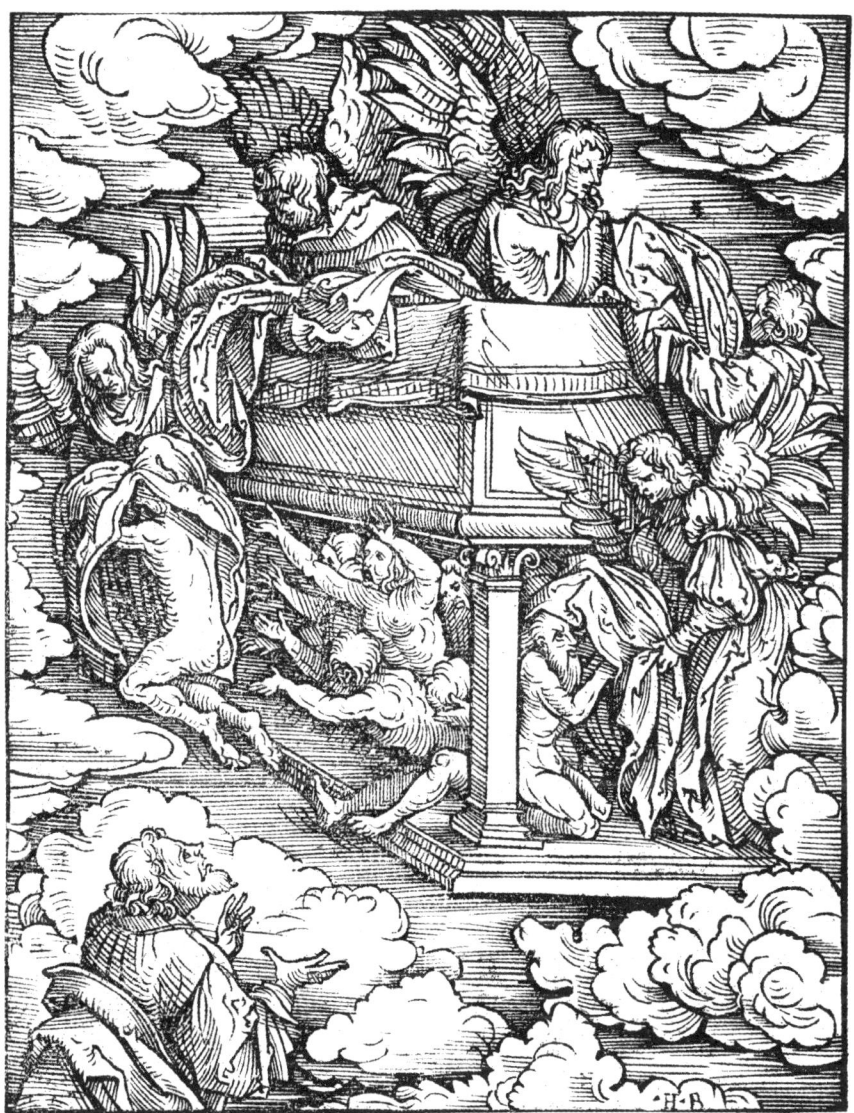

THE CLOTHING OF THE ELECT
HANS BURGKMAIR

CFRC (Creation, Fall, Redemption, and Consummation)
MATTHEW L. CLARK AND NED BUSTARD | LINOCUT

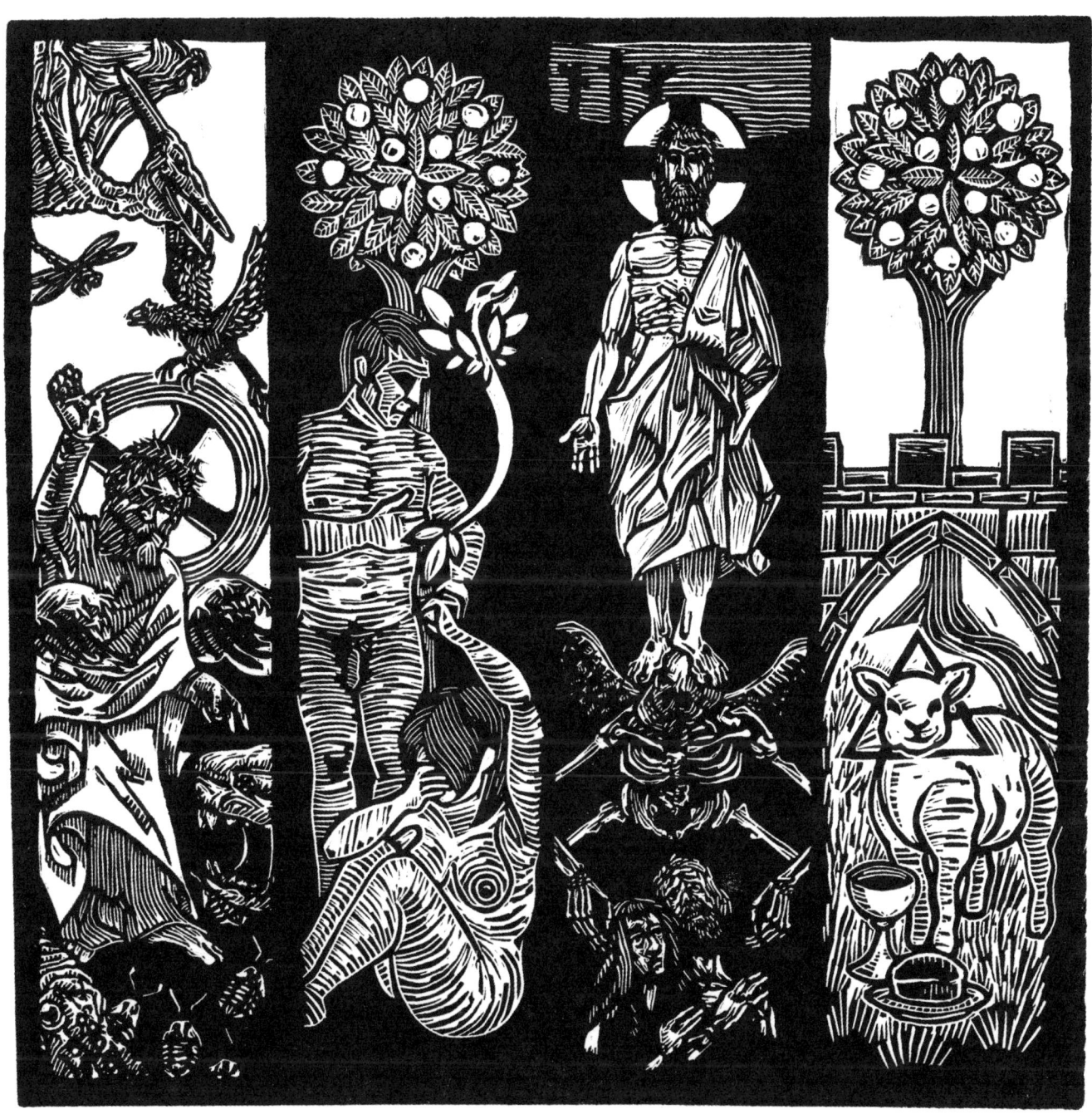

Genesis 2:15–21

THE CREATION OF EVE

The LORD God took the man and put him in the garden of Eden to work it and keep it. And the LORD God commanded the man, saying, "You may surely eat of every tree of the garden, but of the tree of the knowledge of good and evil you shall not eat, for in the day that you eat of it you shall surely die."

   Then the LORD God said, "It is not good that the man should be alone; I will make him a helper fit for him." Now out of the ground the LORD God had formed every beast of the field and every bird of the heavens and brought them to the man to see what he would call them. And whatever the man called every living creature, that was its name. The man gave names to all livestock and to the birds of the heavens and to every beast of the field. But for Adam there was not found a helper fit for him. So the LORD God caused a deep sleep to fall upon the man, and while he slept took one of his ribs and closed up its place with flesh.

Birth of Eve

ANONYMOUS | WOODCUT

This print is from the Cologne Bible. There were two Bibles printed at Cologne between 1478 and 1480. The illustrations in these Bibles served as patterns for many illustrations in later German, Italian, French, Dutch, and English Bibles. In this woodcut God is surrounded by the heavenly hosts as he breathes life into all of Creation—including unicorns and mermaids! In the center of the print God is shown helping Eve to stand, taking her from the rib of Adam. The woman was made to be a helper to the man in carrying out the calling of working in and caring for the Earth. "Helper" in the original Hebrew is the word *ezer*—a strong word used twenty-one times in the Old Testament: twice in the Creation account, three times as a military term, and sixteen times in reference to God himself.

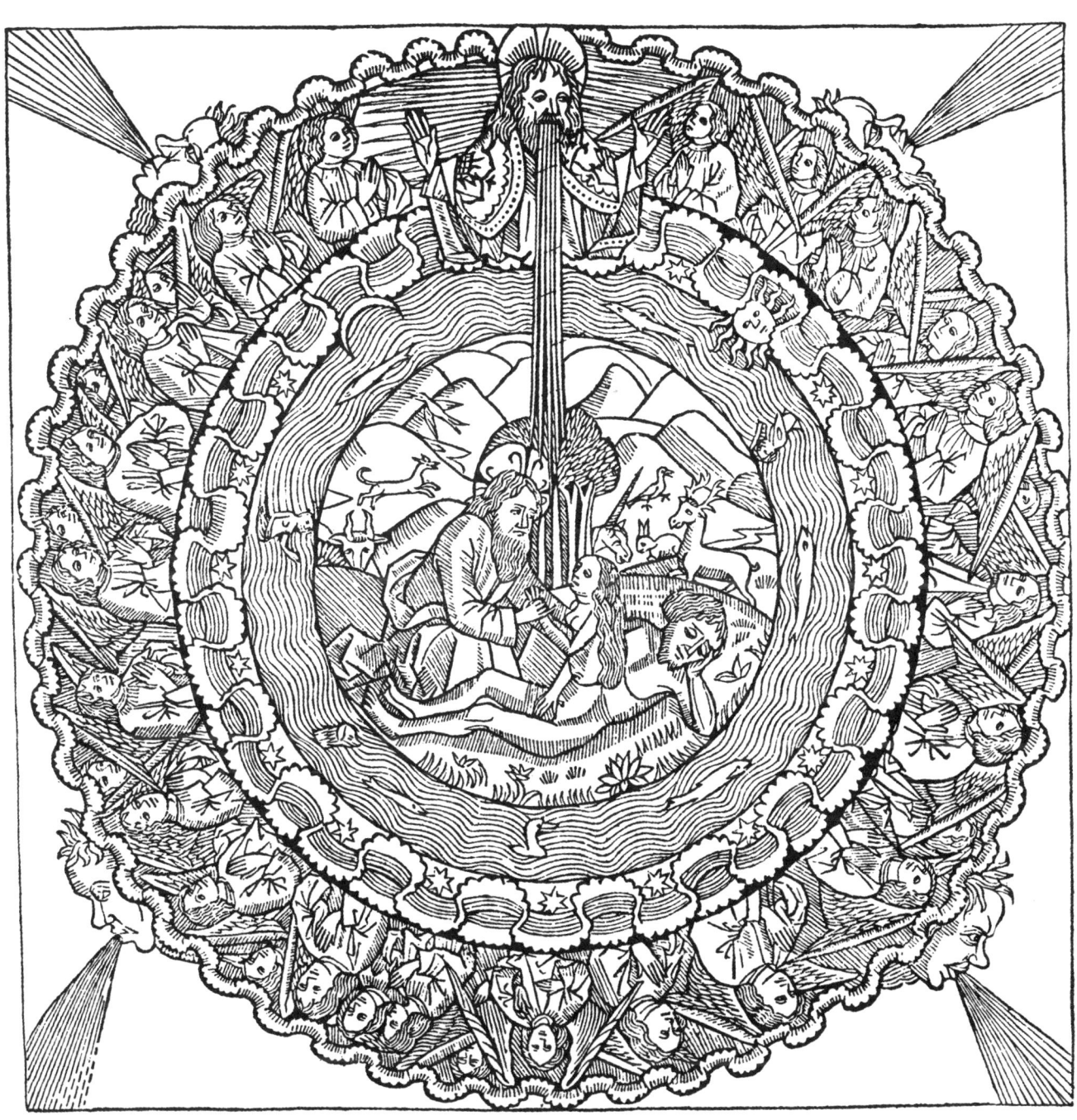

Genesis 2:22–25

TWO BECOME ONE FLESH

And the rib that the LORD God had taken from the man he made into a woman and brought her to the man. Then the man said,

> "This at last is bone of my bones
>   and flesh of my flesh;
> she shall be called Woman,
>   because she was taken out of Man."

Therefore a man shall leave his father and his mother and hold fast to his wife, and they shall become one flesh. And the man and his wife were both naked and were not ashamed.

The Marriage of Adam and Eve
JEAN DUVET | ENGRAVING

The Bible begins and ends with a wedding. This depection by Jean Duvet of that famous first wedding draws heavily on Albrecht Dürer's *Adam and Eve*. Throughout the Creation account God makes complementary pairs—day and night, earth and seas, birds and fish, and so on, ending with the creation of male and female. The end of the chapter concludes with the command to unite the complementary pairs of male and female, consummating the union through sexual intercourse. Jesus pointed to this passage when he expressed his view of marriage in Matthew 19, showing that God's intent for marriage since the dawn of time has been that of establishing a permanent bond (one flesh) between a man and a woman.

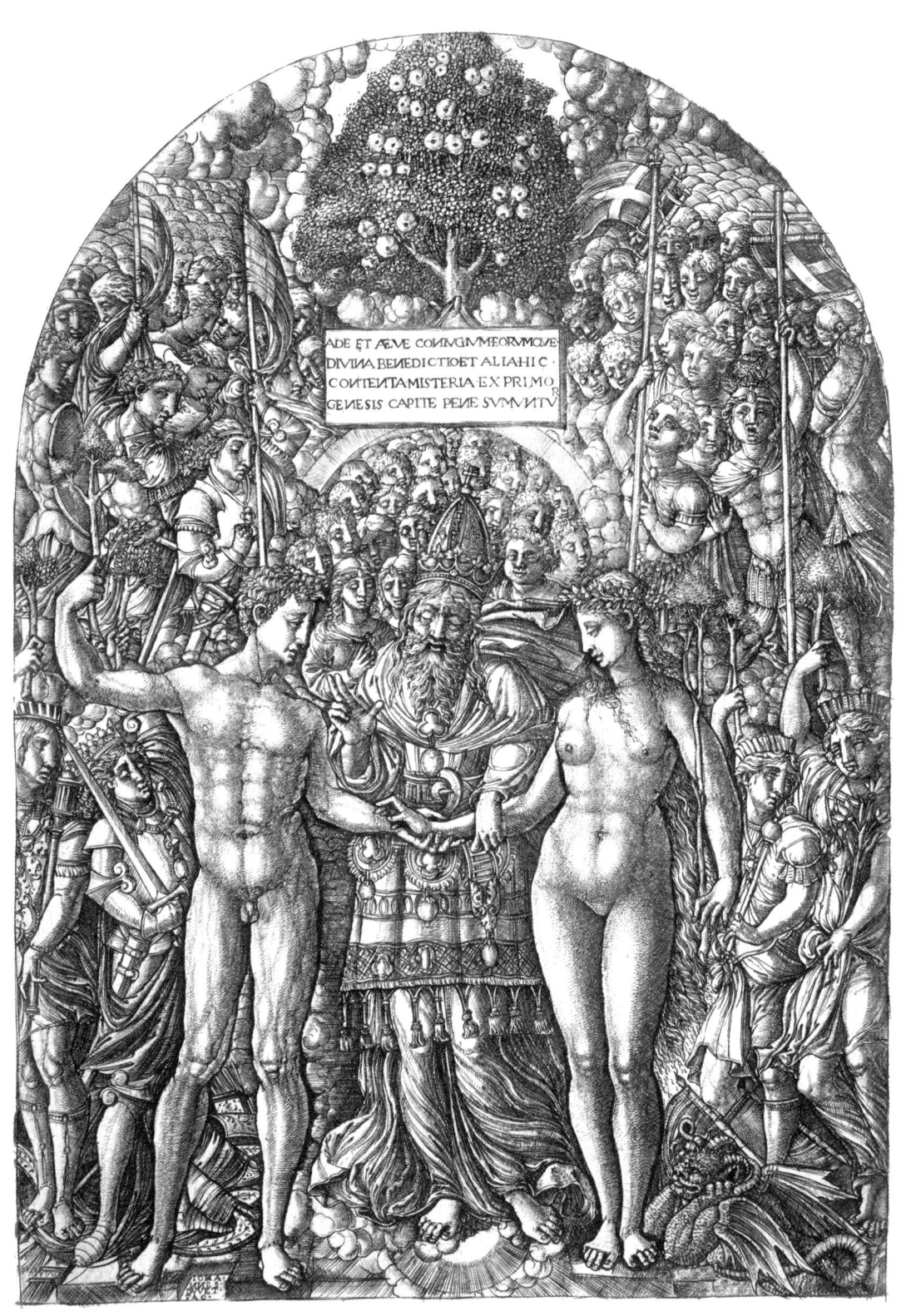

Genesis 3:1–7

THE FALL

Now the serpent was more crafty than any other beast of the field that the Lord God had made.

   He said to the woman, "Did God actually say, 'You shall not eat of any tree in the garden'?" And the woman said to the serpent, "We may eat of the fruit of the trees in the garden, but God said, 'You shall not eat of the fruit of the tree that is in the midst of the garden, neither shall you touch it, lest you die.'" But the serpent said to the woman, "You will not surely die. For God knows that when you eat of it your eyes will be opened, and you will be like God, knowing good and evil." So when the woman saw that the tree was good for food, and that it was a delight to the eyes, and that the tree was to be desired to make one wise, she took of its fruit and ate, and she also gave some to her husband who was with her, and he ate. Then the eyes of both were opened, and they knew that they were naked. And they sewed fig leaves together and made themselves loincloths.

Eve Gives the Fruit
EDWARD KNIPPERS | LINOCUT

On the cover of this book, this linocut is shown next to *Adam Takes the Fruit*. The two prints, originally created to illustrate *The Beginning: A Second Look at the First Sin*, were designed either to stand alone or to work as a diptych. Here Eve is shown holding a piece of fruit. As Eve's outstretched right hand offers Adam the fruit to eat, the Serpent is above her, weaving through the branches of the Tree, tying the two prints together. Unlike many other depictions of this scene throughout art history, Eve is neither cunning nor seductive. Her eyes are downcast and her face in shadows. A once unfallen and good woman is now broken and sadly understands shame.

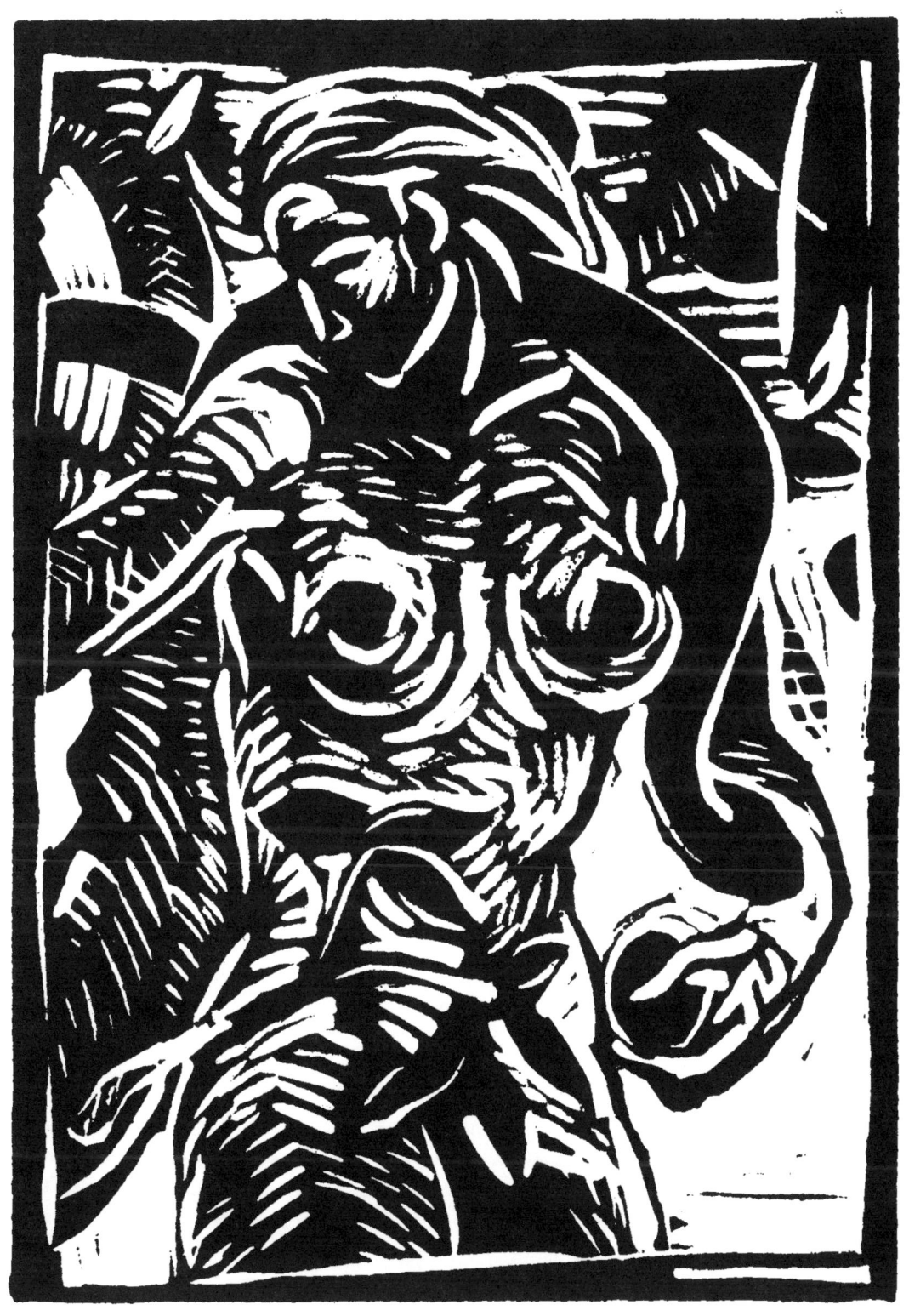

Genesis 3:8–15

THE PROTOEVANGELIUM

And they heard the sound of the Lord God walking in the garden in the cool of the day, and the man and his wife hid themselves from the presence of the Lord God among the trees of the garden. But the Lord God called to the man and said to him, "Where are you?" And he said, "I heard the sound of you in the garden, and I was afraid, because I was naked, and I hid myself." He said, "Who told you that you were naked? Have you eaten of the tree of which I commanded you not to eat?" The man said, "The woman whom you gave to be with me, she gave me fruit of the tree, and I ate." Then the Lord God said to the woman, "What is this that you have done?" The woman said, "The serpent deceived me, and I ate."

    The Lord God said to the serpent, "Because you have done this, cursed are you above all livestock and above all beasts of the field; on your belly you shall go, and dust you shall eat all the days of your life. I will put enmity between you and the woman, and between your offspring and her offspring; he shall bruise your head, and you shall bruise his heel."

God's Confrontation

TANJA BUTLER | LINOCUT

This piece seems to capture all the action of this passage and compresses the sequence down into one image. As an unsophisticated sinner, the Man crudely shifts the blame to his wife. The Woman then blames the Serpent, and the Serpent writhes on the ground under his curse. Amid the punishment, God looks tenderly and gives his children the hope of a coming Savior. Several of the early church fathers (such as Justin Martyr and Irenaeus) regarded verse 15 as the "Protoevangelium"—that is, the first hint of the gospel in the Old Testament: "he shall bruise your head, and you shall bruise his heel." The wound to the woman's offspring (Jesus) would not be ultimately fatal (Jesus would rise again), whereas the blow to the Enemy would destroy his hold over mankind through the victory of Christ over sin and death through the Cross.

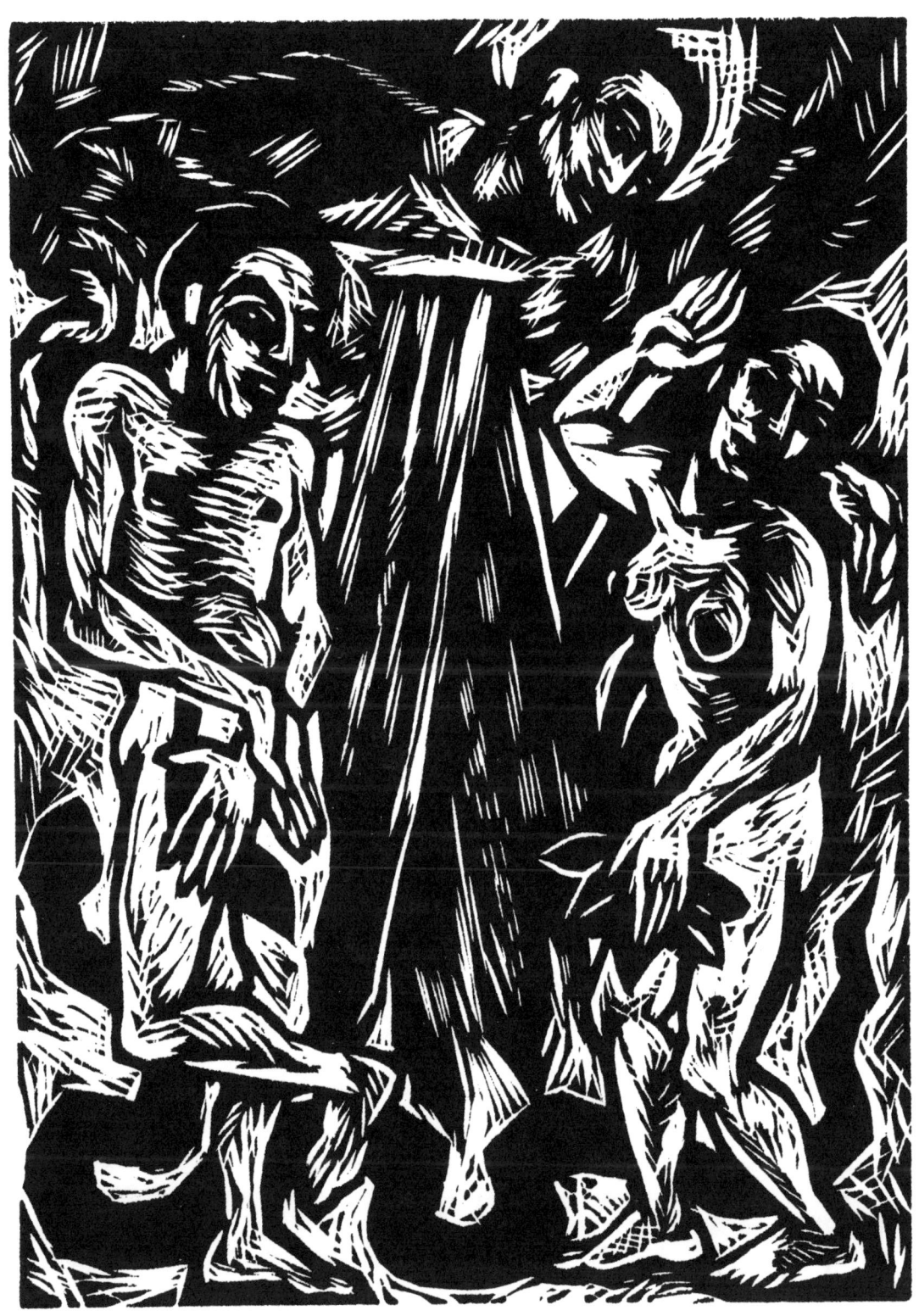

Genesis 4:1–12

THE FIRST MURDER

Now Adam knew Eve his wife, and she conceived and bore Cain, saying, "I have gotten a man with the help of the Lord." And again, she bore his brother Abel. Now Abel was a keeper of sheep, and Cain a worker of the ground. In the course of time Cain brought to the Lord an offering of the fruit of the ground, and Abel also brought of the firstborn of his flock and of their fat portions. And the Lord had regard for Abel and his offering, but for Cain and his offering he had no regard. So Cain was very angry, and his face fell. The Lord said to Cain, "Why are you angry, and why has your face fallen? If you do well, will you not be accepted? And if you do not do well, sin is crouching at the door. Its desire is for you, but you must rule over it."

Cain spoke to Abel his brother. And when they were in the field, Cain rose up against his brother Abel and killed him. Then the Lord said to Cain, "Where is Abel your brother?" He said, "I do not know; am I my brother's keeper?" And the Lord said, "What have you done? The voice of your brother's blood is crying to me from the ground. And now you are cursed from the ground, which has opened its mouth to receive your brother's blood from your hand. When you work the ground, it shall no longer yield to you its strength. You shall be a fugitive and a wanderer on the earth."

Cain and Abel

EDWARD KNIPPERS | WOODCUT

Cain and Abel bring competing offerings to God, each from the work of their hands. It appears from God's interaction with Cain that Cain knew what God required. Like Cain, all of us periodically have better ideas than God about how things should be done. That never turns out well, and often leads to sin crouching at our door. God accepts Abel's animal offering that is similar to the sacrifice required to clothe Adam and Eve. But Cain's offering is not accepted. When Cain was born, Eve thought he was the promised offspring God had said would crush the head of the serpent. Instead, Cain committed the first murder in history. In this piece Abel seems to be already dead on the ground, but Cain continues to bludgeon him in his rage against God. Afterward, like all of us, Cain cried out for mercy. God heard him and protected him.

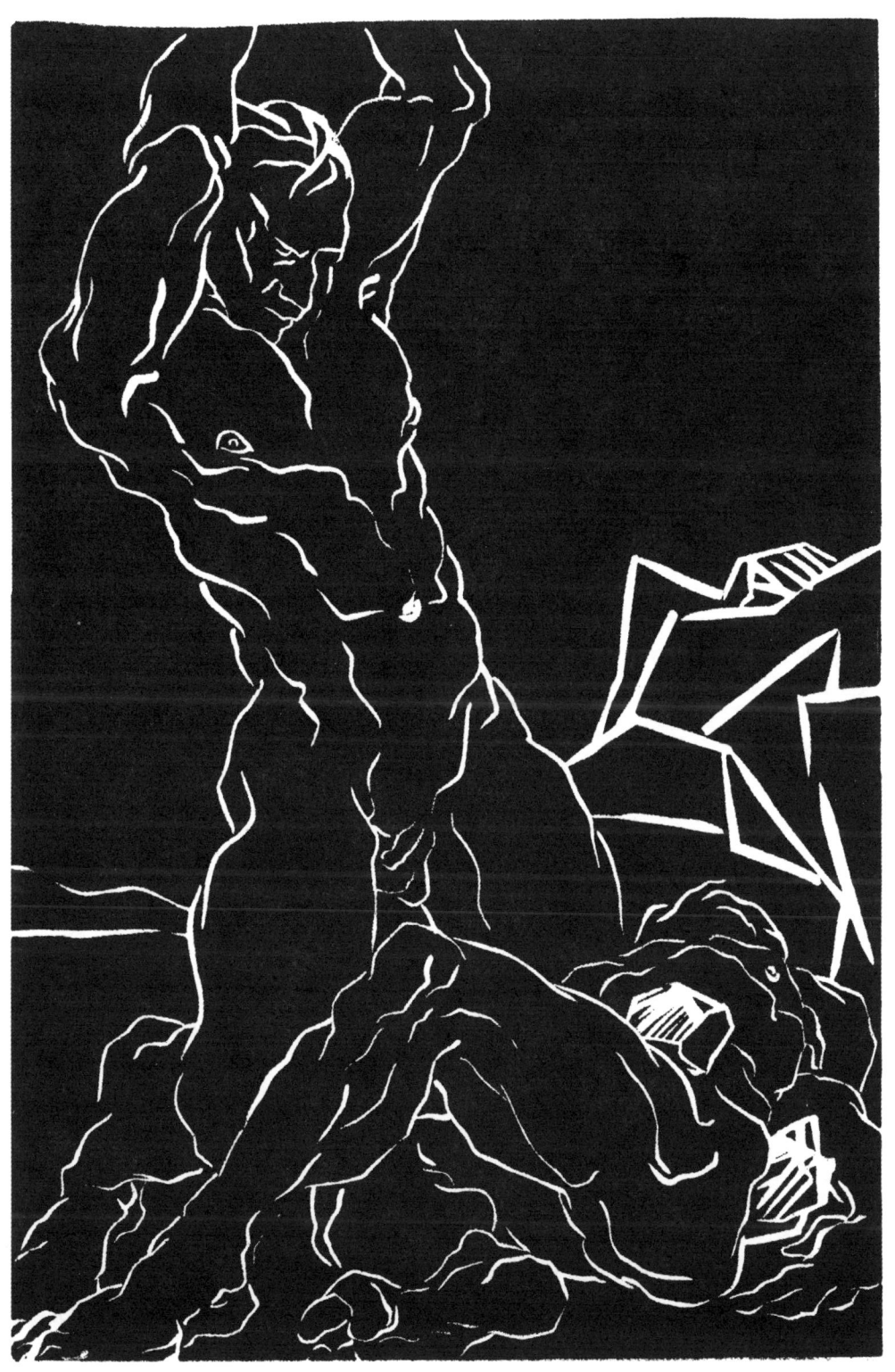

Genesis 5:1–8, 21–29

ENOCH WALKED WITH GOD

This is the book of the generations of Adam. When God created man, he made him in the likeness of God. Male and female he created them, and he blessed them and named them Man when they were created. When Adam had lived 130 years, he fathered a son in his own likeness, after his image, and named him Seth. The days of Adam after he fathered Seth were 800 years; and he had other sons and daughters. Thus all the days that Adam lived were 930 years, and he died.

When Seth had lived 105 years, he fathered Enosh. Seth lived after he fathered Enosh 807 years and had other sons and daughters. Thus all the days of Seth were 912 years, and he died.

* * *

When Enoch had lived 65 years, he fathered Methuselah. Enoch walked with God after he fathered Methuselah 300 years and had other sons and daughters. Thus all the days of Enoch were 365 years. Enoch walked with God, and he was not, for God took him.

When Methuselah had lived 187 years, he fathered Lamech. Methuselah lived after he fathered Lamech 782 years and had other sons and daughters. Thus all the days of Methuselah were 969 years, and he died.

When Lamech had lived 182 years, he fathered a son and called his name Noah, saying, "Out of the ground that the Lord has cursed, this one shall bring us relief from our work and from the painful toil of our hands."

Walking with God

RICK BEERHORST | WOODCUT

The motif of God walking with his people runs throughout the Bible, beginning in Genesis 3, with the Lord walking in the Garden in the cool of the day. In Deuteronomy 5:33 God's people are told to walk in the way that the Lord has commanded, and in 2 Corinthians 5:7 the Bible teaches that this walking with God is by faith, not by sight. In Psalm 23 David describes the experience of walking with God: "The Lord is my shepherd; I shall not want. He makes me lie down in green pastures. He leads me beside still waters. He restores my soul. He leads me in paths of righteousness for his name's sake. Even though I walk through the valley of the shadow of death, I will fear no evil, for you are with me; your rod and your staff, they comfort me. You prepare a table before me in the presence of my enemies; you anoint my head with oil; my cup overflows."

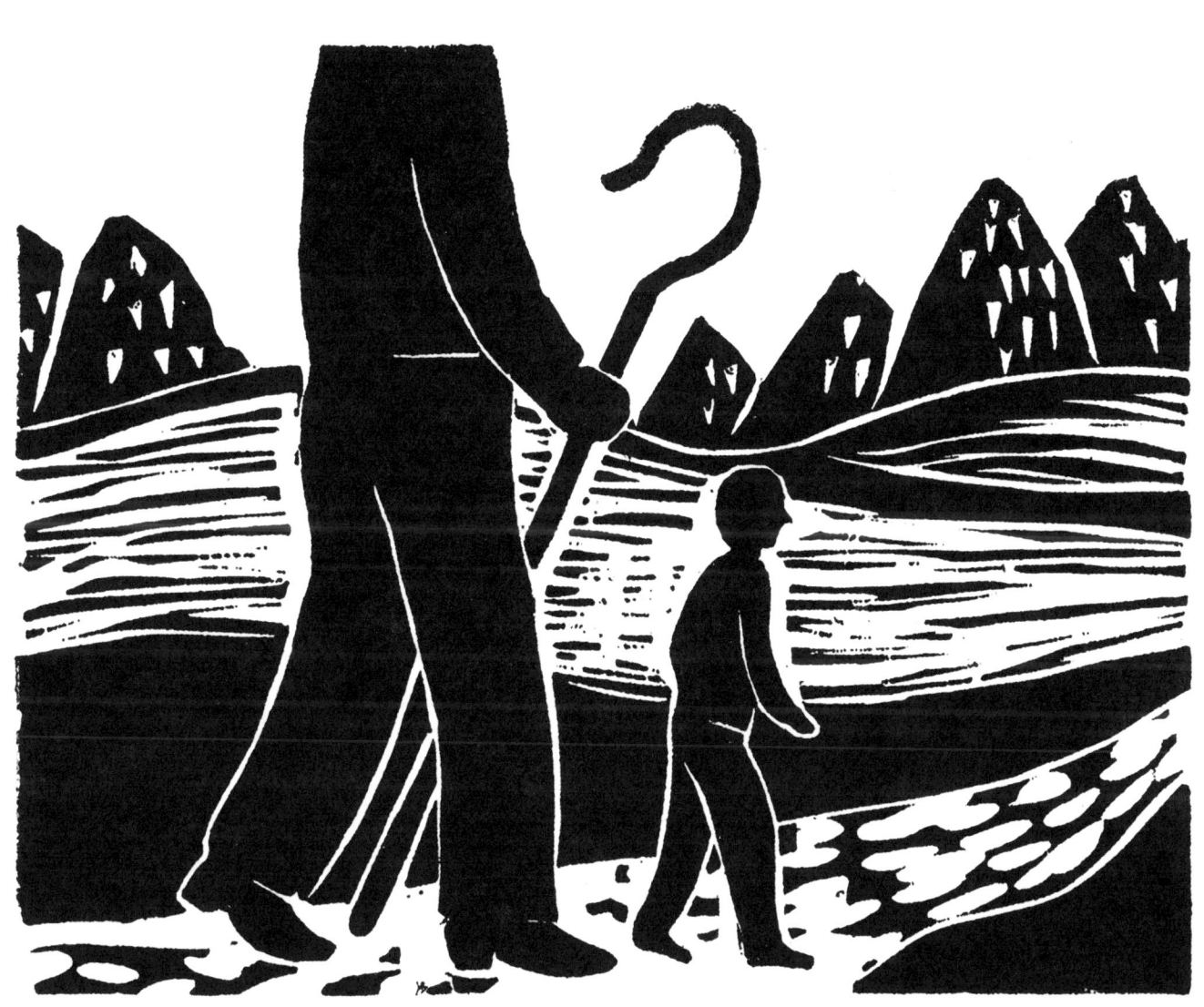

Genesis 7:17–24

THE FLOOD

The flood continued forty days on the earth. The waters increased and bore up the ark, and it rose high above the earth. The waters prevailed and increased greatly on the earth, and the ark floated on the face of the waters. And the waters prevailed so mightily on the earth that all the high mountains under the whole heaven were covered. The waters prevailed above the mountains, covering them fifteen cubits deep. And all flesh died that moved on the earth, birds, livestock, beasts, all swarming creatures that swarm on the earth, and all mankind. Everything on the dry land in whose nostrils was the breath of life died. He blotted out every living thing that was on the face of the ground, man and animals and creeping things and birds of the heavens. They were blotted out from the earth. Only Noah was left, and those who were with him in the ark. And the waters prevailed on the earth 150 days.

And Such Were You

MATTHEW L. CLARK AND NED BUSTARD | WOODCUT

This large woodcut lifts the wave from the famous ukiyo-e woodblock print *The Great Wave off Kanagawa* by Hokusai Katsushika and the ark from a small washi print by Sadao Watanabe to create an image intended to communicate the idea of God's goodness as seen through his preservation and redemption of the unworthy. The animals on this ark are not the cute, innocent animals found in a Noah's Ark playset. According to the traditional symbolism in Christian art, these animals are all evil: the bear (evil influence), the cat (laziness), the goat (the damned), the blackbird (temptation of the flesh), the ape (malice), the leopard (cruelty), the owl (deception), the hog (gluttony) and the fox (guile). The passengers on the ark that God chooses to save are undeserving—as are the people described in 1 Corinthians 6:9–11.

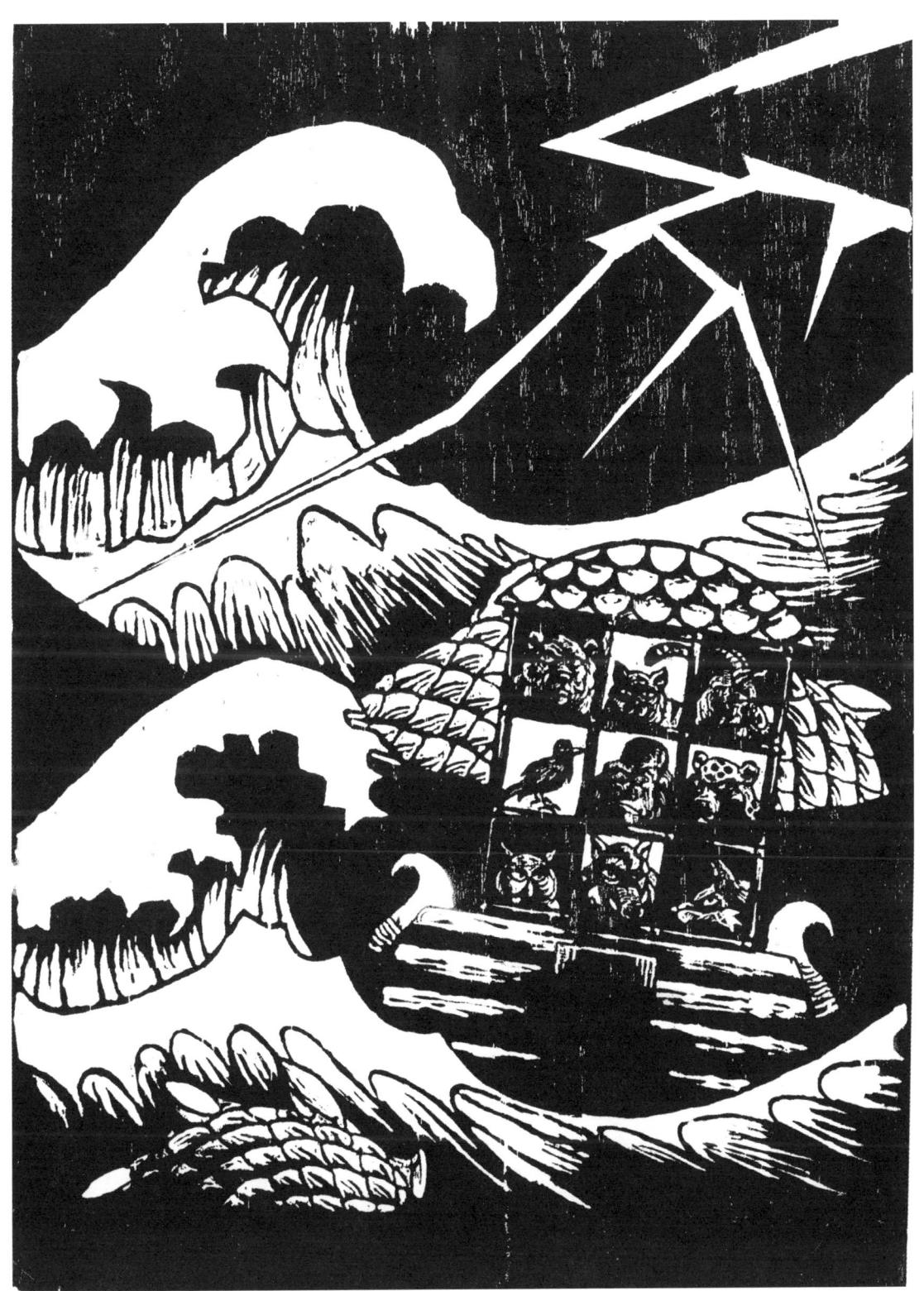

Genesis 9:8–15, 20–23

THE DRUNKENESS OF NOAH

Then God said to Noah and to his sons with him, "Behold, I establish my covenant with you and your offspring after you, and with every living creature that is with you, the birds, the livestock, and every beast of the earth with you, as many as came out of the ark; it is for every beast of the earth. I establish my covenant with you, that never again shall all flesh be cut off by the waters of the flood, and never again shall there be a flood to destroy the earth." And God said, "This is the sign of the covenant that I make between me and you and every living creature that is with you, for all future generations: I have set my bow in the cloud, and it shall be a sign of the covenant between me and the earth. When I bring clouds over the earth and the bow is seen in the clouds, I will remember my covenant that is between me and you and every living creature of all flesh. And the waters shall never again become a flood to destroy all flesh."

. . . .

Noah began to be a man of the soil, and he planted a vineyard. He drank of the wine and became drunk and lay uncovered in his tent. And Ham, the father of Canaan, saw the nakedness of his father and told his two brothers outside. Then Shem and Japheth took a garment, laid it on both their shoulders, and walked backward and covered the nakedness of their father. Their faces were turned backward, and they did not see their father's nakedness.

Failed Savior

NED BUSTARD | LINOCUT

Hebrews 11:7 states that "By faith Noah, being warned by God concerning events as yet unseen, in reverent fear constructed an ark for the saving of his household. By this he condemned the world and became an heir of the righteousness that comes by faith." But although he was instrumental in saving all of the living, Noah was not the promised Savior. Noah is shown here drunk, lying in a cruciform, and with a life preserver forming a halo of sorts around his head. He is an inebriated old man, and the symbol of his saving work is broken and covers him as poorly as the fig leaves covered the shame of Adam and Eve.

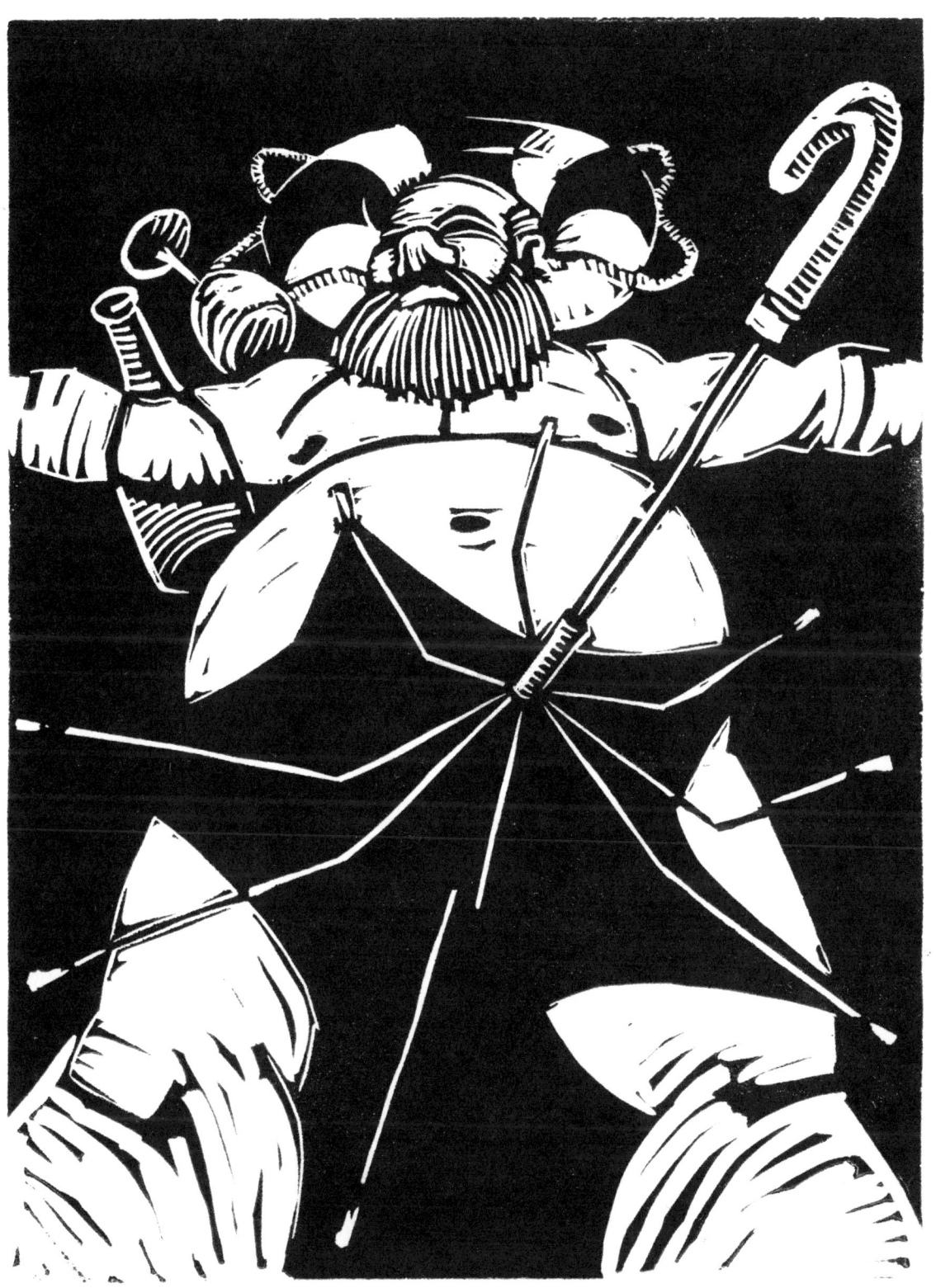

Genesis 15:5–11, 17–18

THE ABRAHAMIC COVENANT

And he brought him outside and said, "Look toward heaven, and number the stars, if you are able to number them." Then he said to him, "So shall your offspring be." And he believed the Lord, and he counted it to him as righteousness.

And he said to him, "I am the Lord who brought you out from Ur of the Chaldeans to give you this land to possess." But he said, "O Lord God, how am I to know that I shall possess it?" He said to him, "Bring me a heifer three years old, a female goat three years old, a ram three years old, a turtledove, and a young pigeon." And he brought him all these, cut them in half, and laid each half over against the other. But he did not cut the birds in half. And when birds of prey came down on the carcasses, Abram drove them away.

* * *

When the sun had gone down and it was dark, behold, a smoking fire pot and a flaming torch passed between these pieces. On that day the Lord made a covenant with Abram, saying, "To your offspring I give this land, from the river of Egypt to the great river, the river Euphrates . . .

A Smoking Pot

MATTHEW L. CLARK | LINOCUT

In faith Abram believed God's promise to receive a land and have descendents. Then God confirmed that promise through a traditional Ancient Near Eastern legal transaction called a covenant. When making a covenant in those days, the two participants would walk between torn animals, symbolizing the consequences if either of them did not honor the agreement. But in this case, God alone passed through the animals, calling a curse upon himself if either he or Abram's people broke the covenant. Abram and his descendents *did* end up breaking the covenant, so Jesus—the Light of the World—died on the Cross. In Galatians 3:13 it is written, "Christ redeemed us from the curse of the law by becoming a curse for us—for it is written, 'Cursed is everyone who is hanged on a tree.'"

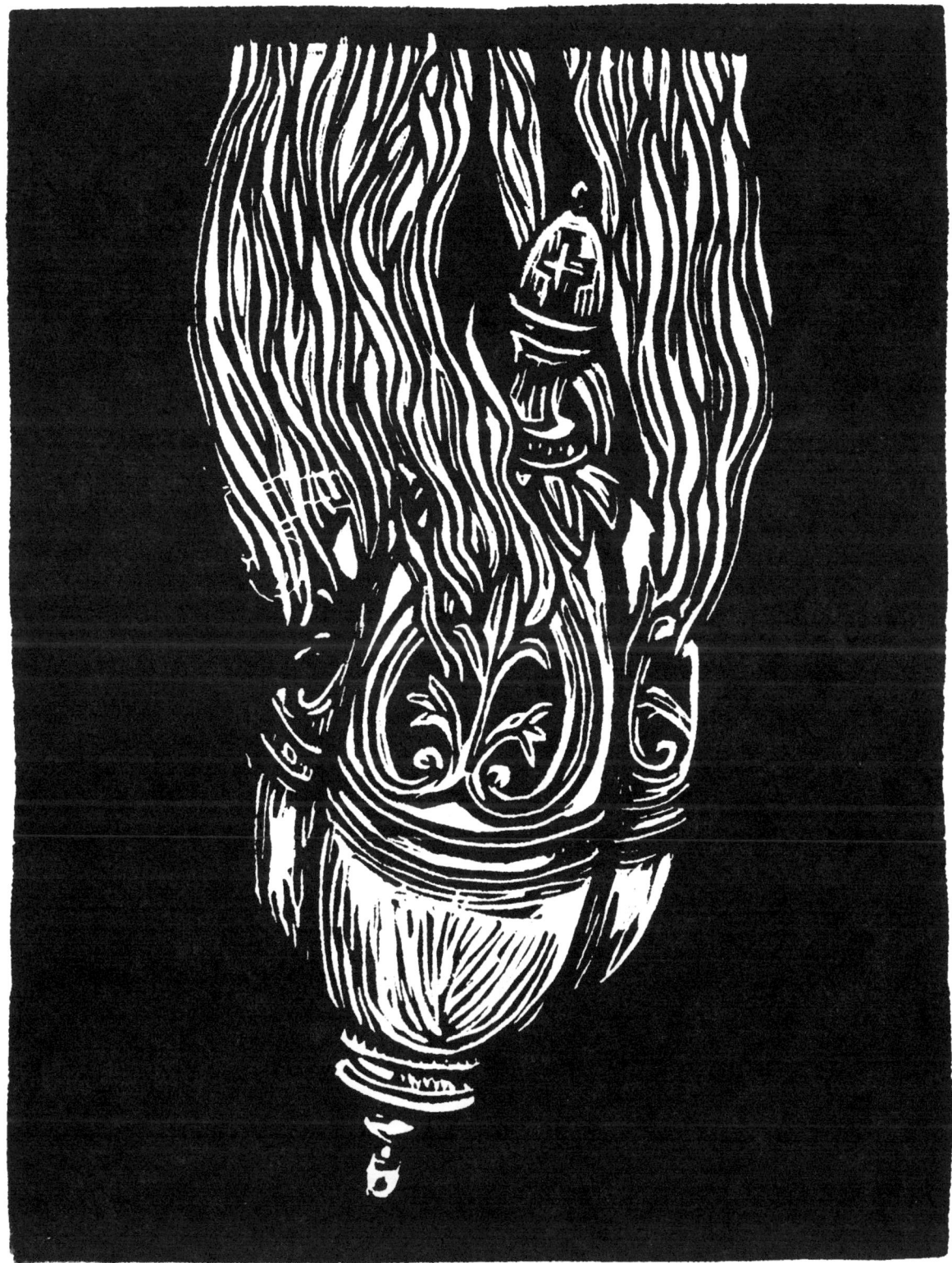

Genesis 19:23–29

SODOM AND GOMORRAH

The sun had risen on the earth when Lot came to Zoar. Then the Lord rained on Sodom and Gomorrah sulfur and fire from the Lord out of heaven. And he overthrew those cities, and all the valley, and all the inhabitants of the cities, and what grew on the ground. But Lot's wife, behind him, looked back, and she became a pillar of salt.

And Abraham went early in the morning to the place where he had stood before the Lord. And he looked down toward Sodom and Gomorrah and toward all the land of the valley, and he looked and, behold, the smoke of the land went up like the smoke of a furnace.

So it was that, when God destroyed the cities of the valley, God remembered Abraham and sent Lot out of the midst of the overthrow when he overthrew the cities in which Lot had lived.

Lot Flees Sodom (Loss)

EDWARD KNIPPERS | WOODCUT

In this woodcut Sodom burns in a chaotic confusion of lines. Lot carries all of his worldly belongings on his back, bent over by the weight. His daughters have hurried ahead of him and as he struggles, his wife looks back and is immediately calcified. Matthew Henry says, "Lot lingered; he trifled. Thus many who are under convictions about their spiritual state, and the necessity of a change, defer that needful work. The salvation of the most righteous men is of God's mercy, not by their own merit. We are saved by grace." The utter destruction of these cities (yet saving Lot), the annihilation of the Flood (yet saving Noah), and the later genocide of the Canaanites (yet saving Rahab) all illustrate God's righteous anger against sin mingled with his mysterious mercy for those he chooses to save.

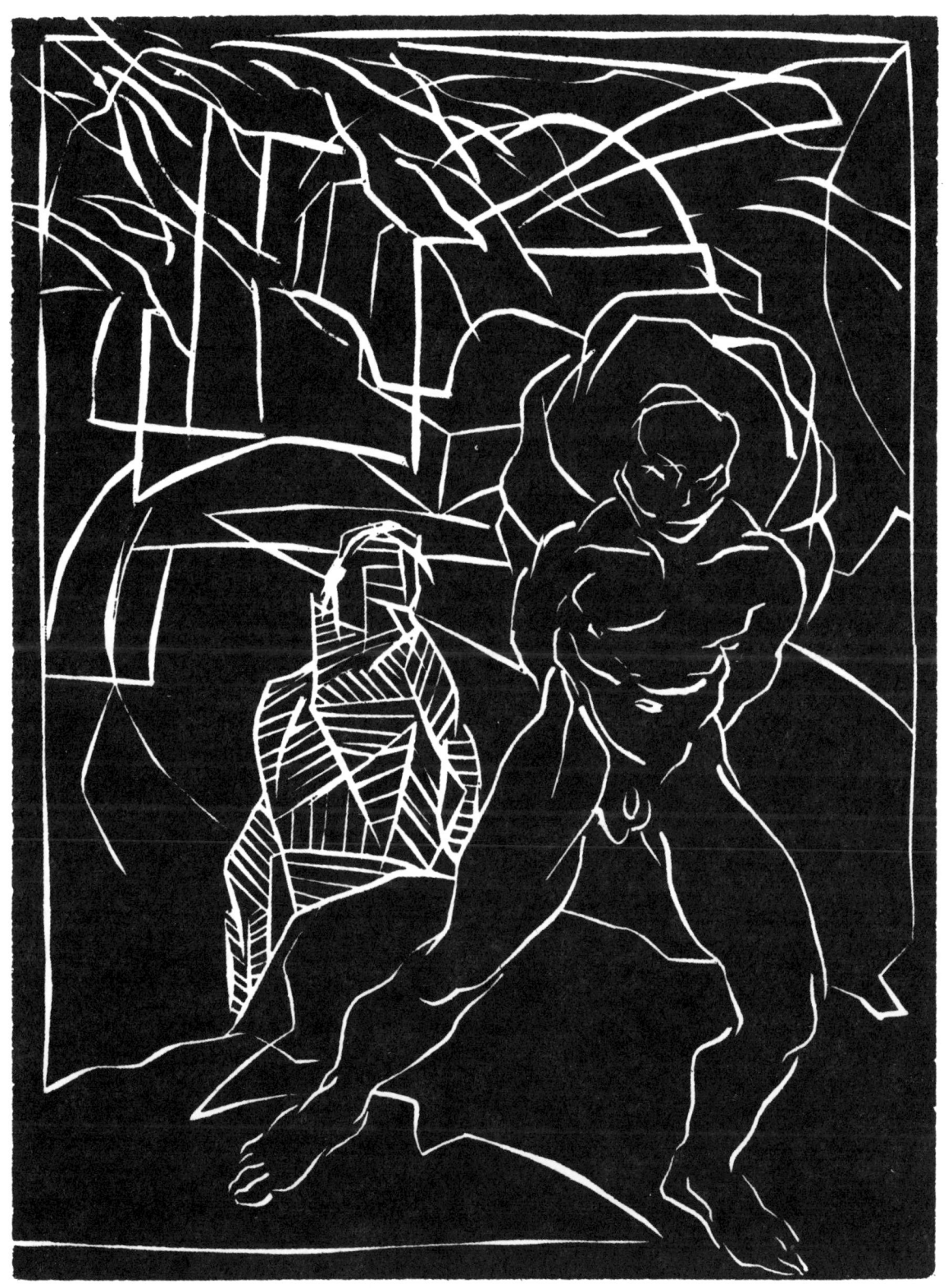

Genesis 19:30–38

THE DAUGHTERS OF LOT

Now Lot went up out of Zoar and lived in the hills with his two daughters, for he was afraid to live in Zoar. So he lived in a cave with his two daughters. And the firstborn said to the younger, "Our father is old, and there is not a man on earth to come in to us after the manner of all the earth. Come, let us make our father drink wine, and we will lie with him, that we may preserve offspring from our father." So they made their father drink wine that night. And the firstborn went in and lay with her father. He did not know when she lay down or when she arose.

The next day, the firstborn said to the younger, "Behold, I lay last night with my father. Let us make him drink wine tonight also. Then you go in and lie with him, that we may preserve offspring from our father." So they made their father drink wine that night also. And the younger arose and lay with him, and he did not know when she lay down or when she arose. Thus both the daughters of Lot became pregnant by their father. The firstborn bore a son and called his name Moab. He is the father of the Moabites to this day. The younger also bore a son and called his name Ben-ammi. He is the father of the Ammonites to this day.

Lot and His Daughters

TANJA BUTLER | LINOCUT

The artist writes, "I found the dramatic gesture for this scene in a painting by Jan Massys, 1563. Massys presented an erotic scene in celebratory mode with sumptuous costumes and lascivious expressions. In contrast, my print represents callous, despairing determination and inebriated weakness." Although Lot was said to be a righteous man and was delivered from the punishment of Sodom, he is still guilty of shocking crimes. He exposed the chastity of his daughters to the men of Sodom, and in this passage his daughters make him drunk and rape him, conceiving grandsons through incest. But is there anything that can't be redeemed? Even in this depraved account there is hope. Ruth, a distant child of Moab, would eventually be grafted into the line of God's chosen people, and ultimately be included in the genealogy of Christ.

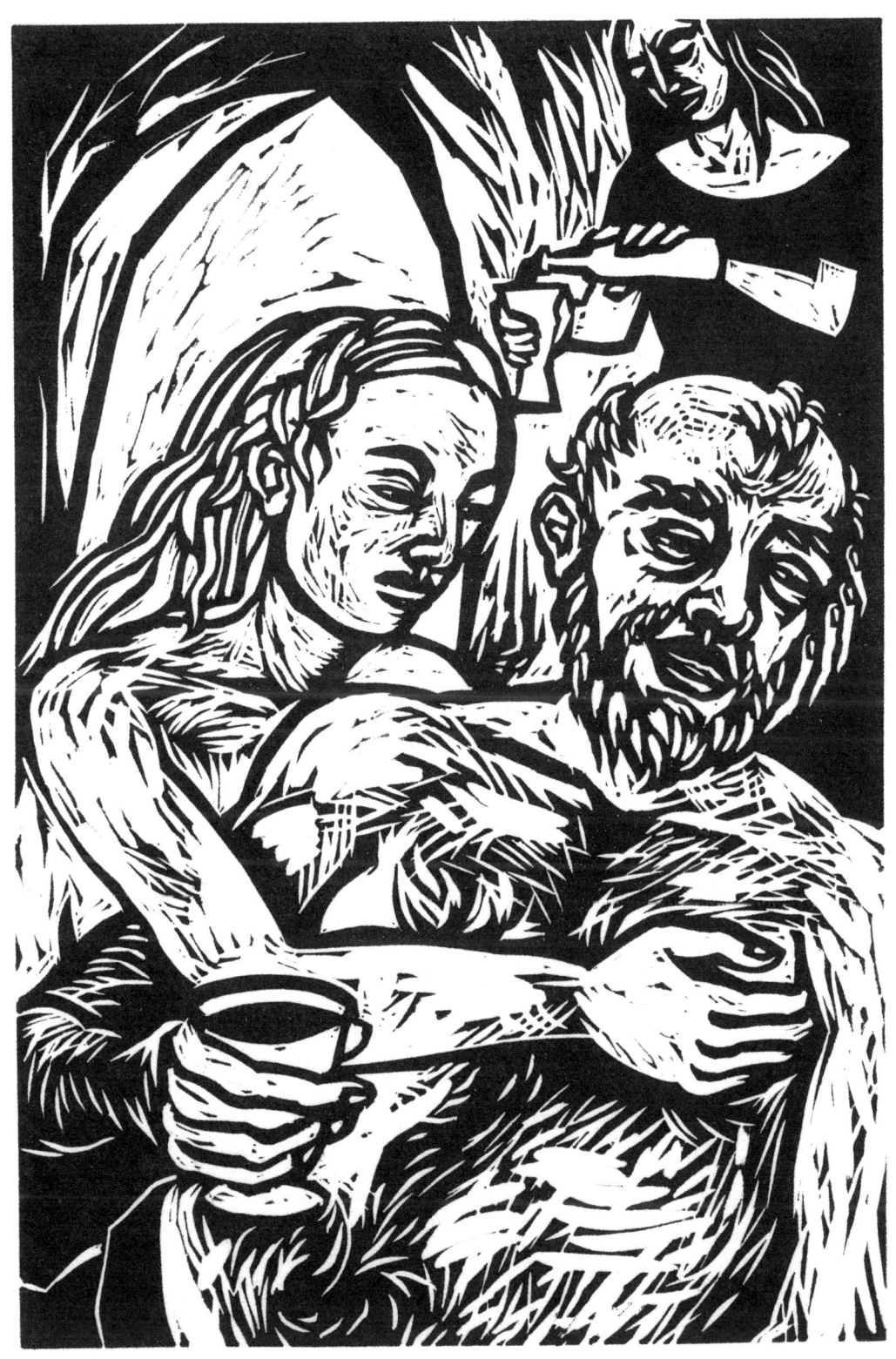

Genesis 22:9–18

THE BINDING

When they came to the place of which God had told him, Abraham built the altar there and laid the wood in order and bound Isaac his son and laid him on the altar, on top of the wood. Then Abraham reached out his hand and took the knife to slaughter his son. But the angel of the Lord called to him from heaven and said, "Abraham, Abraham!" And he said, "Here I am." He said, "Do not lay your hand on the boy or do anything to him, for now I know that you fear God, seeing you have not withheld your son, your only son, from me." And Abraham lifted up his eyes and looked, and behold, behind him was a ram, caught in a thicket by his horns. And Abraham went and took the ram and offered it up as a burnt offering instead of his son. So Abraham called the name of that place, "The Lord will provide"; as it is said to this day, "On the mount of the Lord it shall be provided."

And the angel of the Lord called to Abraham a second time from heaven and said, "By myself I have sworn, declares the Lord, because you have done this and have not withheld your son, your only son, I will surely bless you, and I will surely multiply your offspring as the stars of heaven and as the sand that is on the seashore. And your offspring shall possess the gate of his enemies, and in your offspring shall all the nations of the earth be blessed, because you have obeyed my voice."

Knight of Faith

KEVIN LINDHOLM | LINOCUT

In Hebrews 11 it says, "By faith Abraham, when he was tested, offered up Isaac, and he who had received the promises was in the act of offering up his only son, of whom it was said, 'Through Isaac shall your offspring be named.' He considered that God was able even to raise him from the dead, from which, figuratively speaking, he did receive him back." In his book *Counterfeit Gods*, Tim Keller writes, "God saw Abraham's sacrifice and said, 'Now I know that you love me, because you did not withhold your only son from me.' But how much more can we look at his sacrifice on the cross and say to God, 'Now we know that you love us. For you did not withhold your son, your only son, whom you love, from us.'"

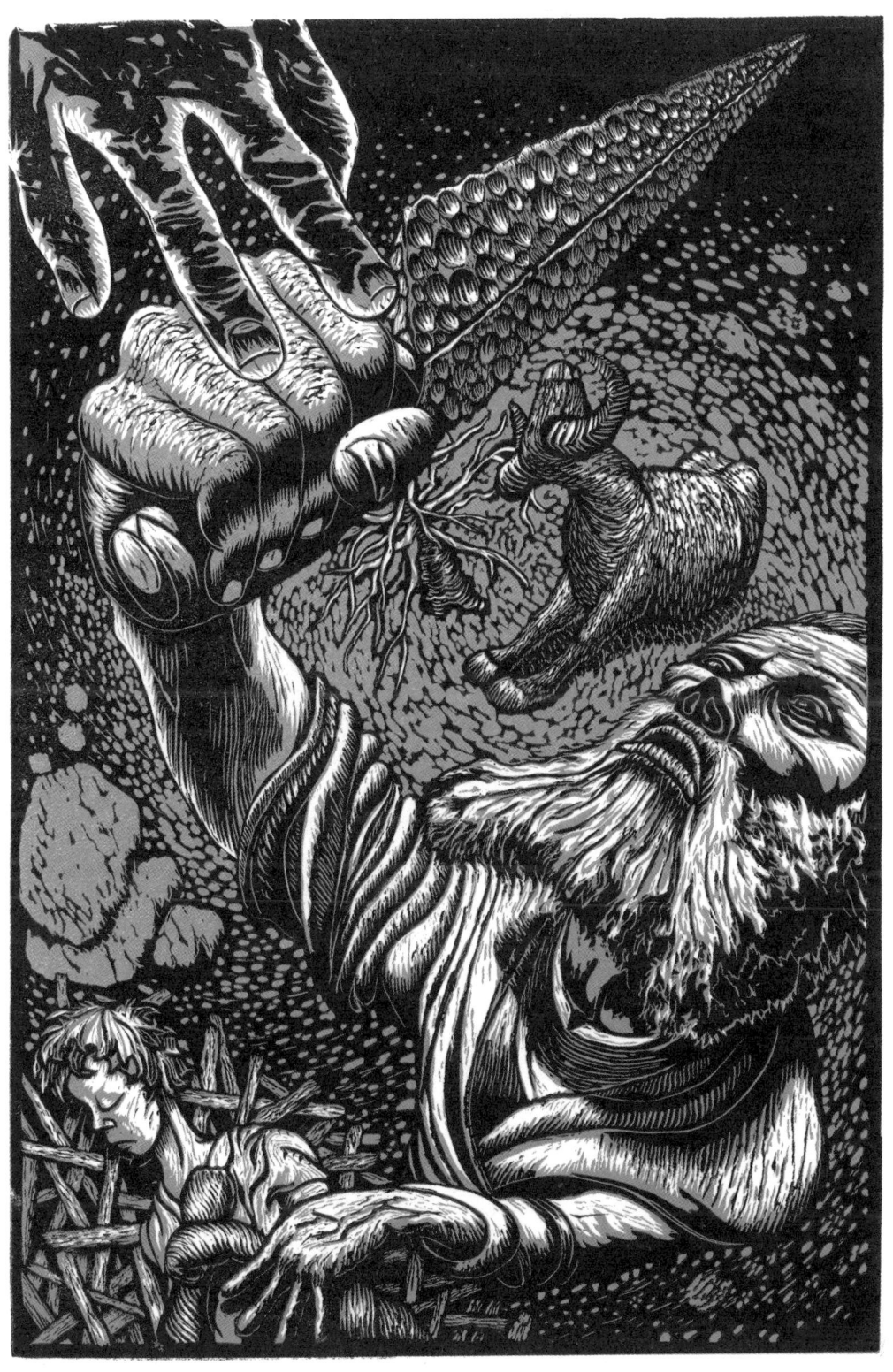

Genesis 27:14–23

THE DECEPTION OF ISAAC

So he went and took them and brought them to his mother, and his mother prepared delicious food, such as his father loved. Then Rebekah took the best garments of Esau her older son, which were with her in the house, and put them on Jacob her younger son. And the skins of the young goats she put on his hands and on the smooth part of his neck. And she put the delicious food and the bread, which she had prepared, into the hand of her son Jacob.

So he went in to his father and said, "My father." And he said, "Here I am. Who are you, my son?" Jacob said to his father, "I am Esau your firstborn. I have done as you told me; now sit up and eat of my game, that your soul may bless me." But Isaac said to his son, "How is it that you have found it so quickly, my son?" He answered, "Because the Lord your God granted me success." Then Isaac said to Jacob, "Please come near, that I may feel you, my son, to know whether you are really my son Esau or not." So Jacob went near to Isaac his father, who felt him and said, "The voice is Jacob's voice, but the hands are the hands of Esau." And he did not recognize him, because his hands were hairy like his brother Esau's hands. So he blessed him.

Isaac Blesses Jacob

WAYNE FORTE | LINCOUT

It is difficult to understand how if God is good and omnipotent, calamities continue to occur, disease runs rampant, and wars rage. It is also challenging to understand why he would choose to bless the manipulations and lies that Rebekah and Jacob cobbled together to swindle Esau of his birthright. Yet Scripture is clear that it was God's will that Jacob receive the blessing, for he said "Jacob I loved, but Esau I hated." Not all who are descended from Abraham are his offspring that God promised to save. In light of this account Paul will ask in Romans 9:14–15, "What shall we say then? Is there injustice on God's part? By no means! For he says to Moses, 'I will have mercy on whom I have mercy, and I will have compassion on whom I have compassion.'"

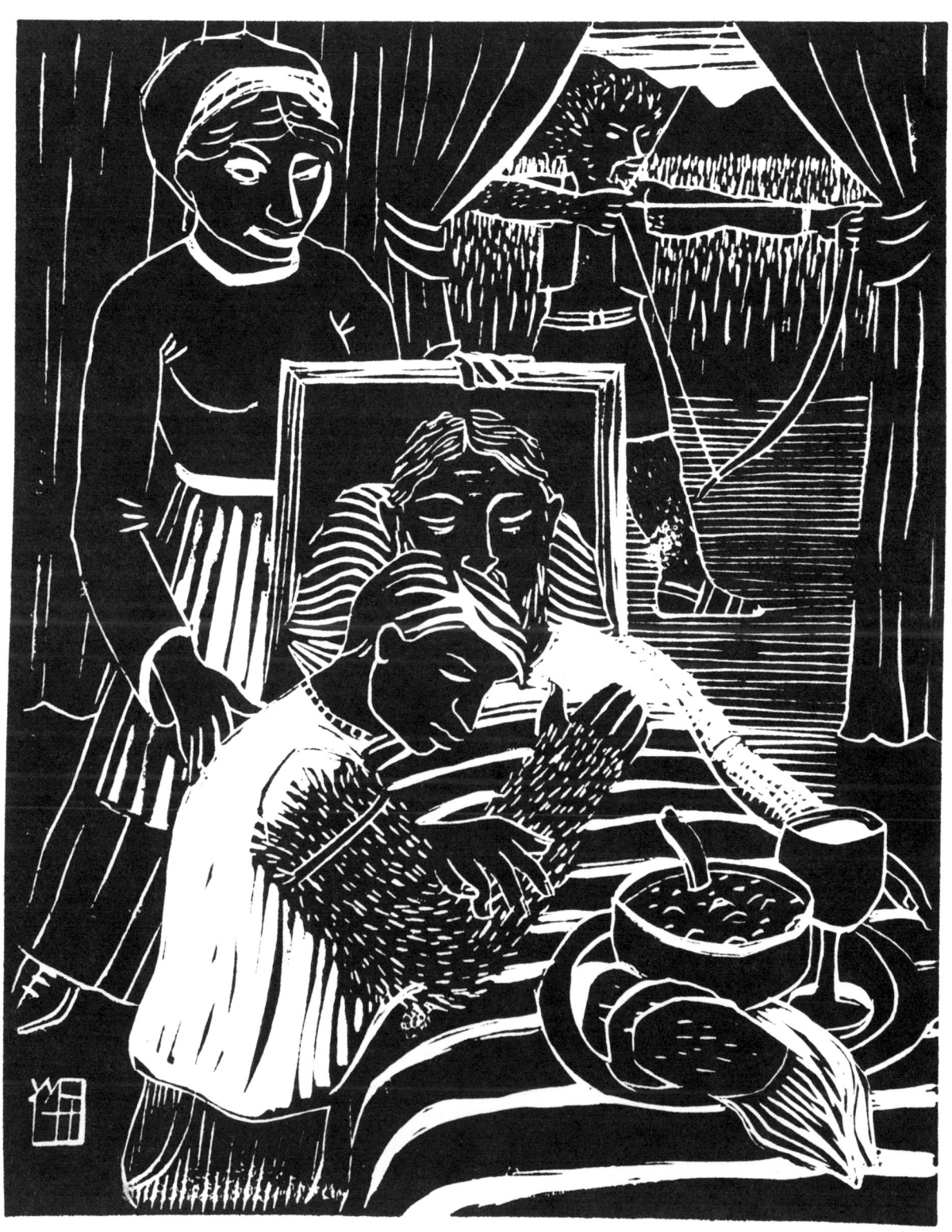

Genesis 28:11–28

THE DREAM AT BETHEL

And he came to a certain place and stayed there that night, because the sun had set. Taking one of the stones of the place, he put it under his head and lay down in that place to sleep. And he dreamed, and behold, there was a ladder set up on the earth, and the top of it reached to heaven. And behold, the angels of God were ascending and descending on it! And behold, the LORD stood above it and said, "I am the LORD, the God of Abraham your father and the God of Isaac. The land on which you lie I will give to you and to your offspring. Your offspring shall be like the dust of the earth, and you shall spread abroad to the west and to the east and to the north and to the south, and in you and your offspring shall all the families of the earth be blessed. Behold, I am with you and will keep you wherever you go, and will bring you back to this land. For I will not leave you until I have done what I have promised you." Then Jacob awoke from his sleep and said, "Surely the LORD is in this place, and I did not know it." And he was afraid and said, "How awesome is this place! This is none other than the house of God, and this is the gate of heaven."

So early in the morning Jacob took the stone that he had put under his head and set it up for a pillar and poured oil on the top of it.

Jacob's Ladder

EDWARD KNIPPERS | WOODCUT

Knippers says, "Art history is never far away from what I am doing." And a prime example of that is found in this piece. The artist explains, "For me, the cubist elements speak for the encounter with another realm of existence." In the biblical account, and in this print, the ladder connects the realms of heaven and earth. And that connection was made by the initiative of God reaching down to Jacob. In the birth of Jesus Christ that connection was again made by God between the two realms for the benefit of mankind. Jesus identifies himself as the ultimate Jacob's Ladder in John 1:51 when he says to Nathaniel, "you will see heaven opened, and the angels of God ascending and descending on the Son of Man."

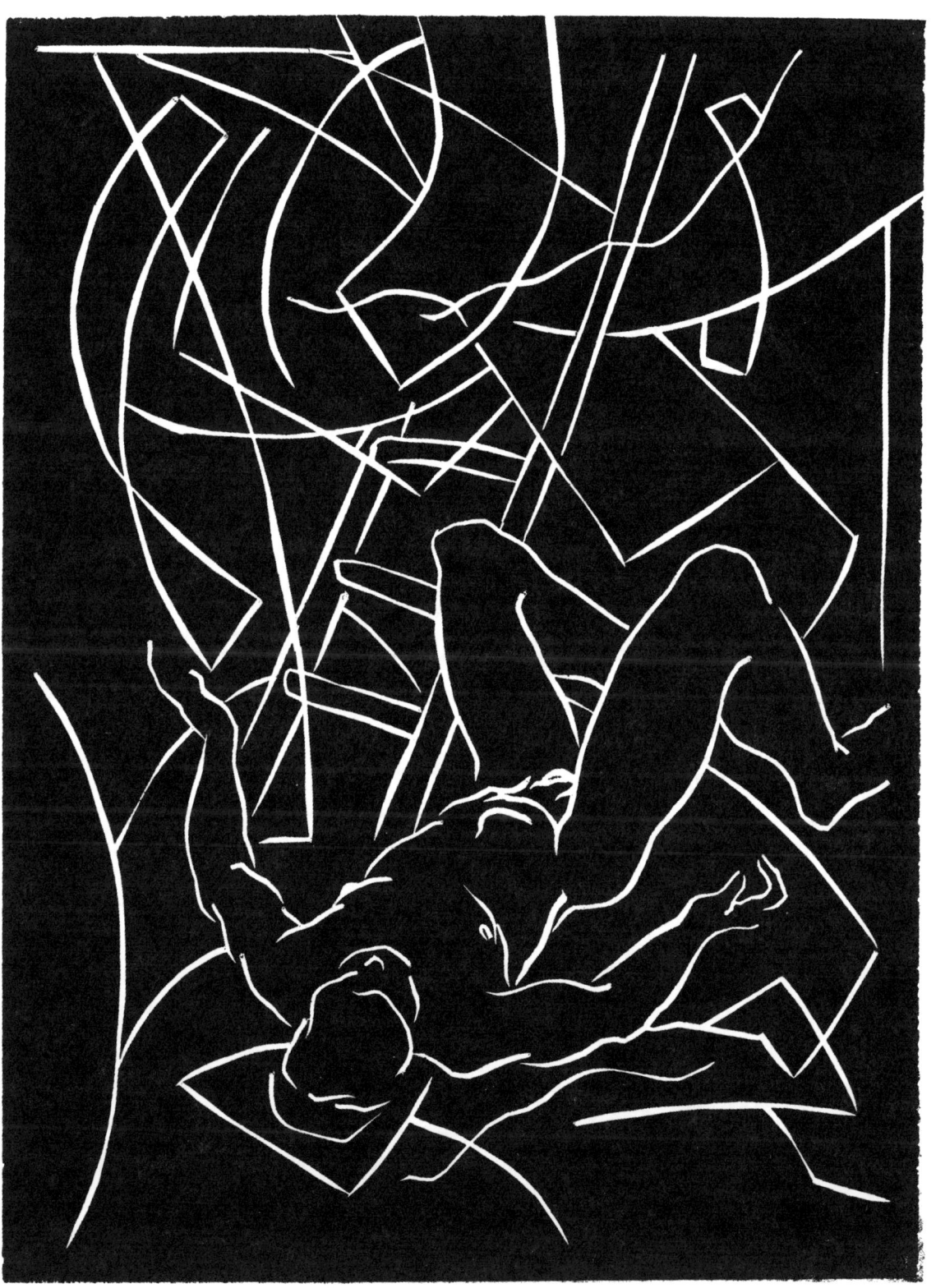

Genesis 39:6b–18

POTIPHAR'S WIFE TEMPTS JOSEPH

Now Joseph was handsome in form and appearance. And after a time his master's wife cast her eyes on Joseph and said, "Lie with me." But he refused and said to his master's wife, "Behold, because of me my master has no concern about anything in the house, and he has put everything that he has in my charge. He is not greater in this house than I am, nor has he kept back anything from me except you, because you are his wife. How then can I do this great wickedness and sin against God?" And as she spoke to Joseph day after day, he would not listen to her, to lie beside her or to be with her.

But one day, when he went into the house to do his work and none of the men of the house was there in the house, she caught him by his garment, saying, "Lie with me." But he left his garment in her hand and fled and got out of the house. And as soon as she saw that he had left his garment in her hand and had fled out of the house, she called to the men of her household and said to them, "See, he has brought among us a Hebrew to laugh at us. He came in to me to lie with me, and I cried out with a loud voice. And as soon as he heard that I lifted up my voice and cried out, he left his garment beside me and fled and got out of the house." Then she laid up his garment by her until his master came home, and she told him the same story, saying, "The Hebrew servant, whom you have brought among us, came in to me to laugh at me. But as soon as I lifted up my voice and cried, he left his garment beside me and fled out of the house."

Joseph Flees Potiphar's Wife

EDWARD KNIPPERS | LITHOGRAPH

In this piece the artist leaves no question in the mind of the viewer about what the temptation was that Joseph was fleeing, nor whether the young man found it tempting. In spite of his body's natural reaction to being seduced by a naked woman, Joseph does not allow himself to be defined or controlled by his desire. He turns and chooses the godly course. But doing the right thing does not always lead to welcome results. Joseph's decision to pursue a holy path in this situation was not without consequence. Aside from unfulfilled desire, his righteous actions resulted in his character being slandered, immediate unemployment, and many years spent wasting away in jail.

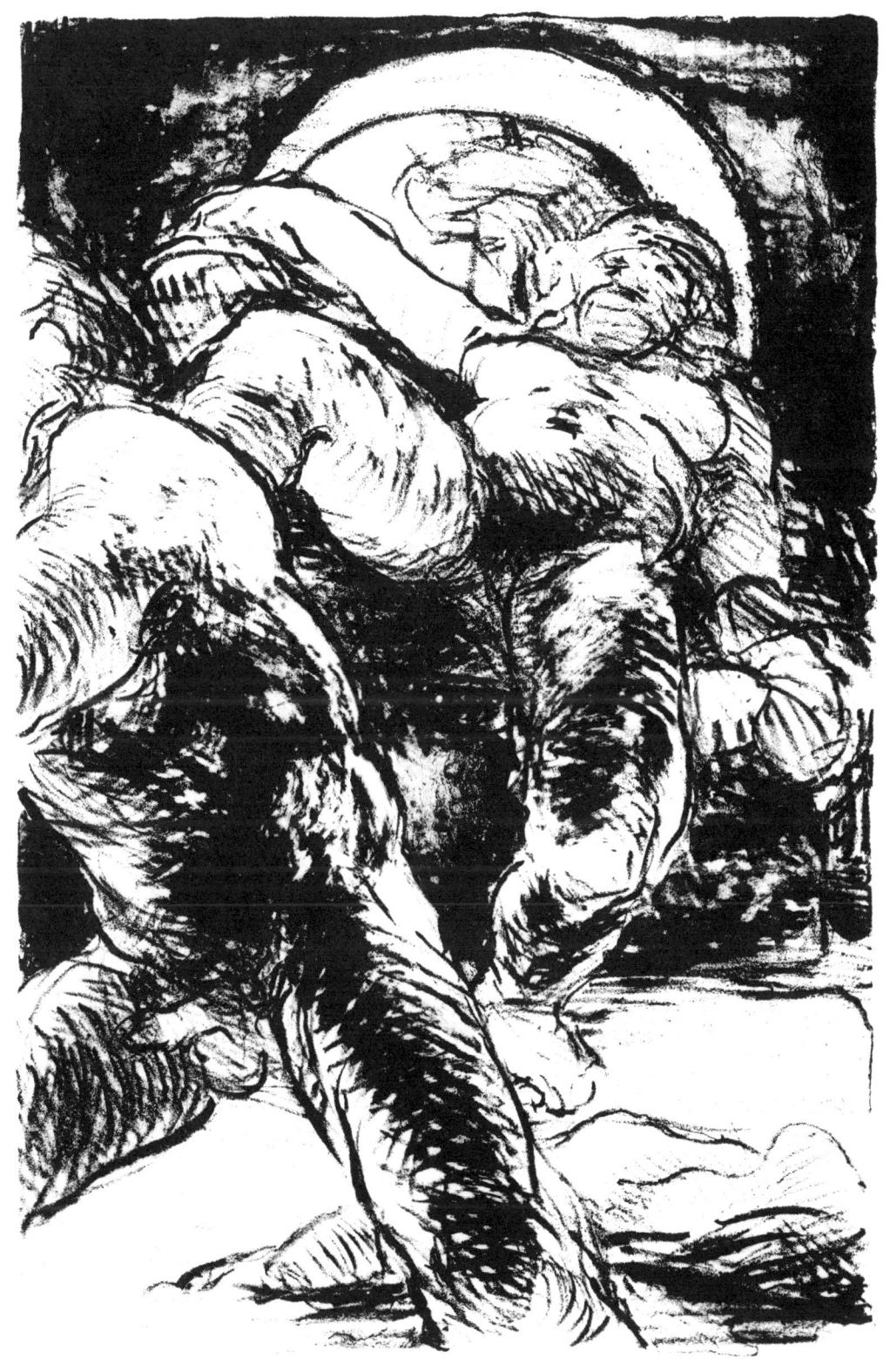

Genesis 41:1–13

INTERPRETATION OF DREAMS

After two whole years, Pharaoh dreamed that he was standing by the Nile, and behold, there came up out of the Nile seven cows attractive and plump, and they fed in the reed grass. And behold, seven other cows, ugly and thin, came up out of the Nile after them, and stood by the other cows on the bank of the Nile. And the ugly, thin cows ate up the seven attractive, plump cows. And Pharaoh awoke. And he fell asleep and dreamed a second time. And behold, seven ears of grain, plump and good, were growing on one stalk. And behold, after them sprouted seven ears, thin and blighted by the east wind. And the thin ears swallowed up the seven plump, full ears. And Pharaoh awoke, and behold, it was a dream. So in the morning his spirit was troubled, and he sent and called for all the magicians of Egypt and all its wise men. Pharaoh told them his dreams, but there was none who could interpret them to Pharaoh.

Then the chief cupbearer said to Pharaoh, "I remember my offenses today. When Pharaoh was angry with his servants and put me and the chief baker in custody in the house of the captain of the guard, we dreamed on the same night, he and I, each having a dream with its own interpretation. A young Hebrew was there with us, a servant of the captain of the guard. When we told him, he interpreted our dreams to us, giving an interpretation to each man according to his dream. And as he interpreted to us, so it came about. I was restored to my office, and the baker was hanged."

Joseph and the Dreams

WAYNE FORTE | LINOCUT

John Piper writes: "Life is not a straight line leading from one blessing to the next and then finally to heaven. Life is a winding and troubled road. Switchback after switchback. And the point of biblical stories like Joseph . . . is to help us feel in our bones (not just know in our heads) that God is for us in all these strange turns. God is not just showing up after the trouble and cleaning it up. He is plotting the course and managing the troubles with far-reaching purposes for our good and for the glory of Jesus Christ." It is often difficult to see the point of the evil circumstances in our lives, but examples like the life of Joseph serve as reminders that God is actively working for our benefit. The sometimes circuitous paths he sets us on are to keep us loving him and depending on him. They are for our good and his glory.

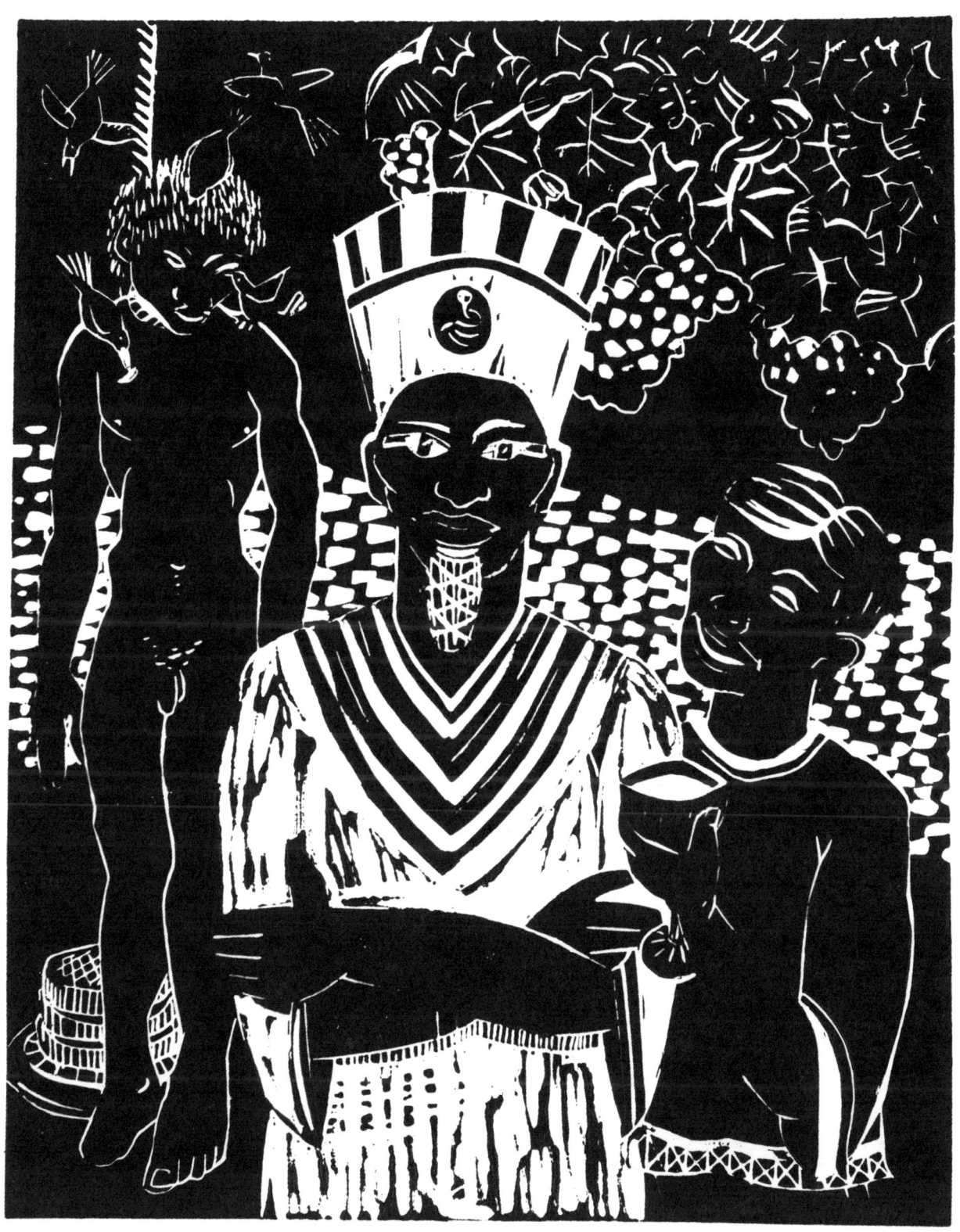

Exodus 2:5–15

MOSES MURDERS

Now the daughter of Pharaoh came down to bathe at the river, while her young women walked beside the river. She saw the basket among the reeds and sent her servant woman, and she took it. When she opened it, she saw the child, and behold, the baby was crying. She took pity on him and said, "This is one of the Hebrews' children." Then his sister said to Pharaoh's daughter, "Shall I go and call you a nurse from the Hebrew women to nurse the child for you?" And Pharaoh's daughter said to her, "Go." So the girl went and called the child's mother. And Pharaoh's daughter said to her, "Take this child away and nurse him for me, and I will give you your wages." So the woman took the child and nursed him. When the child grew older, she brought him to Pharaoh's daughter, and he became her son. She named him Moses, "Because," she said, "I drew him out of the water."

One day, when Moses had grown up, he went out to his people and looked on their burdens, and he saw an Egyptian beating a Hebrew, one of his people. He looked this way and that, and seeing no one, he struck down the Egyptian and hid him in the sand. When he went out the next day, behold, two Hebrews were struggling together. And he said to the man in the wrong, "Why do you strike your companion?" He answered, "Who made you a prince and a judge over us? Do you mean to kill me as you killed the Egyptian?" Then Moses was afraid, and thought, "Surely the thing is known." When Pharaoh heard of it, he sought to kill Moses. But Moses fled from Pharaoh and stayed in the land of Midian. And he sat down by a well.

Moses Kills an Egyptian
MATTHEW L. CLARK | LINOCUT

The artist based this linocut on *Cain Killing Abel*, a woodcut by Albrecht Dürer from 1511. The visual connection underscores the weight of the crime. Often when reading this account the action seems almost justified because the Egyptians were the enemy and Moses was an Israelite. But Moses had been adopted into the royal household. This violent act was as heinous as Cain murdering his brother. Moses would eventually return to Egypt and lead God's people to freedom, but there was blood on his hands. He could never be the holy savior of mankind who was going to crush the Serpent's head, and because of his sins would never reach the Promised Land.

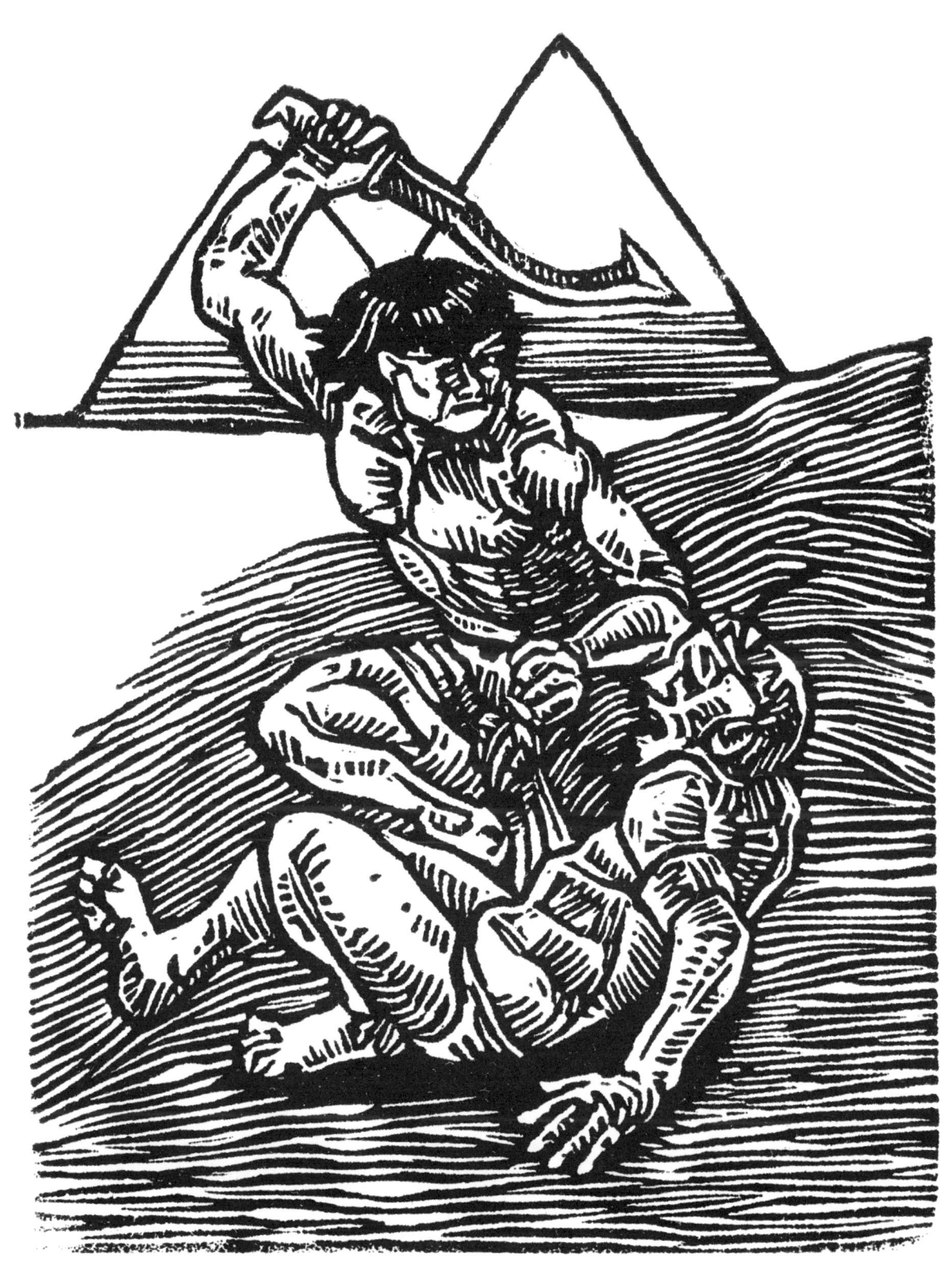

Exodus 8:1–4; 9:22, 23, 27–30

THE PLAGUES

Then the Lord said to Moses, "Go in to Pharaoh and say to him, 'Thus says the Lord, "Let my people go, that they may serve me. But if you refuse to let them go, behold, I will plague all your country with frogs. The Nile shall swarm with frogs that shall come up into your house and into your bedroom and on your bed and into the houses of your servants and your people, and into your ovens and your kneading bowls. The frogs shall come up on you and on your people and on all your servants."'"

. . .

Then the Lord said to Moses, "Stretch out your hand toward heaven, so that there may be hail in all the land of Egypt, on man and beast and every plant of the field, in the land of Egypt." Then Moses stretched out his staff toward heaven, and the Lord sent thunder and hail, and fire ran down to the earth. And the Lord rained hail upon the land of Egypt.

. . .

Then Pharaoh sent and called Moses and Aaron and said to them, "This time I have sinned; the Lord is in the right, and I and my people are in the wrong. Plead with the Lord, for there has been enough of God's thunder and hail. I will let you go, and you shall stay no longer." Moses said to him, "As soon as I have gone out of the city, I will stretch out my hands to the Lord. The thunder will cease, and there will be no more hail, so that you may know that the earth is the Lord's. But as for you and your servants, I know that you do not yet fear the Lord God."

Frog and Hail
ANONYMOUS | WOODCUT

These woodcuts from the Cologne Bible show two of the plagues that were sent upon Egypt. The plagues contrasted the power of the true God with the weaknesses of Egypt's various gods. For example, turning water to blood was an attack on Khnum (guardian of the Nile) and Hapi (spirit of the Nile). Therefore, an inundation of frogs questioned the authority of the frog-headed goddess Heqt, while destructive hail was an ursurping of the control of Seth (an earth god) and Nut (the sky goddess). There is the tradition in art of Moses having horns—as seen in Michelangelo's sculpture *Moses*—and in these prints as well. This is due to a peculiarity in the Vulgate. In Exodus 34:29–35 Moses came down from Mount Sinai and the skin of his face shone because he had been talking with God. St. Jerome translated the word "shone" in the Vulgate as "horned."

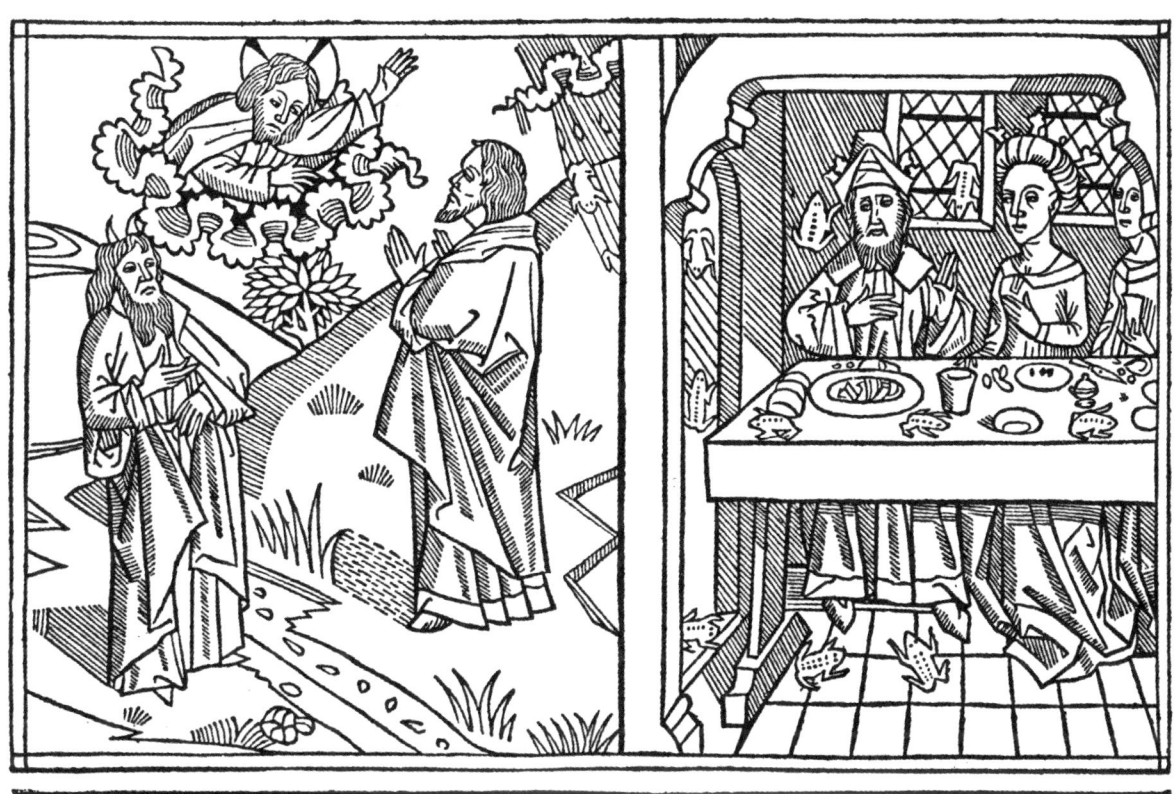
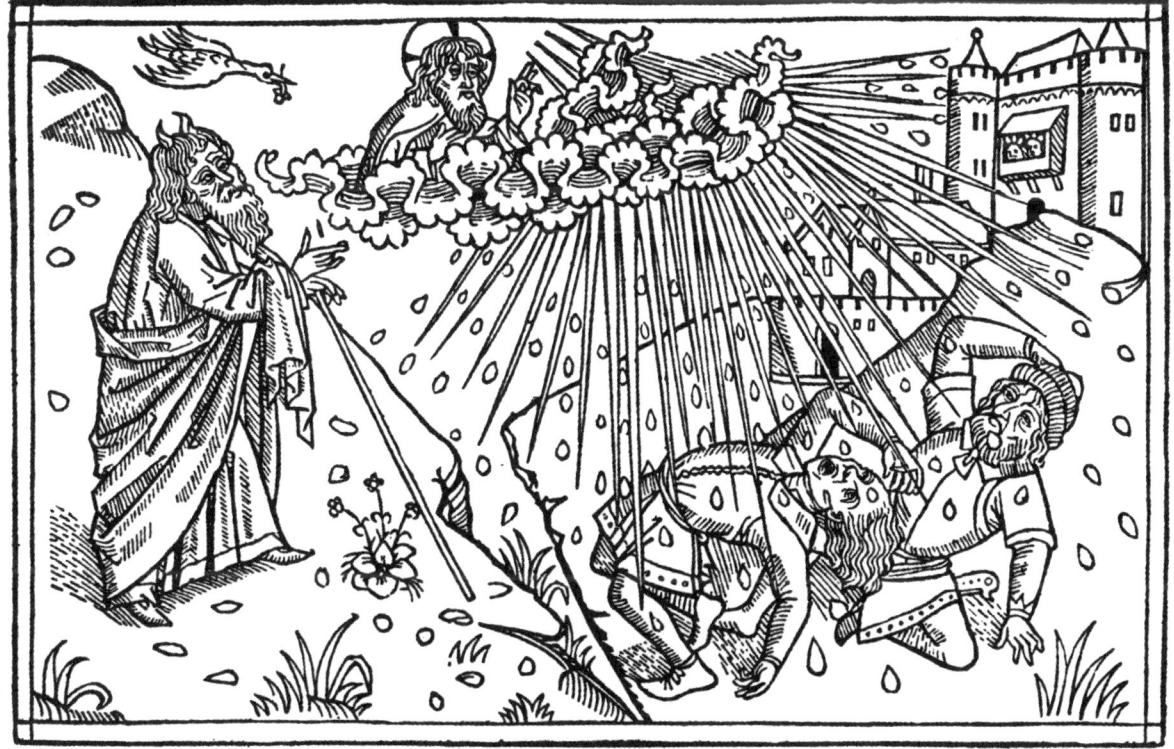

Exodus 12:1–3, 7–14

THE PASSOVER

The Lord said to Moses and Aaron in the land of Egypt, "This month shall be for you the beginning of months. It shall be the first month of the year for you. Tell all the congregation of Israel that on the tenth day of this month every man shall take a lamb according to their fathers' houses, a lamb for a household

. . .

"Then they shall take some of the blood and put it on the two doorposts and the lintel of the houses in which they eat it. They shall eat the flesh that night, roasted on the fire; with unleavened bread and bitter herbs they shall eat it. Do not eat any of it raw or boiled in water, but roasted, its head with its legs and its inner parts. And you shall let none of it remain until the morning; anything that remains until the morning you shall burn. In this manner you shall eat it: with your belt fastened, your sandals on your feet, and your staff in your hand. And you shall eat it in haste. It is the Lord's Passover. For I will pass through the land of Egypt that night, and I will strike all the firstborn in the land of Egypt, both man and beast; and on all the gods of Egypt I will execute judgments: I am the Lord. The blood shall be a sign for you, on the houses where you are. And when I see the blood, I will pass over you, and no plague will befall you to destroy you, when I strike the land of Egypt.

Death Angel

KATHERINE BRIMBERRY | DIRECT POLYMER GRAVURE WITH CHINE COLLÉ

The Passover was the culmination of a series of disasters—flies, gnats, frogs, boils, darkness, and hail. When the final plague came, it required blood. It began with the death of a lamb, blood on the doorframes, and eventually the death of the firstborn. The Jews used hyssop to apply the blood to the doorframes which is reminiscent of the hyssop that was used to give sour wine to Jesus on the cross. The artist writes, "In considering how to represent the Angel of Death I wanted to first show that none of us is immune to death (the phone book page represents all of us). Secondly I wanted to illustrate that even something as fearsome as the *Death Angel* is, in the end, merely an instrument in the hand of God. He is a soldier who is sent out by holy decree, a servant who is subject to God's divine, wise, and loving plans."

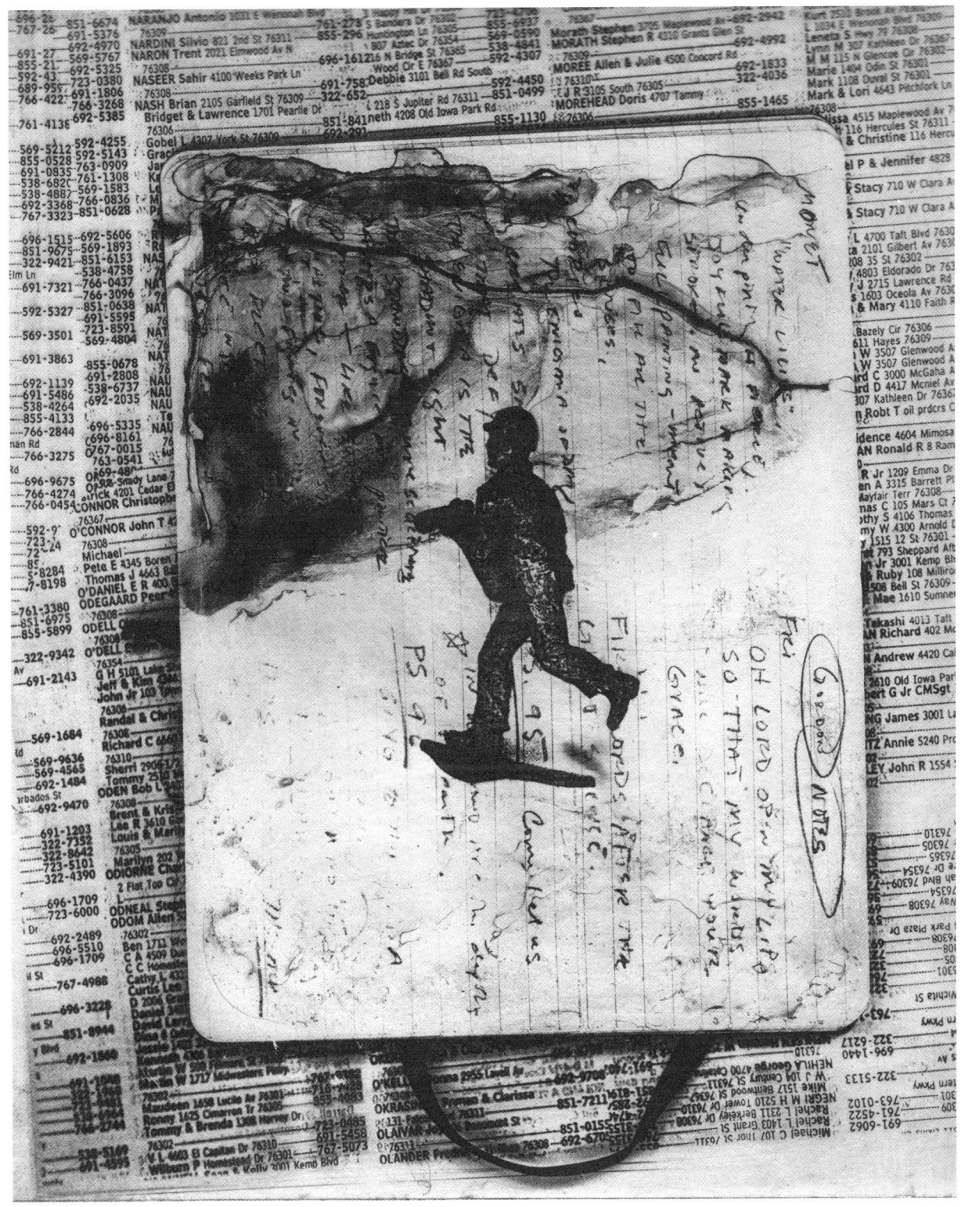

Exodus 14:23–31

AN ARMY IS DESTROYED

The Egyptians pursued and went in after them into the midst of the sea, all Pharaoh's horses, his chariots, and his horsemen. And in the morning watch the Lord in the pillar of fire and of cloud looked down on the Egyptian forces and threw the Egyptian forces into a panic, clogging their chariot wheels so that they drove heavily. And the Egyptians said, "Let us flee from before Israel, for the Lord fights for them against the Egyptians."

Then the Lord said to Moses, "Stretch out your hand over the sea, that the water may come back upon the Egyptians, upon their chariots, and upon their horsemen." So Moses stretched out his hand over the sea, and the sea returned to its normal course when the morning appeared. And as the Egyptians fled into it, the Lord threw the Egyptians into the midst of the sea. The waters returned and covered the chariots and the horsemen; of all the host of Pharaoh that had followed them into the sea, not one of them remained. But the people of Israel walked on dry ground through the sea, the waters being a wall to them on their right hand and on their left.

Thus the Lord saved Israel that day from the hand of the Egyptians, and Israel saw the Egyptians dead on the seashore. Israel saw the great power that the Lord used against the Egyptians, so the people feared the Lord, and they believed in the Lord and in his servant Moses.

Red Sea Carnage

WAYNE FORTE | LINOCUT

The safe crossing through the Red Sea on dry land by the Israelites—along with the subsequent drowning of the Egyptian armies—is a wondrously strange event. Yet theologian B.B. Warfield reminds the reader, "In the infinite wisdom of the Lord of all the earth, each event falls with exact precision into its proper place in the unfolding of his divine plan. Nothing, however small, however strange, occurs without his ordering, or without its particular fitness for its place in the working out of his purpose; and the end of all shall be the manifestation of his glory, and the accumulation of his praise." And it is therefore fitting to take up our tambourines and join with Miriam the sister of Aaron and all the women and sing, "Sing to the Lord, for he has triumphed gloriously; the horse and his rider he has thrown into the sea."

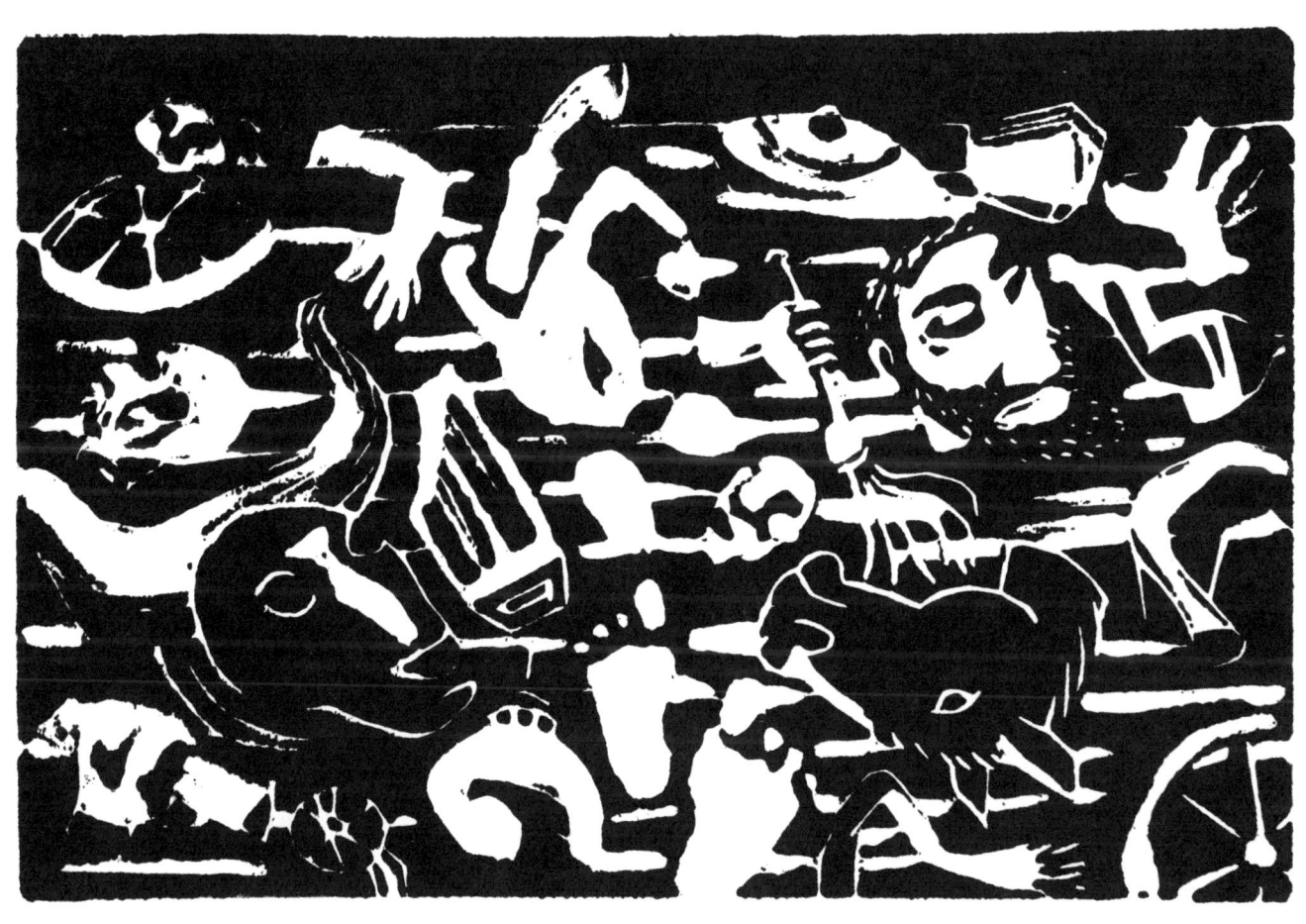

Exodus 24:12–18

THE MOUNTAIN OF GOD

The Lord said to Moses, "Come up to me on the mountain and wait there, that I may give you the tablets of stone, with the law and the commandment, which I have written for their instruction." So Moses rose with his assistant Joshua, and Moses went up into the mountain of God. And he said to the elders, "Wait here for us until we return to you. And behold, Aaron and Hur are with you. Whoever has a dispute, let him go to them."

Then Moses went up on the mountain, and the cloud covered the mountain. The glory of the Lord dwelt on Mount Sinai, and the cloud covered it six days. And on the seventh day he called to Moses out of the midst of the cloud. Now the appearance of the glory of the Lord was like a devouring fire on the top of the mountain in the sight of the people of Israel. Moses entered the cloud and went up on the mountain. And Moses was on the mountain forty days and forty nights.

Moses Receives the Law

EDWARD KNIPPERS | WOODCUT

This print represents a departure from the usual depictions of an old, bearded man holding two arched tablets of stone containing the Law of God. Knippers commented on this piece, saying, "I have tried to show the Law and its complications as weight rather than showing the tablets." Paul writes of this terrible weight in the third chapter of Romans: "For by works of the law no human being will be justified in his sight, since through the law comes knowledge of sin.... there is no distinction: for all have sinned and fall short of the glory of God ..."

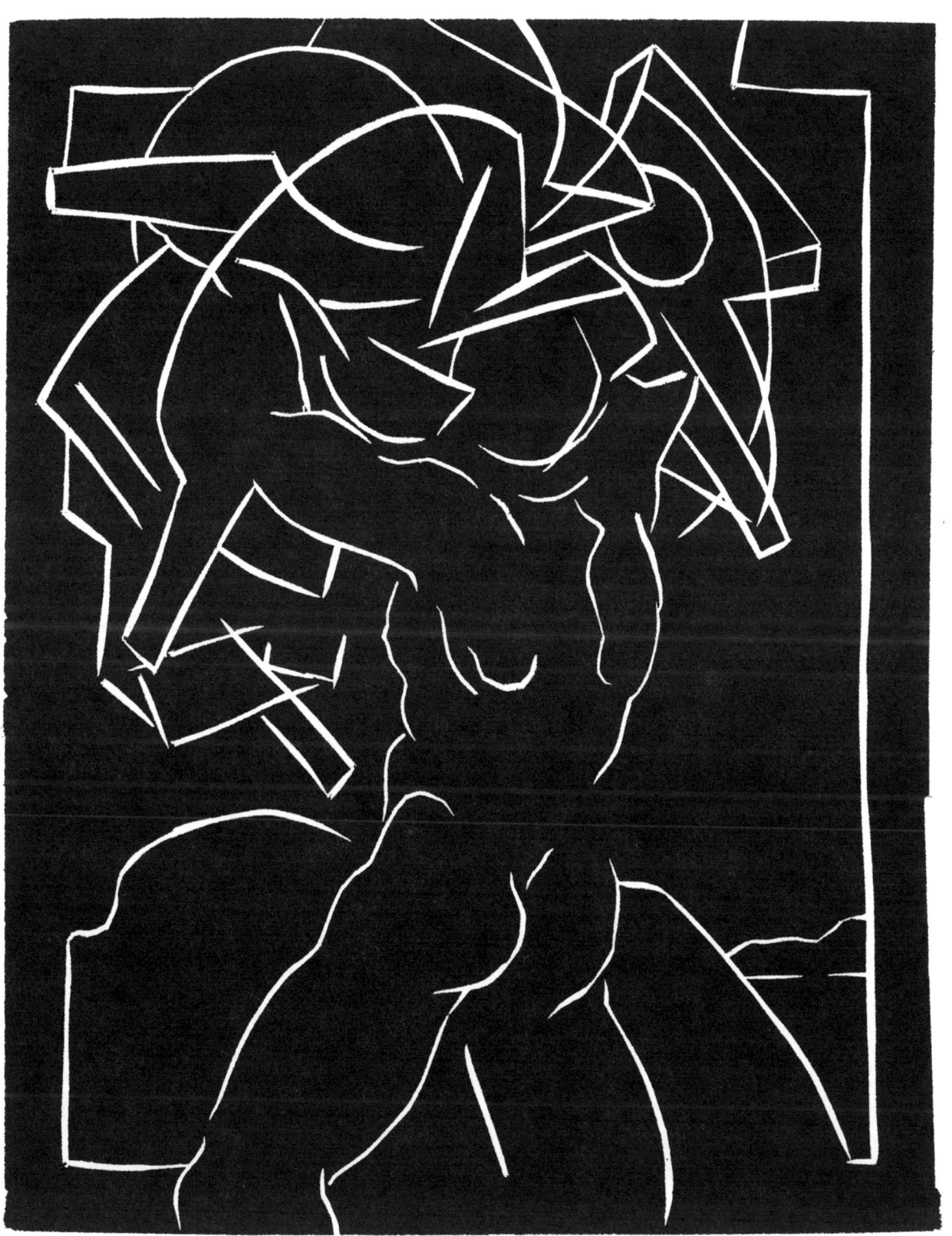

Exodus 16:13–17, 31–35

THE LORD FEEDS HIS PEOPLE

In the evening quail came up and covered the camp, and in the morning dew lay around the camp. And when the dew had gone up, there was on the face of the wilderness a fine, flake-like thing, fine as frost on the ground. When the people of Israel saw it, they said to one another, "What is it?" For they did not know what it was. And Moses said to them, "It is the bread that the Lord has given you to eat. This is what the Lord has commanded: 'Gather of it, each one of you, as much as he can eat. You shall each take an omer, according to the number of the persons that each of you has in his tent.'" And the people of Israel did so. They gathered, some more, some less.

. . .

Now the house of Israel called its name manna. It was like coriander seed, white, and the taste of it was like wafers made with honey. Moses said, "This is what the Lord has commanded: 'Let an omer of it be kept throughout your generations, so that they may see the bread with which I fed you in the wilderness, when I brought you out of the land of Egypt.'" And Moses said to Aaron, "Take a jar, and put an omer of manna in it, and place it before the Lord to be kept throughout your generations." As the Lord commanded Moses, so Aaron placed it before the testimony to be kept. The people of Israel ate the manna forty years, till they came to a habitable land. They ate the manna till they came to the border of the land of Canaan.

Exodus: Bread from Heaven
STEVE PRINCE | LINOCUT

Manna was a mysterious thing provided completely by God for the good of his people. The Israelites were not to hoard it, for it would come to them new each day. This print is from a series that looks at the Old Testament through the lens of a love story. Or as the artist writes, "true love is like an Old Testament made New each day." Here a couple shares some Myrr tea, while locked together in their marriage vows. The premise of this piece is: *If God supplied for the Israelites as they wandered about for forty years, then what will God do for a couple that commits to one another, bound through the covenant of marriage?* God proved faithful to the Israelites in their wilderness, providing for their needs and therefore He will supply this couple's needs as they wander through relational deserts as well as through lands flowing with milk and honey.

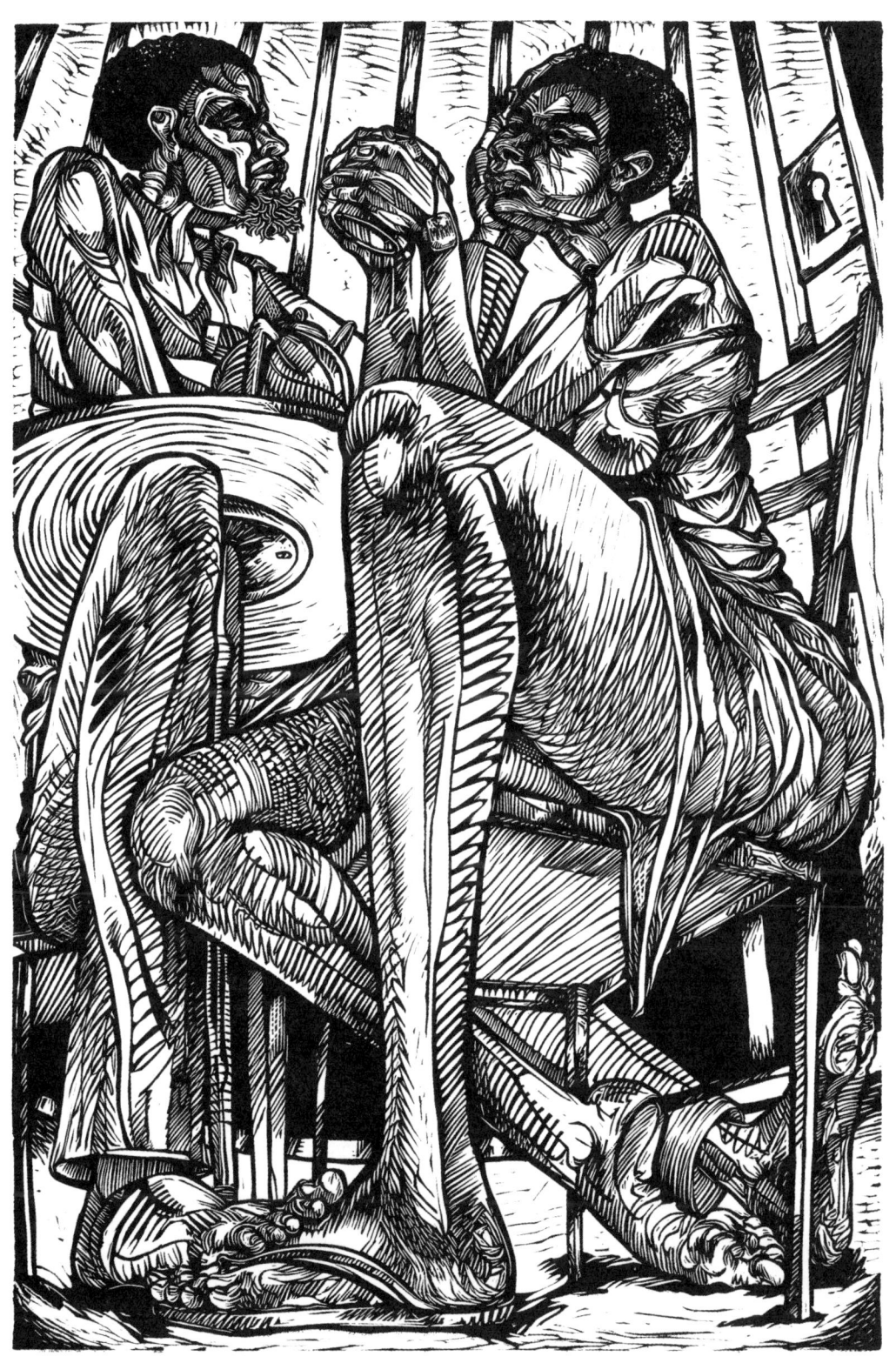

Exodus 31:1–5, 37:1–9

FOR GLORY AND FOR BEAUTY

The Lord said to Moses, "See, I have called by name Bezalel the son of Uri, son of Hur, of the tribe of Judah, and I have filled him with the Spirit of God, with ability and intelligence, with knowledge and all craftsmanship, to devise artistic designs, to work in gold, silver, and bronze, in cutting stones for setting, and in carving wood, to work in every craft.

. . .

Bezalel made the ark of acacia wood. Two cubits and a half was its length, a cubit and a half its breadth, and a cubit and a half its height. And he overlaid it with pure gold inside and outside, and made a molding of gold around it. And he cast for it four rings of gold for its four feet, two rings on its one side and two rings on its other side. And he made poles of acacia wood and overlaid them with gold and put the poles into the rings on the sides of the ark to carry the ark. And he made a mercy seat of pure gold. Two cubits and a half was its length, and a cubit and a half its breadth. And he made two cherubim of gold. He made them of hammered work on the two ends of the mercy seat, one cherub on the one end, and one cherub on the other end. Of one piece with the mercy seat he made the cherubim on its two ends. The cherubim spread out their wings above, overshadowing the mercy seat with their wings, with their faces one to another; toward the mercy seat were the faces of the cherubim.

Bezalel

NED BUSTARD | LINOCUT

The first person in the Bible to be filled with the Holy Spirit was Bezalel, the chief artisan of the Tabernacle. He had skill in engraving precious metals and stones and in wood-carving. He was also a teacher of the arts, and had many apprentices under him (Exodus 35:34–35). Angels were sewn into multicolored curtains and hung from gold hooks. Bronze, silver, and gold were finely fashioned into liturgical objects throughout the Tabernacle. And the priests were clothed in beautiful vestments from head to toe. All of this beauty was made by Bezalel and his apprentices for the glory of God and to be part of the worship offered up by His chosen people. In this print Bezalel is attaching one of the cherubim that sit on either side of the Mercy Seat on the Ark of the Covenant.

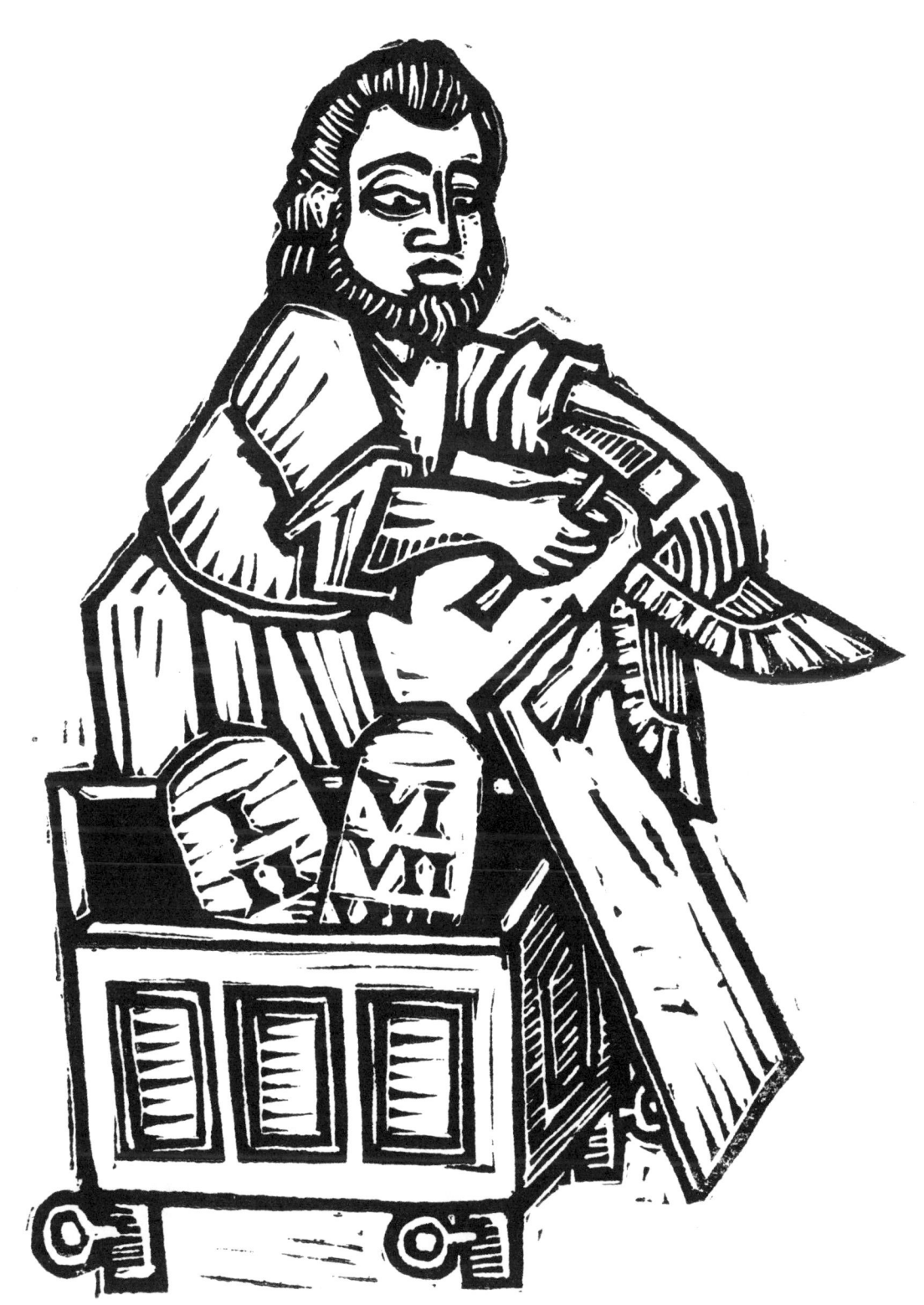

Numbers 21:4–9

THE BRONZE SERPENT

From Mount Hor they set out by the way to the Red Sea, to go around the land of Edom. And the people became impatient on the way. And the people spoke against God and against Moses, "Why have you brought us up out of Egypt to die in the wilderness? For there is no food and no water, and we loathe this worthless food." Then the Lord sent fiery serpents among the people, and they bit the people, so that many people of Israel died. And the people came to Moses and said, "We have sinned, for we have spoken against the Lord and against you. Pray to the Lord, that he take away the serpents from us." So Moses prayed for the people. And the Lord said to Moses, "Make a fiery serpent and set it on a pole, and everyone who is bitten, when he sees it, shall live." So Moses made a bronze serpent and set it on a pole. And if a serpent bit anyone, he would look at the bronze serpent and live.

Desert Serpents

TANJA BUTLER | LINOCUT

Art can be used to the glory of God or as an idol. In this account a metal sculpture of a snake is commissioned by God and is used to save the lives of his people. Later, in 2 Kings 18, the same snake was called Nehushtan and was being used as an idol, so it had to be destroyed by Hezekiah for the sake of the holiness of God's people. And for the holiness of God's people Jesus would one day need to be lifted up, that whoever would look to him would receive eternal life: "For God so loved the world, that he gave his only Son, that whoever believes in him should not perish but have eternal life . . . Whoever believes in him is not condemned, but whoever does not believe is condemned already, because he has not believed in the name of the only Son of God."

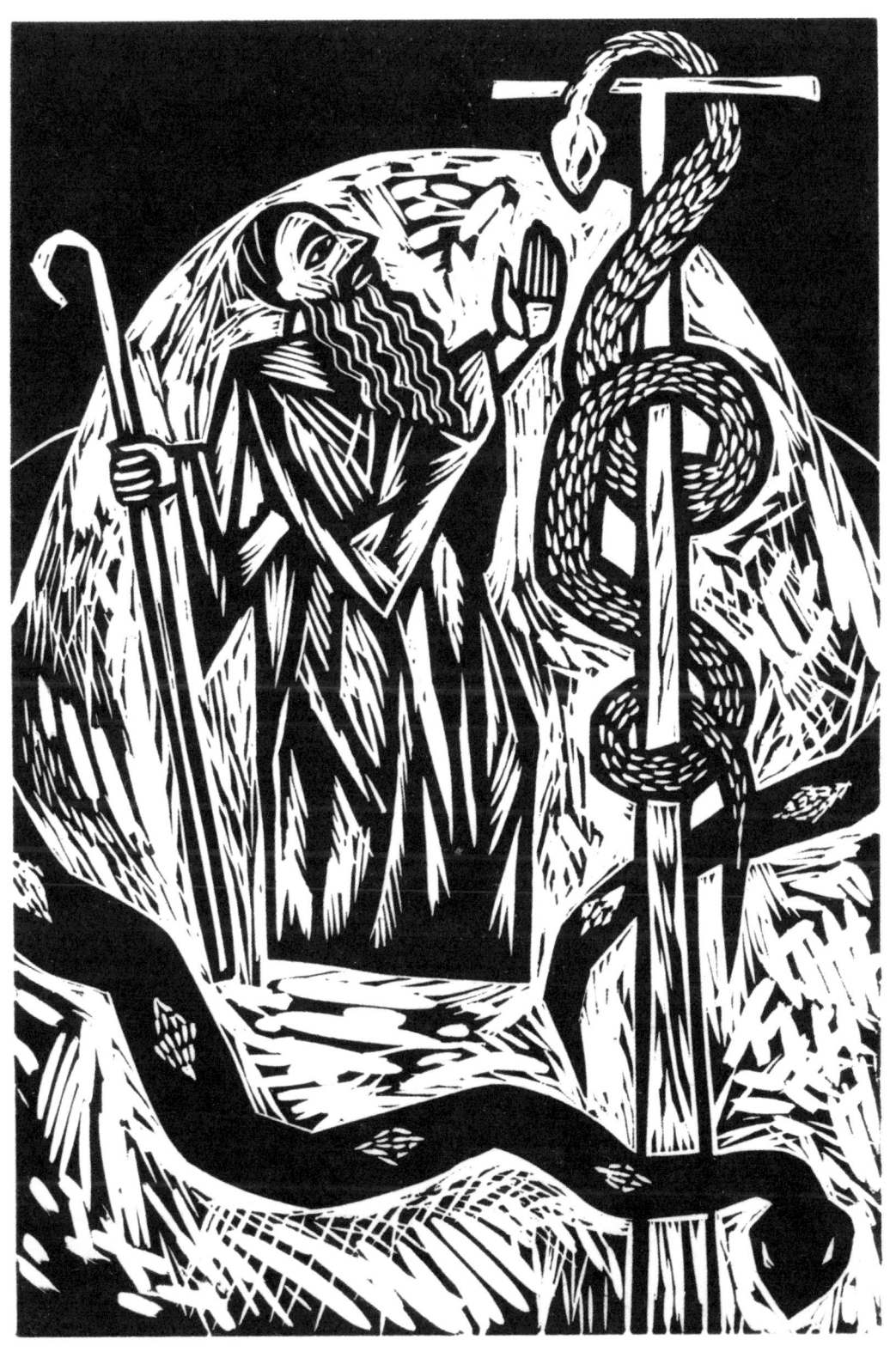

Numbers 25:1–11

ZIMRI AND COZBI

While Israel lived in Shittim, the people began to whore with the daughters of Moab. These invited the people to the sacrifices of their gods, and the people ate and bowed down to their gods. So Israel yoked himself to Baal of Peor. And the anger of the Lord was kindled against Israel. And the Lord said to Moses, "Take all the chiefs of the people and hang them in the sun before the Lord, that the fierce anger of the Lord may turn away from Israel." And Moses said to the judges of Israel, "Each of you kill those of his men who have yoked themselves to Baal of Peor."

And behold, one of the people of Israel came and brought a Midianite woman to his family, in the sight of Moses and in the sight of the whole congregation of the people of Israel, while they were weeping in the entrance of the tent of meeting. When Phinehas the son of Eleazar, son of Aaron the priest, saw it, he rose and left the congregation and took a spear in his hand and went after the man of Israel into the chamber and pierced both of them, the man of Israel and the woman through her belly. Thus the plague on the people of Israel was stopped. Nevertheless, those who died by the plague were twenty-four thousand.

And the Lord said to Moses, "Phinehas the son of Eleazar, son of Aaron the priest, has turned back my wrath from the people of Israel, in that he was jealous with my jealousy among them, so that I did not consume the people of Israel in my jealousy."

Sanctification (The Spear of Phinehas)
NED BUSTARD | MONOPRINT

The grandson of Aaron was jealous for the glory of God and did what was needed to call God's people back to holy living. Being devoted to holiness before God often requires actions that seem harsh. For example, Jesus said if your eye causes you to sin you should tear it out and enter the kingdom of God with one eye instead of being thrown into hell with two eyes. Sadly, the church has not torn out sin in the camp as often as it should. Many see the glorious gospel of Grace as permission to loose and even licentious living. But Paul wrote in Romans 6, "Are we to continue in sin that grace may abound? By no means! How can we who died to sin still live in it?" Christians are called to walk in newness of life. Grace should embolden God's chosen ones to enthusiastic obedience. It is impossible to claim to be a follower of God and not desire to grow in holy living.

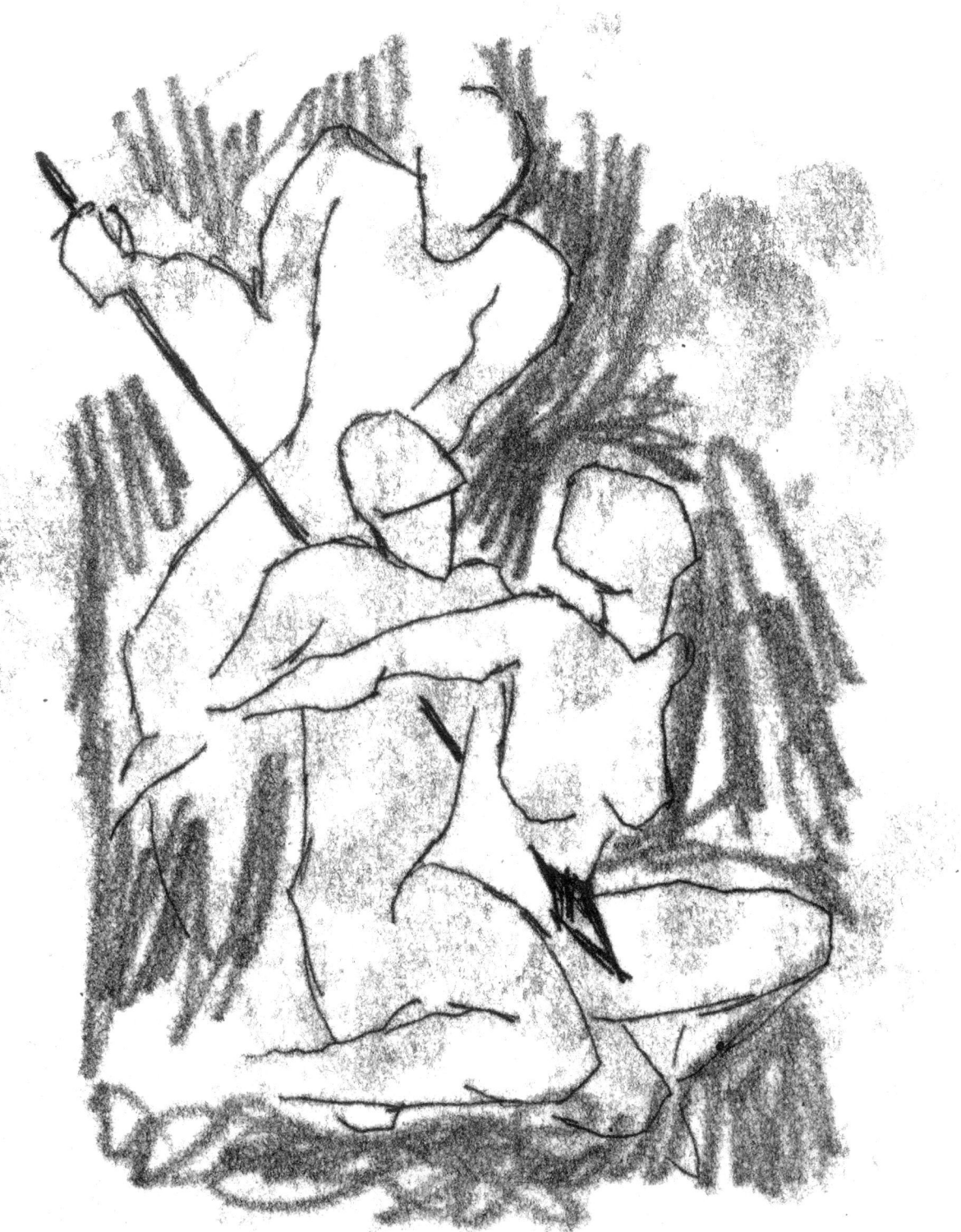

Joshua 2:1, 15–21

RAHAB

And Joshua the son of Nun sent two men secretly from Shittim as spies, saying, "Go, view the land, especially Jericho." And they went and came into the house of a prostitute whose name was Rahab and lodged there.

. . .

Then she let them down by a rope through the window, for her house was built into the city wall, so that she lived in the wall. And she said to them, "Go into the hills, or the pursuers will encounter you, and hide there three days until the pursuers have returned. Then afterward you may go your way." The men said to her, "We will be guiltless with respect to this oath of yours that you have made us swear. Behold, when we come into the land, you shall tie this scarlet cord in the window through which you let us down, and you shall gather into your house your father and mother, your brothers, and all your father's household. Then if anyone goes out of the doors of your house into the street, his blood shall be on his own head, and we shall be guiltless. But if a hand is laid on anyone who is with you in the house, his blood shall be on our head. But if you tell this business of ours, then we shall be guiltless with respect to your oath that you have made us swear." And she said, "According to your words, so be it." Then she sent them away, and they departed. And she tied the scarlet cord in the window.

Rahab

NED BUSTARD | LINOCUT

Denis Haack of *Critique* magazine writes that Rahab is "usually depicted as the scandalously promiscuous woman who was saved by grace, always with the impression given that since someone much more low class and tasteless than I can be saved, there is hope for the likes of me, who is a sinner, but not really all that bad compared to her . . ." But the composition of this print forces the viewer to look up to Rahab, begging the question: are you going to humble yourself and take the salvation offered by this holy hooker? Hebrews 11:31 states that "By faith Rahab the prostitute did not perish with those who were disobedient, because she had given a friendly welcome to the spies." She ended up marrying one of the spies and her son was Boaz, the husband of Ruth—placing her in the genealogical line of Jesus Christ.

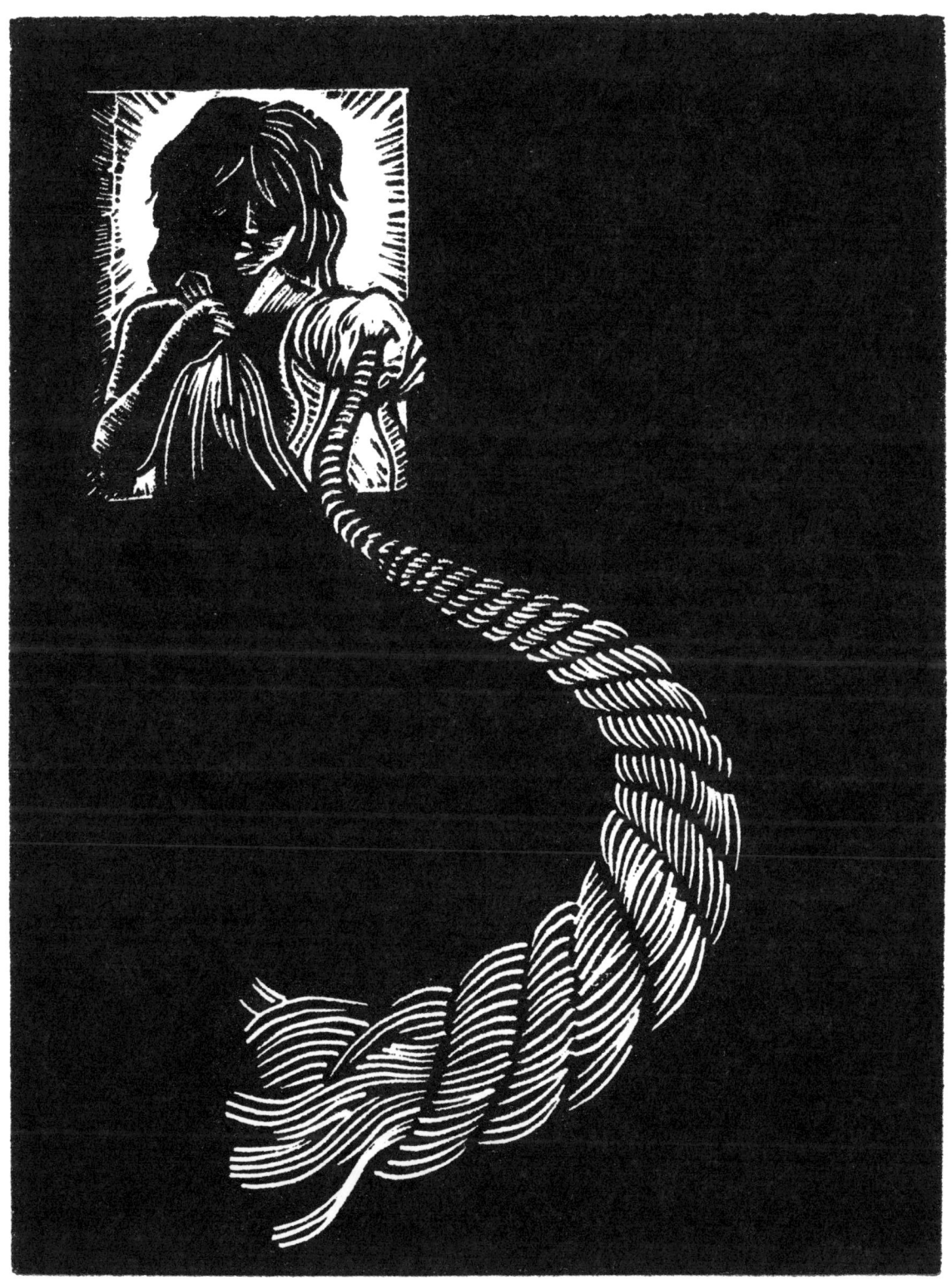

Joshua 10:34–42

GENOCIDE

Then Joshua and all Israel with him passed on from Lachish to Eglon. And they laid siege to it and fought against it. And they captured it on that day, and struck it with the edge of the sword. And he devoted every person in it to destruction that day, as he had done to Lachish.

Then Joshua and all Israel with him went up from Eglon to Hebron. And they fought against it and captured it and struck it with the edge of the sword, and its king and its towns, and every person in it. He left none remaining, as he had done to Eglon, and devoted it to destruction and every person in it.

Then Joshua and all Israel with him turned back to Debir and fought against it and he captured it with its king and all its towns. And they struck them with the edge of the sword and devoted to destruction every person in it; he left none remaining. Just as he had done to Hebron and to Libnah and its king, so he did to Debir and to its king.

So Joshua struck the whole land, the hill country and the Negeb and the lowland and the slopes, and all their kings. He left none remaining, but devoted to destruction all that breathed, just as the Lord God of Israel commanded. And Joshua struck them from Kadesh-barnea as far as Gaza, and all the country of Goshen, as far as Gibeon. And Joshua captured all these kings and their land at one time, because the Lord God of Israel fought for Israel. Then Joshua returned, and all Israel with him, to the camp at Gilgal.

None Remaining/The Edge of the Sword
STEVE HALLA | WOODCUT

Although this piece has a detailed photographic appearance, it is actually a huge woodblock print that was made using a hammer and three nails. "I first started using the nail technique a few years ago while studying the woodcut prints of Käthe Kollwitz and Emil Nolde," comments Halla. "My goal was to somehow combine the bold quality of the woodcut art of the German Expressionists with Albrecht Dürer's attention to detail and my interest in photography." The Bible includes many things that modern readers find hard to reconcile, but perhaps none is more challenging than God's command to kill all of those living in Canaan. There is a temptation to gloss over these passages or even omit them from the narrative. Yet if we are to do justice to the God of Scripture, we must look head-on at all He reveals about himself.

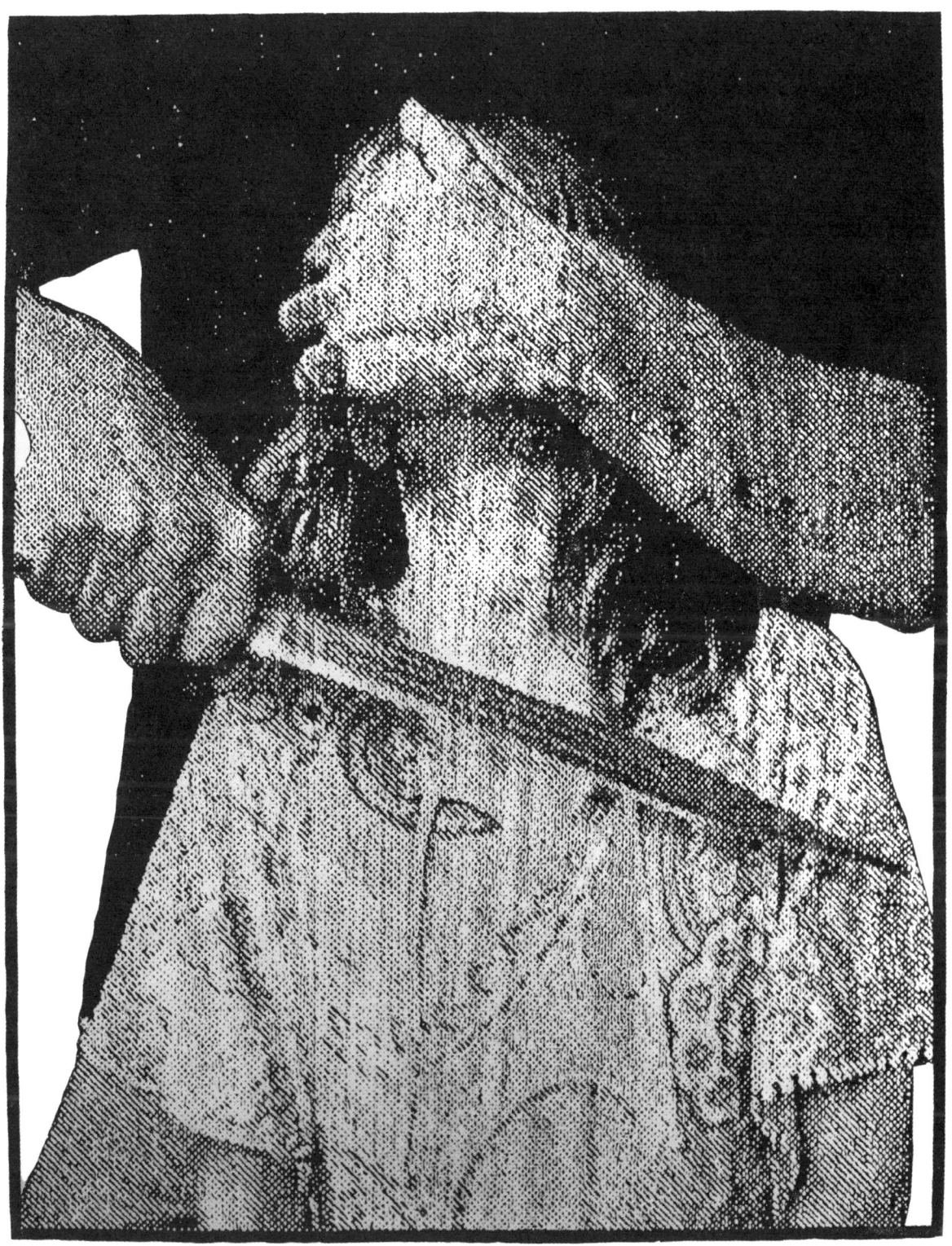

Judges 3:15–25
THE LEFT-HANDED HERO

Then the people of Israel cried out to the Lord, and the Lord raised up for them a deliverer, Ehud, the son of Gera, the Benjaminite, a left-handed man. The people of Israel sent tribute by him to Eglon the king of Moab. And Ehud made for himself a sword with two edges, a cubit in length, and he bound it on his right thigh under his clothes. And he presented the tribute to Eglon king of Moab. Now Eglon was a very fat man. And when Ehud had finished presenting the tribute, he sent away the people who carried the tribute. But he himself turned back at the idols near Gilgal and said, "I have a secret message for you, O king." And he commanded, "Silence." And all his attendants went out from his presence. And Ehud came to him as he was sitting alone in his cool roof chamber. And Ehud said, "I have a message from God for you." And he arose from his seat. And Ehud reached with his left hand, took the sword from his right thigh, and thrust it into his belly. And the hilt also went in after the blade, and the fat closed over the blade, for he did not pull the sword out of his belly; and the dung came out. Then Ehud went out into the porch and closed the doors of the roof chamber behind him and locked them.

When he had gone, the servants came, and when they saw that the doors of the roof chamber were locked, they thought, "Surely he is relieving himself in the closet of the cool chamber." And they waited till they were embarrassed. But when he still did not open the doors of the roof chamber, they took the key and opened them, and there lay their lord dead on the floor.

Ehud
RYAN STANDER | LITHOGRAPH

Stander interprets the story of Ehud by drawing on pop culture icons as varied as Jabba the Hutt and James Bond. This account has all the trappings of a classic spy thriller (except the girl). Ehud has a Q Branch gadget strapped to his leg before he enters the lair of the bulbous megalomaniac. He uses clever wordplay to get in close enough for the kill, and then the villain dies in a gratuitously graphic disgorgement of fecal matter. Ehud exits, and some potty humor is included in the story that delays the discovery of the corpse. Back in the hill country of Ephraim, Ehud blows his theme song on a trumpet (ba-da-da-dahh, da-da-da!) and the special-ops of Israel go roaring in. There is an explosive battle to wrap up the story, around 10,000 Moabite soldiers are wiped out, and Ehud lives to *Die Another Day*.

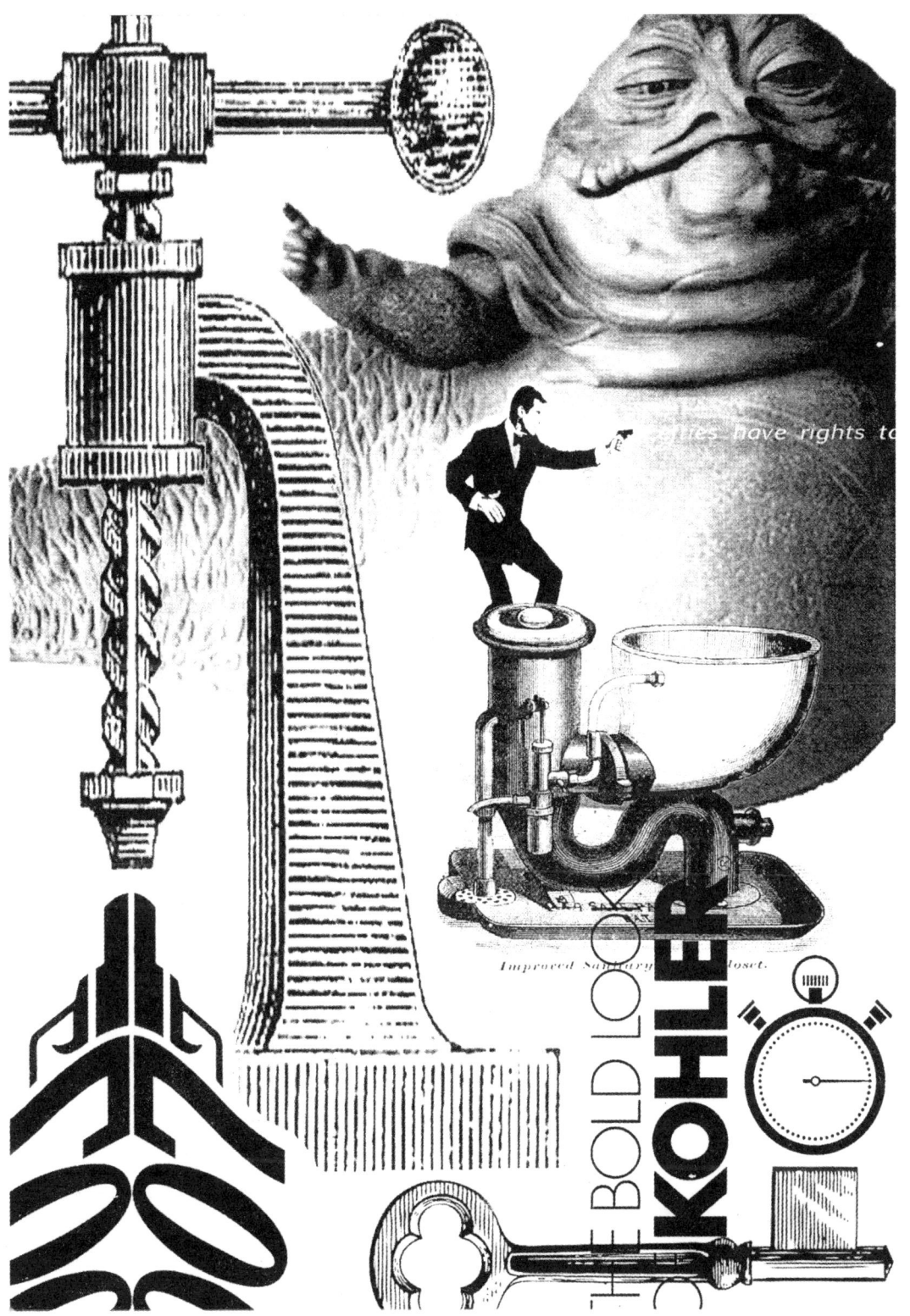

Judges 4:17–22
THE DEATH OF SISERA

But Sisera fled away on foot to the tent of Jael, the wife of Heber the Kenite, for there was peace between Jabin the king of Hazor and the house of Heber the Kenite. And Jael came out to meet Sisera and said to him, "Turn aside, my lord; turn aside to me; do not be afraid." So he turned aside to her into the tent, and she covered him with a rug. And he said to her, "Please give me a little water to drink, for I am thirsty." So she opened a skin of milk and gave him a drink and covered him. And he said to her, "Stand at the opening of the tent, and if any man comes and asks you, 'Is anyone here?' say, 'No.'" But Jael the wife of Heber took a tent peg, and took a hammer in her hand. Then she went softly to him and drove the peg into his temple until it went down into the ground while he was lying fast asleep from weariness. So he died. And behold, as Barak was pursuing Sisera, Jael went out to meet him and said to him, "Come, and I will show you the man whom you are seeking." So he went in to her tent, and there lay Sisera dead, with the tent peg in his temple.

Jael
WAYNE FORTE | LINOCUT

According to Deborah's song in the fifth chapter of Judges, Sisera's mother thinks her son is late in returning home because he is busy raping women and stealing embroidered garments from the dead. But instead Sisera lies on the ground with an impaled temple. The judge sings, "Most blessed of women be Jael, the wife of Heber the Kenite, of tent-dwelling women most blessed." Curiously, the only other woman called "most blessed of women" in the Bible was the Virgin Mary. Jewish commentaries present various theories debating to what degree Jael was *not* a virgin, but they all agree that the Israelites were saved through her violent act. Jael is responsible for killing Sisera and gets the credit for delivering God's people (rather than Deborah or Barak), while God gets the glory.

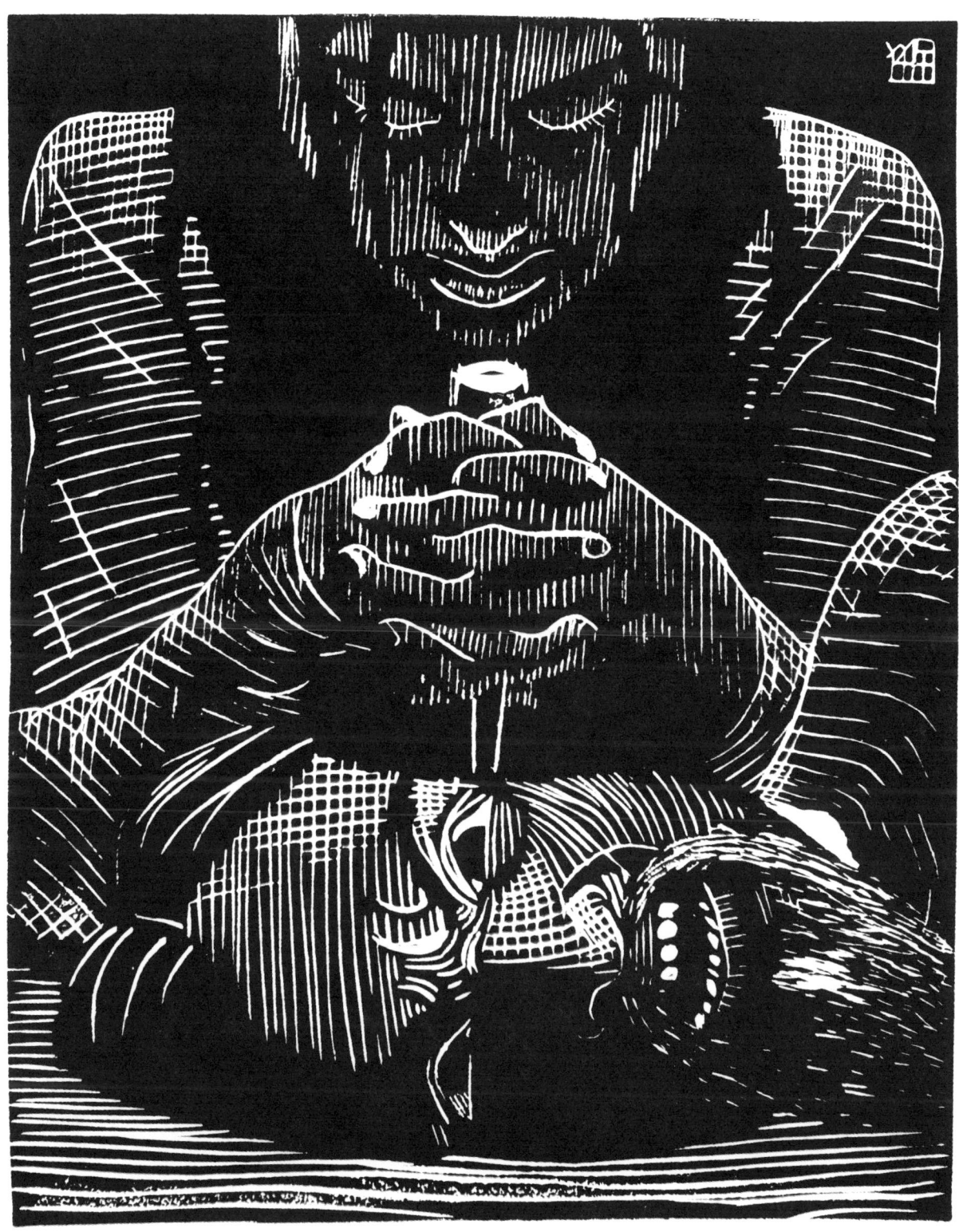

Judges 20:4–12

THE MAIL-ORDER BRIDE

And the Levite, the husband of the woman who was murdered, answered and said, "I came to Gibeah that belongs to Benjamin, I and my concubine, to spend the night. And the leaders of Gibeah rose against me and surrounded the house against me by night. They meant to kill me, and they violated my concubine, and she is dead. So I took hold of my concubine and cut her in pieces and sent her throughout all the country of the inheritance of Israel, for they have committed abomination and outrage in Israel. Behold, you people of Israel, all of you, give your advice and counsel here."

And all the people arose as one man, saying, "None of us will go to his tent, and none of us will return to his house. But now this is what we will do to Gibeah: we will go up against it by lot, and we will take ten men of a hundred throughout all the tribes of Israel, and a hundred of a thousand, and a thousand of ten thousand, to bring provisions for the people, that when they come they may repay Gibeah of Benjamin, for all the outrage that they have committed in Israel." So all the men of Israel gathered against the city, united as one man.

And the tribes of Israel sent men through all the tribe of Benjamin, saying, "What evil is this that has taken place among you?

What Evil is This?

NED BUSTARD | LINOCUT

The look of this print was inspired by the 1959 movie poster for *Anatomy of a Murder* by graphic designer Saul Bass. The print illustrates the story of a woman who was gang-raped by a group of men and left for dead. The Benjamites were as evil as the people of Sodom and Gomorrah, and this event illuminated Israel's spiritual state. In response, the woman was cut up in pieces by her husband and sent around to the different regions of Israel to call them to action. It was a shocking crime . . . and a callous response. But upon reflection, it is easy to see that this biblical account isn't too far removed from how women are being treated today. Through pornography, women are still cut into merely their body parts and shipped around. The internet simply delivers the pieces faster.

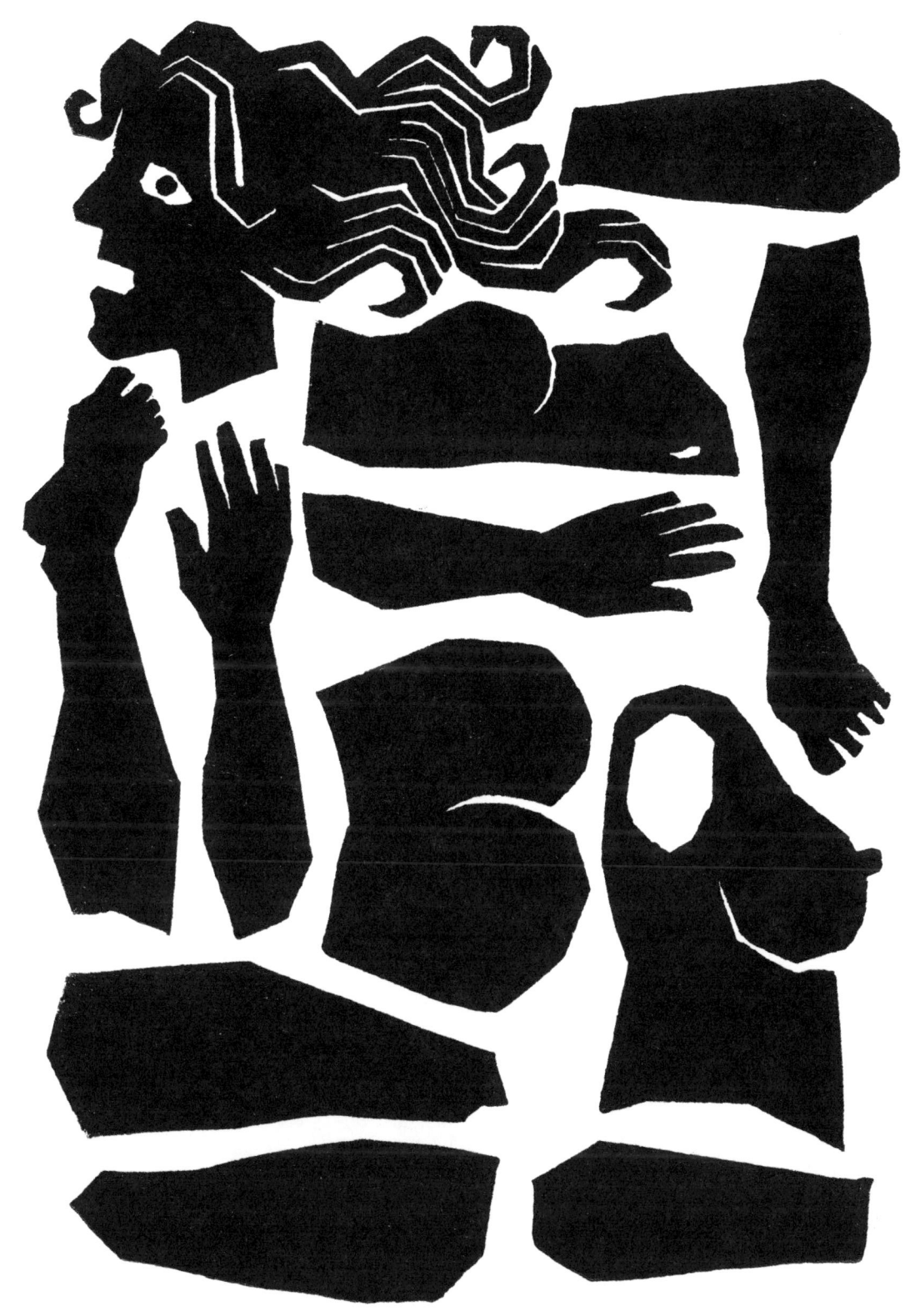

Judges 16:4–6, 15–18

SAMSON AND DELILAH

After this he loved a woman in the Valley of Sorek, whose name was Delilah. And the lords of the Philistines came up to her and said to her, "Seduce him, and see where his great strength lies, and by what means we may overpower him, that we may bind him to humble him. And we will each give you 1,100 pieces of silver." So Delilah said to Samson, "Please tell me where your great strength lies, and how you might be bound, that one could subdue you."

* * *

And she said to him, "How can you say, 'I love you,' when your heart is not with me? You have mocked me these three times, and you have not told me where your great strength lies." And when she pressed him hard with her words day after day, and urged him, his soul was vexed to death. And he told her all his heart, and said to her, "A razor has never come upon my head, for I have been a Nazirite to God from my mother's womb. If my head is shaved, then my strength will leave me, and I shall become weak and be like any other man."

When Delilah saw that he had told her all his heart, she sent and called the lords of the Philistines, saying, "Come up again, for he has told me all his heart." Then the lords of the Philistines came up to her and brought the money in their hands.

The Failed Redeemer

NED BUSTARD | LINOCUT

In some ways Samson prefigures Christ: he was betrayed by one he loved, was tortured and mocked by his people's oppressors, and died with outstretched arms. Samson was given supernatural strength to defeat the enemies of God's people. The Spirit of the Lord rushed upon him and he was able to kill a lion with his bare hands, slay an army with the jawbone of an ass, and destroy a pagan temple. But he is forever known as a failed redeemer because of his libido. Samson was supposed to protect and righteously judge God's people, but instead he gave away everything to be with a prostitute. This print could have been a scene of tender intimacy but instead is one of wicked betrayal. Samson sleeps blissfully while Delilah slowly takes out the shears that will rob Samson of his God-given strength.

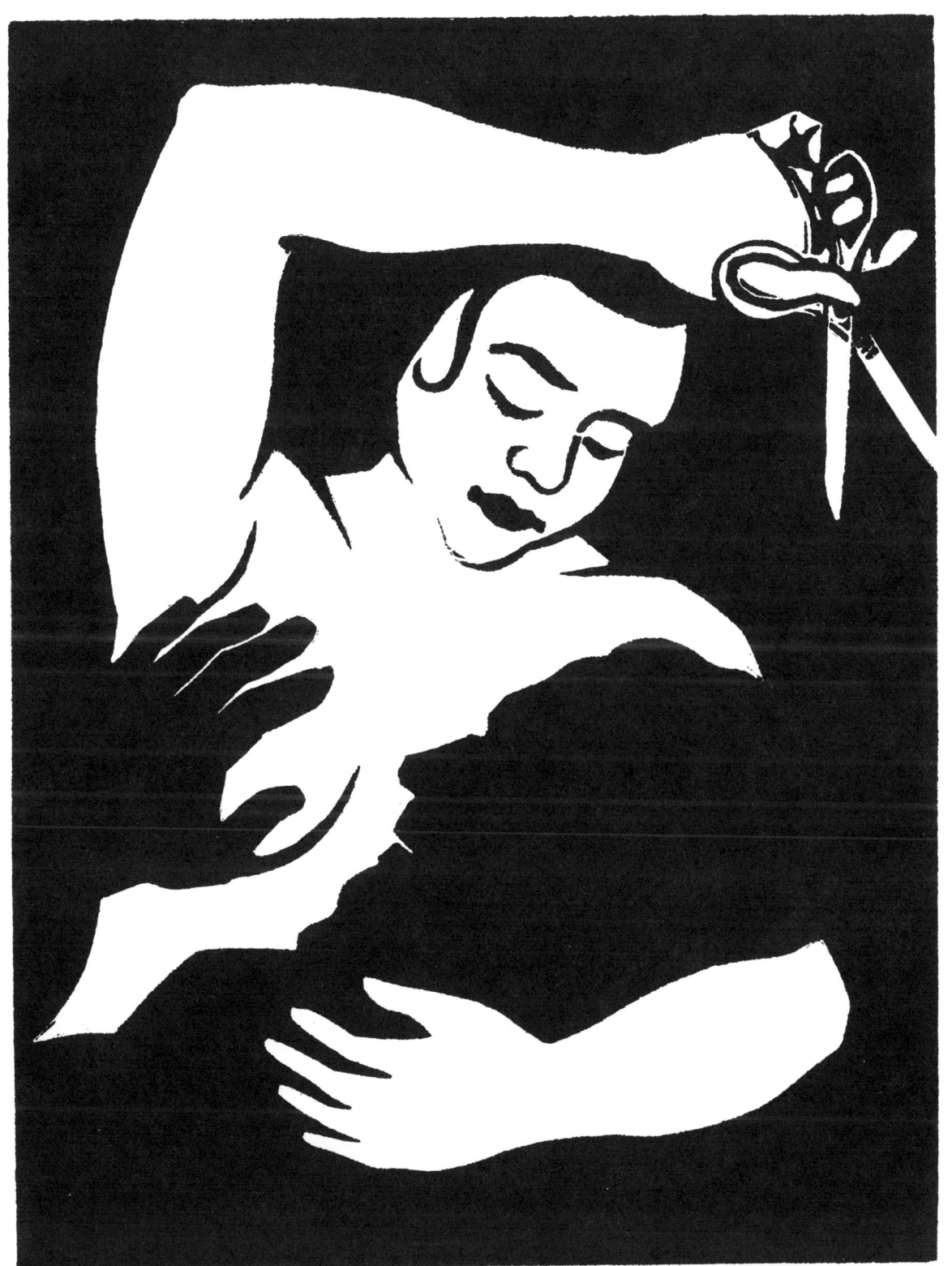

Ruth 3:6–13

THE THRESHING FLOOR

So she went down to the threshing floor and did just as her mother-in-law had commanded her. And when Boaz had eaten and drunk, and his heart was merry, he went to lie down at the end of the heap of grain. Then she came softly and uncovered his feet and lay down. At midnight the man was startled and turned over, and behold, a woman lay at his feet! He said, "Who are you?" And she answered, "I am Ruth, your servant. Spread your wings over your servant, for you are a redeemer." And he said, "May you be blessed by the Lord, my daughter. You have made this last kindness greater than the first in that you have not gone after young men, whether poor or rich. And now, my daughter, do not fear. I will do for you all that you ask, for all my fellow townsmen know that you are a worthy woman. And now it is true that I am a redeemer. Yet there is a redeemer nearer than I. Remain tonight, and in the morning, if he will redeem you, good; let him do it. But if he is not willing to redeem you, then, as the Lord lives, I will redeem you. Lie down until the morning."

Ruth and Boaz (after Ben Zion)
NED BUSTARD | LINOCUT

Ben-Zion Weinman (1897–1987) was a sculptor, painter, and printmaker. An emigrant from Ukraine, he came to the United States in 1920 and was a founding member of a 1930's avant-garde group called "The Ten." During the 1950s he completed several portfolios of expressionistic etchings/aquatints. This print is a reworking of one of those pieces from *The Books of Ruth, Job, and Song of Songs* portfolio. The Bible is ambiguous about what may or may not have happened that night on the threshing floor. Weinman leaves the way open for either reading of the passage in his visualization of the famous night. He depicts both people asleep under the starlight, the future great-grandmother of King David under a blanket at the feet of Boaz, who snores against a heap of grain.

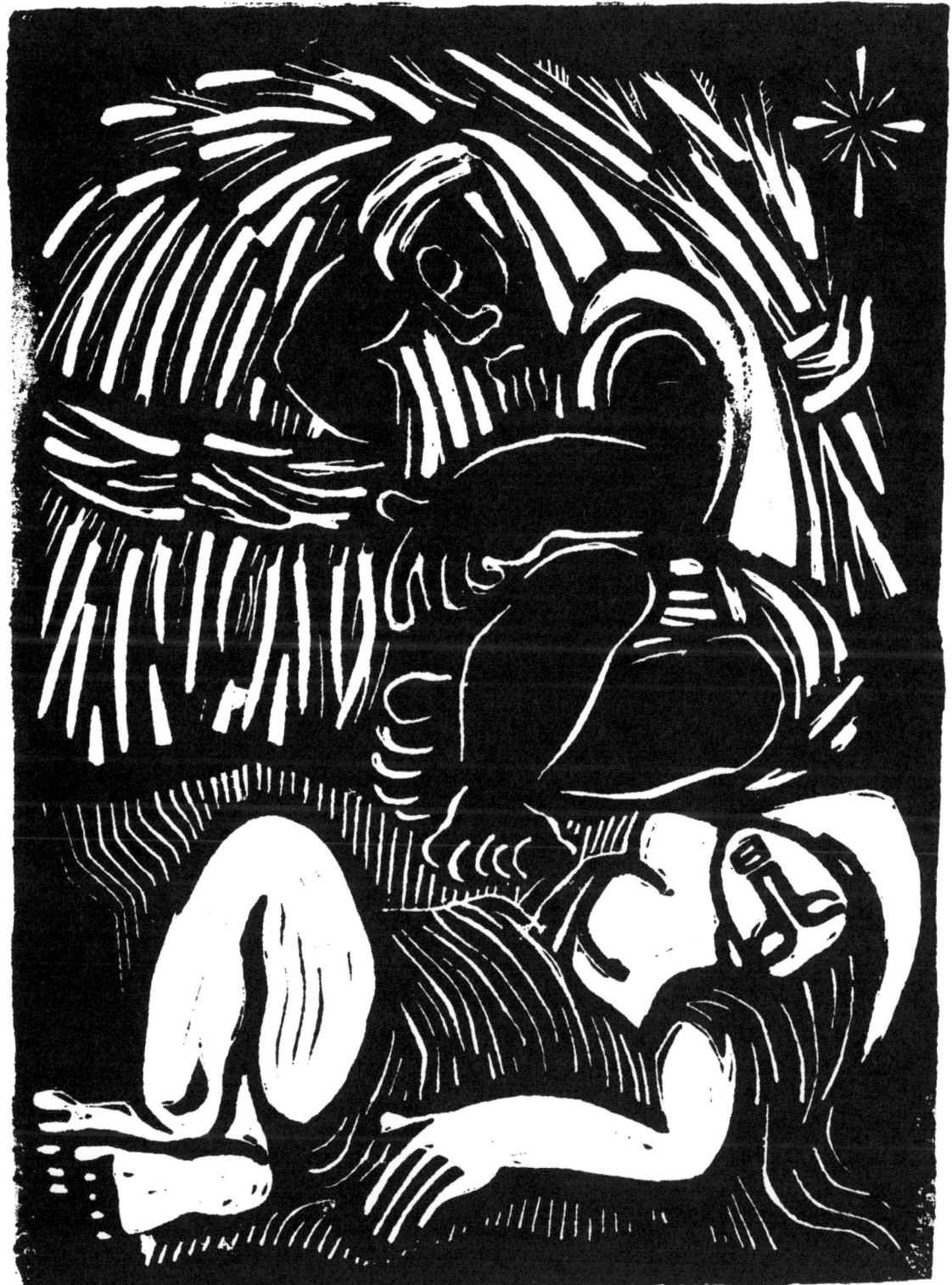

1 Samuel 1:1–8

WHY DO YOU WEEP?

There was a certain man of Ramathaim-zophim of the hill country of Ephraim whose name was Elkanah the son of Jeroham, son of Elihu, son of Tohu, son of Zuph, an Ephrathite. He had two wives. The name of the one was Hannah, and the name of the other, Peninnah. And Peninnah had children, but Hannah had no children.

    Now this man used to go up year by year from his city to worship and to sacrifice to the Lord of hosts at Shiloh, where the two sons of Eli, Hophni and Phinehas, were priests of the Lord. On the day when Elkanah sacrificed, he would give portions to Peninnah his wife and to all her sons and daughters. But to Hannah he gave a double portion, because he loved her, though the Lord had closed her womb. And her rival used to provoke her grievously to irritate her, because the Lord had closed her womb. So it went on year by year. As often as she went up to the house of the Lord, she used to provoke her. Therefore Hannah wept and would not eat. And Elkanah, her husband, said to her, "Hannah, why do you weep? And why do you not eat? And why is your heart sad? Am I not more to you than ten sons?"

Hannah

ERIN CROSS | LINOCUT

The suffering felt by Hannah over her dark womb is clearly etched in her face in this print. She knows that bearing children is good and, as it says in Psalms 127, the fruit of the womb are like "arrows in the hand of a warrior . . . Blessed is the man who fills his quiver with them!" But although children are a blessing from God, it must be remembered they are *from* God and his provision of them to us is subject to his sovereignty. God works through our tragedies to write his great story of redemption for his glory and, ultimately, for our good. Infertility, like other trials God puts in our way, are there to test us and to help us grow into the likeness of Christ. Like Hannah, these struggles should drive us to prayer. For we must not forget that prayer is God's appointed means of working out his grand design in his world and in our lives.

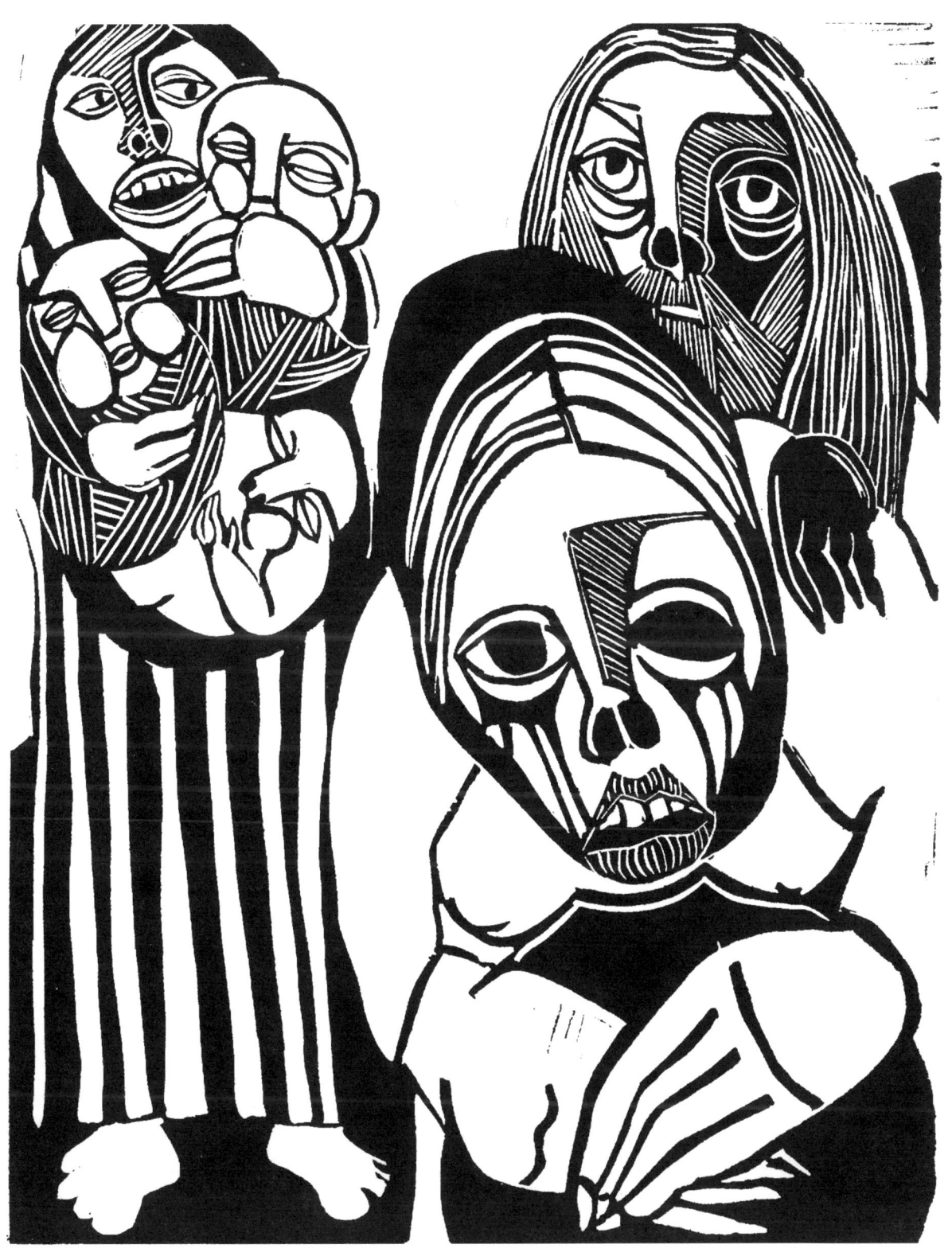

1 Samuel 17:44–51

THE BATTLE IS THE LORD'S

The Philistine said to David, "Come to me, and I will give your flesh to the birds of the air and to the beasts of the field." Then David said to the Philistine, "You come to me with a sword and with a spear and with a javelin, but I come to you in the name of the Lord of hosts, the God of the armies of Israel, whom you have defied. This day the Lord will deliver you into my hand, and I will strike you down and cut off your head. And I will give the dead bodies of the host of the Philistines this day to the birds of the air and to the wild beasts of the earth, that all the earth may know that there is a God in Israel, and that all this assembly may know that the Lord saves not with sword and spear. For the battle is the Lord's, and he will give you into our hand."

When the Philistine arose and came and drew near to meet David, David ran quickly toward the battle line to meet the Philistine. And David put his hand in his bag and took out a stone and slung it and struck the Philistine on his forehead. The stone sank into his forehead, and he fell on his face to the ground.

So David prevailed over the Philistine with a sling and with a stone, and struck the Philistine and killed him. There was no sword in the hand of David. Then David ran and stood over the Philistine and took his sword and drew it out of its sheath and killed him and cut off his head with it. When the Philistines saw that their champion was dead, they fled.

David and Goliath

EDWARD KNIPPERS | WOODCUT

Art often shapes our understanding of the Bible. A classic example of this fact is the common perception—based on countless Sunday school worksheets—that David was a little boy when he fought Goliath. Children's storybook Bibles are usually guilty of this error as well. Theologian A.D. Bauer asks, "What responsible adult would allow a young boy to go fight a giant? He was no child. Before David fought the giant, he fought (and killed) bears and lions. In the text David is described as 'a brave man and a warrior' and served as an armor bearer for Saul." Knippers has studied the text and therefore depicts Goliath as a huge man and David as a soldier in his prime, for there is no way that the giant was decapitated by a child.

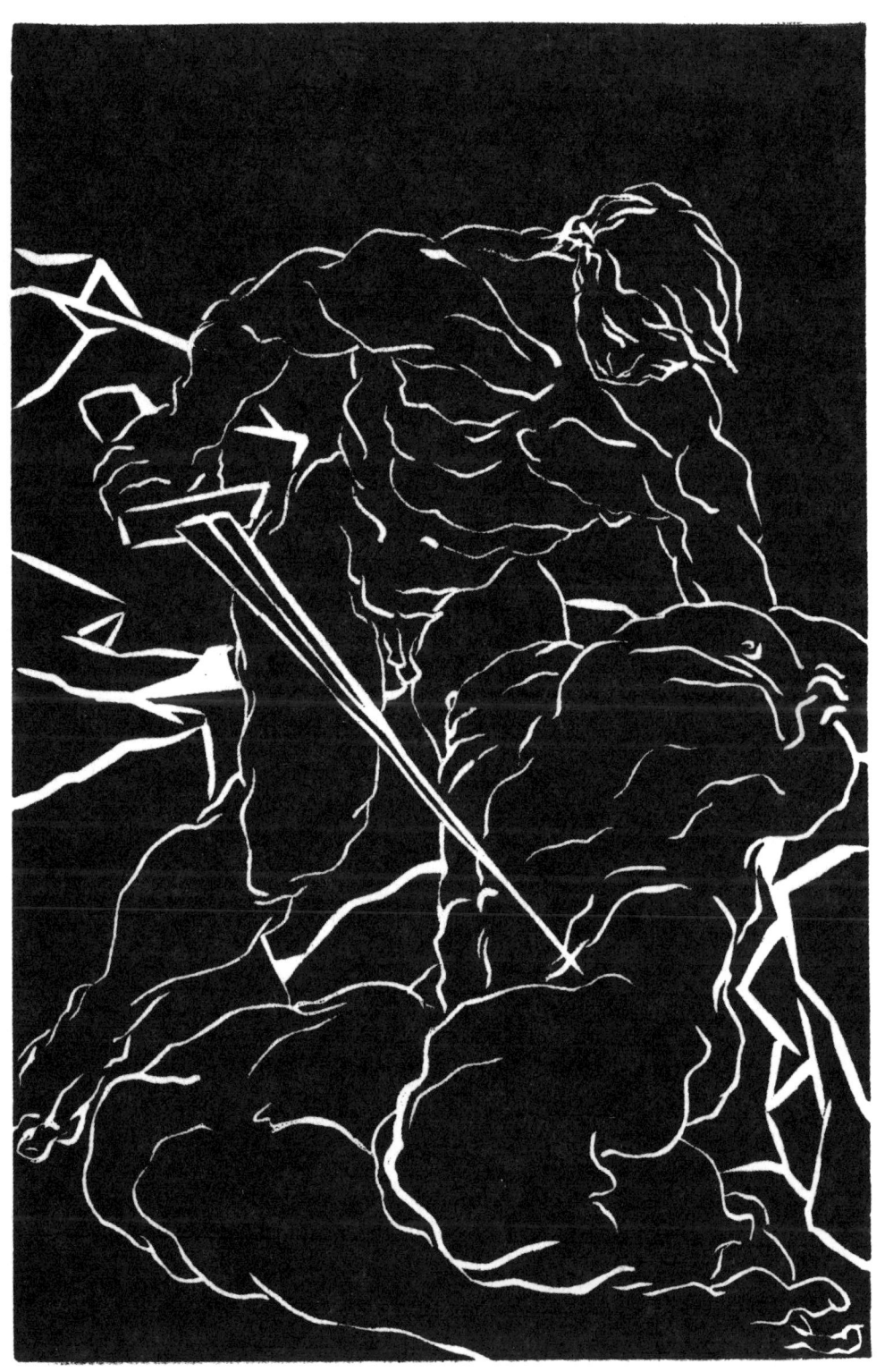

2 Samuel 11:1–5

DAVID AND BATHSHEBA

In the spring of the year, the time when kings go out to battle, David sent Joab, and his servants with him, and all Israel. And they ravaged the Ammonites and besieged Rabbah. But David remained at Jerusalem.

It happened, late one afternoon, when David arose from his couch and was walking on the roof of the king's house, that he saw from the roof a woman bathing; and the woman was very beautiful. And David sent and inquired about the woman. And one said, "Is not this Bathsheba, the daughter of Eliam, the wife of Uriah the Hittite?" So David sent messengers and took her, and she came to him, and he lay with her. (Now she had been purifying herself from her uncleanness.) Then she returned to her house. And the woman conceived, and she sent and told David, "I am pregnant."

Violation

NED BUSTARD | LINOCUT

Bathsheba is a faithful wife who is bathing in "a garden locked," as it says in the fourth chapter of the Song of Solomon. An apple tree grows in her garden, along with grapes, alluding to Song of Solomon 2:5, where apples and raisins are aphrodisiacs. Bathsheba's thoughts (and toes) are directed toward her husband, Uriah. From the king's lecherous smile, it is obvious that even before he had conjugal knowledge of her, David had stolen Bathsheba from Uriah and used her as a pin-up playmate in his mind. Chronologically Uriah is not yet in Jerusalem at this point of the biblical account. Yet in this print he loyally stands guard over the leering king, his spear pointing to the ultimate cost of David's voyeurism and infidelity—the sacrificial Lamb who would die outside of the city, on the Hill of the Skull.

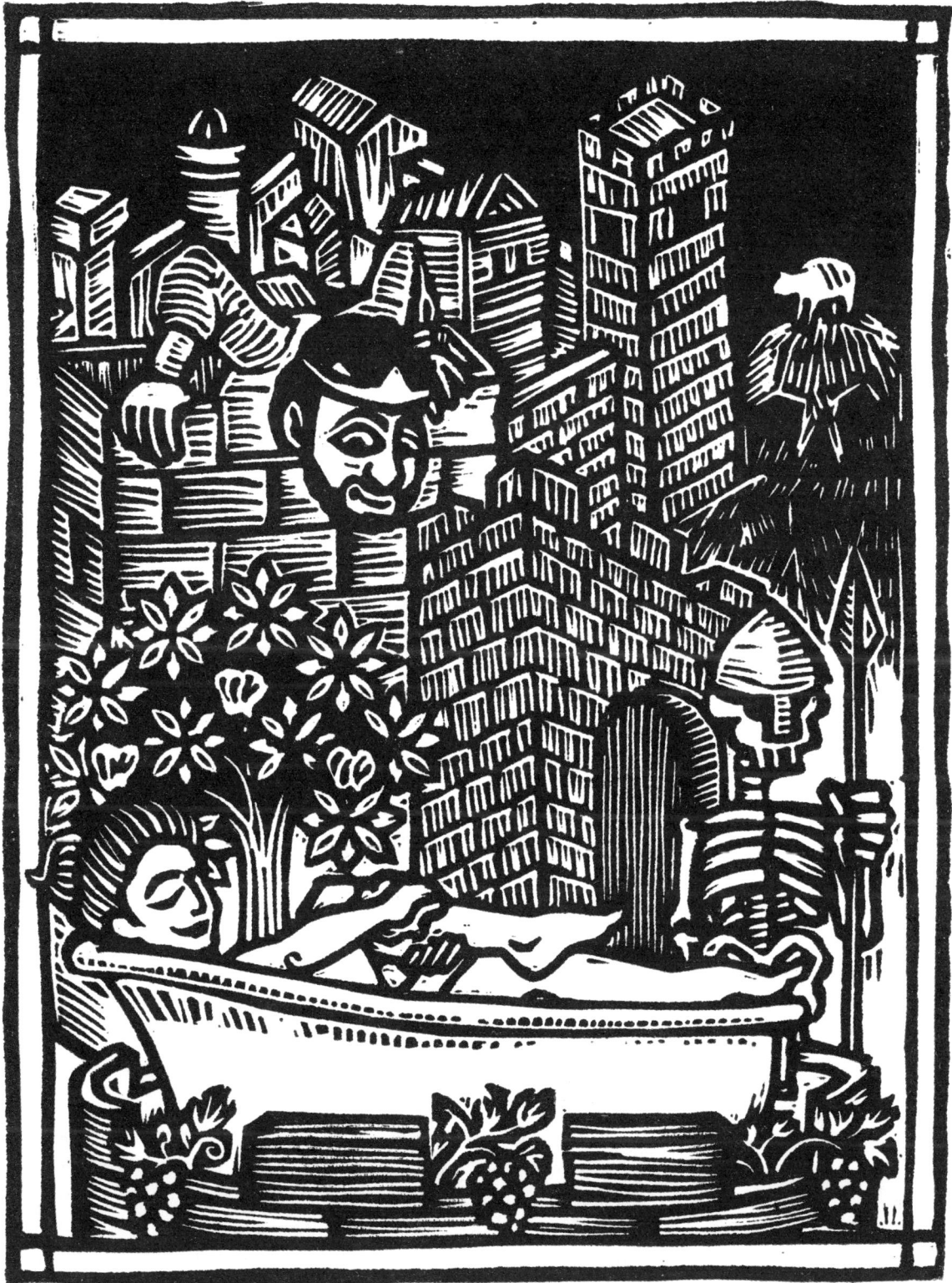

2 Samuel 13:1–2, 11b–19
THE LUST OF AMNON

Now Absalom, David's son, had a beautiful sister, whose name was Tamar. And after a time Amnon, David's son, loved her. And Amnon was so tormented that he made himself ill because of his sister Tamar, for she was a virgin, and it seemed impossible to Amnon to do anything to her.

. . . he took hold of her and said to her, "Come, lie with me, my sister." She answered him, "No, my brother, do not violate me, for such a thing is not done in Israel; do not do this outrageous thing. As for me, where could I carry my shame? And as for you, you would be as one of the outrageous fools in Israel. Now therefore, please speak to the king, for he will not withhold me from you." But he would not listen to her, and being stronger than she, he violated her and lay with her.

Then Amnon hated her with very great hatred, so that the hatred with which he hated her was greater than the love with which he had loved her. And Amnon said to her, "Get up! Go!" But she said to him, "No, my brother, for this wrong in sending me away is greater than the other that you did to me." But he would not listen to her. He called the young man who served him and said, "Put this woman out of my presence and bolt the door after her." Now she was wearing a long robe with sleeves, for thus were the virgin daughters of the king dressed. So his servant put her out and bolted the door after her. And Tamar put ashes on her head and tore the long robe that she wore. And she laid her hand on her head and went away, crying aloud as she went.

Rape of Tamar
ERIN CROSS | LINOCUT

James the Just, in the first chapter of his epistle, wrote: "But each person is tempted when he is lured and enticed by his own desire. Then desire when it has conceived gives birth to sin, and sin when it is fully grown brings forth death." Like his father David, Amnon let his lust control him. He made an idol of his sister's body, raped her, and then hated her. The passage demonstrates how God's good gift of sexual intercourse can be a destructive weapon when it is used outside of his design for drawing men and women together within the covenant of marriage. Instead of being a good gift, it killed Amnon's desire and destroyed Tamar's life. Tamar is described as beautiful, obedient, wise, and kind. Yet due to Amnon's sins, she ends her days disgraced and desolate, living in her other brother's house, unmarried and unloved.

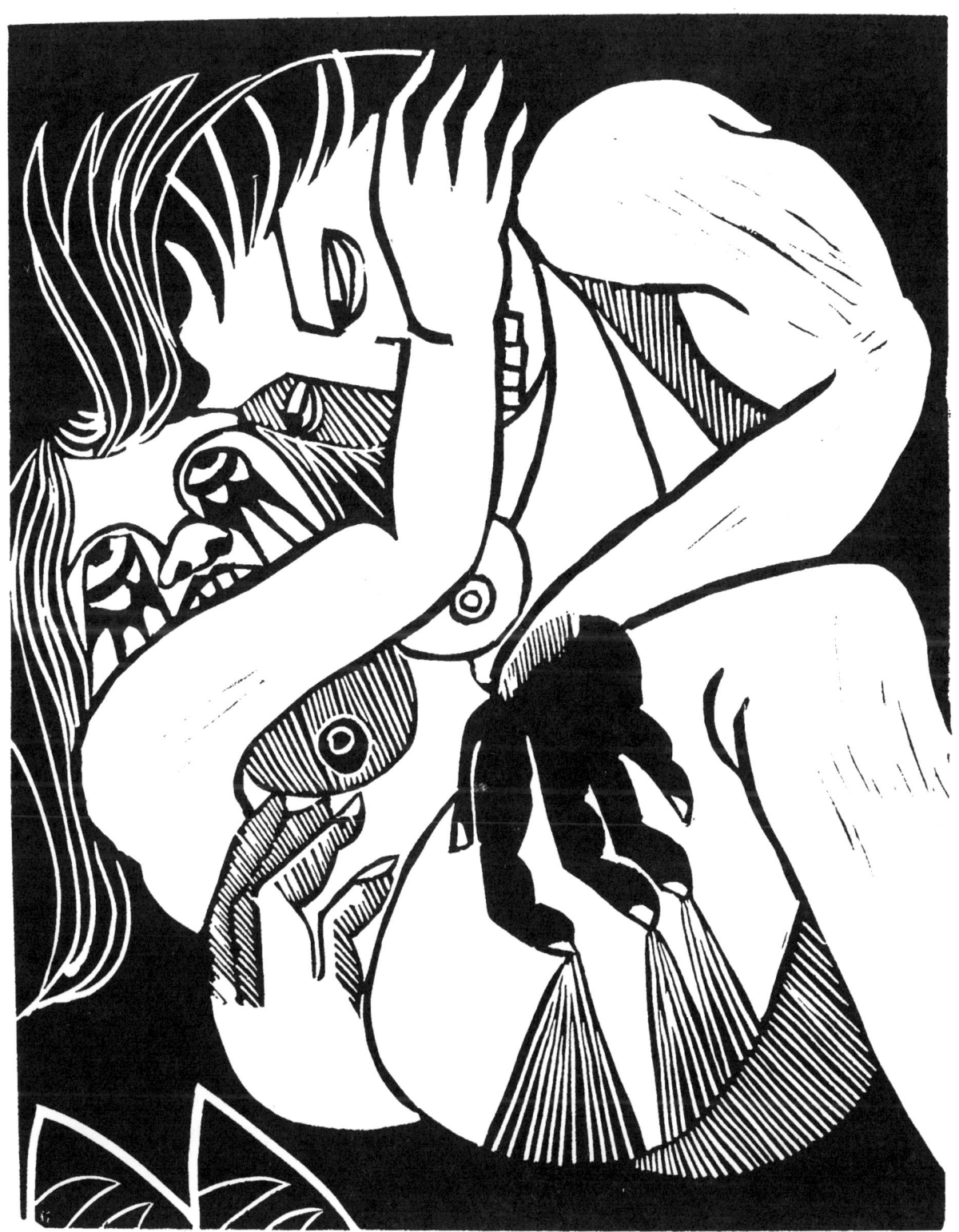

1 Kings 18:25–29, 36–39

THE MOCKERY OF BAAL

Then Elijah said to the prophets of Baal, "Choose for yourselves one bull and prepare it first, for you are many, and call upon the name of your god, but put no fire to it." And they took the bull that was given them, and they prepared it and called upon the name of Baal from morning until noon, saying, "O Baal, answer us!" But there was no voice, and no one answered. And they limped around the altar that they had made. And at noon Elijah mocked them, saying, "Cry aloud, for he is a god. Either he is musing, or he is relieving himself, or he is on a journey, or perhaps he is asleep and must be awakened." And they cried aloud and cut themselves after their custom with swords and lances, until the blood gushed out upon them. And as midday passed, they raved on until the time of the offering of the oblation, but there was no voice. No one answered; no one paid attention.

. . . .

And at the time of the offering of the oblation, Elijah the prophet came near and said, "O Lord, God of Abraham, Isaac, and Israel, let it be known this day that you are God in Israel, and that I am your servant, and that I have done all these things at your word. Answer me, O Lord, answer me, that this people may know that you, O Lord, are God, and that you have turned their hearts back." Then the fire of the Lord fell and consumed the burnt offering and the wood and the stones and the dust, and licked up the water that was in the trench. And when all the people saw it, they fell on their faces and said, "The Lord, he is God; the Lord, he is God."

Prophets of Baal

DIEGO JOURDAN PEREIRA | WOODCUT

The Israelites had drifted away from the commands and teachings of Moses and had instead embraced their culture's idea of good and evil. They saw themselves on the right side of history by following Baal, the storm-and-fertility god. But Elijah challenged their inverted ideas of worship, calling them back to true holiness. D.A. Carson writes, "People do not drift toward Holiness. Apart from grace-driven effort, people do not gravitate toward godliness, prayer, obedience to Scripture, faith, and delight in the Lord. We drift toward compromise and call it tolerance; we drift toward disobedience and call it freedom; we drift toward superstition and call it faith . . . we slide toward godlessness and convince ourselves we have been liberated."

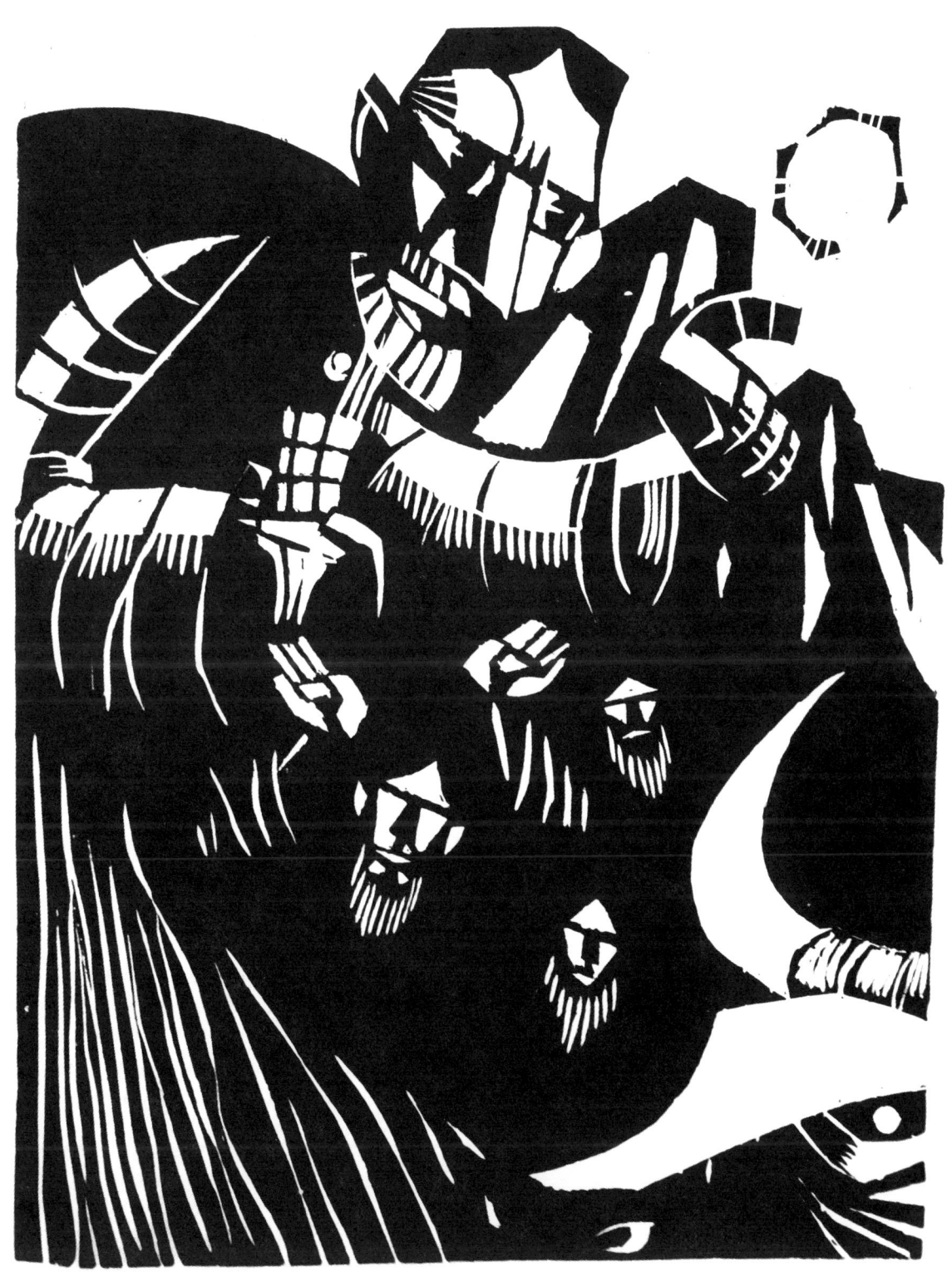

1 Kings 19:11–18

ELIJAH STANDS BEFORE THE LORD

And he said, "Go out and stand on the mount before the Lord." And behold, the Lord passed by, and a great and strong wind tore the mountains and broke in pieces the rocks before the Lord, but the Lord was not in the wind. And after the wind an earthquake, but the Lord was not in the earthquake. And after the earthquake a fire, but the Lord was not in the fire. And after the fire the sound of a low whisper. And when Elijah heard it, he wrapped his face in his cloak and went out and stood at the entrance of the cave. And behold, there came a voice to him and said, "What are you doing here, Elijah?" He said, "I have been very jealous for the Lord, the God of hosts. For the people of Israel have forsaken your covenant, thrown down your altars, and killed your prophets with the sword, and I, even I only, am left, and they seek my life, to take it away." And the Lord said to him, "Go, return on your way to the wilderness of Damascus. And when you arrive, you shall anoint Hazael to be king over Syria. And Jehu the son of Nimshi you shall anoint to be king over Israel, and Elisha the son of Shaphat of Abel-meholah you shall anoint to be prophet in your place. And the one who escapes from the sword of Hazael shall Jehu put to death, and the one who escapes from the sword of Jehu shall Elisha put to death. Yet I will leave seven thousand in Israel, all the knees that have not bowed to Baal, and every mouth that has not kissed him."

A Gentle Whisper

JUSTIN SORENSEN | LINOCUT

The artist writes, "I've always been interested in how the spectacle of the fire or earthquake didn't touch Elijah at his core the way the gentleness of a whisper did. The ordinariness of the whisper really strikes me. My tendency is always to look for God in the places I expect to find him. The whisper seems to suggest that God can't be controlled, and that he can manifest himself however he likes. I think the whisper is God's way of saying to Elijah that he is everywhere, and that he is moving in ways we can't see. It's not that God wasn't whispering up until that point, it's that Elijah then became aware of it."

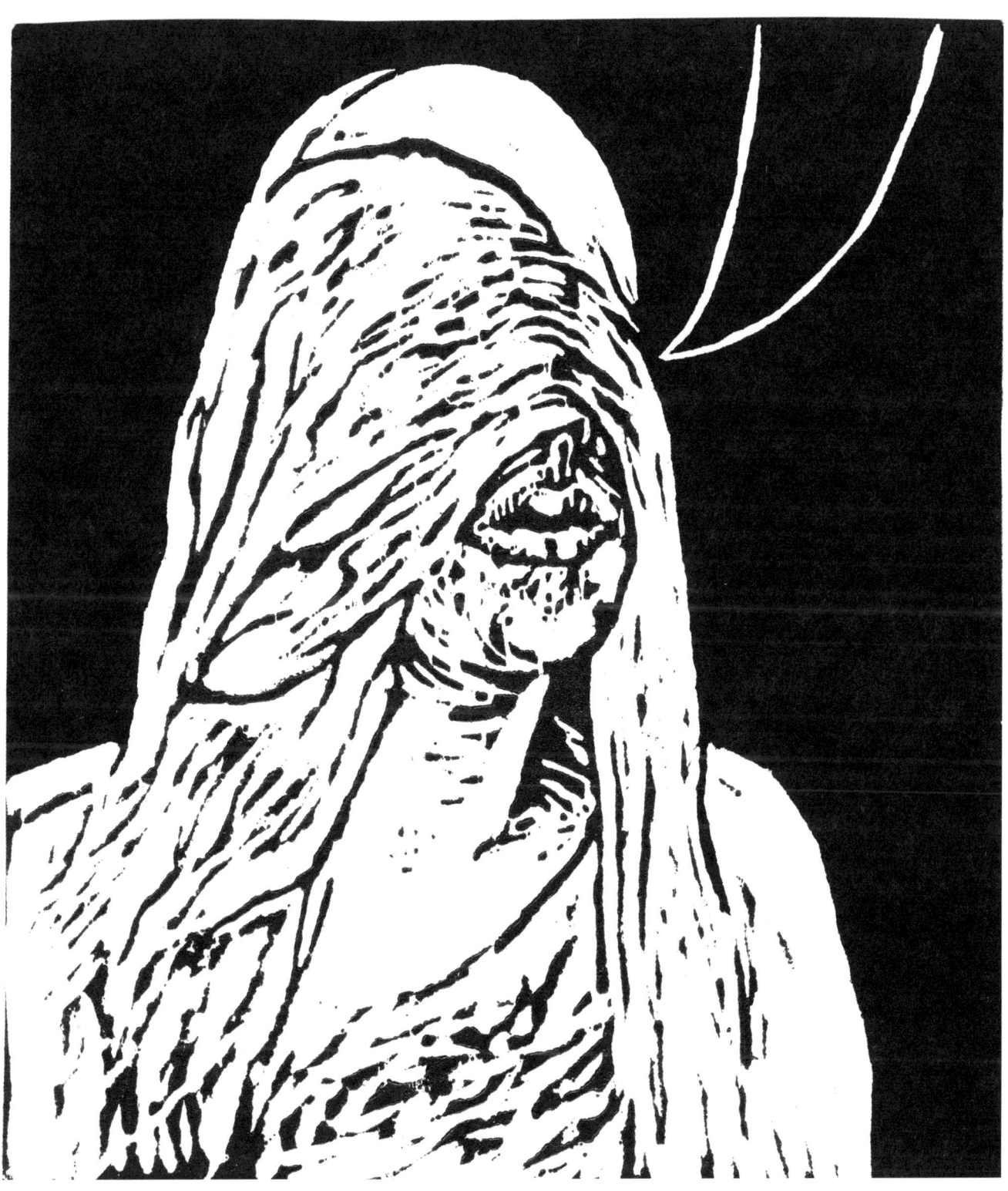

2 Kings 2:9–14

ELIJAH AND THE WHIRLWIND

When they had crossed, Elijah said to Elisha, "Ask what I shall do for you, before I am taken from you." And Elisha said, "Please let there be a double portion of your spirit on me." And he said, "You have asked a hard thing; yet, if you see me as I am being taken from you, it shall be so for you, but if you do not see me, it shall not be so." And as they still went on and talked, behold, chariots of fire and horses of fire separated the two of them. And Elijah went up by a whirlwind into heaven. And Elisha saw it and he cried, "My father, my father! The chariots of Israel and its horsemen!" And he saw him no more.

    Then he took hold of his own clothes and tore them in two pieces. And he took up the cloak of Elijah that had fallen from him and went back and stood on the bank of the Jordan. Then he took the cloak of Elijah that had fallen from him and struck the water, saying, "Where is the Lord, the God of Elijah?" And when he had struck the water, the water was parted to the one side and to the other, and Elisha went over.

The Translation of Elijah

EDWARD KNIPPERS | WOODCUT

In the book *Objects of Grace: Conversations on Creativity and Faith*, Knippers says, "In representing these Biblical figures in the nude, I am trying to show that these characters were individual people, just like we are. I am challenging the viewer to come to grips with their own physicality in order to have the fullness of life that God has given us. . . . The only way I can relate to the past is to think that somebody was there; some body was there. The main relationship that I have to those people—my ancestors—is not sociological or in terms of the way they dress but that they had bodies. As I read the scriptures and realize that those people had bodies, like I have a body, and that God spoke to them, even taking on a body himself, then I realize that God can speak to me."

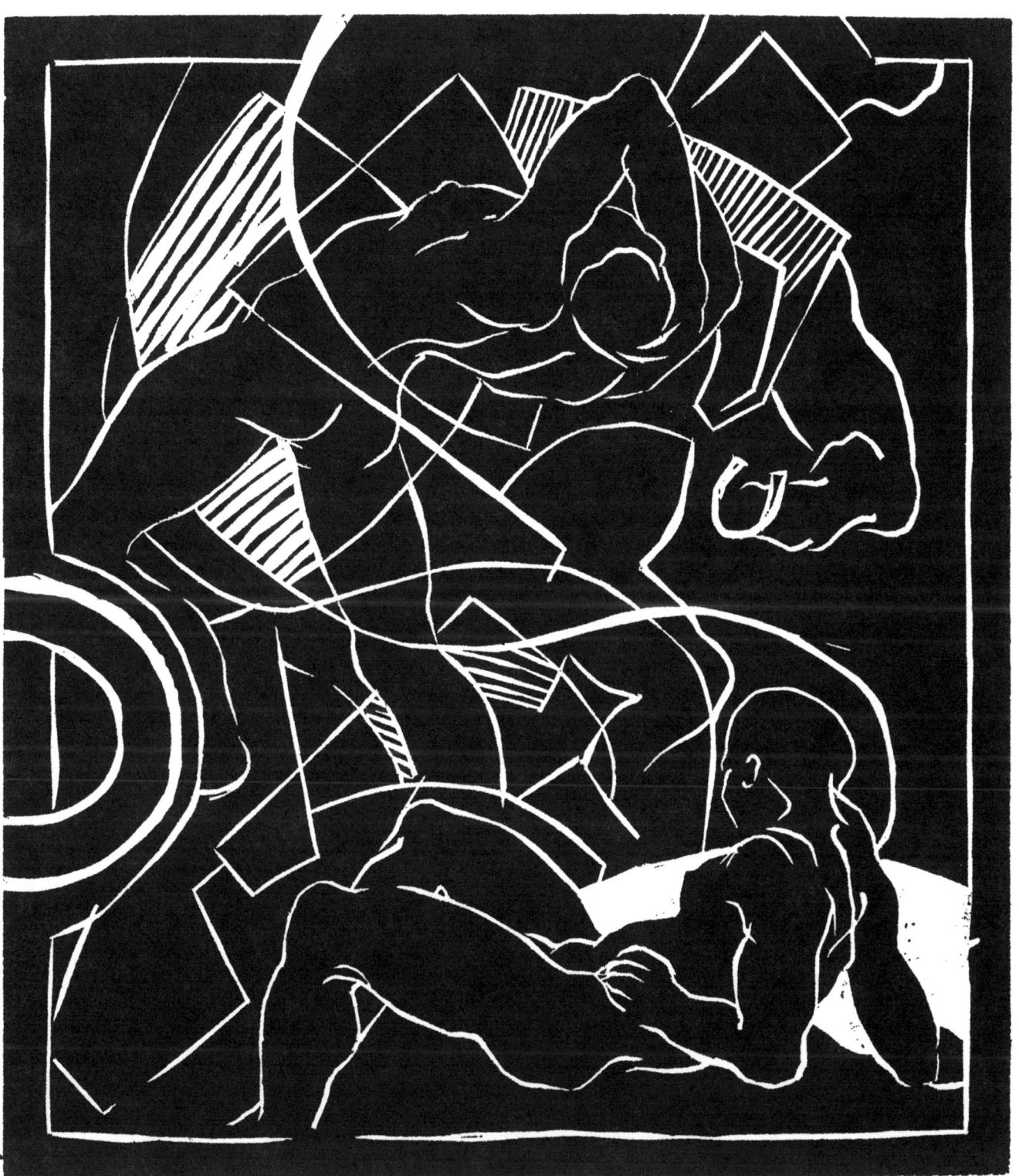

2 Kings 9:30–37
THE DEATH OF JEZEBEL

When Jehu came to Jezreel, Jezebel heard of it. And she painted her eyes and adorned her head and looked out of the window. And as Jehu entered the gate, she said, "Is it peace, you Zimri, murderer of your master?" And he lifted up his face to the window and said, "Who is on my side? Who?" Two or three eunuchs looked out at him. He said, "Throw her down." So they threw her down. And some of her blood spattered on the wall and on the horses, and they trampled on her. Then he went in and ate and drank. And he said, "See now to this cursed woman and bury her, for she is a king's daughter." But when they went to bury her, they found no more of her than the skull and the feet and the palms of her hands. When they came back and told him, he said, "This is the word of the Lord, which he spoke by his servant Elijah the Tishbite: 'In the territory of Jezreel the dogs shall eat the flesh of Jezebel, and the corpse of Jezebel shall be as dung on the face of the field in the territory of Jezreel, so that no one can say, This is Jezebel.'"

Jezebel
ERIN CROSS | LINOCUT

The dogs in this print tear at Jezebel's flesh like Amnon tore at Tamar in the artwork accompanying 2 Samuel 13. But Jezebel is the polar opposite of Tamar. The Phoenician princess was a strong-minded, licentious woman. A controlling, manipulative woman, she led Ahab and his people into zealous worship of Baal and Ashtaroth with two pagan temples built and over 800 priests employed. So extraordinary was the force of her will, that even after the great defeat recorded in 1 Kings 18, in the face of Jezebel's murderous raging, Elijah fled for his life. But for all of her idolatry, wicked deeds, and political machinations, in the end Elijah's prophecy, "The dogs shall eat Jezebel by the wall of Jezreel," was fulfilled to the very letter.

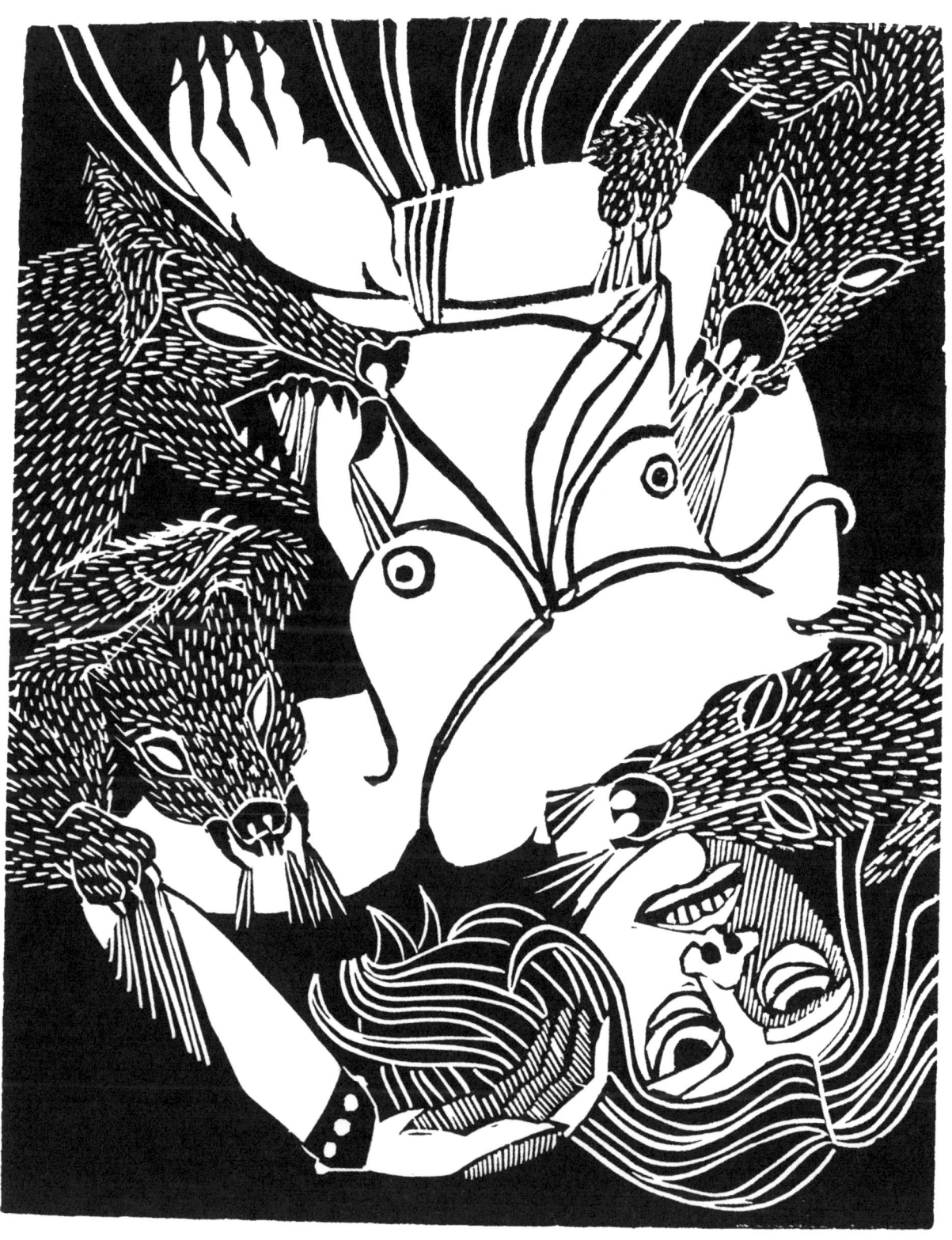

Nehemiah 13:23–31

CONFRONTING SIN

In those days also I saw the Jews who had married women of Ashdod, Ammon, and Moab. And half of their children spoke the language of Ashdod, and they could not speak the language of Judah, but only the language of each people. And I confronted them and cursed them and beat some of them and pulled out their hair. And I made them take an oath in the name of God, saying, "You shall not give your daughters to their sons, or take their daughters for your sons or for yourselves. Did not Solomon king of Israel sin on account of such women? Among the many nations there was no king like him, and he was beloved by his God, and God made him king over all Israel. Nevertheless, foreign women made even him to sin. Shall we then listen to you and do all this great evil and act treacherously against our God by marrying foreign women?"

And one of the sons of Jehoiada, the son of Eliashib the high priest, was the son-in-law of Sanballat the Horonite. Therefore I chased him from me. Remember them, O my God, because they have desecrated the priesthood and the covenant of the priesthood and the Levites.

Thus I cleansed them from everything foreign, and I established the duties of the priests and Levites, each in his work; and I provided for the wood offering at appointed times, and for the firstfruits.

Remember me, O my God, for good.

Nehemiah 13:25

NED BUSTARD | LINOCUT

Who shouts curses at people while also beating them and pulling out their hair? It is easy to be offended by such behavior, but by starting with the last sentence, "Remember me, O my God, for good," the preceding verses may make more sense. Nehemiah was zealous for God's holiness.

Rather than taking offense at Nehemiah's extreme actions, how would it be if instead we brought our souls to task for ignoring God's holiness or desecrating his house? Have we forgotten what the holiness of God secured on the Cross? Or have we so shrunk in our understanding of "Holy, holy, holy is the Lord of hosts; the whole earth is full of his glory" that our knees fail to tremble? As the thief on the cross said, "Jesus, remember me when you come into your kingdom," so we say, "Remember us, O God, for good."

Esther 2:12–18

ONE NIGHT WITH THE KING

Now when the turn came for each young woman to go in to King Ahasuerus, after being twelve months under the regulations for the women, since this was the regular period of their beautifying, six months with oil of myrrh and six months with spices and ointments for women—when the young woman went in to the king in this way, she was given whatever she desired to take with her from the harem to the king's palace. In the evening she would go in, and in the morning she would return to the second harem in custody of Shaashgaz, the king's eunuch, who was in charge of the concubines. She would not go in to the king again, unless the king delighted in her and she was summoned by name.

When the turn came for Esther the daughter of Abihail the uncle of Mordecai, who had taken her as his own daughter, to go in to the king, she asked for nothing except what Hegai the king's eunuch, who had charge of the women, advised. Now Esther was winning favor in the eyes of all who saw her. And when Esther was taken to King Ahasuerus, into his royal palace, in the tenth month, which is the month of Tebeth, in the seventh year of his reign, the king loved Esther more than all the women, and she won grace and favor in his sight more than all the virgins, so that he set the royal crown on her head and made her queen instead of Vashti. Then the king gave a great feast for all his officials and servants; it was Esther's feast. He also granted a remission of taxes to the provinces and gave gifts with royal generosity.

Esther and the King (after Marc Chagall)

NED BUSTARD | LINOCUT

This print combines into one piece Esther and the King from two separate lithographs by Marc Chagall. A Belarussian-Russian-French artist, Chagall created works in a variety of mediums including painting, book illustrations, stained glass, stage sets, ceramic, tapestries and fine art prints. He once remarked, "Since my early youth, I have been fascinated by the Bible. It has always seemed to me still that it is the greatest source of poetry of all time." The story of Esther is certainly poetic, though not prescriptive. It describes how God saved his people, but doesn't mention God. It extolls a Israelite woman, but the woman was part of a harem. Yet God can work out his plan of salvation in any situation . . . even through a marriage like Esther's. As Paul writes in 1 Corinthians, "For how do you know, wife, whether you will save your husband?"

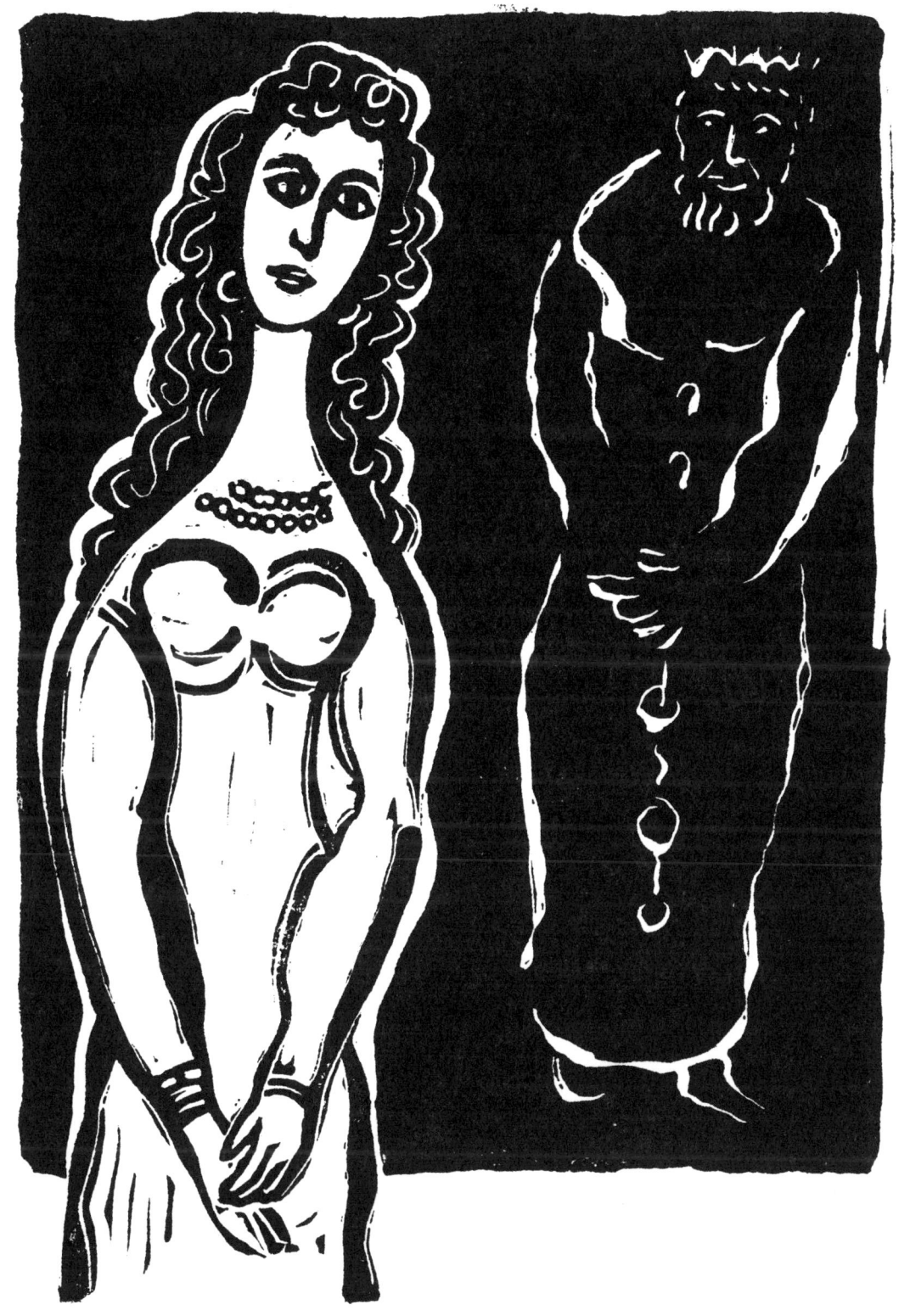

Job 40:15–18, 41:1–5

BEHEMOTH AND LEVIATHAN

"Behold, Behemoth,
    which I made as I made you;
    he eats grass like an ox.
Behold, his strength in his loins,
    and his power in the muscles of his belly.
He makes his tail stiff like a cedar;
    the sinews of his thighs are knit together.
His bones are tubes of bronze,
    his limbs like bars of iron.

. . .

"Can you draw out Leviathan with a fishhook
    or press down his tongue with a cord?
Can you put a rope in his nose
    or pierce his jaw with a hook?
Will he make many pleas to you?
    Will he speak to you soft words?
Will he make a covenant with you
    to take him for your servant forever?
Will you play with him as with a bird,
    or will you put him on a leash for your girls?

Behemoth and Leviathan

WILLIAM BLAKE | ENGRAVING

This is the fifteenth in a series of twenty-two engraved prints from William Blake's *Illustrations of the Book of Job*. The Book of Job focuses on the question of suffering and evil. In this piece God reaches down from heaven and points out the Behemoth and the Leviathan to Job, his wife, and Job's friends. He does this to "answer" Job and his questions about why he has suffered. These two monsters serve as visual aides to illustrate the Lord's point that human beings know so little of creation and could not begin to understand God or his ways. Yet we know that God set a plan in motion at the beginning of time to eliminate evil. At the Cross he began, as it says in Revelation, "to make all things new." All of the suffering in the world will be transformed into joy, all the ugliness into beauty, and all the hate into love.

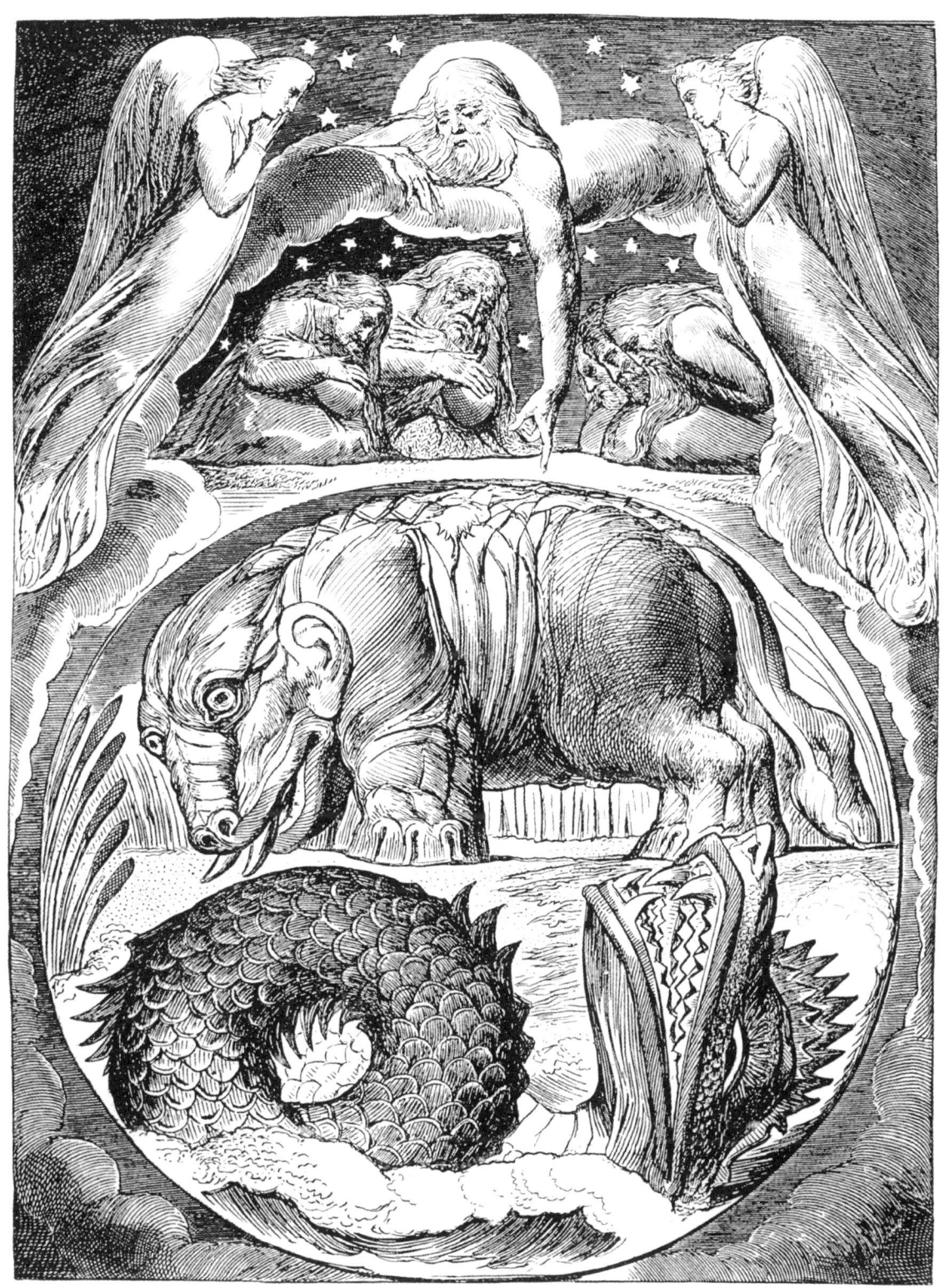

Psalm 5:1–2, 38:1–2, 41:9, 130:1–2

SONGS OF DESPAIR

Give ear to my words, O Lord;
    consider my groaning.
Give attention to the sound of my cry,
    my King and my God,
    for to you do I pray.

. . .

O Lord, rebuke me not in your anger,
    nor discipline me in your wrath!
For your arrows have sunk into me,
    and your hand has come down on me.

. . .

Even my close friend in whom I trusted,
    who ate my bread, has lifted his heel against me.

. . .

Out of the depths I cry to you, O Lord!
    O Lord, hear my voice!
Let your ears be attentive
    to the voice of my pleas for mercy!

Psalm 5, 38, 41, 130 (left to right/top to bottom)
KREG YINGST | LINOCUT

Luke Le Duc has written that "To be fully human, to be fully honest with our Creator and each other, to truly love God and each other with all our being, we must not present a version of our lives either to God or to each other that suppresses the reality that 'life isn't right' in our world. It is the language of sorrow and lament that gives us words to speak to God that reflect the brokenness and pain and disorientation that is embedded in our world and so deeply a part of each of us." These four prints are from *Psalms in Block Prints and Light from Darkness: Portraits and Prayer* and visually address the laments and doubts and griefs that are part of the life of faith. Even Christ is not exempt from these things, as seen in the print on the lower left.

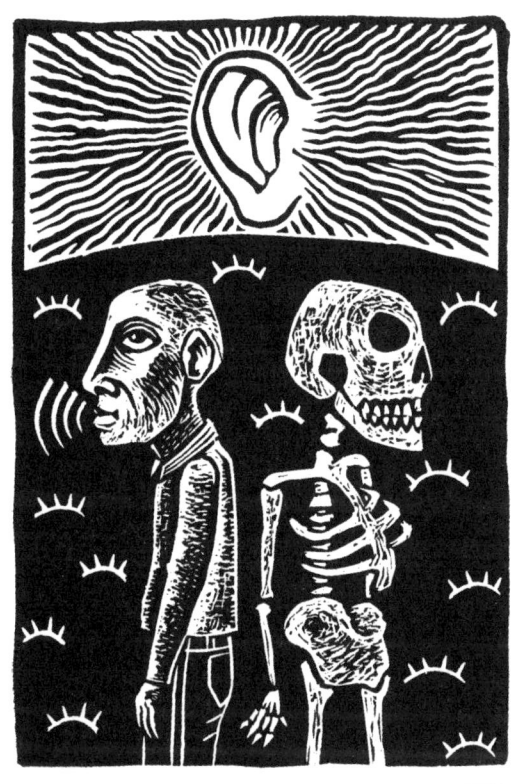
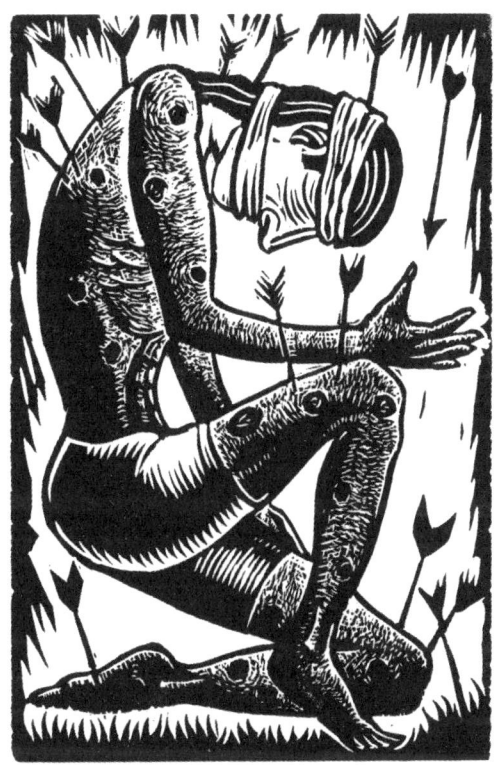
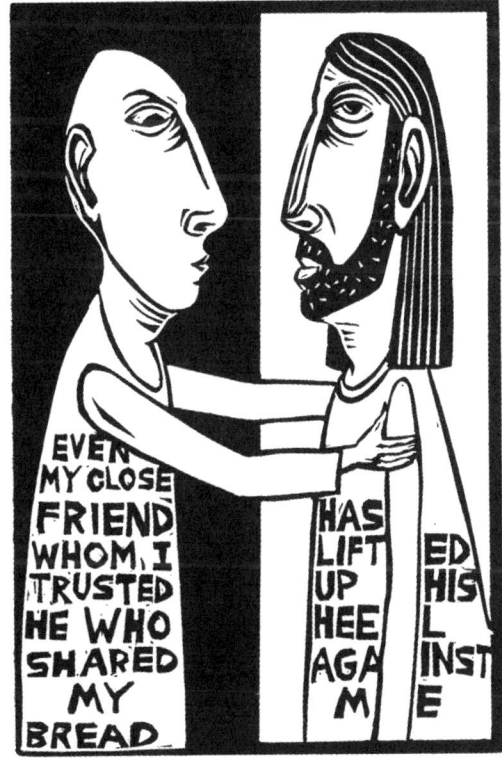
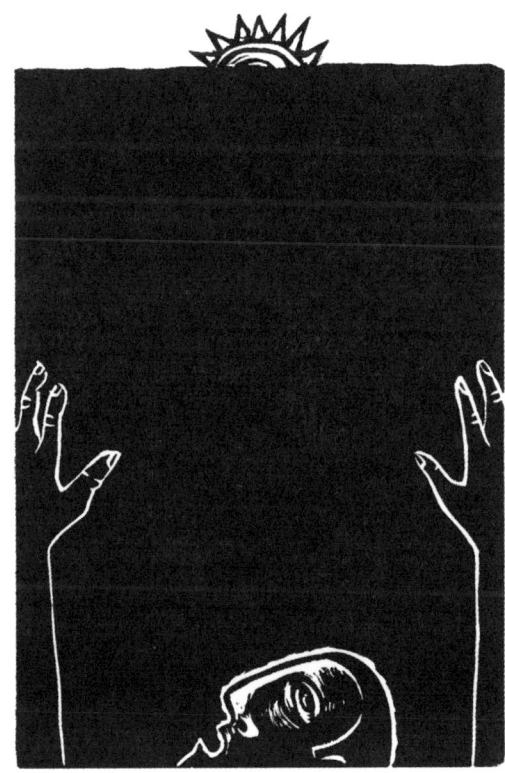

Proverbs 5:15–23

THE WIFE OF YOUR YOUTH

Drink water from your own cistern,
    flowing water from your own well.
Should your springs be scattered abroad,
    streams of water in the streets?
Let them be for yourself alone,
    and not for strangers with you.
Let your fountain be blessed,
    and rejoice in the wife of your youth,
    a lovely deer, a graceful doe.
Let her breasts fill you at all times with delight;
    be intoxicated always in her love.
Why should you be intoxicated, my son, with a forbidden woman
    and embrace the bosom of an adulteress?
For a man's ways are before the eyes of the Lord,
    and he ponders all his paths.
The iniquities of the wicked ensnare him,
    and he is held fast in the cords of his sin.
He dies for lack of discipline,
    and because of his great folly he is led astray.

The White Shirt (Man and Wife)

EDWARD KNIPPERS | MONOPRINT

In *The Gospel and Sex*, Tim Keller writes, "The Bible is full of covenant renewal ceremonies.... The ultimate covenant renewal ceremony is the Lord's Supper. The sacrament of the Lord's Supper renews the covenant made at baptism; through the breaking of bread and the pouring out of wine it reenacts the selfless sacrifice of Jesus to us.... In the same way, marriage is a covenant, one that creates a place of security for vulnerability. But though covenant is necessary for sex, sex is also necessary for covenant. The covenant will grow stale unless we continually revisit and reenact it. Sex is a covenant renewal ceremony for marriage, the physical reenactment of the inseparable oneness in all other areas—economic, legal, personal, psychological—created by the marriage covenant. Sex renews and revitalizes the marriage covenant."

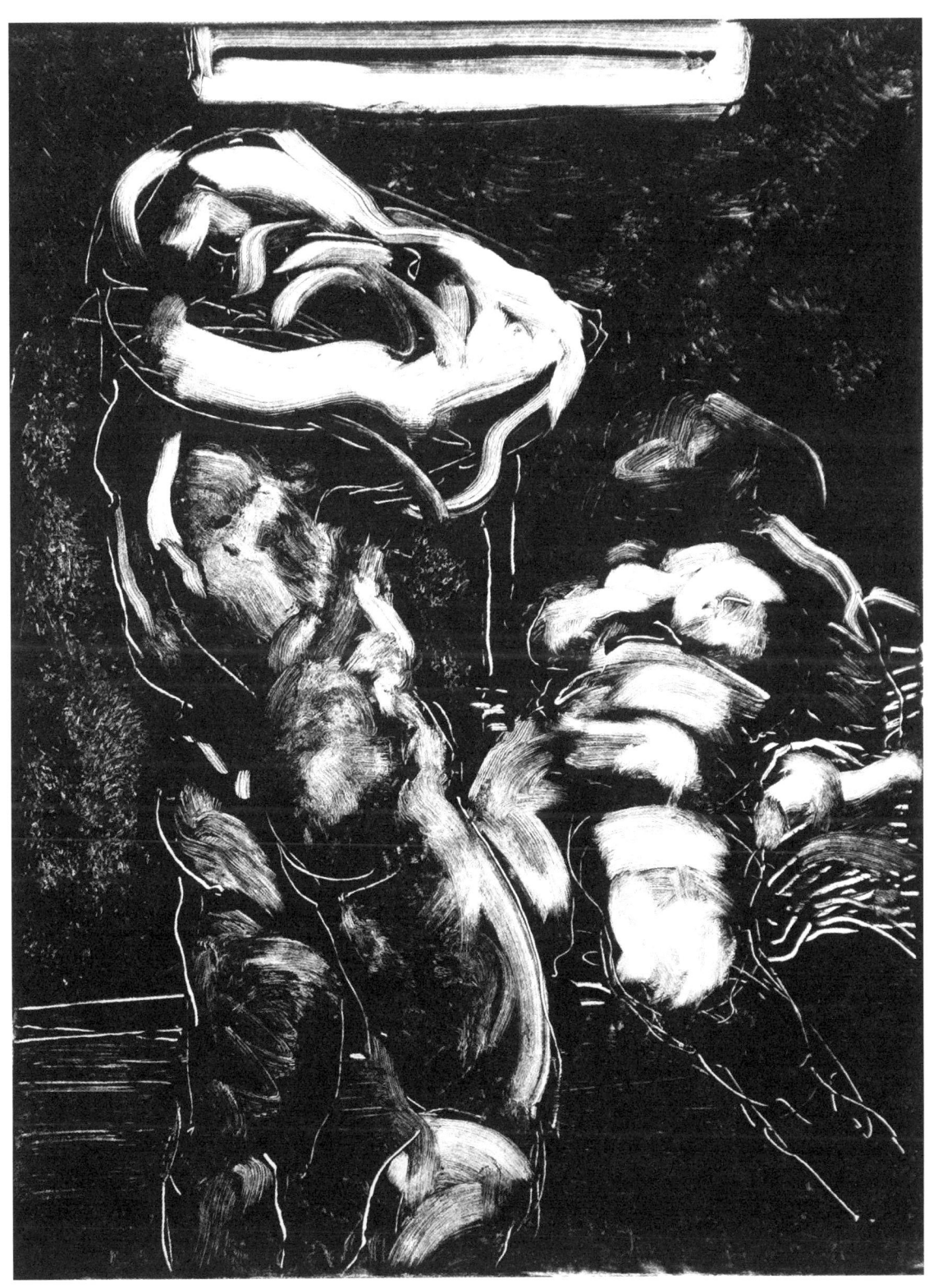

Ecclesiastes 9:1–10

MADNESS IN THEIR HEARTS

But all this I laid to heart, examining it all, how the righteous and the wise and their deeds are in the hand of God. Whether it is love or hate, man does not know; both are before him. It is the same for all, since the same event happens to the righteous and the wicked, to the good and the evil, to the clean and the unclean, to him who sacrifices and him who does not sacrifice. As the good one is, so is the sinner, and he who swears is as he who shuns an oath. This is an evil in all that is done under the sun, that the same event happens to all. Also, the hearts of the children of man are full of evil, and madness is in their hearts while they live, and after that they go to the dead. But he who is joined with all the living has hope, for a living dog is better than a dead lion. For the living know that they will die, but the dead know nothing, and they have no more reward, for the memory of them is forgotten. Their love and their hate and their envy have already perished, and forever they have no more share in all that is done under the sun.

Go, eat your bread with joy, and drink your wine with a merry heart, for God has already approved what you do.

Let your garments be always white. Let not oil be lacking on your head.

Enjoy life with the wife whom you love, all the days of your vain life that he has given you under the sun, because that is your portion in life and in your toil at which you toil under the sun. Whatever your hand finds to do, do it with your might, for there is no work or thought or knowledge or wisdom in Sheol, to which you are going.

Blessed Excess

MARK T. SMITH | LINOCUT

The artist spotlights the evil, madness, and excesses that consume the children of man—all mindless pursuits that are rendered meaningless in the face of Death. The composition of the print alludes to old maps, but in the upper corner where there should be a jolly anthropomorphic cloud blowing wind, Death is throwing lighting bolts. Another common element of nautical charts is a mermaid. Here she symbolizes the human experience of being "amphibians," as it says in *The Screwtape Letters*. That is, humans are both Spirit and Animal. As she swims across the page, the body of the mermaid morphs into good things that are often fouled up or perverted through selfish overindulgence and abuse: Alchohol (the bottle), Sex (the triple-X), Power (the crown), and Work (the V8 engine).

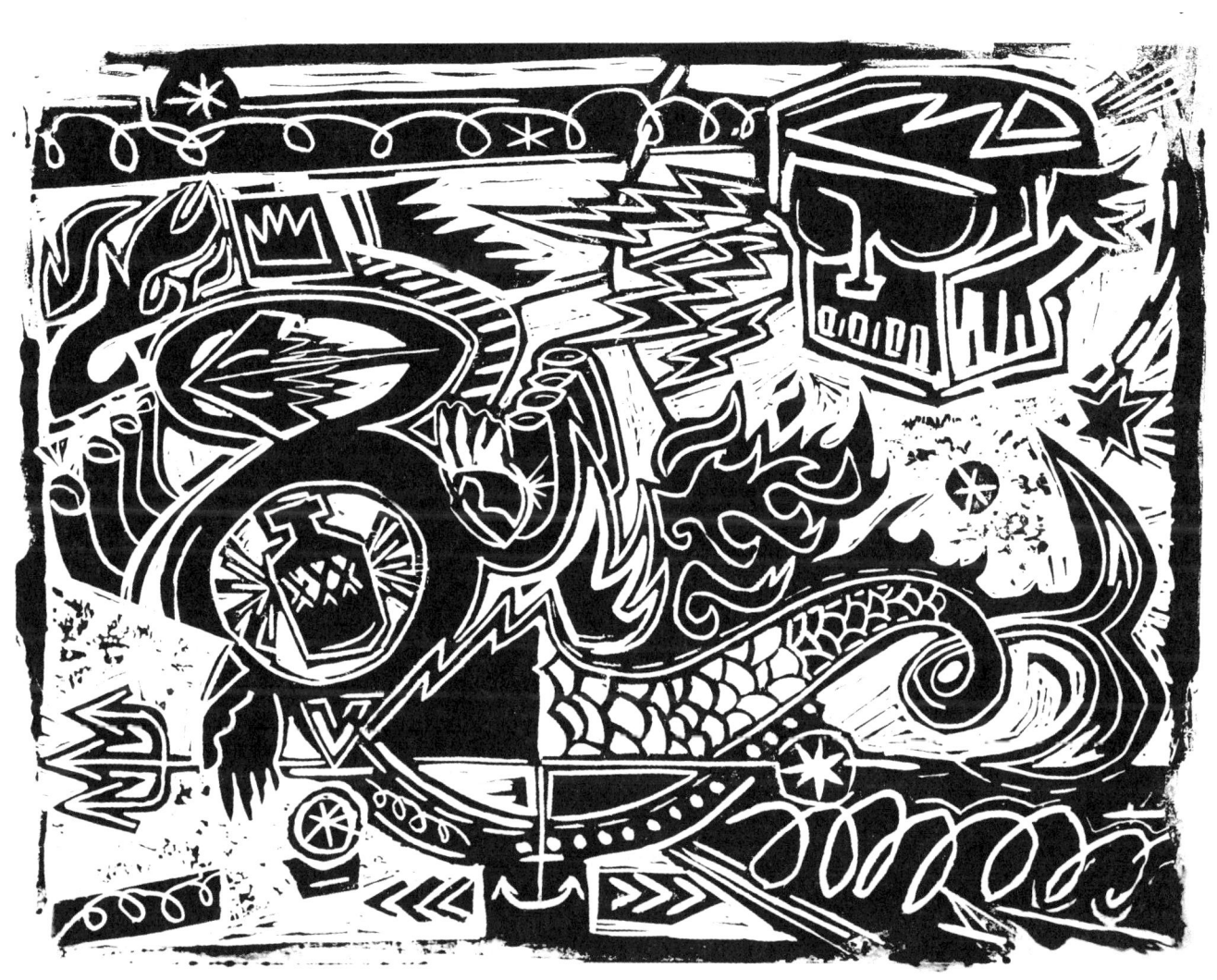

Song of Songs 1:2, 6:2–3, 7:6–9
IN THE GARDEN OF LOVE

She

Let him kiss me with the kisses of his mouth!
For your love is better than wine;

My beloved has gone down to his garden
    to the beds of spices,
to graze in the gardens
    and to gather lilies.
I am my beloved's and my beloved is mine;
    he grazes among the lilies.

He

How beautiful and pleasant you are,
    O loved one, with all your delights!
Your stature is like a palm tree,
    and your breasts are like its clusters.
I say I will climb the palm tree
    and lay hold of its fruit.
Oh may your breasts be like clusters of the vine,
    and the scent of your breath like apples,
and your mouth like the best wine.

Kisses

TANJA BUTLER | LINOCUT

Martin Luther is said to have quipped: "Twice a week, hundred-four a year, should give neither cause to fear." For Luther, conjugal love was to be praised and marital faithfulness championed. He advised: "Where conjugal chastity is to be maintained, husband and wife must, above all things, live together in love and harmony, so that one cherishes the other wholeheartedly and with complete fidelity." John Piper asserts that to aid married people in maintaining conjugal chastity, "faith makes use of sexual intercourse as a means of grace. For the people God leads into marriage, sexual relations are a God-ordained means of overcoming temptation to sin . . . [Therefore] faith wields the weapon of sexual intercourse against Satan. A married couple gives a severe blow to the head of that ancient serpent when they aim to give as much sexual satisfaction to each other as possible."

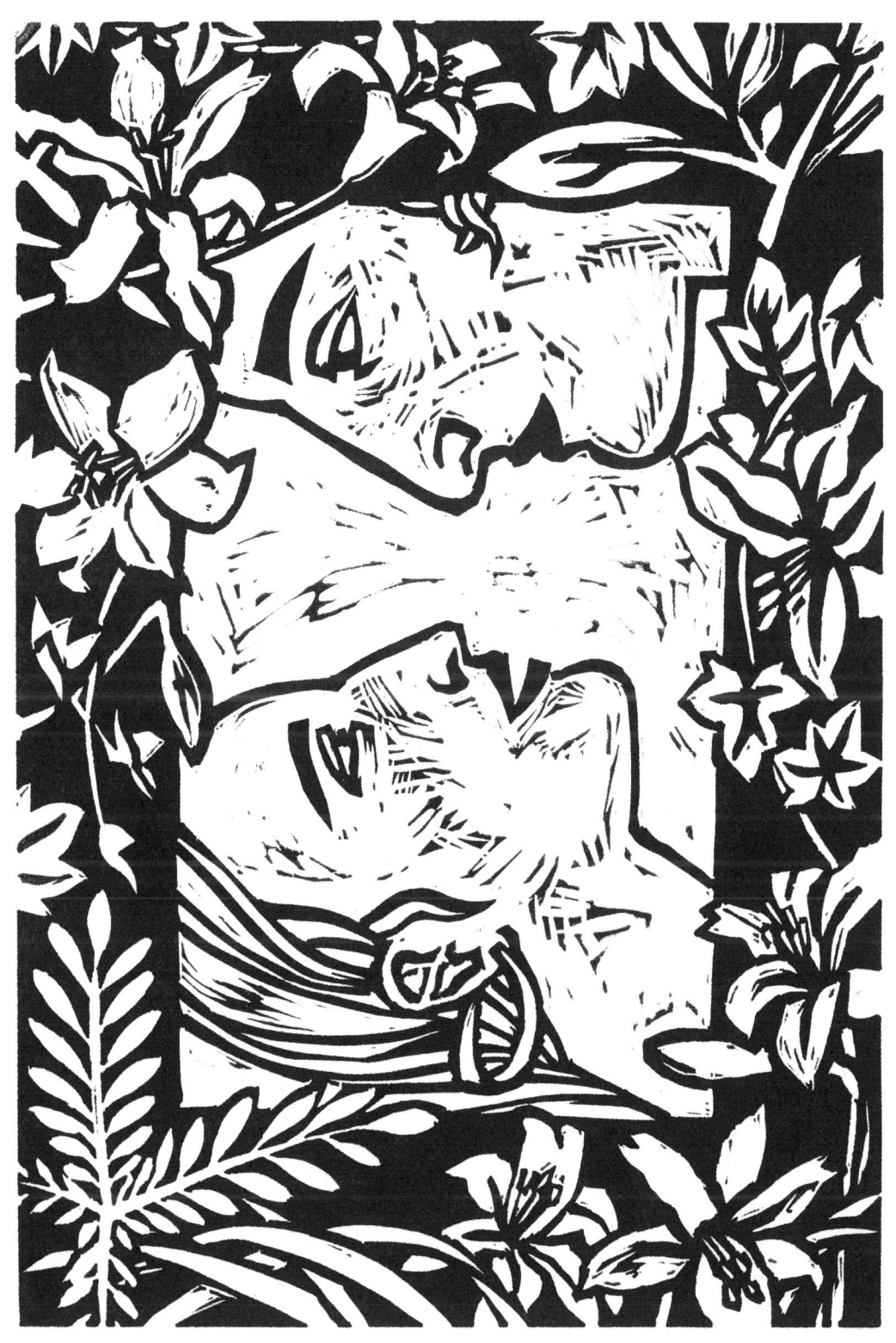

Isaiah 6:1–8

UNCLEAN LIPS

In the year that King Uzziah died I saw the Lord sitting upon a throne, high and lifted up; and the train of his robe filled the temple. Above him stood the seraphim. Each had six wings: with two he covered his face, and with two he covered his feet, and with two he flew. And one called to another and said:

> "Holy, holy, holy is the Lord of hosts;
> the whole earth is full of his glory!"

And the foundations of the thresholds shook at the voice of him who called, and the house was filled with smoke. And I said: "Woe is me! For I am lost; for I am a man of unclean lips, and I dwell in the midst of a people of unclean lips; for my eyes have seen the King, the Lord of hosts!"

Then one of the seraphim flew to me, having in his hand a burning coal that he had taken with tongs from the altar. And he touched my mouth and said: "Behold, this has touched your lips; your guilt is taken away, and your sin atoned for."

And I heard the voice of the Lord saying, "Whom shall I send, and who will go for us?" Then I said, "Here I am! Send me."

Isaiah 6

WAYNE FORTE | LINOCUT

It is easy to imagine an artist choosing to illustrate the spectacle of the six-winged seraphim calling out to each other from this passage. But instead, Forte identifies with the prophet: "Woe is me! For I am lost; for I am a man of unclean lips, and I dwell in the midst of a people of unclean lips." This print focuses on the mercy of God and the work of sanctification in the life of a believer. What is truly amazing to learn about in the Bible is not multi-winged angels or mysterious visions. Rather, it is that through the work of Christ on the Cross dying for our sins, our guilt is taken away and our sin is atoned for.

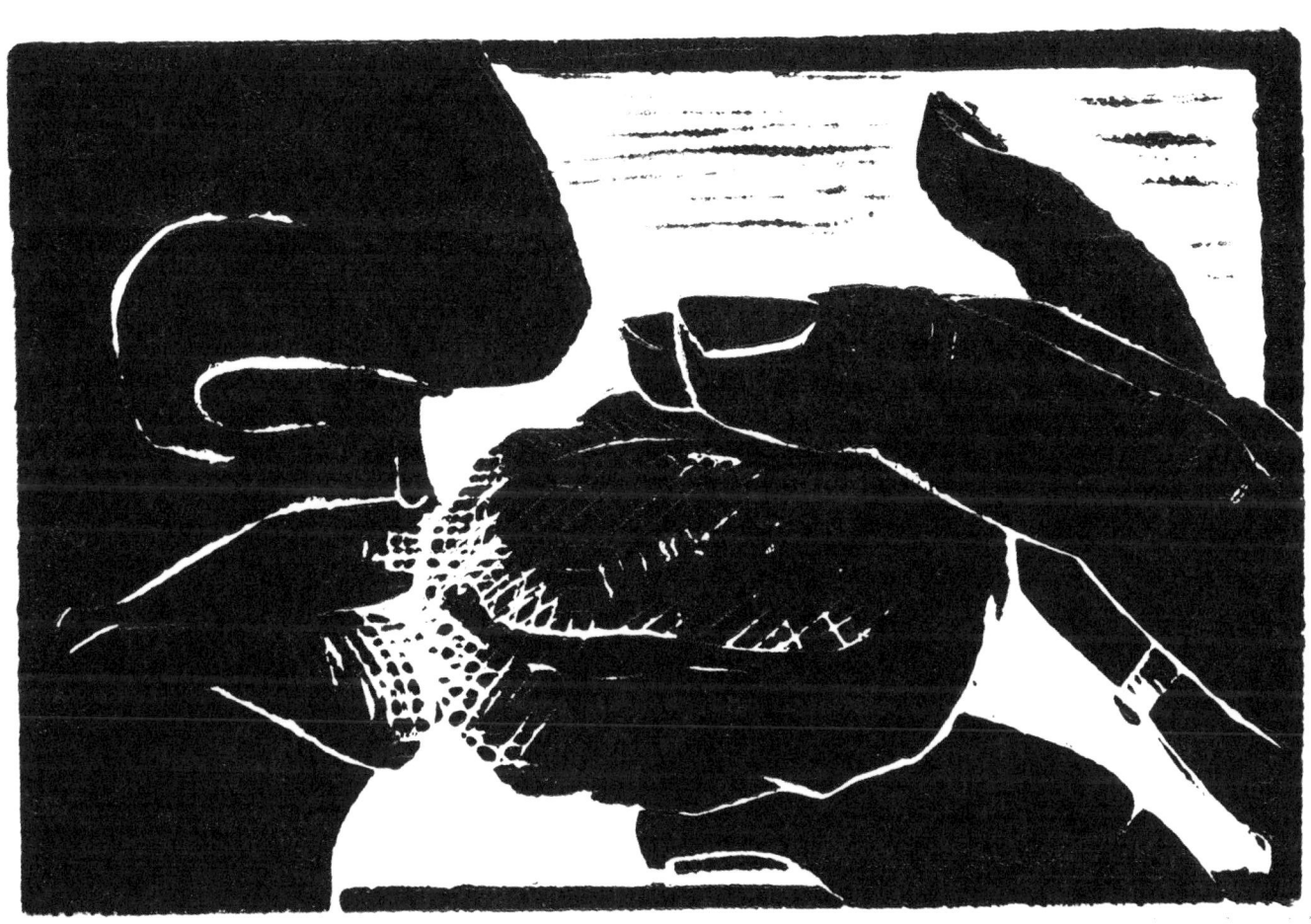

Isaiah 53:1–6

HE HAS BORNE OUR GRIEFS

Who has believed what he has heard from us?
    And to whom has the arm of the Lord been revealed?
For he grew up before him like a young plant,
    and like a root out of dry ground;
he had no form or majesty that we should look at him,
    and no beauty that we should desire him.
He was despised and rejected by men;
    a man of sorrows, and acquainted with grief;
and as one from whom men hide their faces
    he was despised, and we esteemed him not.
Surely he has borne our griefs
    and carried our sorrows;
yet we esteemed him stricken,
    smitten by God, and afflicted.
But he was pierced for our transgressions;
    he was crushed for our iniquities;
upon him was the chastisement that brought us peace,
    and with his wounds we are healed.
All we like sheep have gone astray;
    we have turned—every one—to his own way;
and the Lord has laid on him
    the iniquity of us all.

En Agonie (after Rouault)

NED BUSTARD | LINOCUT

This print is based on *Jesus sera en agonie jusqu'a la fin du mond*, a piece that can be found in *Rouault-Fujimura: Soliloquies*. In that book, artist Makoto Fujimura writes that the works by Georges Rouault "transport us to a past beyond the fragmentation of Modernism into the enchantment and mysteries of a medieval aesthetic, before rationality was segregated from passion and our hearts divorced from faith." When this print has been exhibited, some have been unable to decipher the image: a torn and battered Christ hanging on the Cross. Perhaps this is because the contemporary church resists a broken savior. But Rouault embraced him. Fujimura says that Rouault showed in his art "a suffering servant who took on the broken condition of our souls, the historic Jesus of Nazareth, who chose to walk into darkness claiming to be the 'light of the world.'"

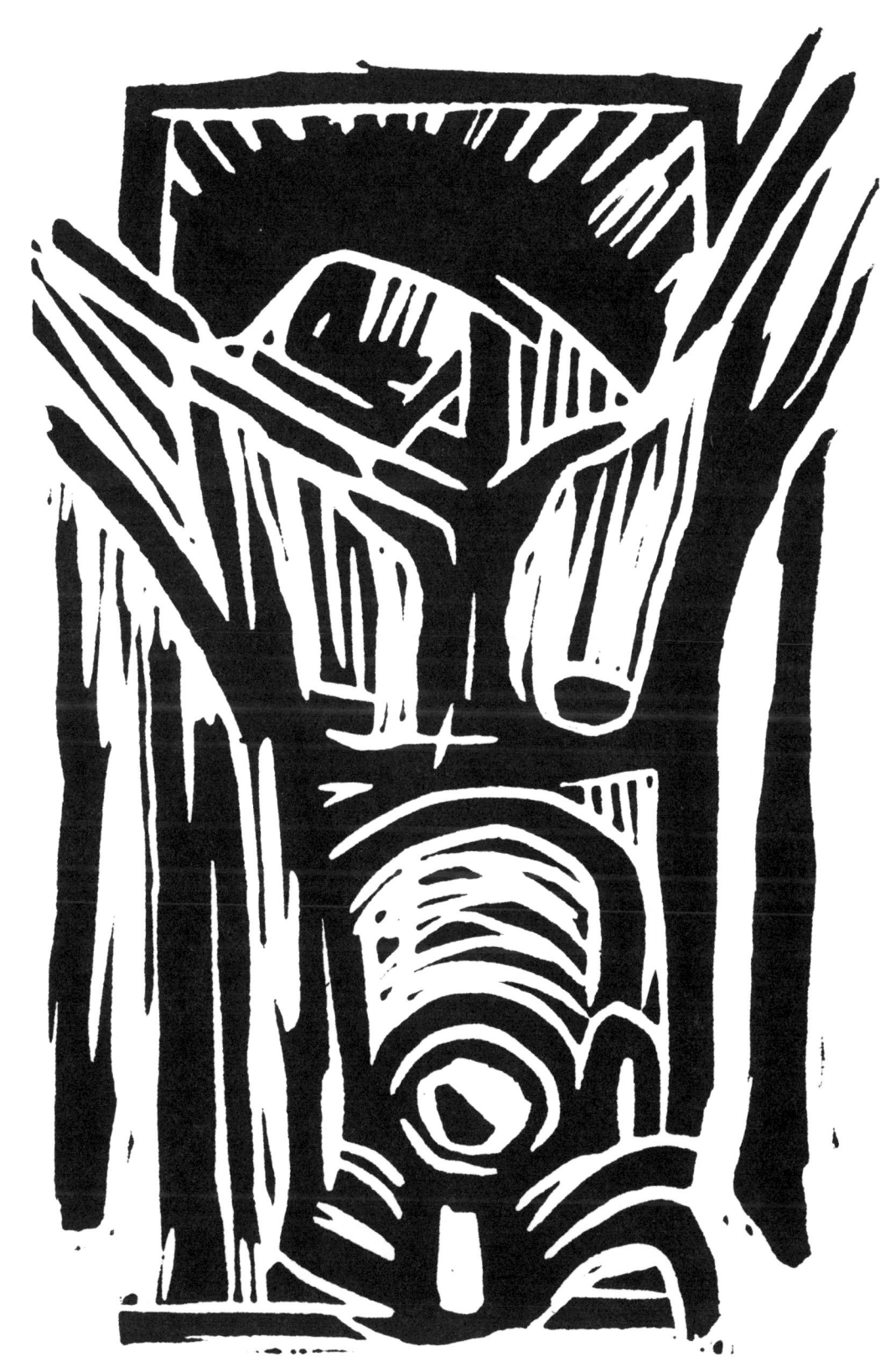

Jeremiah 29:1–8

SEEK THE WELFARE OF THE CITY

These are the words of the letter that Jeremiah the prophet sent from Jerusalem to the surviving elders of the exiles, and to the priests, the prophets, and all the people, whom Nebuchadnezzar had taken into exile from Jerusalem to Babylon. This was after King Jeconiah and the queen mother, the eunuchs, the officials of Judah and Jerusalem, the craftsmen, and the metal workers had departed from Jerusalem. The letter was sent by the hand of Elasah the son of Shaphan and Gemariah the son of Hilkiah, whom Zedekiah king of Judah sent to Babylon to Nebuchadnezzar king of Babylon. It said: "Thus says the Lord of hosts, the God of Israel, to all the exiles whom I have sent into exile from Jerusalem to Babylon: Build houses and live in them; plant gardens and eat their produce. Take wives and have sons and daughters; take wives for your sons, and give your daughters in marriage, that they may bear sons and daughters; multiply there, and do not decrease. But seek the welfare of the city where I have sent you into exile, and pray to the Lord on its behalf, for in its welfare you will find your welfare.

Song of the City

RICK BEERHORST | WOODCUT

Followers of God are exiles, caught between the Garden of Eden and the City of God in the restored earth. And like the exiles in Babylon, we are called to work and pray for the common good of our cities—while also nurturing our faith so that we do not assimilate the idolatrous aspects of our culture. Eric Jacobsen believes that cities are a crucible for our sanctification in preparation for life in the New Jerusalem. In *Sidewalks in the Kingdom* he writes, "Cities force us to live, work, and play near people to whom we may need to show love, gentleness, and kindness. In the suburban ideal of a large house surrounded by a large lot, we don't ever have to see others, let alone interact with them. Cities are filled with physical, historical, and relational contingencies that require patience and self control on our part."

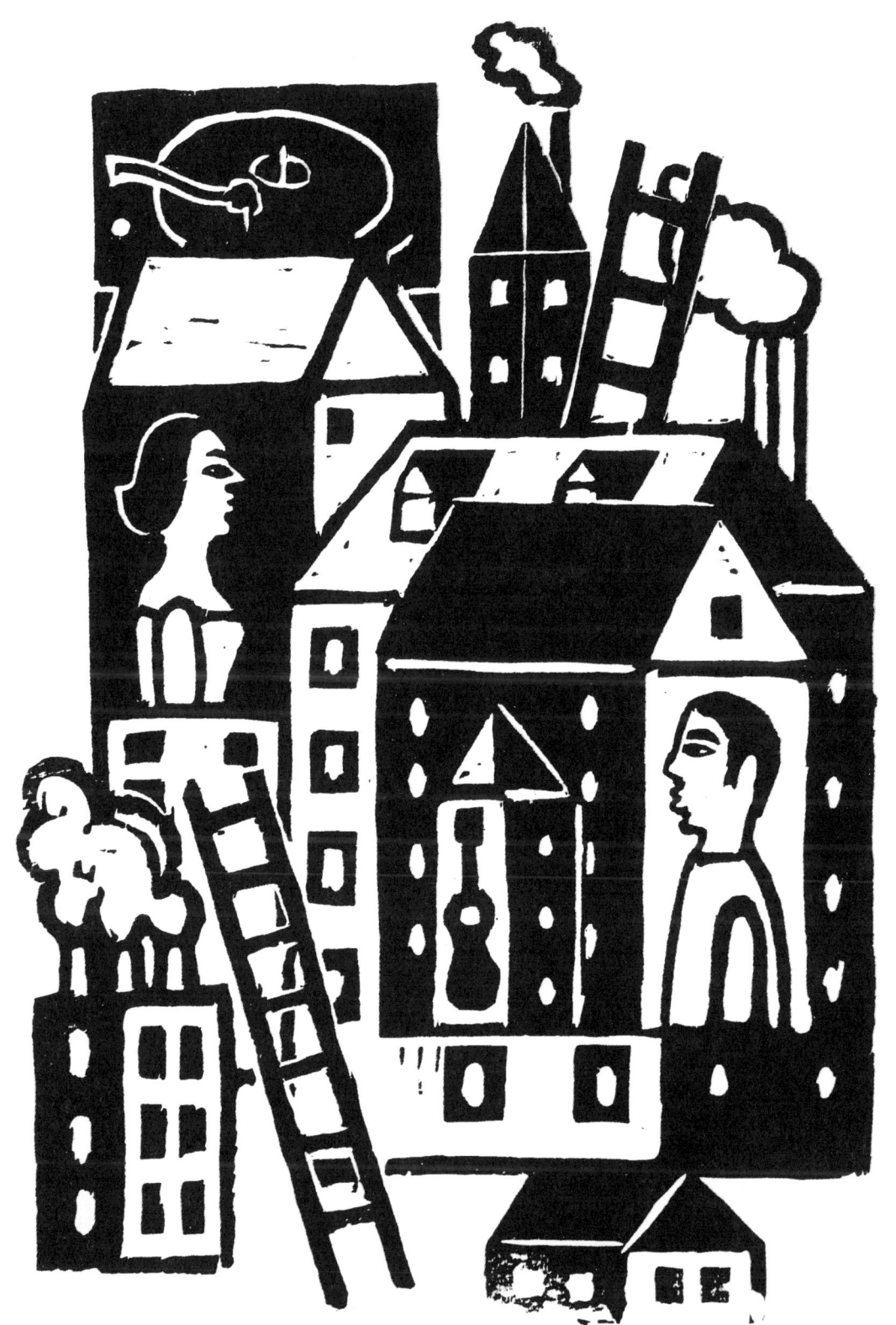

Lamentations 3:14–24

THE FAITHFULNESS OF GOD

I have become the laughingstock of all peoples,
    the object of their taunts all day long.
He has filled me with bitterness;
    he has sated me with wormwood.
He has made my teeth grind on gravel,
    and made me cower in ashes;
my soul is bereft of peace;
    I have forgotten what happiness is;
so I say, "My endurance has perished;
    so has my hope from the Lord."
Remember my affliction and my wanderings,
    the wormwood and the gall!
My soul continually remembers it
    and is bowed down within me.
But this I call to mind,
    and therefore I have hope:
The steadfast love of the Lord never ceases;
    his mercies never come to an end;
they are new every morning;
    great is your faithfulness.
"The Lord is my portion," says my soul,
    "therefore I will hope in him."

Lamentations: Send Your Rain

STEVE PRINCE | LINOCUT

This print is from the same series as *Exodus: Bread from Heaven* and therefore is intended to be a look at an Old Testament passage through the lens of a love story. This image shows a couple walking through a storm, which is symbolic of the suffering, pain, and destruction documented in the book of Lamentations. The husband clings to his wife as they move in faith through the storm. In the midst of the raindrops three elongated figural forms (alluding to the Trinity/Holy Spirit) create a covering over the couple. The woman clutching her abdomen is a symbol of hope and renewal as it represents the imminent arrival of a child. The presence of the Cross is created by the subtle placement of the woman's finger overlapping the rod of the umbrella. It is by faith they walk, and the Holy Spirit amplifies their love through the storms of life.

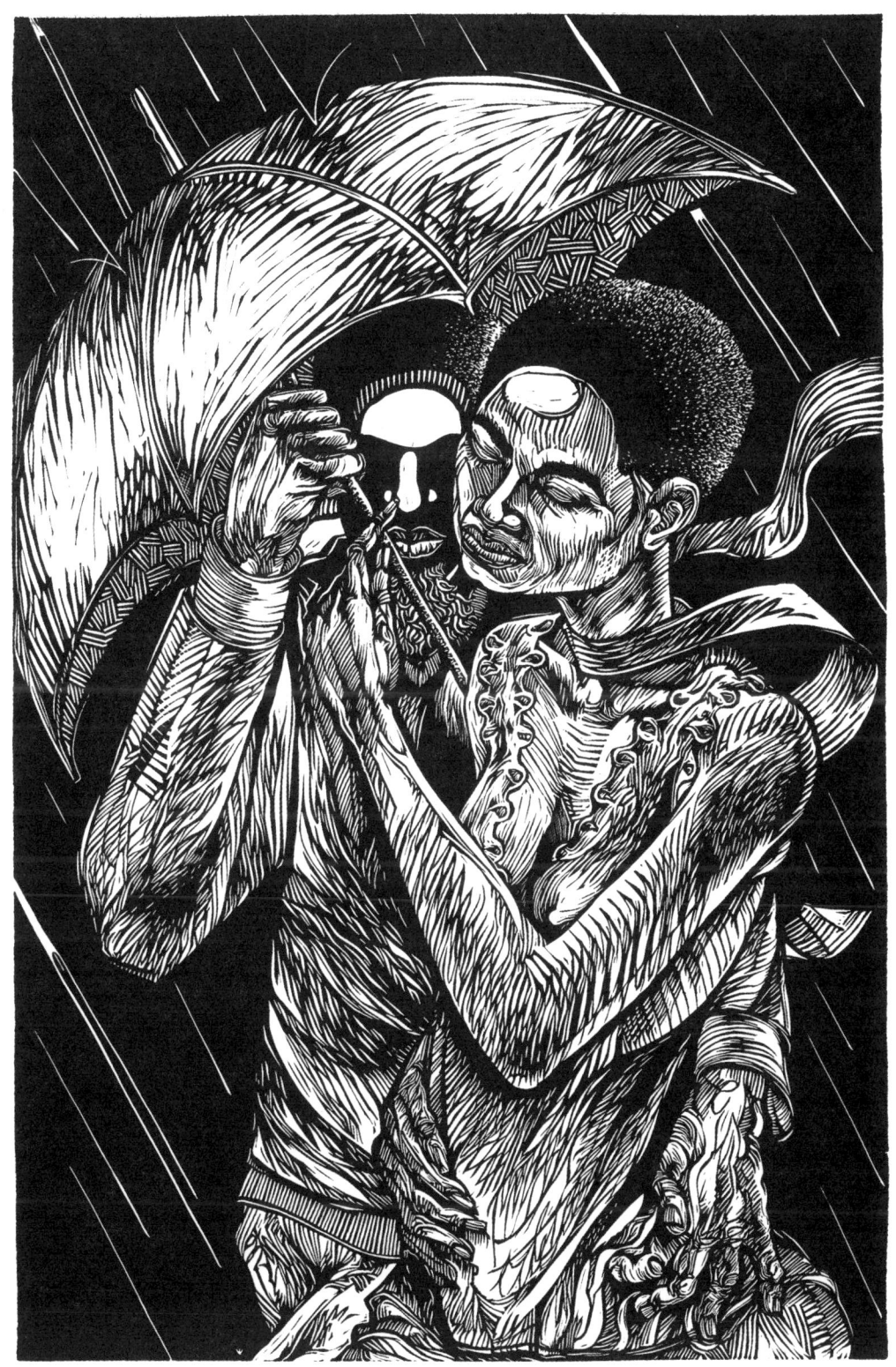

Ezekiel 1:1–12

A VISION OF HEAVEN

In the thirtieth year, in the fourth month, on the fifth day of the month, as I was among the exiles by the Chebar canal, the heavens were opened, and I saw visions of God. On the fifth day of the month (it was the fifth year of the exile of King Jehoiachin), the word of the Lord came to Ezekiel the priest, the son of Buzi, in the land of the Chaldeans by the Chebar canal, and the hand of the Lord was upon him there.

As I looked, behold, a stormy wind came out of the north, and a great cloud, with brightness around it, and fire flashing forth continually, and in the midst of the fire, as it were gleaming metal. And from the midst of it came the likeness of four living creatures. And this was their appearance: they had a human likeness, but each had four faces, and each of them had four wings. Their legs were straight, and the soles of their feet were like the sole of a calf's foot. And they sparkled like burnished bronze. Under their wings on their four sides they had human hands. And the four had their faces and their wings thus: their wings touched one another. Each one of them went straight forward, without turning as they went. As for the likeness of their faces, each had a human face. The four had the face of a lion on the right side, the four had the face of an ox on the left side, and the four had the face of an eagle. Such were their faces. And their wings were spread out above. Each creature had two wings, each of which touched the wing of another, while two covered their bodies. And each went straight forward. Wherever the spirit would go, they went, without turning as they went.

Ezekiel's Vision

TANJA BUTLER | LINOCUT

This passage is one of overwhelming intensity and disorientation, and the artist conveys these sensations through the swirling composition of this print. As in *God's Confrontation* earlier in this book, in this print Butler has compressed a great deal of the story into one image. The stormy wind and flashing fire with four living creatures from Ezekiel's vision are represented in the angelic figure in upper left, wheel on right, and seven stars representing fire flashing forth. Ezekiel's response to seeing the glory of God is shown in the three central figures: the prophet fell on his face and the Spirit set him on his feet—then the Spirit gave him a scroll and told him to eat it. When the vision was completed, Ezekiel sat among the exiles, stunned and sick, for seven days. His despair is shown through the frieze of figures along the bottom.

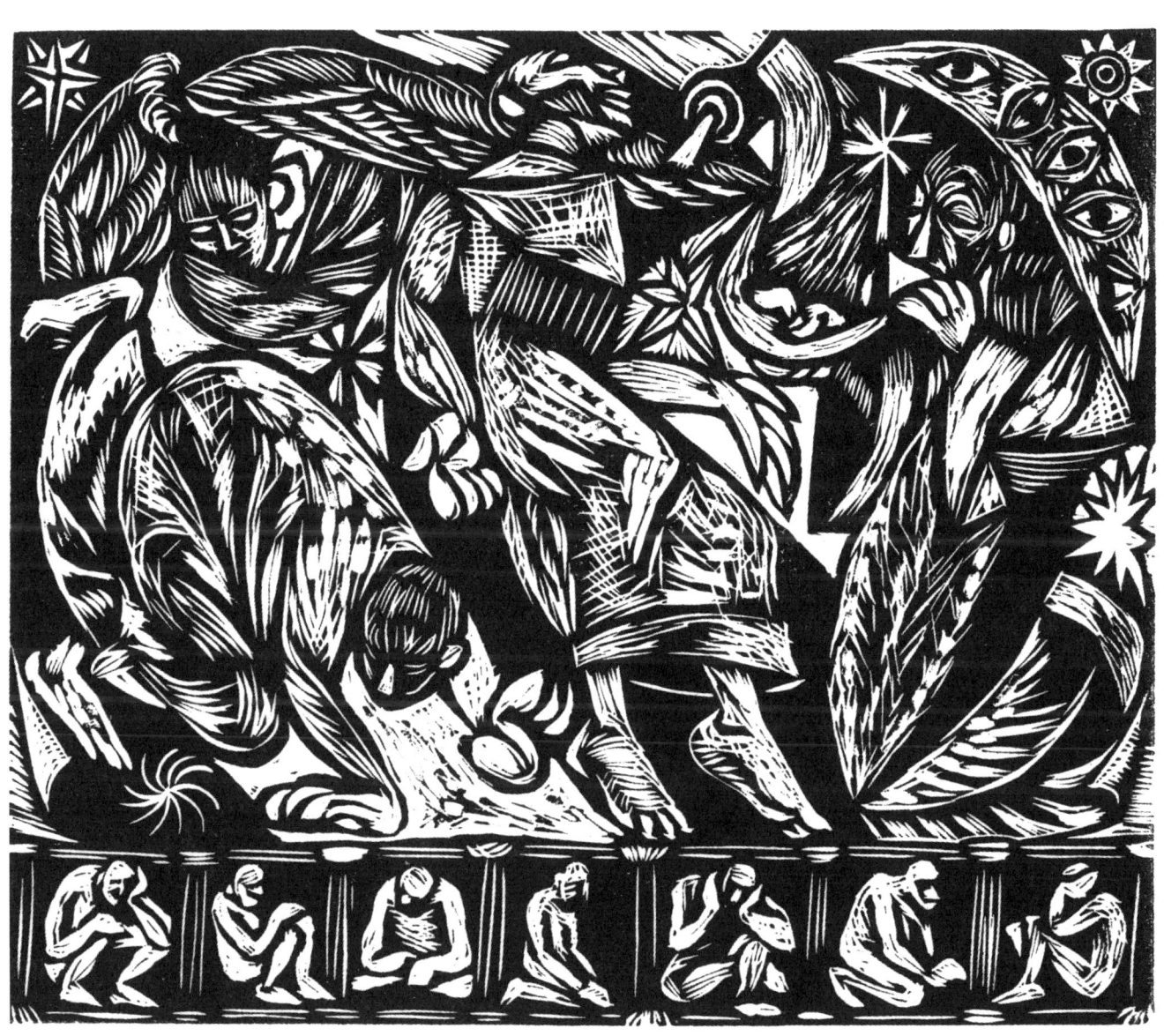

Ezekiel 23:1–7, 11, 18–21

OHOLAH AND OHOLIBAH

The word of the Lord came to me: "Son of man, there were two women, the daughters of one mother. They played the whore in Egypt; they played the whore in their youth; there their breasts were pressed and their virgin bosoms handled. Oholah was the name of the elder and Oholibah the name of her sister. They became mine, and they bore sons and daughters. As for their names, Oholah is Samaria, and Oholibah is Jerusalem.

"Oholah played the whore while she was mine, and she lusted after her lovers the Assyrians, warriors clothed in purple, governors and commanders, all of them desirable young men, horsemen riding on horses. She bestowed her whoring upon them, the choicest men of Assyria all of them, and she defiled herself with all the idols of everyone after whom she lusted.

. . .

Her sister Oholibah saw this, and she became more corrupt than her sister in her lust and in her whoring, which was worse than that of her sister.

. . .

When she carried on her whoring so openly and flaunted her nakedness, I turned in disgust from her, as I had turned in disgust from her sister. Yet she increased her whoring, remembering the days of her youth, when she played the whore in the land of Egypt and lusted after her lovers there, whose members were like those of donkeys, and whose issue was like that of horses. Thus you longed for the lewdness of your youth, when the Egyptians handled your bosom and pressed your young breasts."

Straatmuzikanten

HENRI VAN STRATEN | LINOCUT

The artist was probably not thinking of Ezekiel 23 when he carved this block of buskers, but it has been repurposed for that function here. When viewed through the lens of Ezekiel 23, the piece works very well as an illustration for a passage condemning idolatry, described as lascivious unfaithfulness to God. The two sisters Oholah and Oholibah dance in the lower left corner of the print and Oholibah leers at the men in uniform (here street performers instead of the purple-robed Assyrian officials). Oholibah's occupation as a prostitute is clearly established by looking over the trumpeter's shoulder, where the viewer can see that this is the red-light district of the city.

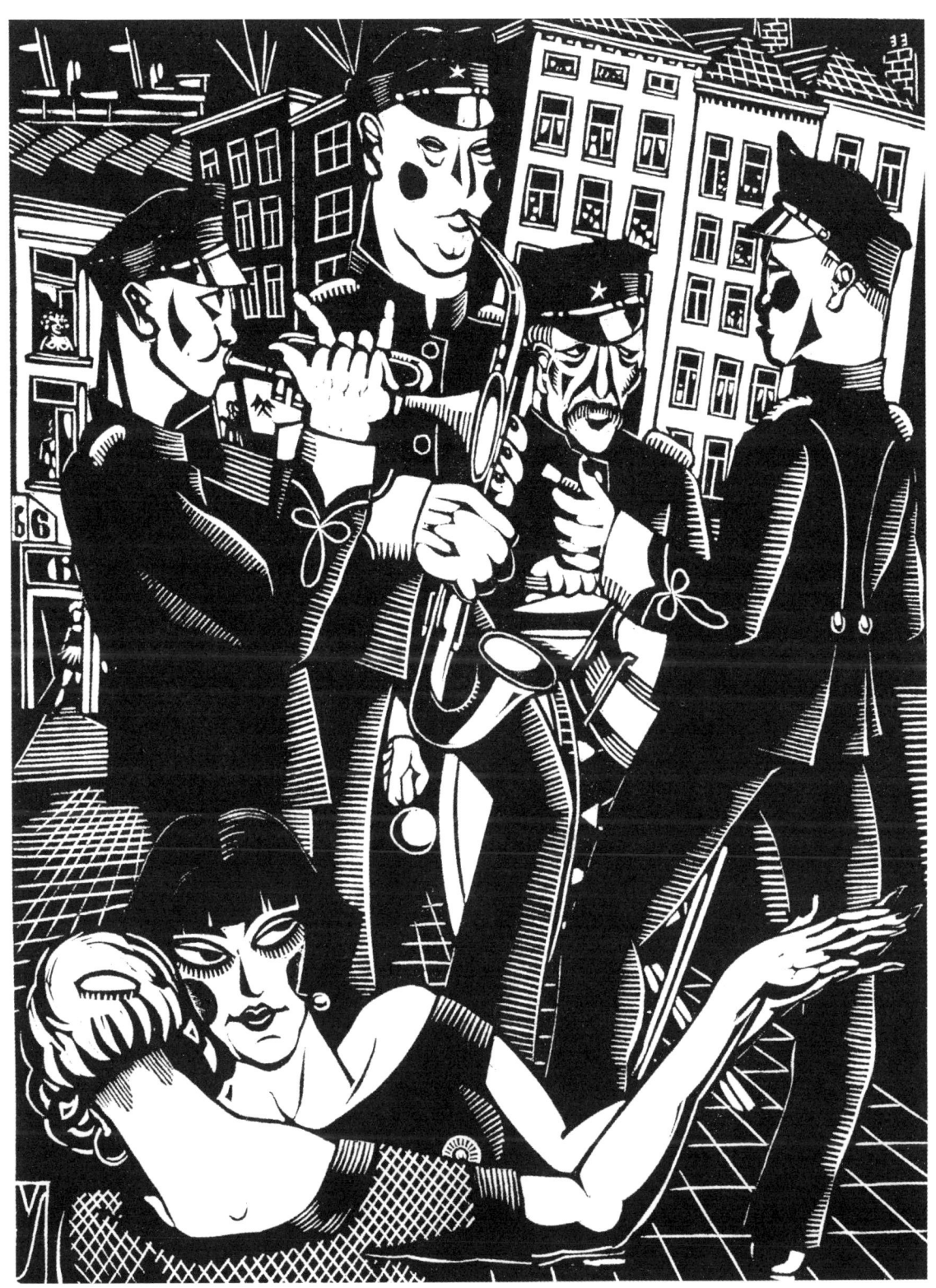

Ezekiel 37:1–10

DRY BONES

The hand of the Lord was upon me, and he brought me out in the Spirit of the Lord and set me down in the middle of the valley; it was full of bones. And he led me around among them, and behold, there were very many on the surface of the valley, and behold, they were very dry. And he said to me, "Son of man, can these bones live?" And I answered, "O Lord God, you know." Then he said to me, "Prophesy over these bones, and say to them, O dry bones, hear the word of the Lord. Thus says the Lord God to these bones: Behold, I will cause breath to enter you, and you shall live. And I will lay sinews upon you, and will cause flesh to come upon you, and cover you with skin, and put breath in you, and you shall live, and you shall know that I am the Lord."

So I prophesied as I was commanded. And as I prophesied, there was a sound, and behold, a rattling, and the bones came together, bone to its bone. And I looked, and behold, there were sinews on them, and flesh had come upon them, and skin had covered them. But there was no breath in them. Then he said to me, "Prophesy to the breath; prophesy, son of man, and say to the breath, Thus says the Lord God: Come from the four winds, O breath, and breathe on these slain, that they may live." So I prophesied as he commanded me, and the breath came into them, and they lived and stood on their feet, an exceedingly great army.

Valley of Bones

DIEGO JOURDAN PEREIRA | WOODCUT

In this vision the prophet walks through the valley of the shadow of death wearing his ceremonial robes—the knots in the wood forming decorative elements that may allude to the Urim and Thummim worn by the high priest. But because the Israelites are in exile, the young Levite has no hope to ever wear such robes and get to serve in the Temple. Yet in spite of their current bleak conditions, there is hope for the people of God. There is hope because God has made promises to his people, and he keeps his word. Barely visible on Ezekiel's left and right are skulls, and in the foreground a rib cage is visible. The bones represent the house of Israel. And God says: "Behold, I will open your graves and raise you from your graves, O my people . . . And I will put my Spirit within you, and you shall live . . ."

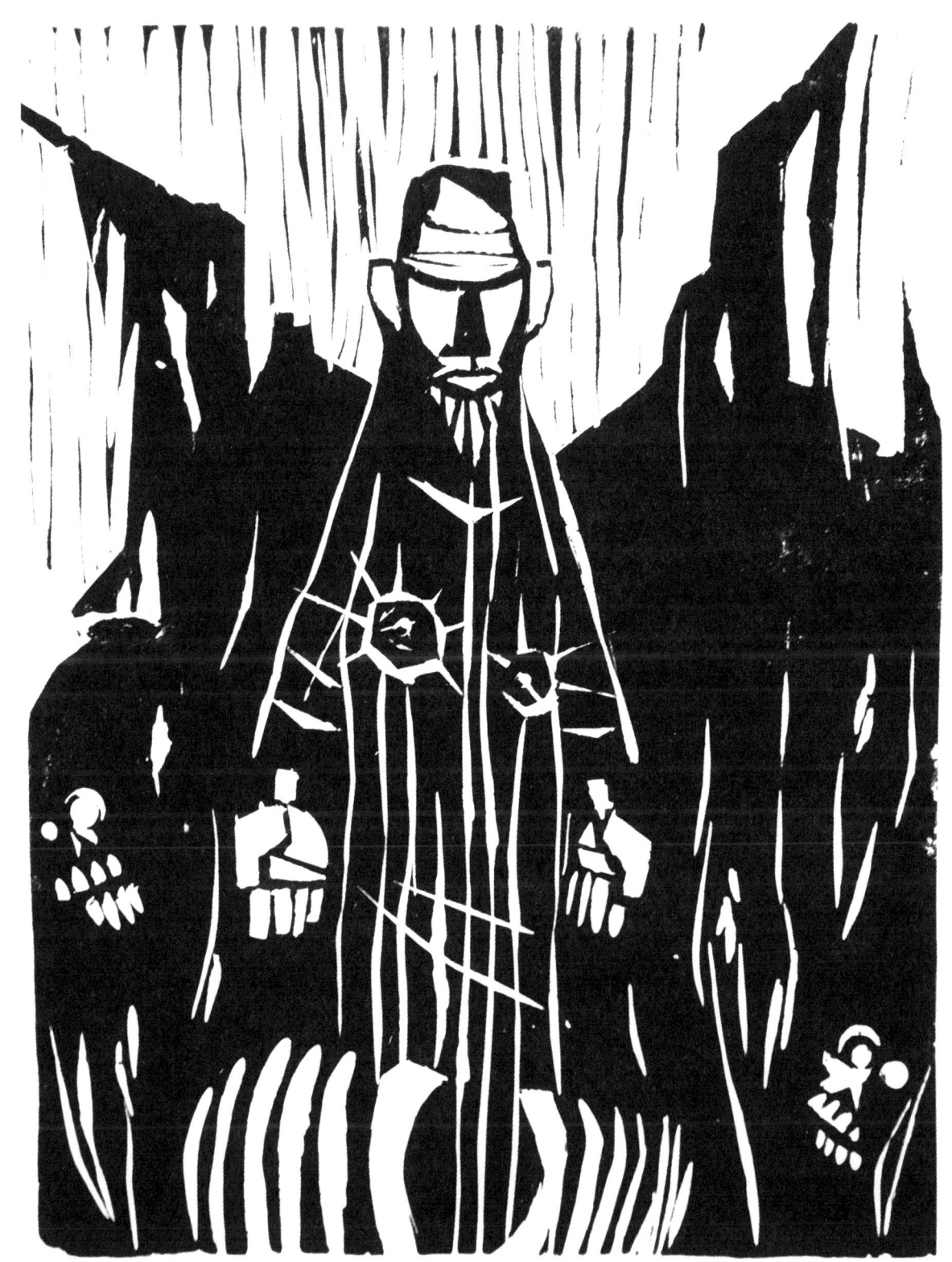

Daniel 3:14–19, 22–23

THE FIERY FURNACE

"Is it true, O Shadrach, Meshach, and Abednego, that you do not serve my gods or worship the golden image that I have set up? Now if you are ready when you hear the sound of the horn, pipe, lyre, trigon, harp, bagpipe, and every kind of music, to fall down and worship the image that I have made, well and good. But if you do not worship, you shall immediately be cast into a burning fiery furnace. And who is the god who will deliver you out of my hands?"

Shadrach, Meshach, and Abednego answered and said to the king, "O Nebuchadnezzar, we have no need to answer you in this matter. If this be so, our God whom we serve is able to deliver us from the burning fiery furnace, and he will deliver us out of your hand, O king. But if not, be it known to you, O king, that we will not serve your gods or worship the golden image that you have set up."

Then Nebuchadnezzar was filled with fury, and the expression of his face was changed against Shadrach, Meshach, and Abednego. He ordered the furnace heated seven times more than it was usually heated . . . Because the king's order was urgent and the furnace overheated, the flame of the fire killed those men who took up Shadrach, Meshach, and Abednego. And these three men, Shadrach, Meshach, and Abednego, fell bound into the burning fiery furnace.

Even If

NED BUSTARD | LINOCUT

The title for this piece comes from a different translation of the "But if not" protest against Nebuchadnezzar made by these three young men in this passage. And at the end of the passage above it looks like God will *not* save them. The poor Persian soldier on furnace duty that day lies on the ground, burned halfway to the bones by the incredible heat, and Shadrach, Meshach, and Abednego are doomed to be burned to death. But then the king was astonished to see four men unbound, walking unhurt in the fire. God had chosen to save them. He protected them from the king, from the heat, and from death. The appearance of the fourth man in the fire represents a *theophany*—God revealing himself in human form before the Incarnation. Other such appearances include Genesis 32:24–30 and Joshua 5:13–15.

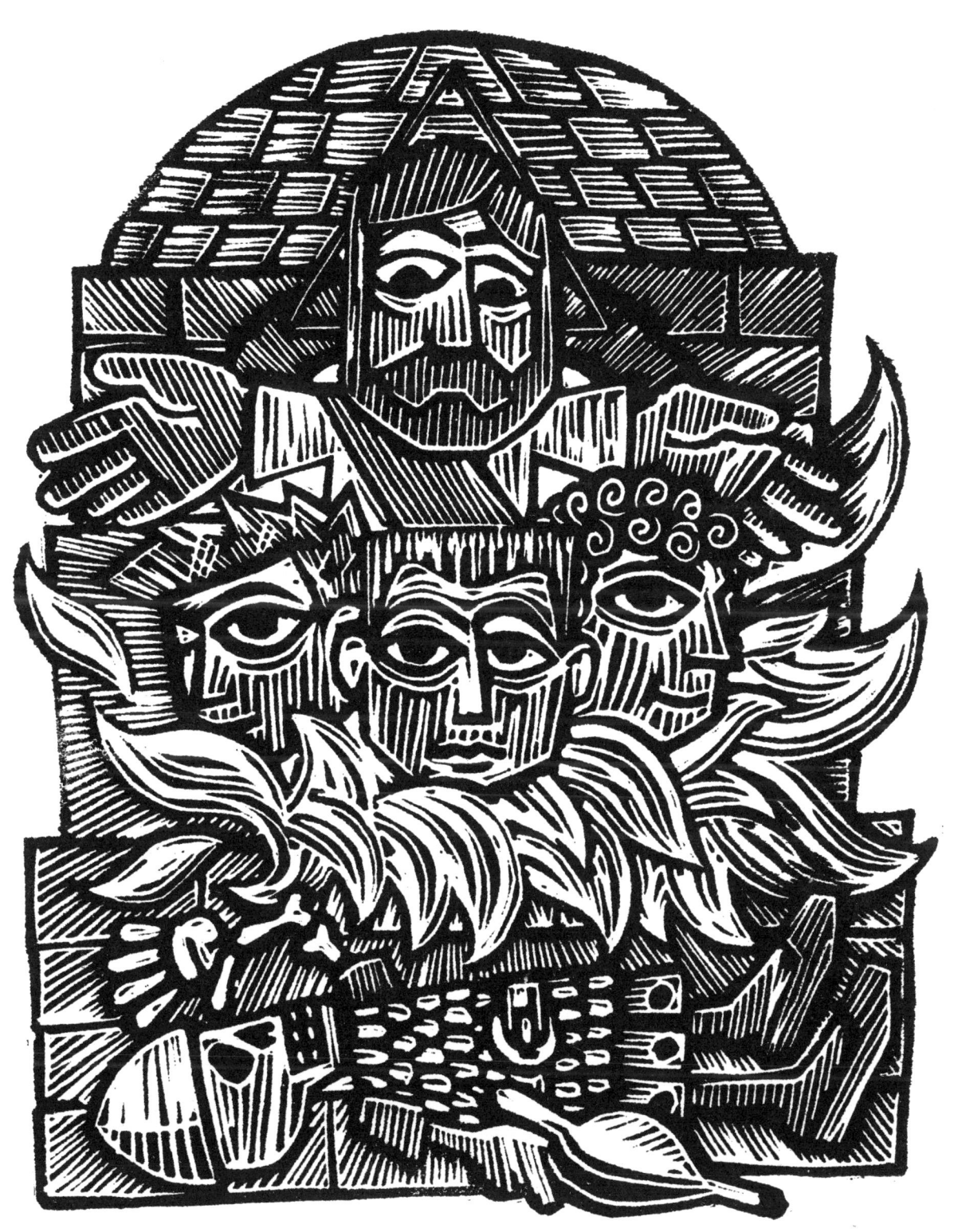

Daniel 6:16–24

DANIEL IN THE LIONS' DEN

Then the king commanded, and Daniel was brought and cast into the den of lions. The king declared to Daniel, "May your God, whom you serve continually, deliver you!" And a stone was brought and laid on the mouth of the den, and the king sealed it with his own signet and with the signet of his lords, that nothing might be changed concerning Daniel. Then the king went to his palace and spent the night fasting; no diversions were brought to him, and sleep fled from him.

Then, at break of day, the king arose and went in haste to the den of lions. As he came near to the den where Daniel was, he cried out in a tone of anguish. The king declared to Daniel, "O Daniel, servant of the living God, has your God, whom you serve continually, been able to deliver you from the lions?" Then Daniel said to the king, "O king, live forever! My God sent his angel and shut the lions' mouths, and they have not harmed me, because I was found blameless before him; and also before you, O king, I have done no harm." Then the king was exceedingly glad, and commanded that Daniel be taken up out of the den. So Daniel was taken up out of the den, and no kind of harm was found on him, because he had trusted in his God. And the king commanded, and those men who had maliciously accused Daniel were brought and cast into the den of lions—they, their children, and their wives. And before they reached the bottom of the den, the lions overpowered them and broke all their bones in pieces.

The Angel

MARGARET BUSTARD | LINOCUT, COLLAGE

Billy Graham wrote in *Angels: God's Secret Agents*, "In the den, Daniel's sight evidently perceived the angelic presence, and the lions' strength more than met its match in the power of the angel. In most instances, angels, when appearing visibly, are so glorious and impressively beautiful as to stun and amaze men who witness their presence." For example, in Revelation 19 the apostle John falls down at the feet of an angel to worship him, causing the angel to have to rebuke him. Inspired by the descriptions of angels in Ezekiel, nineteenth-century engravings were cut up and collaged over a repeating pattern of linocut lions to illustrate Daniel's famous den. In the story the lions are supposed to be scary, but here they are shown to be cute and cuddly by comparison with the terrifying unworldly servant of the Lord.

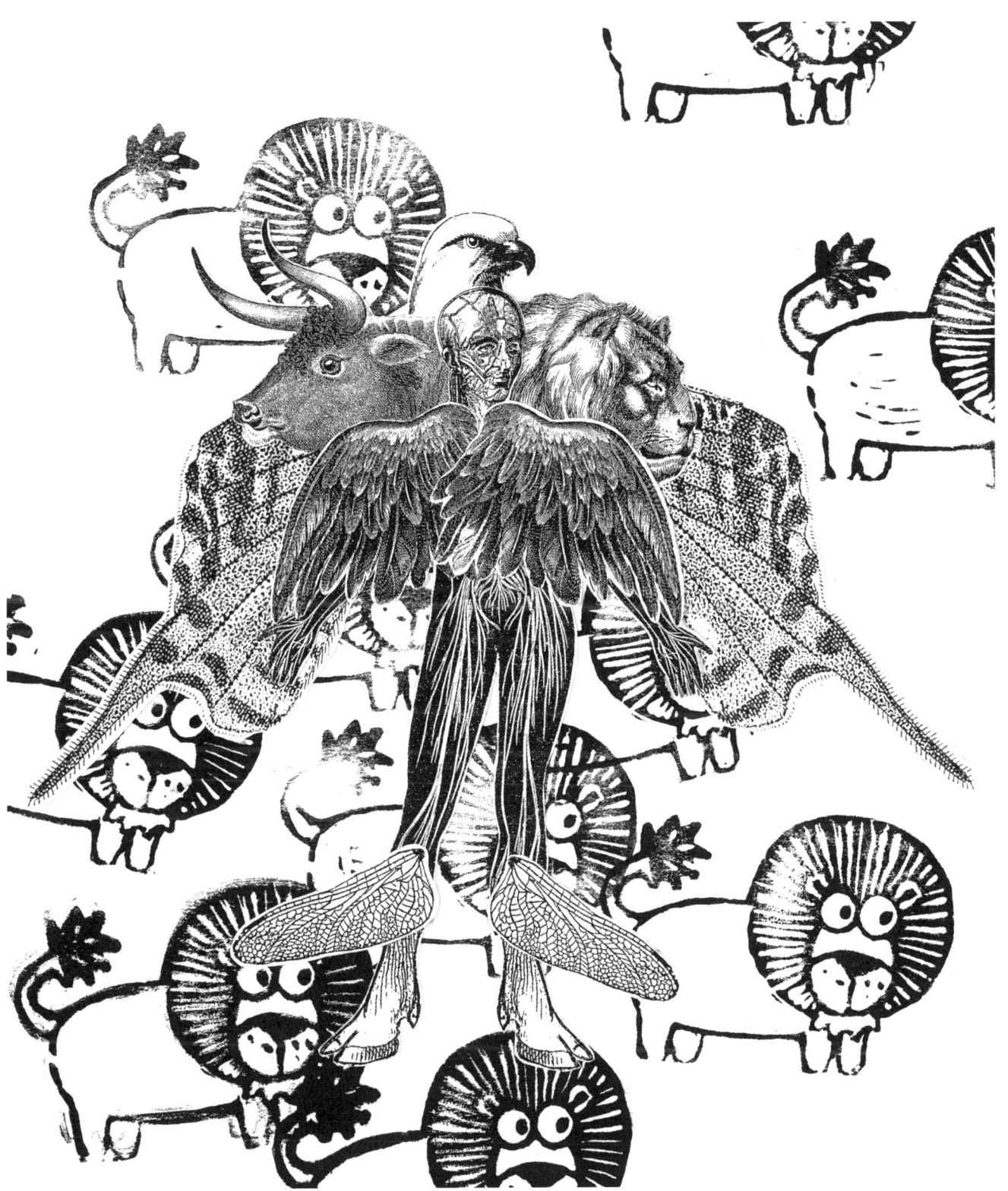

Daniel 4:24–32

THE CRAZY KING

". . . this is the interpretation, O king: It is a decree of the Most High, which has come upon my lord the king, that you shall be driven from among men, and your dwelling shall be with the beasts of the field. You shall be made to eat grass like an ox, and you shall be wet with the dew of heaven, and seven periods of time shall pass over you, till you know that the Most High rules the kingdom of men and gives it to whom he will. And as it was commanded to leave the stump of the roots of the tree, your kingdom shall be confirmed for you from the time that you know that Heaven rules. Therefore, O king, let my counsel be acceptable to you: break off your sins by practicing righteousness, and your iniquities by showing mercy to the oppressed, that there may perhaps be a lengthening of your prosperity."

All this came upon King Nebuchadnezzar. At the end of twelve months he was walking on the roof of the royal palace of Babylon, and the king answered and said, "Is not this great Babylon, which I have built by my mighty power as a royal residence and for the glory of my majesty?" While the words were still in the king's mouth, there fell a voice from heaven, "O King Nebuchadnezzar, to you it is spoken: The kingdom has departed from you, and you shall be driven from among men, and your dwelling shall be with the beasts of the field. And you shall be made to eat grass like an ox, and seven periods of time shall pass over you, until you know that the Most High rules the kingdom of men and gives it to whom he will."

The Madness of King Nebuchadnezzar
MATTHEW L. CLARK | LINOCUT

Verse 33 continues with, "Immediately the word was fulfilled against Nebuchadnezzar. He was driven from among men and ate grass like an ox, and his body was wet with the dew of heaven till his hair grew as long as eagles' feathers, and his nails were like birds' claws." The artist writes, "The 'horns of divinity' appear in many ancient Sumerian and Babylonian idols. Also, the ancient peoples often thought of crazy people as touched by divinity. So, ironically, Nebuchadnezzar achieved what he desired to accomplish in chapter three when he commissioned the golden statue of himself—but not exactly the way he wanted!" Ultimately the king recovered his sanity and could "praise and extol and honor the King of heaven, for all his works are right and his ways are just; and those who walk in pride he is able to humble."

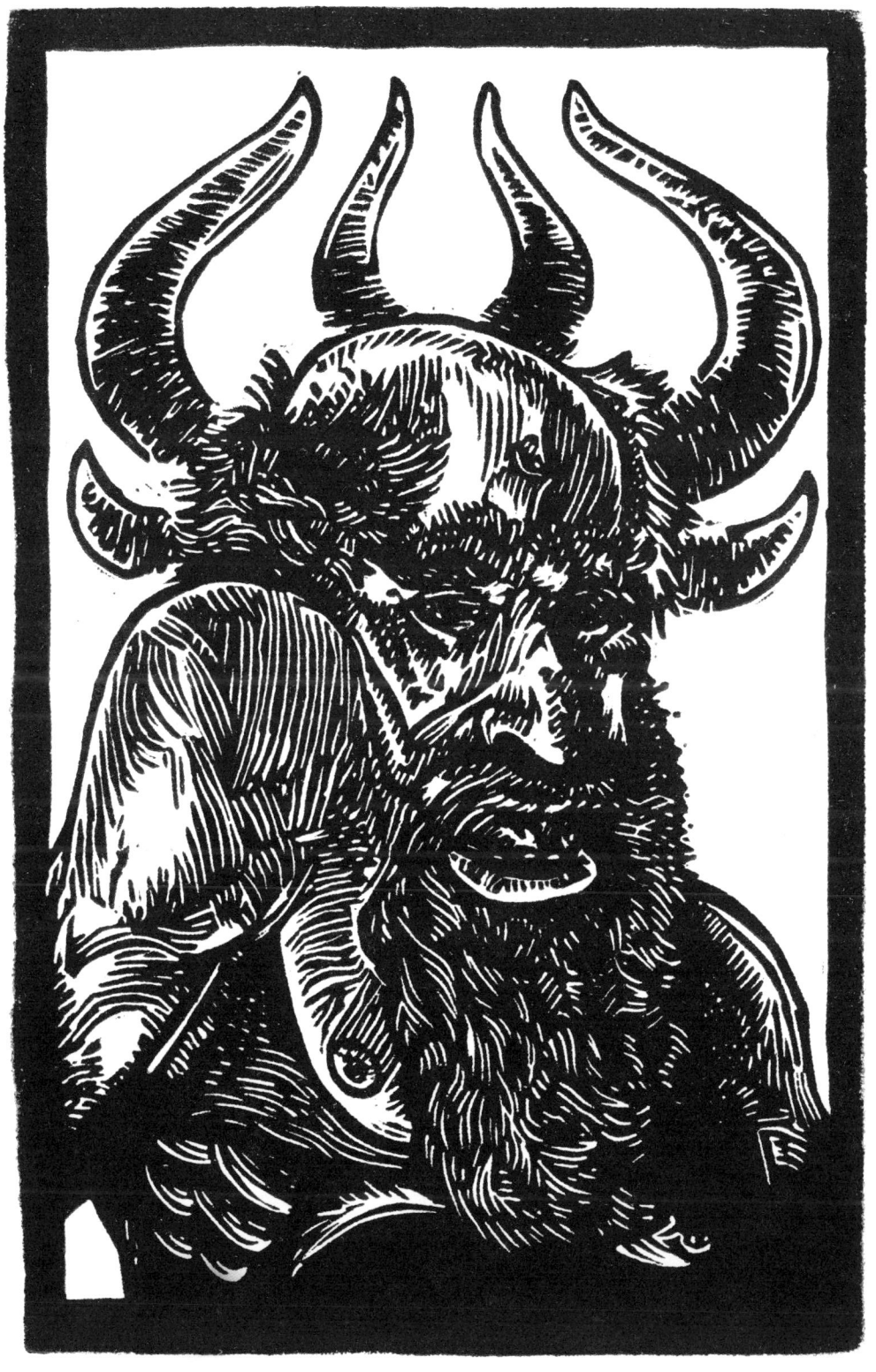

Hosea 3

THE REDEMPTION OF GOMER

And the Lord said to me, "Go again, love a woman who is loved by another man and is an adulteress, even as the Lord loves the children of Israel, though they turn to other gods and love cakes of raisins." So I bought her for fifteen shekels of silver and a homer and a lethech of barley. And I said to her, "You must dwell as mine for many days. You shall not play the whore, or belong to another man; so will I also be to you." For the children of Israel shall dwell many days without king or prince, without sacrifice or pillar, without ephod or household gods. Afterward the children of Israel shall return and seek the Lord their God, and David their king, and they shall come in fear to the Lord and to his goodness in the latter days.

Bride and Groom

NED BUSTARD | LINOCUT

In this piece a spurned husband dresses up in a tuxedo and comes out to the street corner with a wedding ring and an offer of marriage to his unfaithful wife who is standing under the street light, working as a prostitute. Gomer/Israel is a whore who is following after other lovers/gods, as alluded to in the "love cakes of raisins"—a reference to the fertility rituals in which raisin cakes were shaped into the form of a female goddess and used in pagan worship. But in spite of the offense and in spite of the great cost, Hosea pays for his wayward wife and takes her home. Through this amazing act of love Hosea is shown to be a model of Christ, as he paid the ultimate price for his wayward Bride.

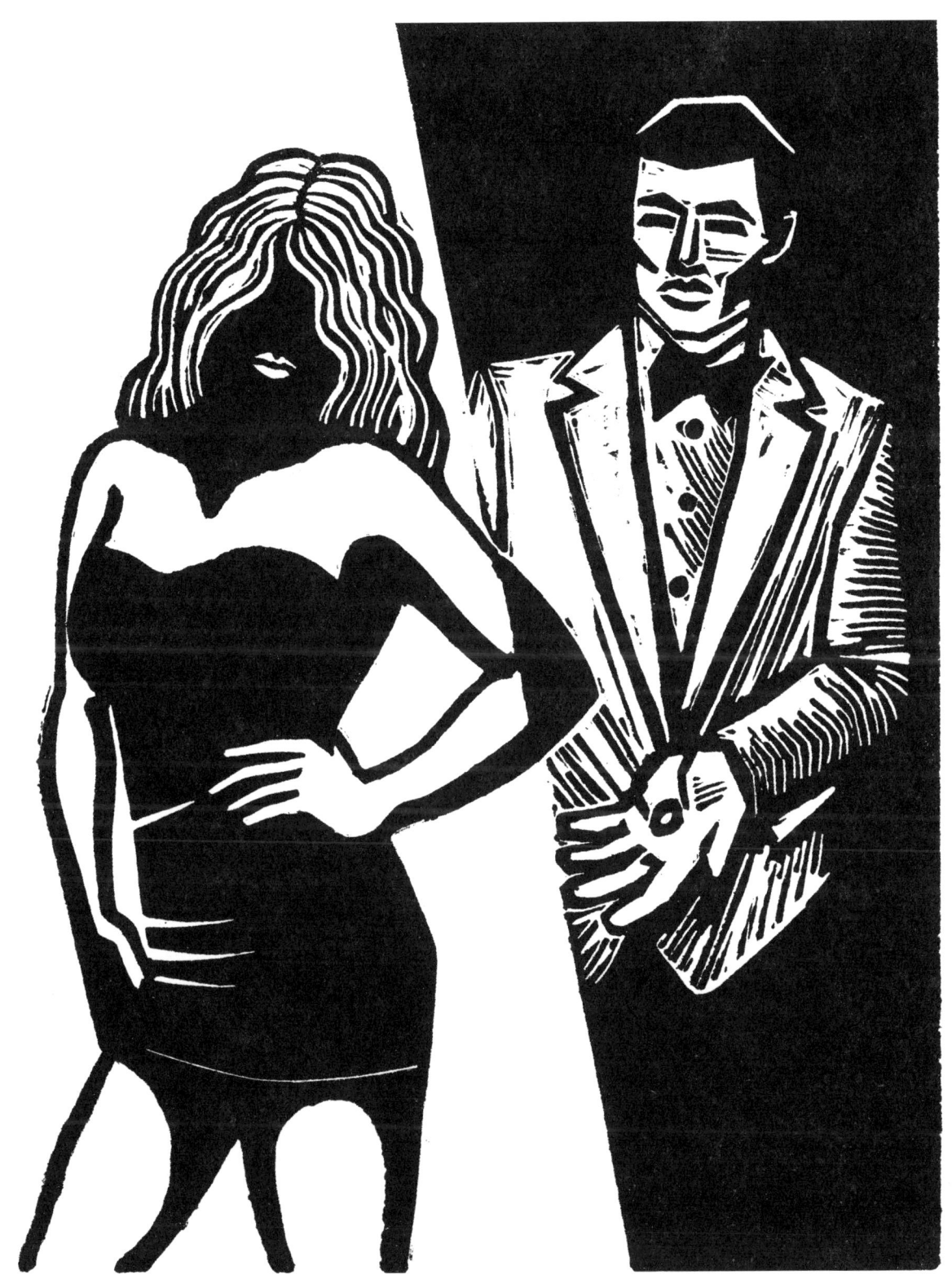

Joel 2:25–29

THE LOCUST YEARS

I will restore to you the years
    that the swarming locust has eaten,
the hopper, the destroyer, and the cutter,
    my great army, which I sent among you.

You shall eat in plenty and be satisfied,
    and praise the name of the Lord your God,
    who has dealt wondrously with you.
And my people shall never again be put to shame.
You shall know that I am in the midst of Israel,
    and that I am the Lord your God and there is none else.
And my people shall never again be put to shame.

And it shall come to pass afterward,
    that I will pour out my Spirit on all flesh;
your sons and your daughters shall prophesy,
    your old men shall dream dreams,
    and your young men shall see visions.
Even on the male and female servants
    in those days I will pour out my Spirit.

Locusts

MATTHEW L. CLARK | ETCHING

Swarming locusts are the image of loss. Sometimes we tell ourselves that what is lost in our lives is lost forever. We are powerless against those who devour and gorge themselves, as a great army sent to destroy what took us years to build. But if God sends the locust, then He and He alone has the power to restore that which has been lost to destruction. He and He alone is the Lord our God who is to be praised. The shame endured through loss is taken away by none other than our God. Come, Holy Spirit, come, and replace our loss with your Spirit until we see visions, dream dreams, and declare your wonders.

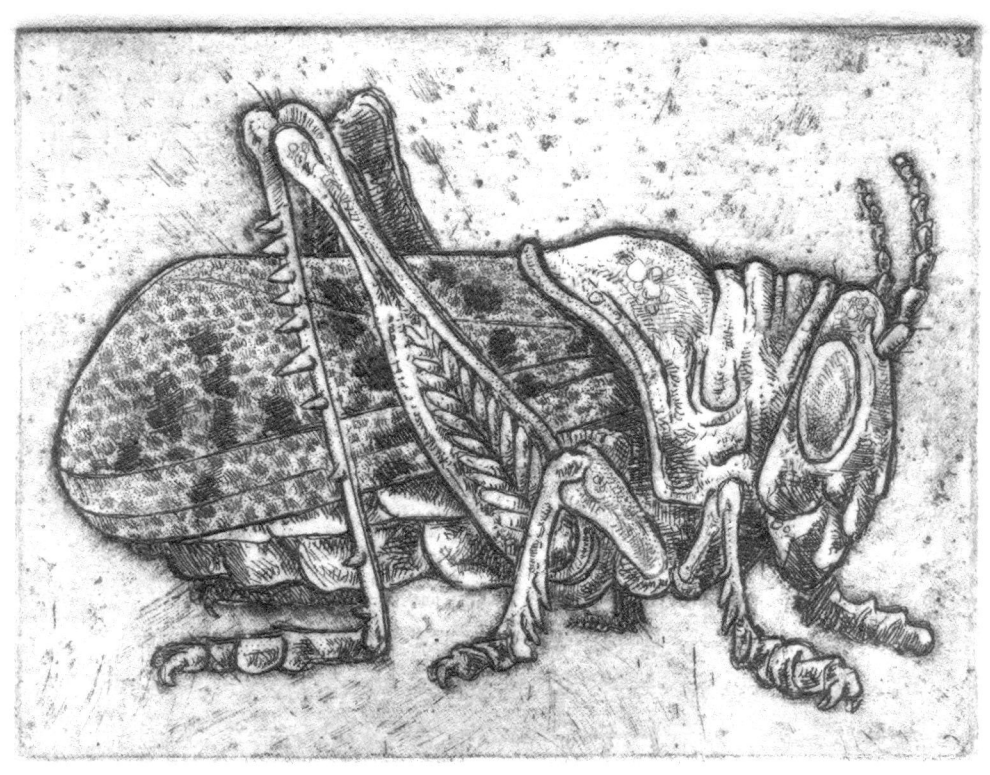
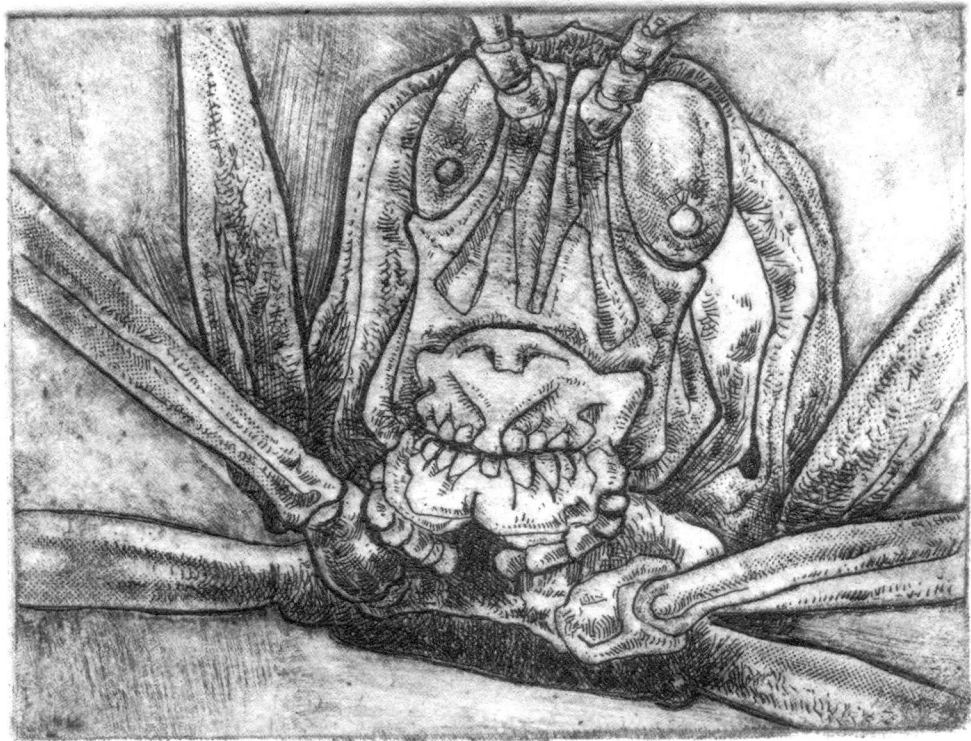

Jonah 1:11–2:3

IN THE BELLY OF THE FISH

Then they said to him, "What shall we do to you, that the sea may quiet down for us?" For the sea grew more and more tempestuous. He said to them, "Pick me up and hurl me into the sea; then the sea will quiet down for you, for I know it is because of me that this great tempest has come upon you." Nevertheless, the men rowed hard to get back to dry land, but they could not, for the sea grew more and more tempestuous against them. Therefore they called out to the LORD, "O LORD, let us not perish for this man's life, and lay not on us innocent blood, for you, O LORD, have done as it pleased you." So they picked up Jonah and hurled him into the sea, and the sea ceased from its raging. Then the men feared the LORD exceedingly, and they offered a sacrifice to the LORD and made vows.

And the LORD appointed a great fish to swallow up Jonah. And Jonah was in the belly of the fish three days and three nights.

Then Jonah prayed to the LORD his God from the belly of the fish, saying,

"I called out to the LORD, out of my distress,
    and he answered me;
out of the belly of Sheol I cried,
    and you heard my voice.
For you cast me into the deep,
    into the heart of the seas,
    and the flood surrounded me;
all your waves and your billows
    passed over me.

Psalm 30

KREG YINGST | LINOCUT

The psalmist and Jonah both understand what it is to be brought up from Sheol and to have life restored. Therefore it makes sense that the artist would visually connect Psalm 30 with the miracle of Jonah and the great fish. But Sinclair Ferguson writes that "too much discussion about the great fish can divert us from the real issue. The narrative is not really about the fish at all. It has only a 'walk-on part' in this gripping drama. Focus on the great fish and we may lose sight of the great God." Instead, this story is one about God lavishly pouring out his grace on the undeserving. Jonah knew that God was "slow to anger and abounding in steadfast love," and knowing that God was merciful made the prophet very angry. But it is clear throughout the Bible that God "has mercy on whomever he wills, and he hardens whomever he wills."

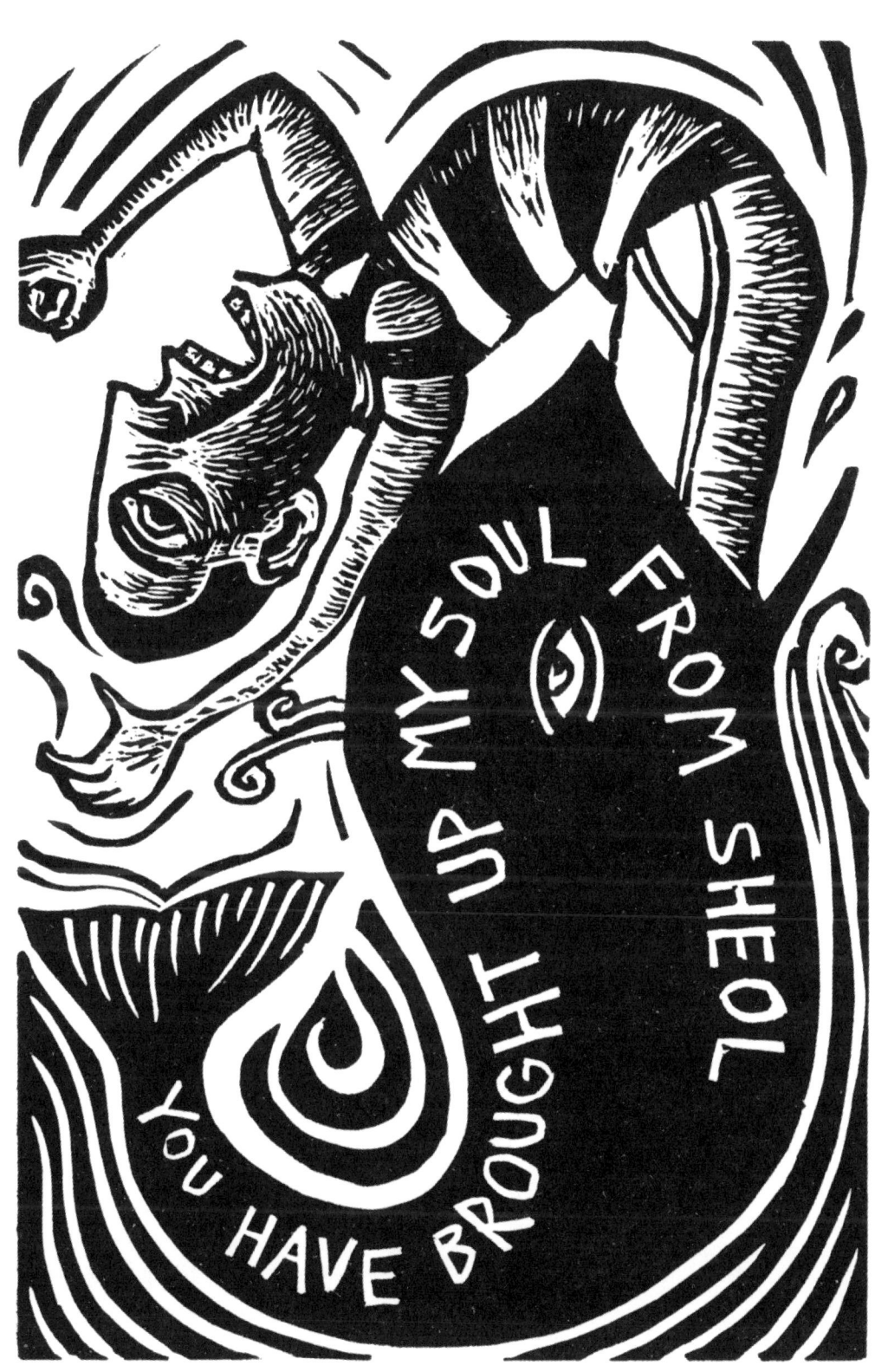

Micah 5:1–6

THE COMING SHEPHERD

Now muster your troops, O daughter of troops;
    siege is laid against us;
with a rod they strike the judge of Israel
    on the cheek.
But you, O Bethlehem Ephrathah,
    who are too little to be among the clans of Judah,
from you shall come forth for me
    one who is to be ruler in Israel,
whose coming forth is from of old,
    from ancient days.
Therefore he shall give them up until the time
    when she who is in labor has given birth;
then the rest of his brothers shall return
    to the people of Israel.
And he shall stand and shepherd his flock in the strength of the Lord,
    in the majesty of the name of the Lord his God.
And they shall dwell secure, for now he shall be great
    to the ends of the earth.
And he shall be their peace.

Shepherd King

TANJA BUTLER | LINOCUT

This passage looks forward to the coming of an eternal ruler who would bring peace and shepherd God's people. In John 10:14-16, 27-30 Jesus claimed to be this majestic shepherd: "I am the good shepherd. I know my own and my own know me, just as the Father knows me and I know the Father; and I lay down my life for the sheep. And I have other sheep that are not of this fold. I must bring them also, and they will listen to my voice. So there will be one flock, one shepherd. . . . My sheep hear my voice, and I know them, and they follow me. I give them eternal life, and they will never perish, and no one will snatch them out of my hand. My Father, who has given them to me, is greater than all, and no one is able to snatch them out of the Father's hand. I and the Father are one."

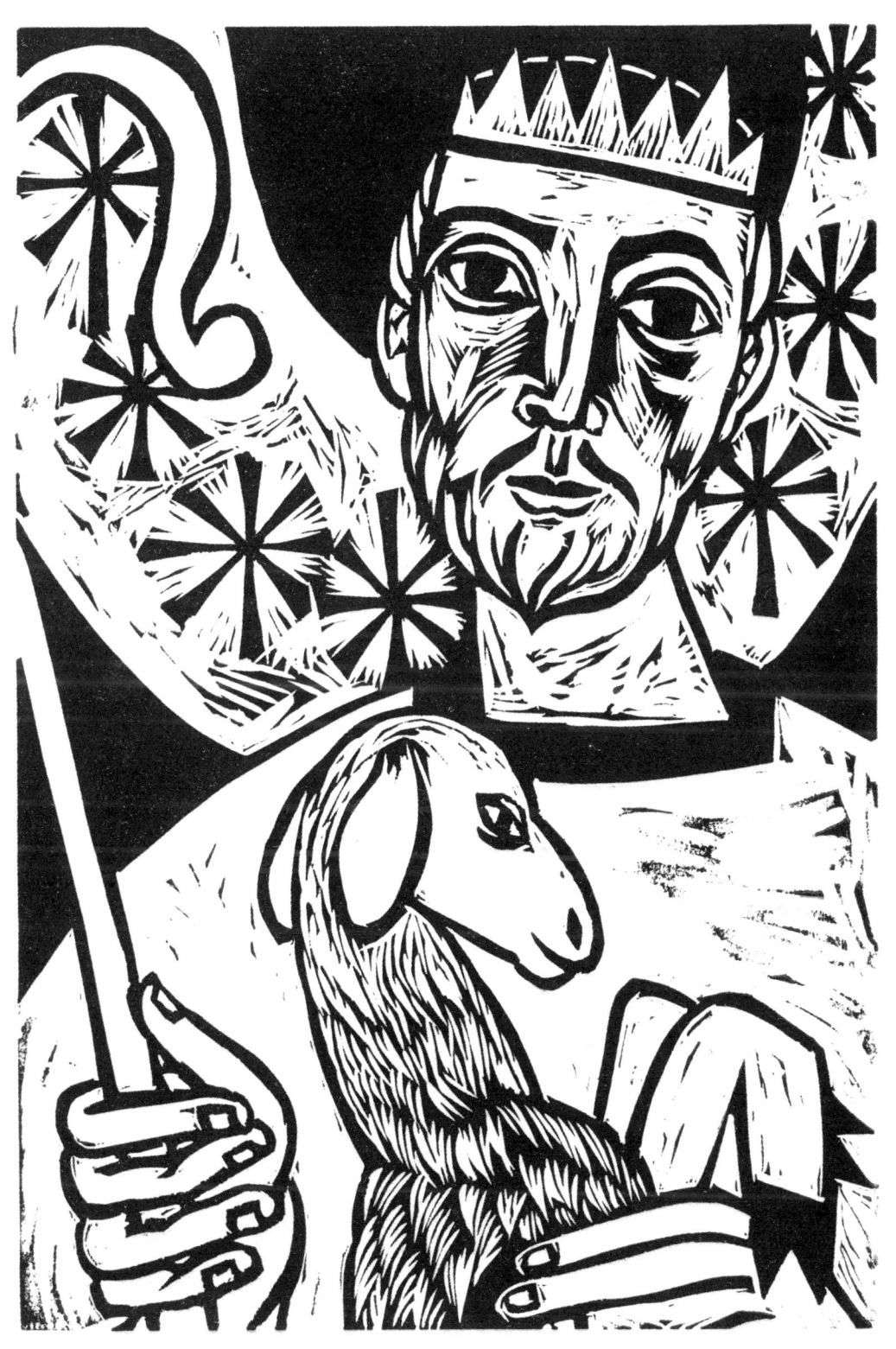

Habakkuk 3:17–19

YET I WILL REJOICE

Though the fig tree should not blossom,
    nor fruit be on the vines,
the produce of the olive fail
    and the fields yield no food,
the flock be cut off from the fold
    and there be no herd in the stalls,
yet I will rejoice in the Lord;
    I will take joy in the God of my salvation.
God, the Lord, is my strength;
    he makes my feet like the deer's;
    he makes me tread on my high places . . .

Habakkuk 3:17–19

NED BUSTARD | LINOCUT

The fig trees, olives, and flocks in this passage represent the monetary securities for the Israelites. In the face of the coming destruction of the nation by the Babylonians and the accompanying material disasters, the prophet raises up his hands and says that he will trust God. Yahweh is his strength. A broken piggy bank replaces the fig trees, olives, and flocks to represent a contemporary concept of fiscal disaster. The words around the image are from Habakkuk 2:4, they are repeated by Paul in Romans 1:17, and those same words would eventually become the central teaching during the Reformation.

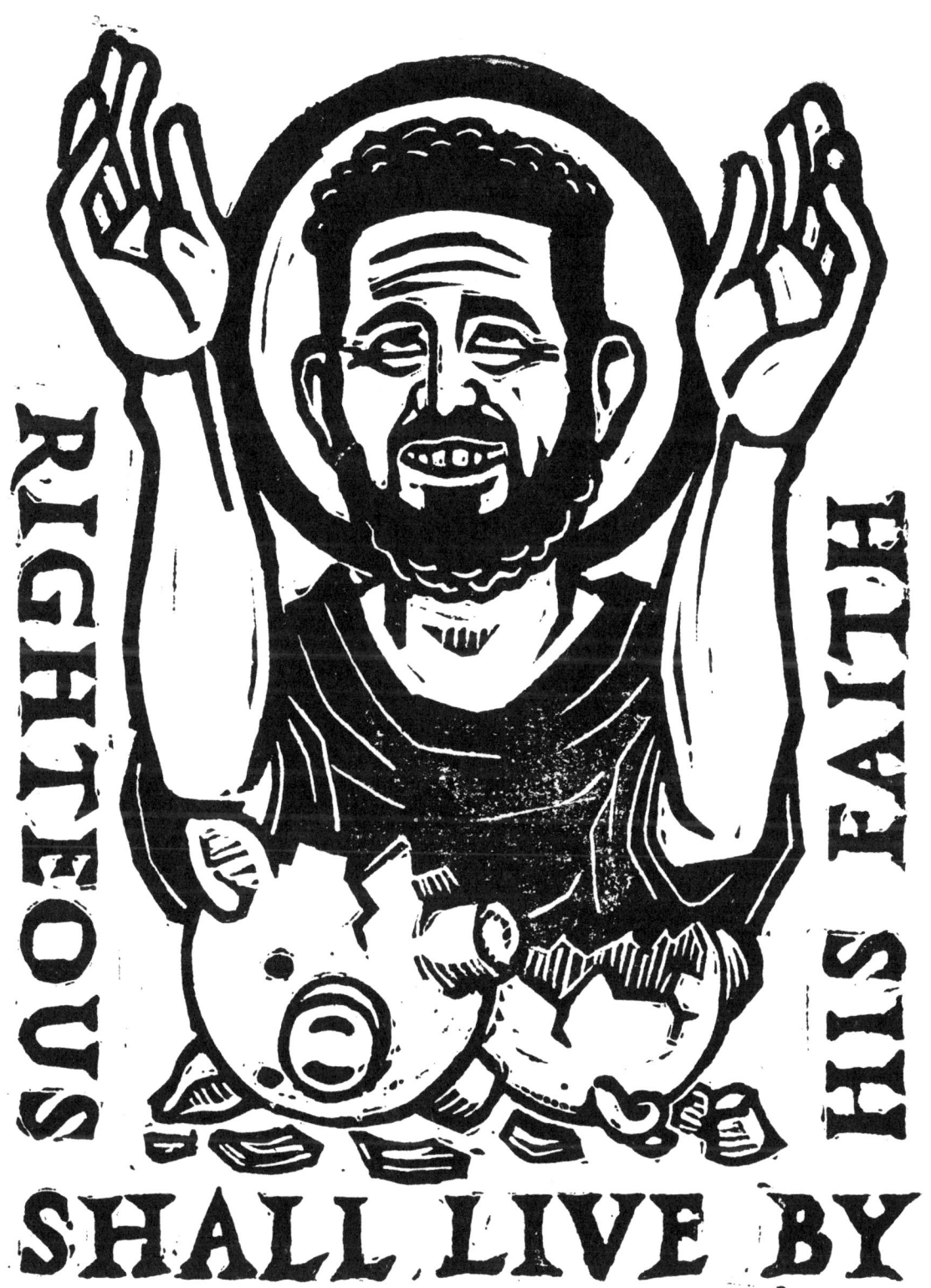

Zephaniah 1:14–18

THE DAY OF THE LORD

The great day of the Lord is near,
    near and hastening fast;
the sound of the day of the Lord is bitter;
    the mighty man cries aloud there.
A day of wrath is that day,
    a day of distress and anguish,
a day of ruin and devastation,
    a day of darkness and gloom,
a day of clouds and thick darkness,
    a day of trumpet blast and battle cry
against the fortified cities
    and against the lofty battlements.
I will bring distress on mankind,
    so that they shall walk like the blind,
    because they have sinned against the Lord;
their blood shall be poured out like dust,
    and their flesh like dung.
Neither their silver nor their gold
    shall be able to deliver them on the day of the wrath of the Lord.
In the fire of his jealousy,
    all the earth shall be consumed;
for a full and sudden end
    he will make of all the inhabitants of the earth.

The Whore of Babylon

ALBRECHT DÜRER | WOODCUT

The last book in the Bible is known for violent descriptions of the chaotic judgement that will be coming on the Day of the Lord, but the term stretches way back into the Old Testament to the Book of Isaiah. According to *The End: A Readers' Guide to Revelation*, "The description of the day of the Lord in the Old Testament typically refers to God's judgment which will have a devastating effect on Israel or on some other nation. In the New Testament, the Day of the Lord refers to God's final judgment which believers look forward to with anticipation." Dürer became famous when he published his large woodcuts of the Day of the Lord, *The Apocalypse*. This image is the last in that series. It illustrates Revelation 17:3–4.

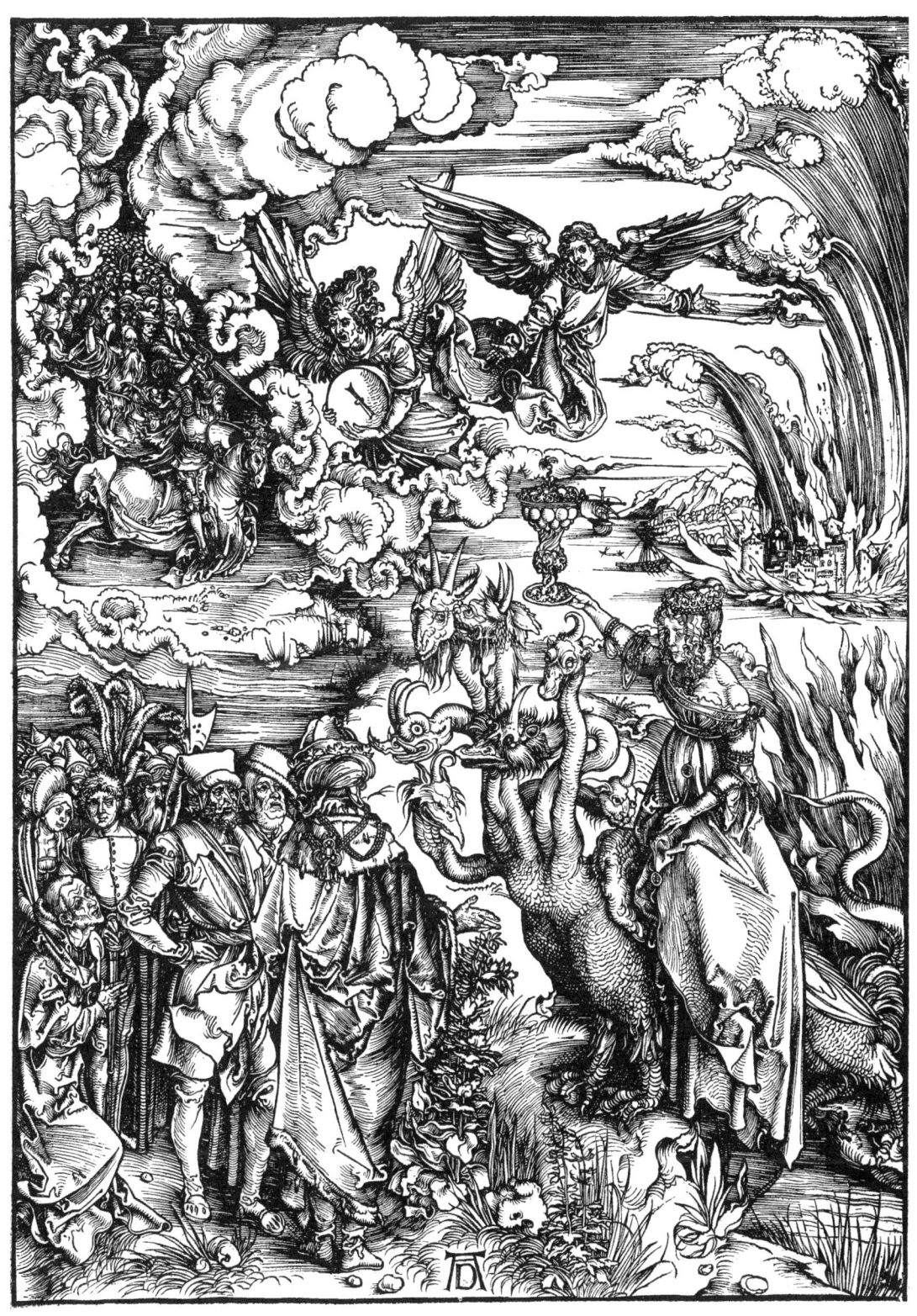

Malachi 4

THE BIRTH OF JOHN FORETOLD

"For behold, the day is coming, burning like an oven, when all the arrogant and all evildoers will be stubble. The day that is coming shall set them ablaze, says the Lord of hosts, so that it will leave them neither root nor branch. But for you who fear my name, the sun of righteousness shall rise with healing in its wings. You shall go out leaping like calves from the stall. And you shall tread down the wicked, for they will be ashes under the soles of your feet, on the day when I act, says the Lord of hosts.

"Remember the law of my servant Moses, the statutes and rules that I commanded him at Horeb for all Israel.

"Behold, I will send you Elijah the prophet before the great and awesome day of the Lord comes. And he will turn the hearts of fathers to their children and the hearts of children to their fathers, lest I come and strike the land with a decree of utter destruction."

Intertestamental Angel *(left detail)*
MATTHEW L. CLARK | LINOCUT

The fires of judgment are burning hotter than in Nebuchadnezzar's fiery furnace, but the healing wings of the angel are extended to offer protection for those who fear the the Lord. This print is one half of a diptych, and with its other half form one work of art to help convey the idea that the Old and New Testaments form one story. Between them is an intermission of sorts in the story. The intermission—or intertestamental period—is sometimes called the "400 Silent Years," but it was in no way quiet. The Old Testament was translated into Greek (now known as the Septuagint), the Synagogue was established in Jewish religious life, Alexander the Great brought Hellenistic language and culture to the land, the Second Temple was built, the Maccabean revolt occured, the Romans took over, and the Dead Sea Scrolls were written.

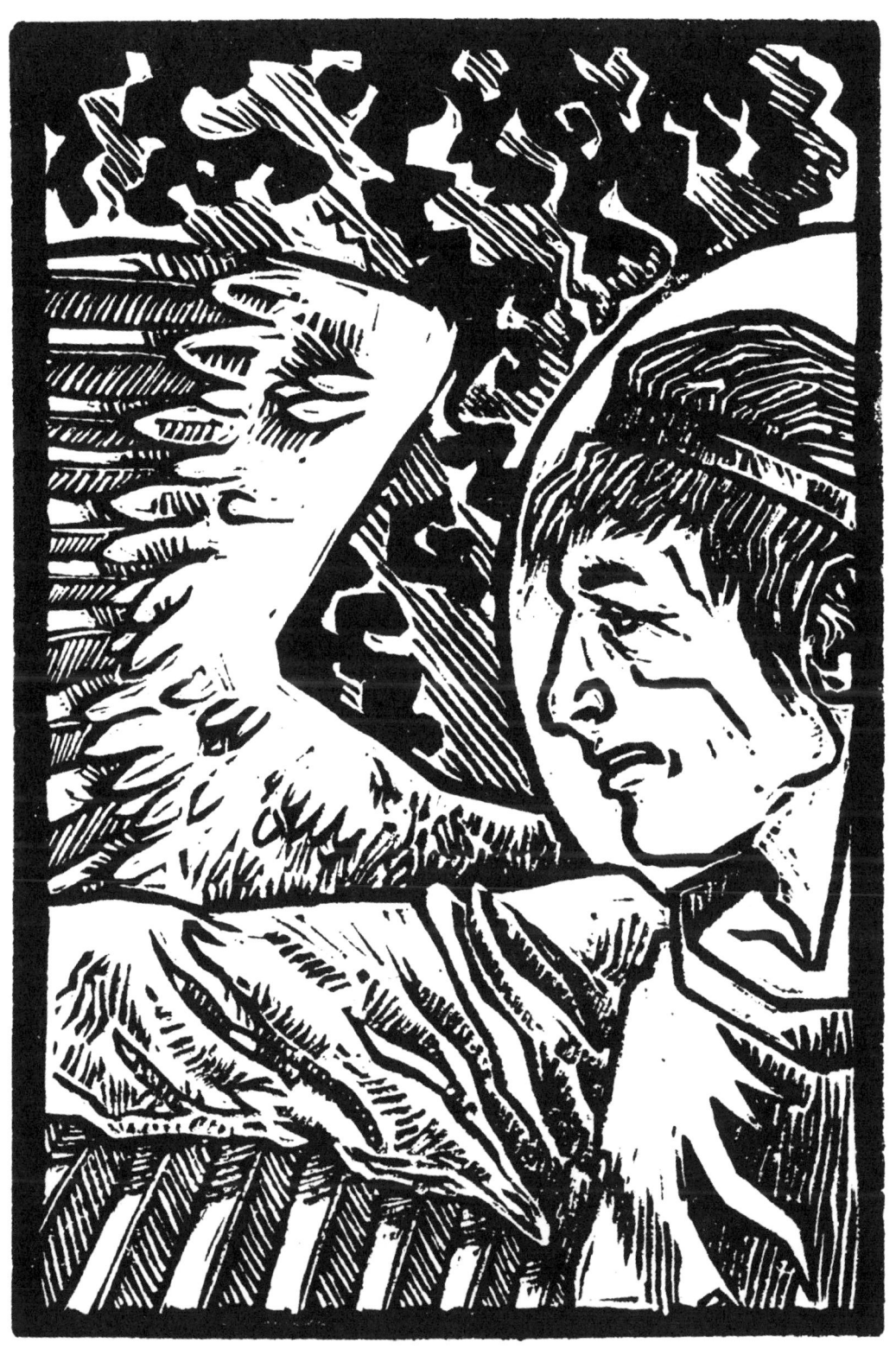

Luke 1:8–20

THE BIRTH OF JOHN FORETOLD

Now while [Zechariah] was serving as priest before God when his division was on duty, according to the custom of the priesthood, he was chosen by lot to enter the temple of the Lord and burn incense. And the whole multitude of the people were praying outside at the hour of incense. And there appeared to him an angel of the Lord standing on the right side of the altar of incense. And Zechariah was troubled when he saw him, and fear fell upon him. But the angel said to him, "Do not be afraid, Zechariah, for your prayer has been heard, and your wife Elizabeth will bear you a son, and you shall call his name John. And you will have joy and gladness, and many will rejoice at his birth, for he will be great before the Lord. And he must not drink wine or strong drink, and he will be filled with the Holy Spirit, even from his mother's womb. And he will turn many of the children of Israel to the Lord their God, and he will go before him in the spirit and power of Elijah, to turn the hearts of the fathers to the children, and the disobedient to the wisdom of the just, to make ready for the Lord a people prepared."

And Zechariah said to the angel, "How shall I know this? For I am an old man, and my wife is advanced in years." And the angel answered him, "I am Gabriel. I stand in the presence of God, and I was sent to speak to you and to bring you this good news. And behold, you will be silent and unable to speak until the day that these things take place, because you did not believe my words, which will be fulfilled in their time."

Intertestamental Angel *(right detail)*
MATTHEW L. CLARK | LINOCUT

As Zechariah went about carrying out the worship in the Temple, offering up the prayers of God's people, a response came from God in the form of one of his unhuman messengers. As with other appearances of angels in the Bible, Zechariah was terrified by the sight of the heavenly creature. The angel had come to tell Zechariah that his son would be the Elijah whose arrival had been prophesied about hundreds of years earlier in Malachi 4.

The bee is a symbol in church art for work, good order, vigilance, and zeal in acquiring virtue, as well as sweetness and religious eloquence. Zechariah's son, John, would later eat honey and preach with eloquence a hard message of repentance and the sweet good news that the Messiah was coming.

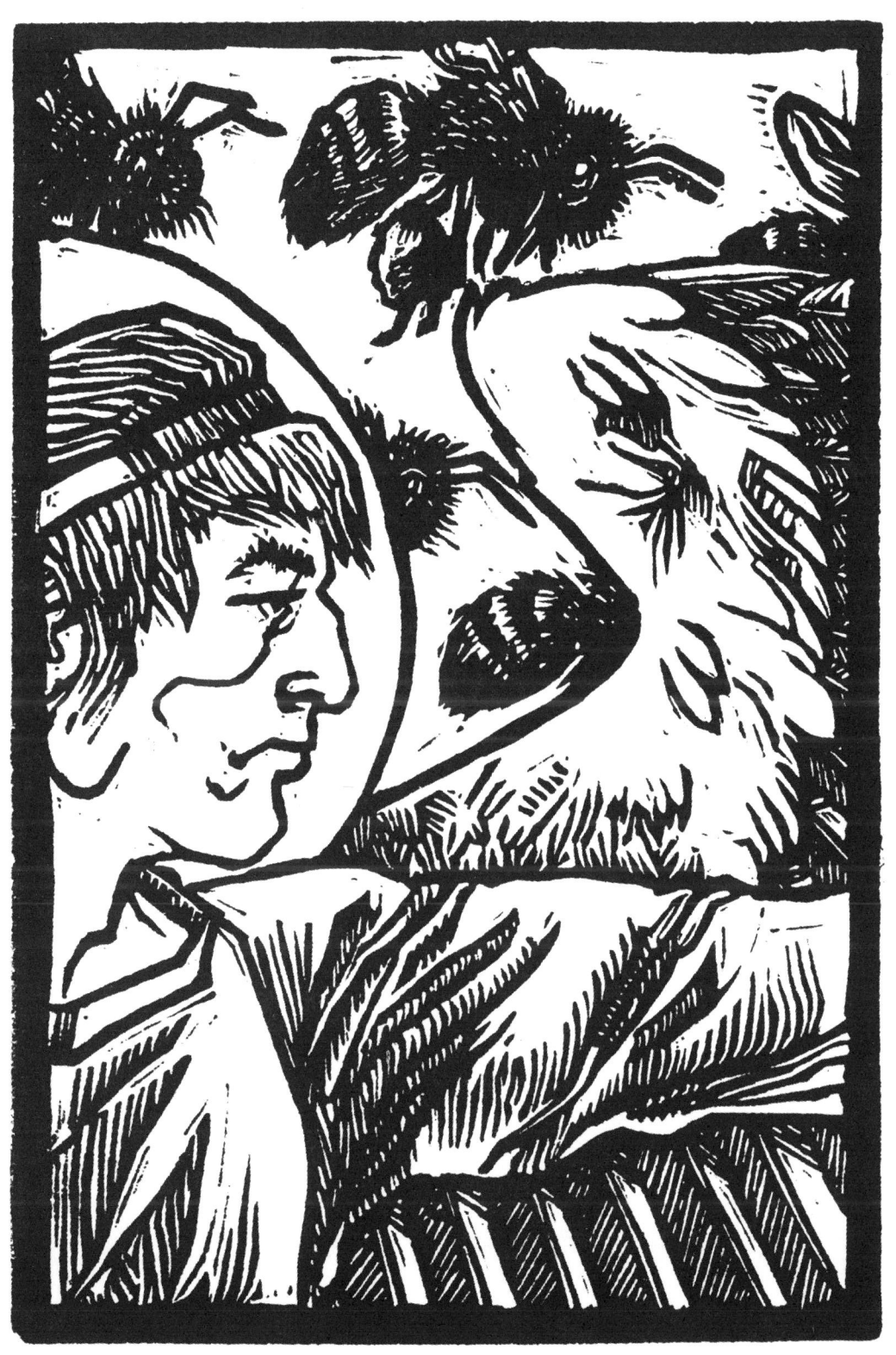

Luke 1:26–38

THE ANGEL VISITS MARY

In the sixth month the angel Gabriel was sent from God to a city of Galilee named Nazareth, to a virgin betrothed to a man whose name was Joseph, of the house of David. And the virgin's name was Mary. And he came to her and said, "Greetings, O favored one, the Lord is with you!" But she was greatly troubled at the saying, and tried to discern what sort of greeting this might be. And the angel said to her, "Do not be afraid, Mary, for you have found favor with God. And behold, you will conceive in your womb and bear a son, and you shall call his name Jesus. He will be great and will be called the Son of the Most High. And the Lord God will give to him the throne of his father David, and he will reign over the house of Jacob forever, and of his kingdom there will be no end."

And Mary said to the angel, "How will this be, since I am a virgin?"

And the angel answered her, "The Holy Spirit will come upon you, and the power of the Most High will overshadow you; therefore the child to be born will be called holy—the Son of God. And behold, your relative Elizabeth in her old age has also conceived a son, and this is the sixth month with her who was called barren. For nothing will be impossible with God." And Mary said, "Behold, I am the servant of the Lord; let it be to me according to your word." And the angel departed from her.

Annunciation

FRANZ MARC | WOODCUT

Artwork about the Annunciation is usually some combination of a devout Mary interrupted from her prayers by a serene angel Gabriel—perhaps with a lily close by. But in this print, Marc throws tradition out the window and depicts a startling event. The Holy Spirit is overshadowing the blessed virgin, and the moment is so terrifyingly glorious that Gabriel must avert his gaze. Poet Luci Shaw writes about that event:

> the Angel in the room, the impossible demand,
> the response without reflection. Only one
> word of curiosity, echoing Zechariah's *How?*

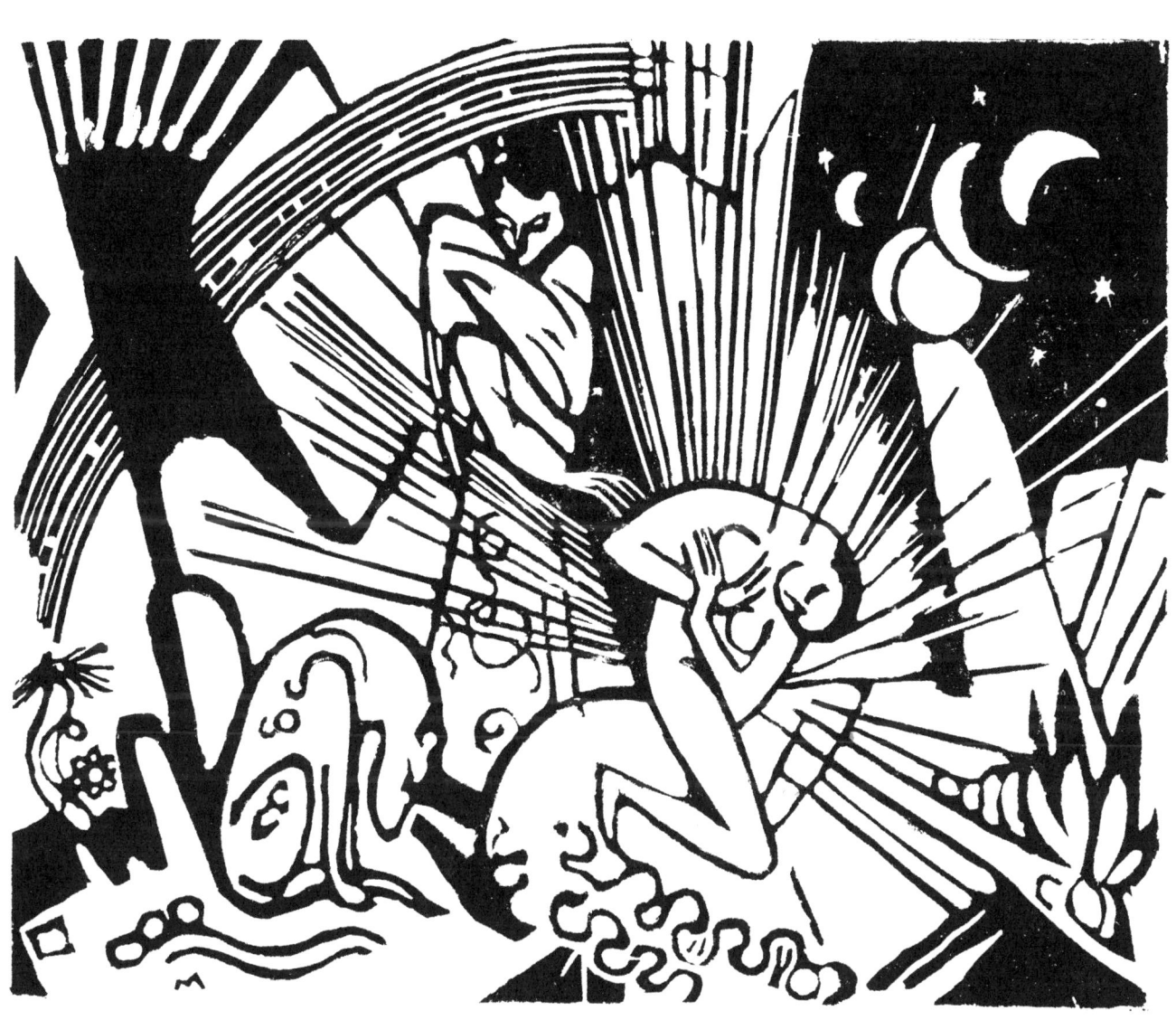

Luke 2:1–14

THE NATIVITY

In those days a decree went out from Caesar Augustus that all the world should be registered. This was the first registration when Quirinius was governor of Syria. And all went to be registered, each to his own town. And Joseph also went up from Galilee, from the town of Nazareth, to Judea, to the city of David, which is called Bethlehem, because he was of the house and lineage of David, to be registered with Mary, his betrothed, who was with child. And while they were there, the time came for her to give birth. And she gave birth to her firstborn son and wrapped him in swaddling cloths and laid him in a manger, because there was no place for them in the inn.

And in the same region there were shepherds out in the field, keeping watch over their flock by night. And an angel of the Lord appeared to them, and the glory of the Lord shone around them, and they were filled with great fear. And the angel said to them, "Fear not, for behold, I bring you good news of great joy that will be for all the people. For unto you is born this day in the city of David a Savior, who is Christ the Lord. And this will be a sign for you: you will find a baby wrapped in swaddling cloths and lying in a manger." And suddenly there was with the angel a multitude of the heavenly host praising God and saying,

> "Glory to God in the highest,
> and on earth peace among those with whom he is pleased!"

The Glorious Form

CHRIS STOFFEL OVERVOORDE | WOODCUT

In a poem titled *On the Morning of Christ's Nativity*, John Milton wrote, "That Glorious Form forsook the courts of everlasting life . . . and choose with us a house of mortal clay." In this print the artist wanted to attempt to capture the idea of the Incarnation as well as the pain and suffering of childbirth. The second person of the Trinity came into the world through a birth canal just like everyone. The twenty-four elders and the four beasts mentioned in Revelation 19:4 are here along with the seven-fold Spirit—and an in utero infant. Bono of U2 writes: "The Christmas story has a crazy good plot with an even crazier premise—the idea goes, if there is a force of love and logic behind the universe, then how amazing would it be if that incomprehensible power chose to express itself as a child born in shit and straw poverty."

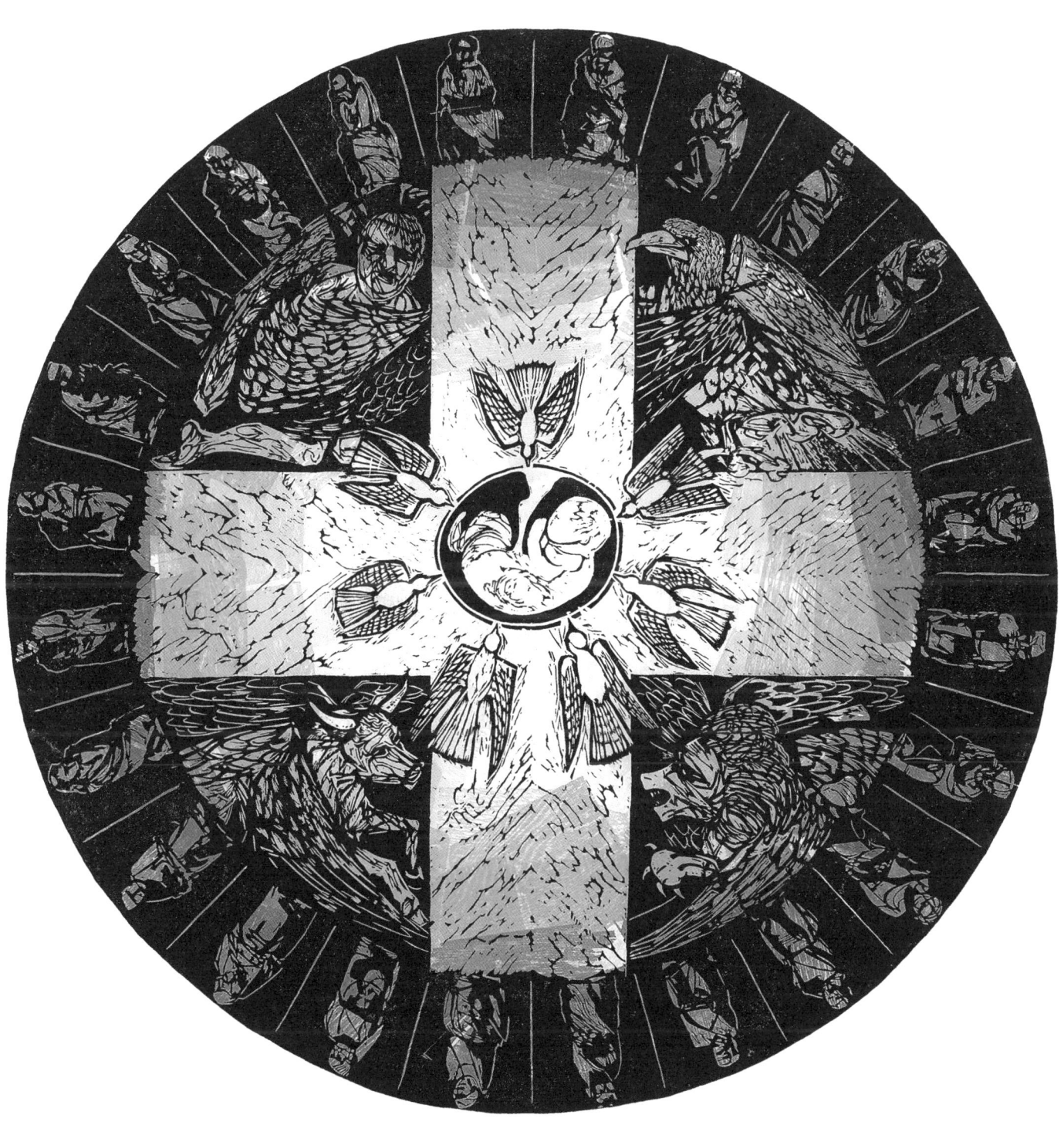

Matthew 2:7–15

FLIGHT INTO EGYPT

Then Herod summoned the wise men secretly and ascertained from them what time the star had appeared. And he sent them to Bethlehem, saying, "Go and search diligently for the child, and when you have found him, bring me word, that I too may come and worship him." After listening to the king, they went on their way. And behold, the star that they had seen when it rose went before them until it came to rest over the place where the child was. When they saw the star, they rejoiced exceedingly with great joy. And going into the house they saw the child with Mary his mother, and they fell down and worshiped him. Then, opening their treasures, they offered him gifts, gold and frankincense and myrrh. And being warned in a dream not to return to Herod, they departed to their own country by another way.

Now when they had departed, behold, an angel of the Lord appeared to Joseph in a dream and said, "Rise, take the child and his mother, and flee to Egypt, and remain there until I tell you, for Herod is about to search for the child, to destroy him." And he rose and took the child and his mother by night and departed to Egypt and remained there until the death of Herod. This was to fulfill what the Lord had spoken by the prophet, "Out of Egypt I called my son."

Rest on the Flight to Egypt

TANJA BUTLER | LINOCUT

There is no violin-playing angel in this piece as in Caravaggio's *Rest on the Flight into Egypt* or a gaggle of cherubic playmates as in *Rest on the Flight into Egypt* by Lucas Cranach the Elder. Instead in this piece there is only Joseph, Mary, and the young Jesus—just a poor family, afraid and huddled in the dark. Butler says that the "peasant figures bundled against the cold recall the frantic flight of my father's family across the European continent during the last months of a world war." Christmas carols such as *Away in a Manger* and *The Little Drummer Boy* tend to romanticize the Nativity and gloss over the fear, danger, and isolation that the poor family experienced during the early years in the life of Jesus.

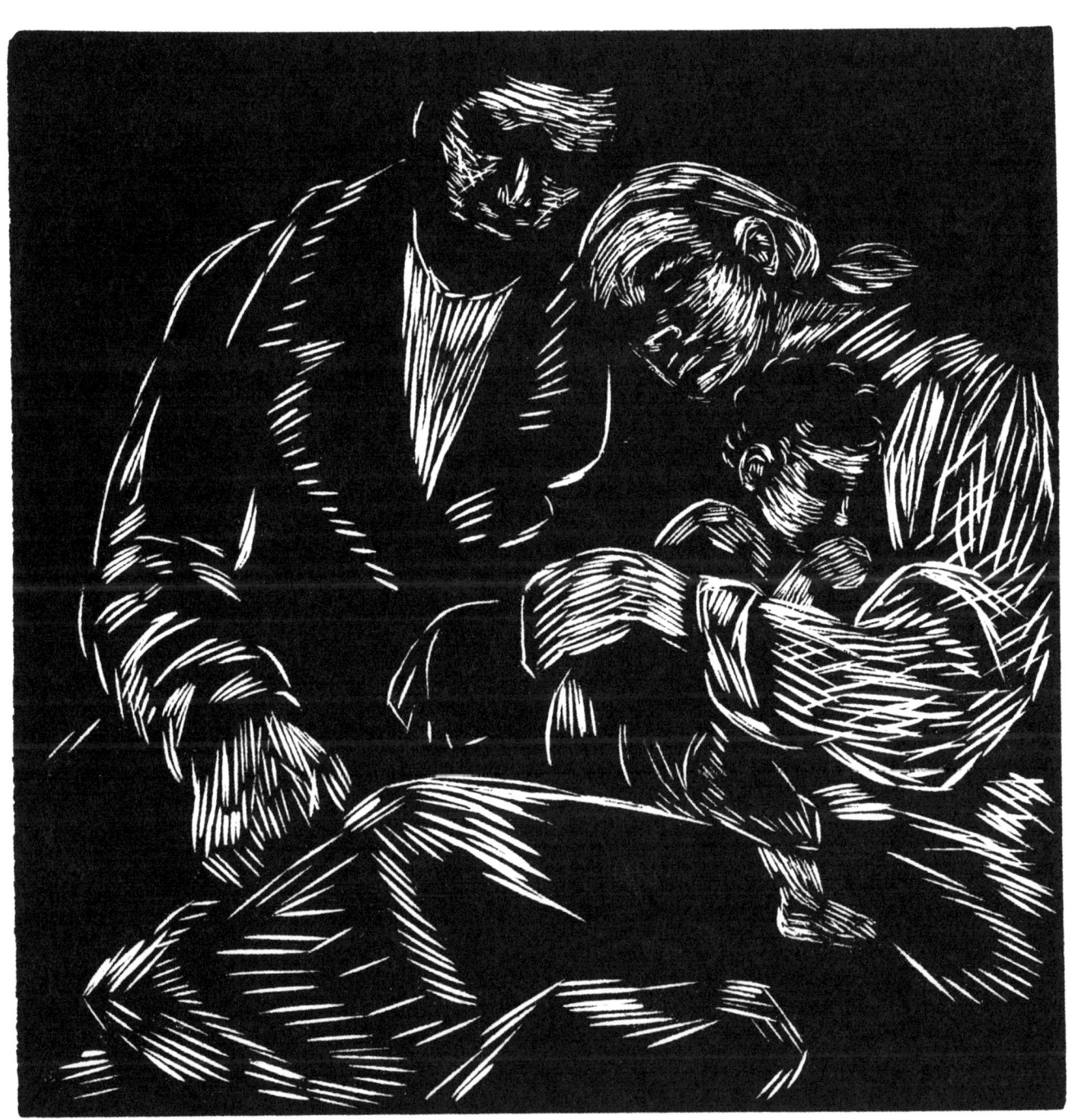

Matthew 2:16–23

MASSACRE OF THE INNOCENTS

Then Herod, when he saw that he had been tricked by the wise men, became furious, and he sent and killed all the male children in Bethlehem and in all that region who were two years old or under, according to the time that he had ascertained from the wise men. Then was fulfilled what was spoken by the prophet Jeremiah:

> "A voice was heard in Ramah,
>   weeping and loud lamentation,
> Rachel weeping for her children;
>   she refused to be comforted, because they are no more."

But when Herod died, behold, an angel of the Lord appeared in a dream to Joseph in Egypt, saying, "Rise, take the child and his mother and go to the land of Israel, for those who sought the child's life are dead." And he rose and took the child and his mother and went to the land of Israel. But when he heard that Archelaus was reigning over Judea in place of his father Herod, he was afraid to go there, and being warned in a dream he withdrew to the district of Galilee. And he went and lived in a city called Nazareth, so that what was spoken by the prophets might be fulfilled, that he would be called a Nazarene.

The Massacre of the Innocents

EDWARD KNIPPERS | WOODCUT

Herod the Great was an evil man and a ruthless politician. To maintain his power he went so far as to murder several of his sons, and even his wife! Therefore, when the wise men told him about the birth of a rival prince—a young boy whose birth was heralded by the stars and confirmed in prophetic writings—he had no qualms about immediately sending in armed men to kill all the children in Bethlehem two years old or under. The soldier in this print has shoved "Rachel" to the ground, with his foot forced between her legs and a salacious smile on his face. His attention is on the infant's mother and appears to have very little concern about killing an infant. Sadly, this callous disregard of children is historically accurate. Infanticide in ancient Greece and Rome was almost as common as abortion is in our day.

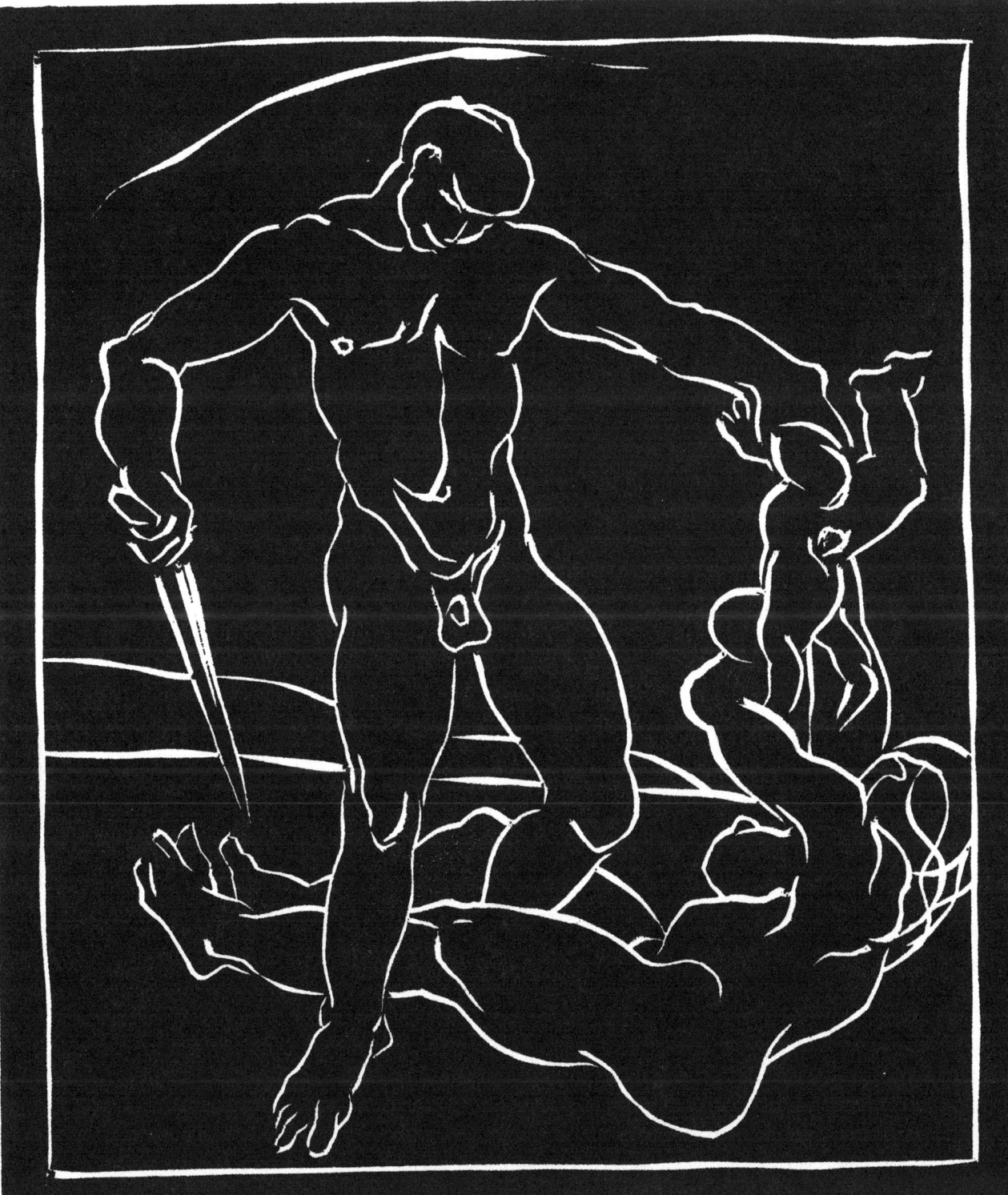

Matthew 3:1–2, 11–17

THE BAPTISM OF CHRIST

In those days John the Baptist came preaching in the wilderness of Judea, "Repent, for the kingdom of heaven is at hand."

. . .

"I baptize you with water for repentance, but he who is coming after me is mightier than I, whose sandals I am not worthy to carry. He will baptize you with the Holy Spirit and fire. His winnowing fork is in his hand, and he will clear his threshing floor and gather his wheat into the barn, but the chaff he will burn with unquenchable fire."

Then Jesus came from Galilee to the Jordan to John, to be baptized by him. John would have prevented him, saying, "I need to be baptized by you, and do you come to me?" But Jesus answered him, "Let it be so now, for thus it is fitting for us to fulfill all righteousness." Then he consented. And when Jesus was baptized, immediately he went up from the water, and behold, the heavens were opened to him, and he saw the Spirit of God descending like a dove and coming to rest on him; and behold, a voice from heaven said, "This is my beloved Son, with whom I am well pleased."

Baptism (after Otto Dix)
NED BUSTARD | LINOCUT

Dix (1891–1969) was a German artist, painter, and print maker known for his harshly realistic depictions of the brutality of war, but his post-World War II work was largely religious in nature. This linocut is based on *Baptism of Jesus*, a lithograph from *Matthäus Evangelium*. Art historian James Romaine observed that the Holy Spirit is funneled through the hand of John like a sieve, baptizing Jesus in both water and in the Spirit. About the Bible, Dix is quoted to have said, "You have to read every single word. For the Bible is a wonderful history book. There is great truth in all of it. Most people don't read the Bible, but reading the Bible, reading it as it is, in all of its realism, including the Old Testament: it's quite a book. Quite a book, you might even say it is the book of books . . . simply magnificent!"

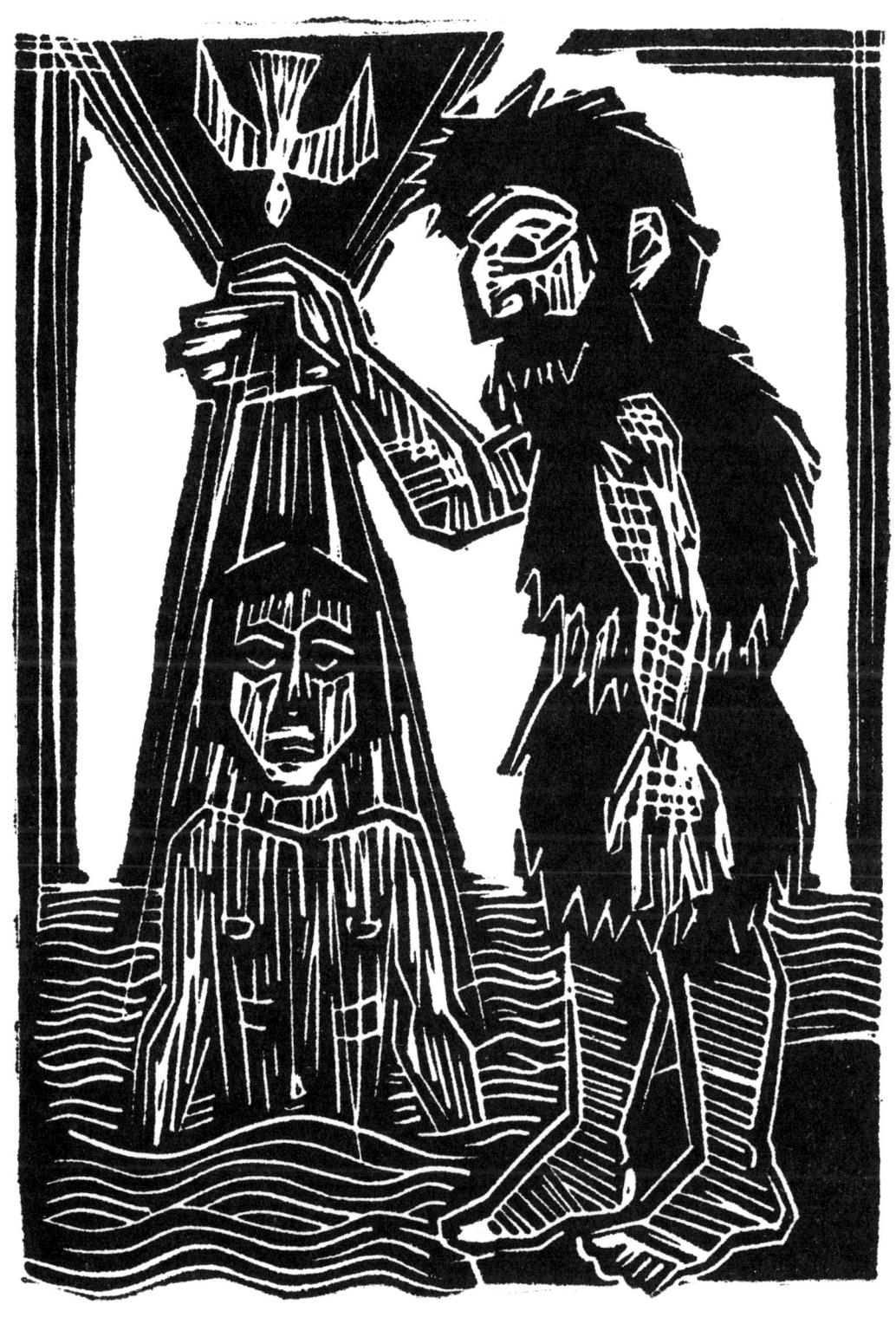

Matthew 4:1–10

THE TEMPTATION OF CHRIST

Then Jesus was led up by the Spirit into the wilderness to be tempted by the devil. And after fasting forty days and forty nights, he was hungry. And the tempter came and said to him, "If you are the Son of God, command these stones to become loaves of bread." But he answered, "It is written,

> "'Man shall not live by bread alone,
> but by every word that comes from the mouth of God.'"

Then the devil took him to the holy city and set him on the pinnacle of the temple and said to him, "If you are the Son of God, throw yourself down, for it is written,

> "'He will command his angels concerning you,' and

> "'On their hands they will bear you up,
> lest you strike your foot against a stone.'"

Jesus said to him, "Again it is written, 'You shall not put the Lord your God to the test.'" Again, the devil took him to a very high mountain and showed him all the kingdoms of the world and their glory. And he said to him, "All these I will give you, if you will fall down and worship me." Then Jesus said to him, "Be gone, Satan! For it is written,

> "'You shall worship the Lord your God
> and him only shall you serve.'"

Temptation

MATTHEW L. CLARK | LINOCUT

Satan comes to Jesus in this piece as a Jewish holy man, whispering reasonable words of comforting temptation, shown as black voice bubbles slithering into the ears of the Son of Man. The artist wrote about this piece, "I think an important thing not to overlook here is the fact that this was a *real* temptation. Jesus had to really be tempted if this episode was to have any significant meaning. As such, I tried to show him emaciated and weak. At least physically weak. I have no idea if forty days of fasting leaves one spiritually weakened or strengthened. But I assume it would be immediately weakening or Satan would not have chosen that time to act." The little bat-winged speech bubble is not quoting any scripture, rather it is a line spoken by Boromir in *The Fellowship of the Ring*.

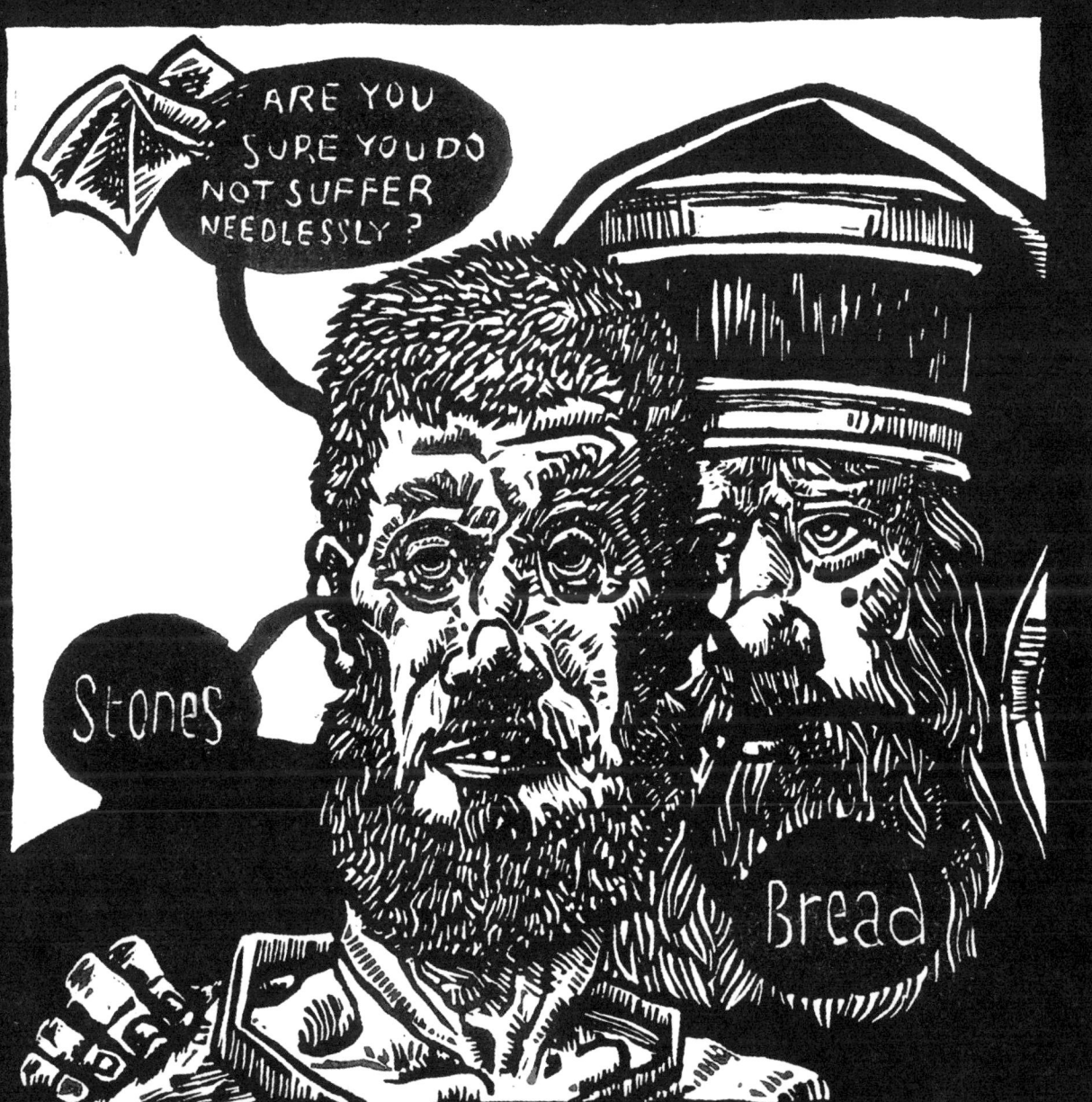

John 2:1–11

THE WEDDING AT CANA

On the third day there was a wedding at Cana in Galilee, and the mother of Jesus was there. Jesus also was invited to the wedding with his disciples. When the wine ran out, the mother of Jesus said to him, "They have no wine." And Jesus said to her, "Woman, what does this have to do with me? My hour has not yet come." His mother said to the servants, "Do whatever he tells you."

Now there were six stone water jars there for the Jewish rites of purification, each holding twenty or thirty gallons. Jesus said to the servants, "Fill the jars with water." And they filled them up to the brim. And he said to them, "Now draw some out and take it to the master of the feast." So they took it. When the master of the feast tasted the water now become wine, and did not know where it came from (though the servants who had drawn the water knew), the master of the feast called the bridegroom and said to him, "Everyone serves the good wine first, and when people have drunk freely, then the poor wine. But you have kept the good wine until now." This, the first of his signs, Jesus did at Cana in Galilee, and manifested his glory. And his disciples believed in him.

The Wedding

ERIC CROSS | LINOCUT

Jesus seems to be rather cheeky, telling his mother he will do his work in his own time. Then the over-abundance of God's grace is felt as Jesus makes well over 100 gallons of the best wine—near the *end* of the party. Usually Jesus is in the foreground in artistic depictions of his first miracle. But in this image Jesus stands off in the background. Appropriately, the bride and groom are in the center of things, enjoying the celebration. Imagine the kindness of the Lord. He cares about our marriages, our celebrations and the love expressed between married couples. Christ's first miracle was at a wedding, underscoring from beginning to end, the Bible is a story about marriage. The Bible begins with the marriage of Adam and Eve and ends with the wedding of the Lamb. Marriage is a love relationship reflecting the union of God with the church.

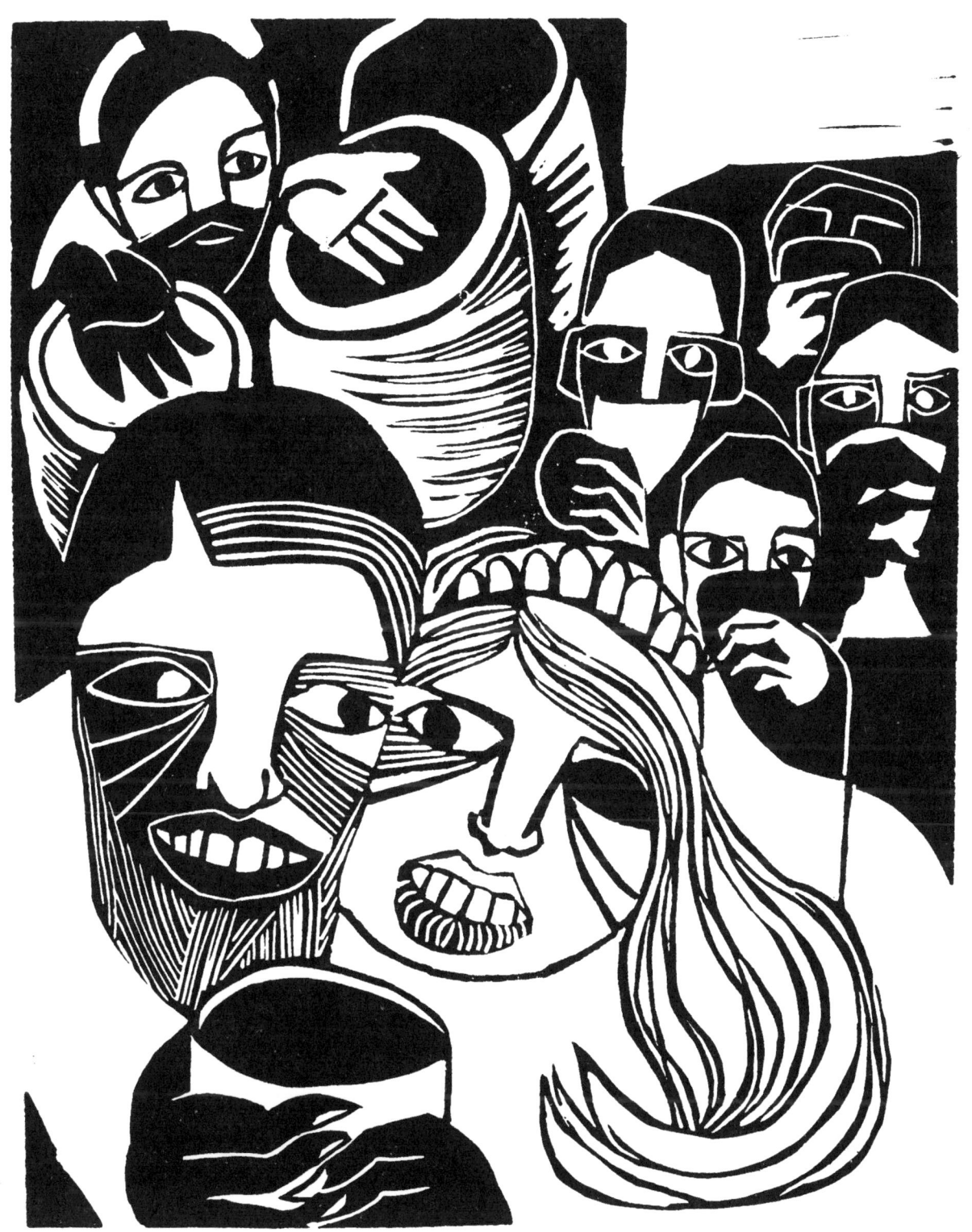

John 4:13–26

THE WOMAN AT THE WELL

Jesus said to her, "Everyone who drinks of this water will be thirsty again, but whoever drinks of the water that I will give him will never be thirsty again. The water that I will give him will become in him a spring of water welling up to eternal life." The woman said to him, "Sir, give me this water, so that I will not be thirsty or have to come here to draw water."

Jesus said to her, "Go, call your husband, and come here." The woman answered him, "I have no husband." Jesus said to her, "You are right in saying, 'I have no husband'; for you have had five husbands, and the one you now have is not your husband. What you have said is true." The woman said to him, "Sir, I perceive that you are a prophet. Our fathers worshiped on this mountain, but you say that in Jerusalem is the place where people ought to worship." Jesus said to her, "Woman, believe me, the hour is coming when neither on this mountain nor in Jerusalem will you worship the Father. You worship what you do not know; we worship what we know, for salvation is from the Jews. But the hour is coming, and is now here, when the true worshipers will worship the Father in spirit and truth, for the Father is seeking such people to worship him. God is spirit, and those who worship him must worship in spirit and truth." The woman said to him, "I know that Messiah is coming (he who is called Christ). When he comes, he will tell us all things." Jesus said to her, "I who speak to you am he."

Woman at the Well

DIEGO JOURDAN PEREIRA | WOODCUT

The composition of this piece is unusual in that the viewer can actually see the water that Jesus and the woman are discussing. The circle of Christ's halo is repeated in the well, connecting the water with the Living Water. In this passage Jesus asks for a drink of water from a Samaritan, specifically from a woman who was viewed by Samaritans as an adulteress. Even knowing her whole story, Jesus expresses a love for her that leads her to tell the whole town about him. Jews had no dealings with Samaritans because Jews viewed Samaritans as half Jews. In fact, a Jew wouldn't even drink from a cup that had been touched by a Samaritan. Yet Jesus loved the Samaritan woman, setting an example to his church of showing love to those who struggle with sin. What would it look like for believers to emulate how Jesus engaged and loved imperfect people?

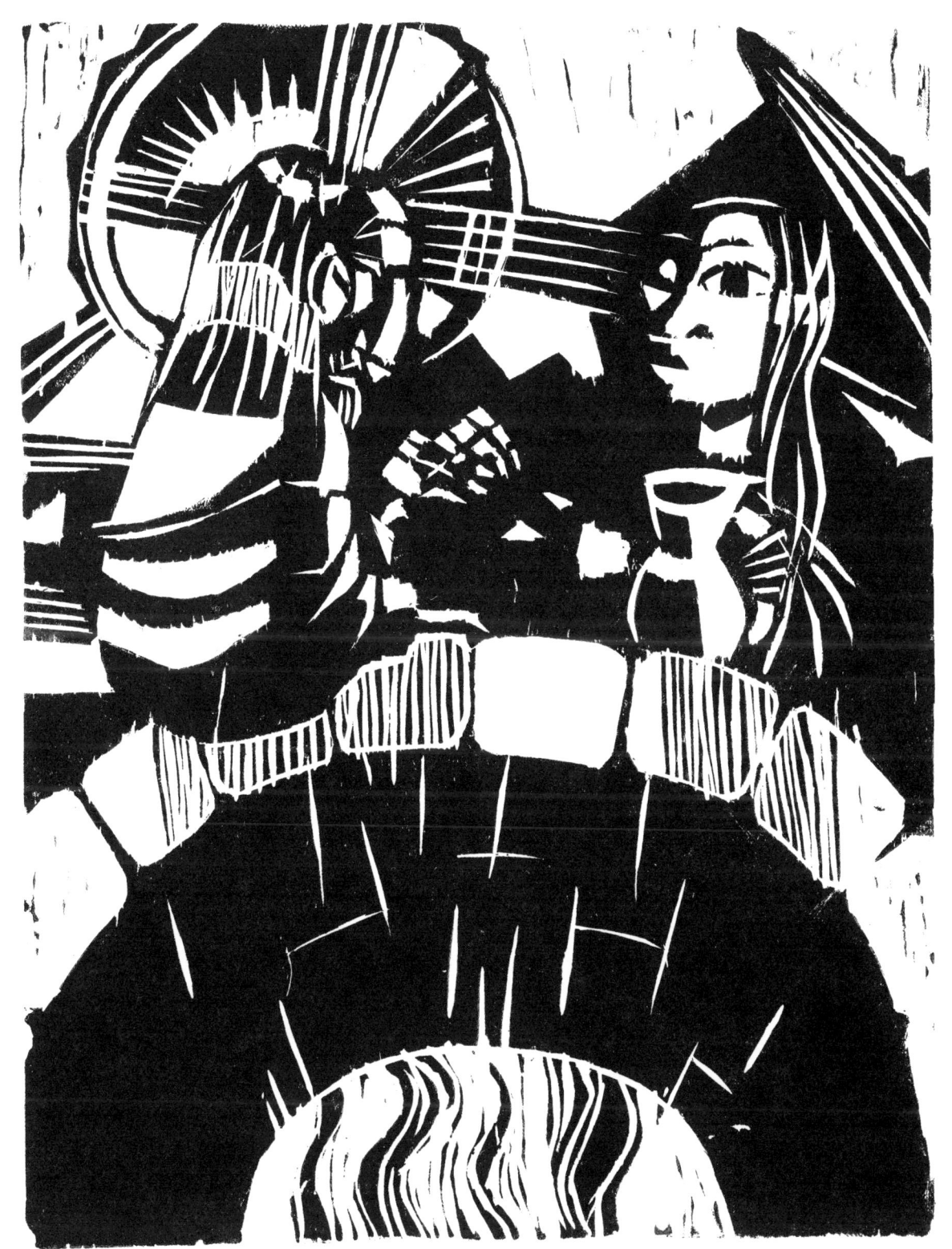

John 5:19–29

FROM DEATH TO LIFE

So Jesus said to them, "Truly, truly, I say to you, the Son can do nothing of his own accord, but only what he sees the Father doing. For whatever the Father does, that the Son does likewise. For the Father loves the Son and shows him all that he himself is doing. And greater works than these will he show him, so that you may marvel. For as the Father raises the dead and gives them life, so also the Son gives life to whom he will. The Father judges no one, but has given all judgment to the Son, that all may honor the Son, just as they honor the Father. Whoever does not honor the Son does not honor the Father who sent him. Truly, truly, I say to you, whoever hears my word and believes him who sent me has eternal life. He does not come into judgment, but has passed from death to life.

"Truly, truly, I say to you, an hour is coming, and is now here, when the dead will hear the voice of the Son of God, and those who hear will live. For as the Father has life in himself, so he has granted the Son also to have life in himself. And he has given him authority to execute judgment, because he is the Son of Man. Do not marvel at this, for an hour is coming when all who are in the tombs will hear his voice and come out, those who have done good to the resurrection of life, and those who have done evil to the resurrection of judgment.

Christ Preaching (La petite Tombe)

REMBRANDT HARMENSZOON VAN RIJN | ETCHING, DRYPOINT, AND ENGRAVING

The name of this etching ('La petite Tombe') is thought to refer to Nicolaes de La Tombe, who probably commissioned this piece. In this print Jesus preaches to young and old, rich and poor, men and women, and space is made in the composition for even the viewer of the print to be part of the crowd. As Jesus taught, everyone was challenged by his words. His words were different from the other religious leaders of his day. He was wise, true, and . . . offensive. Some of his followers turned away, while others embraced his teachings as the words of eternal life. On the final day all will hear his voice and come out of the grave. But not everyone will arise to the same destiny. Jesus is life and he is justice. All are called to consider the question—will we rise to a resurrection of life or will we rise to a resurrection of judgment?

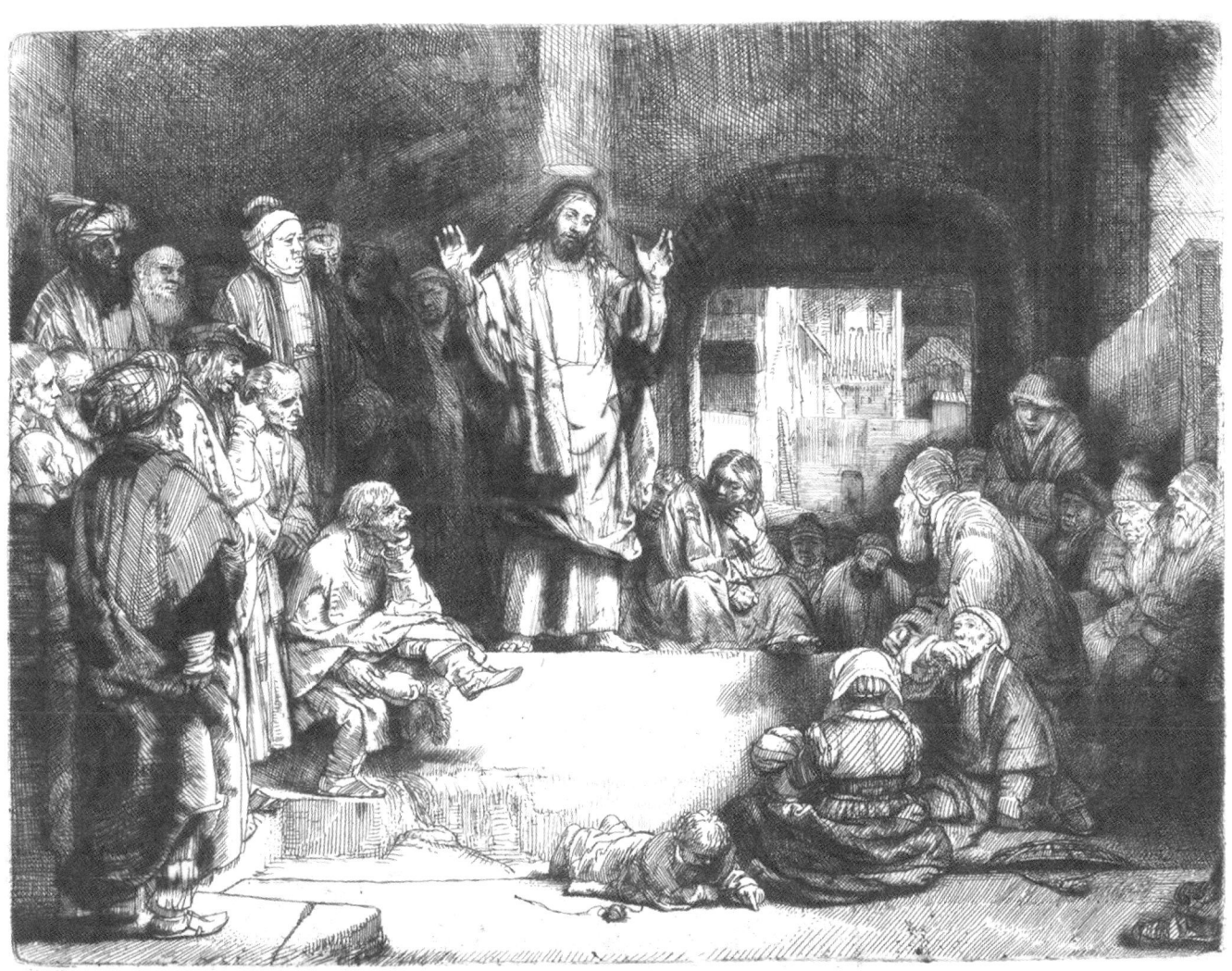

Mark 4:1–13

THE SOWER

Again he began to teach beside the sea. And a very large crowd gathered about him, so that he got into a boat and sat in it on the sea, and the whole crowd was beside the sea on the land. And he was teaching them many things in parables, and in his teaching he said to them: "Listen! Behold, a sower went out to sow. And as he sowed, some seed fell along the path, and the birds came and devoured it. Other seed fell on rocky ground, where it did not have much soil, and immediately it sprang up, since it had no depth of soil. And when the sun rose, it was scorched, and since it had no root, it withered away. Other seed fell among thorns, and the thorns grew up and choked it, and it yielded no grain. And other seeds fell into good soil and produced grain, growing up and increasing and yielding thirtyfold and sixtyfold and a hundredfold." And he said, "He who has ears to hear, let him hear."

And when he was alone, those around him with the twelve asked him about the parables. And he said to them, "To you has been given the secret of the kingdom of God, but for those outside everything is in parables, so that

"they may indeed see but not perceive,
 and may indeed hear but not understand,
 lest they should turn and be forgiven."

And he said to them, "Do you not understand this parable? How then will you understand all the parables?"

Sower (after van Gogh)
NED BUSTARD | LINOCUT

This print drew its inspiration from a painting by Vincent van Gogh. In turn, van Gogh's inspiration came from a painting by Jean-François Millet. Art historian James Romaine has written that "Vincent felt an intense bond with Millet's art. Both Vincent and Millet were Christians and the former regarded the latter's work as a preeminent example of 'Christian' art. For Vincent this meant an art that breathed the spirit of Christ, a spirit of peace and redemption, into a troubled world." The sower graciously sows the same seed on all the soils. But some soils are open to God's message and respond while others have a focus on the physical world and its pleasures and dangers. The seed falling on the soils bears different fruit depending on the heart of the hearer. The seed is always there in abundance. The gospel is always available.

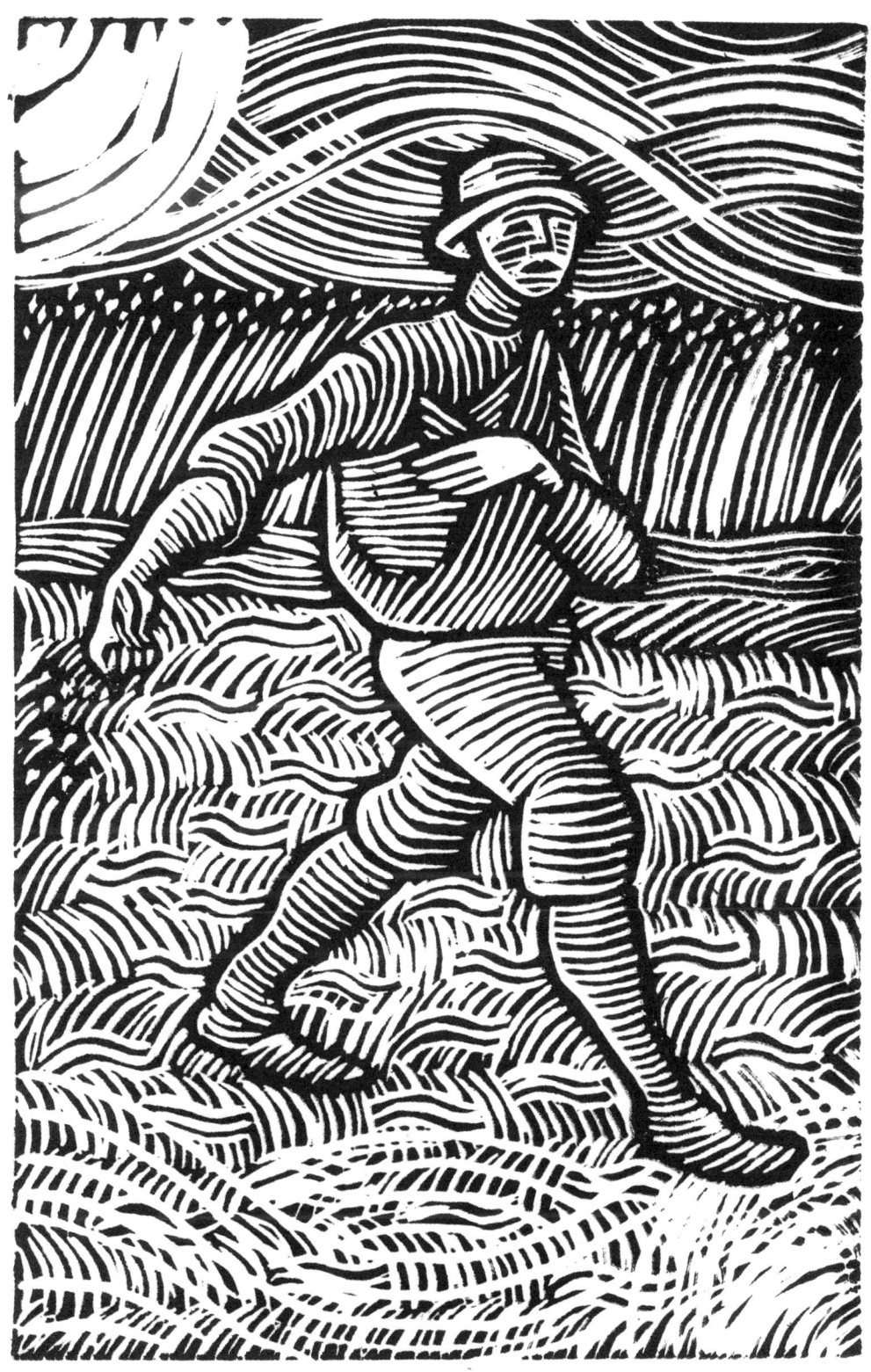

Mark 6:18–29

SALOME

For John had been saying to Herod, "It is not lawful for you to have your brother's wife." And Herodias had a grudge against him and wanted to put him to death. But she could not, for Herod feared John, knowing that he was a righteous and holy man, and he kept him safe. When he heard him, he was greatly perplexed, and yet he heard him gladly.

But an opportunity came when Herod on his birthday gave a banquet for his nobles and military commanders and the leading men of Galilee. For when Herodias's daughter came in and danced, she pleased Herod and his guests. And the king said to the girl, "Ask me for whatever you wish, and I will give it to you." And he vowed to her, "Whatever you ask me, I will give you, up to half of my kingdom." And she went out and said to her mother, "For what should I ask?" And she said, "The head of John the Baptist." And she came in immediately with haste to the king and asked, saying, "I want you to give me at once the head of John the Baptist on a platter." And the king was exceedingly sorry, but because of his oaths and his guests he did not want to break his word to her. And immediately the king sent an executioner with orders to bring John's head. He went and beheaded him in the prison and brought his head on a platter and gave it to the girl, and the girl gave it to her mother. When his disciples heard of it, they came and took his body and laid it in a tomb.

John's Halo (after Felixmüller and Clark)

NED BUSTARD | LINOCUT

Herodias' daughter danced and pleased king Herod and his guests. Herod promised her anything she wanted, but he was shocked when she asked for John the Baptist's head on a platter. He allowed murder to occur rather than breaking a promise and feeling foolish in front of his guests. How often do concerns about keeping up appearances trump extending mercy and showing humility? The gospel calls for selflessness in the place of pride. It calls for right to be done even in the face of embarrassment. Conrad Felixmüller (1897–1977) was a German expressionist painter and printmaker. This piece is based on one of his woodcuts, but the head of John has been replaced with one based on a woodcut self-portrait of Matthew L. Clark. The angle of the silver platter allows it to serve as both a vessel for conveyance and as a halo.

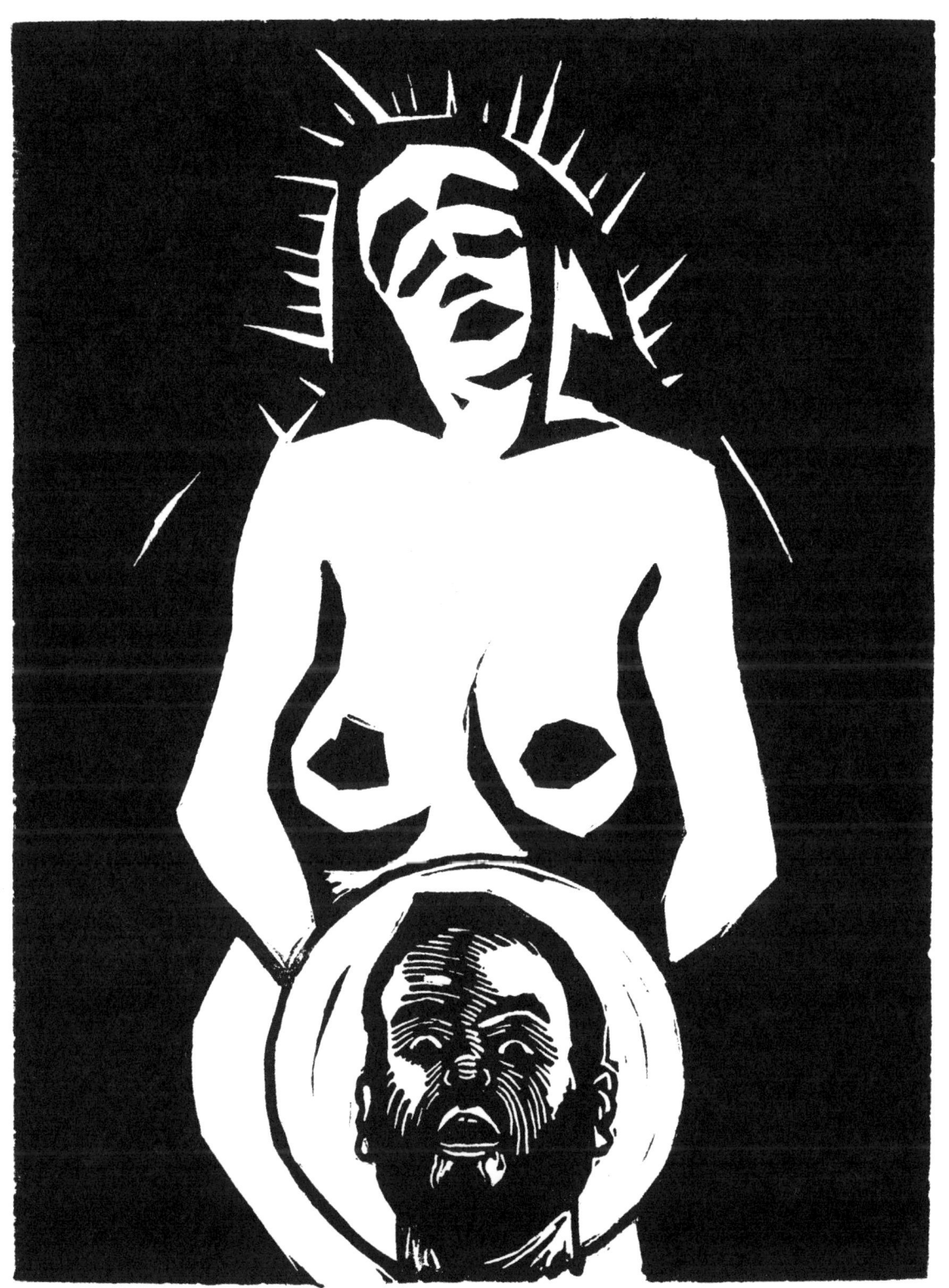

John 6:1–14

FEEDING THE MULTITUDE

After this Jesus went away to the other side of the Sea of Galilee, which is the Sea of Tiberias. And a large crowd was following him, because they saw the signs that he was doing on the sick. Jesus went up on the mountain, and there he sat down with his disciples. Now the Passover, the feast of the Jews, was at hand. Lifting up his eyes, then, and seeing that a large crowd was coming toward him, Jesus said to Philip, "Where are we to buy bread, so that these people may eat?" He said this to test him, for he himself knew what he would do. Philip answered him, "Two hundred denarii worth of bread would not be enough for each of them to get a little." One of his disciples, Andrew, Simon Peter's brother, said to him, "There is a boy here who has five barley loaves and two fish, but what are they for so many?" Jesus said, "Have the people sit down." Now there was much grass in the place. So the men sat down, about five thousand in number. Jesus then took the loaves, and when he had given thanks, he distributed them to those who were seated. So also the fish, as much as they wanted. And when they had eaten their fill, he told his disciples, "Gather up the leftover fragments, that nothing may be lost." So they gathered them up and filled twelve baskets with fragments from the five barley loaves left by those who had eaten. When the people saw the sign that he had done, they said, "This is indeed the Prophet who is to come into the world!"

Miracle No. 4 (Jesus Feeds the Five Thousand)

CRAIG HAWKINS | MONOPRINT

Hawkins writes, "For this monoprint I composed slices of bread and two fish in a way that mimics the anaphase of mitosis. I don't pretend to understand this miracle, but I do believe that the same one who multiplied fish and bread to feed us now works in us to physically grow and spiritually mature us."
In this passage Jesus the healer and Jesus the teacher shows more of who he is. The miracle is amazing like the other miracles he did. But what may be surprising to the reader is that Jesus cares so deeply about people he doesn't even know. Jesus thinks about a relatively mundane issue like food and abundantly provides for these strangers. It is the Lord who divided the loaves and fishes. And it is the Lord who knows and cares for fulfilling our deepest needs.

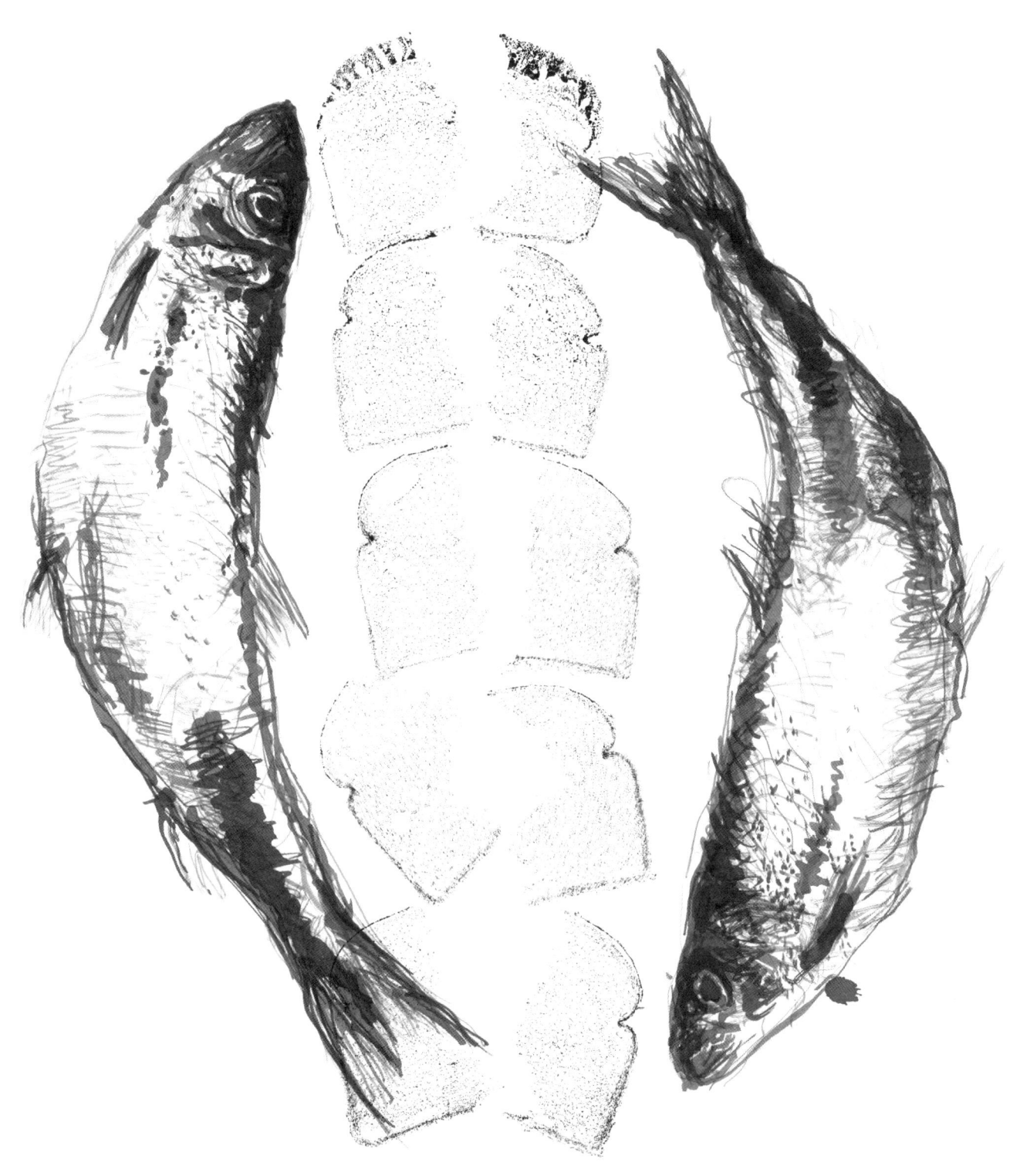

Mark 9:42–48

THE FIRES OF HELL

"Whoever causes one of these little ones who believe in me to sin, it would be better for him if a great millstone were hung around his neck and he were thrown into the sea. And if your hand causes you to sin, cut it off. It is better for you to enter life crippled than with two hands to go to hell, to the unquenchable fire. And if your foot causes you to sin, cut it off. It is better for you to enter life lame than with two feet to be thrown into hell. And if your eye causes you to sin, tear it out. It is better for you to enter the kingdom of God with one eye than with two eyes to be thrown into hell, 'where their worm does not die and the fire is not quenched.'

The Devil Belial before the Gates of Hell
ANONYMOUS | WOODCUT

In spite of the famous lyrics by Charles Wesley describing him as "Gentle Jesus, meek and mild," Jesus often spoke of hell. What is disturbing about the point made by Jesus in this text is that to end up in hell is so much to be avoided self mutilation is preferable. It shocks us to believe that a God of love would send people to hell to experience eternal fire, isolation, utter darkness, and ravenous worms. But according to the Bible, hell isn't a place to which one is sent to, but rather a destination of choice. J.I. Packer wrote: "Scripture sees hell as self-chosen . . . [H]ell appears as God's gesture of respect for human choice. All receive what they actually chose, either to be with God forever, worshipping him, or without God forever, worshipping themselves."

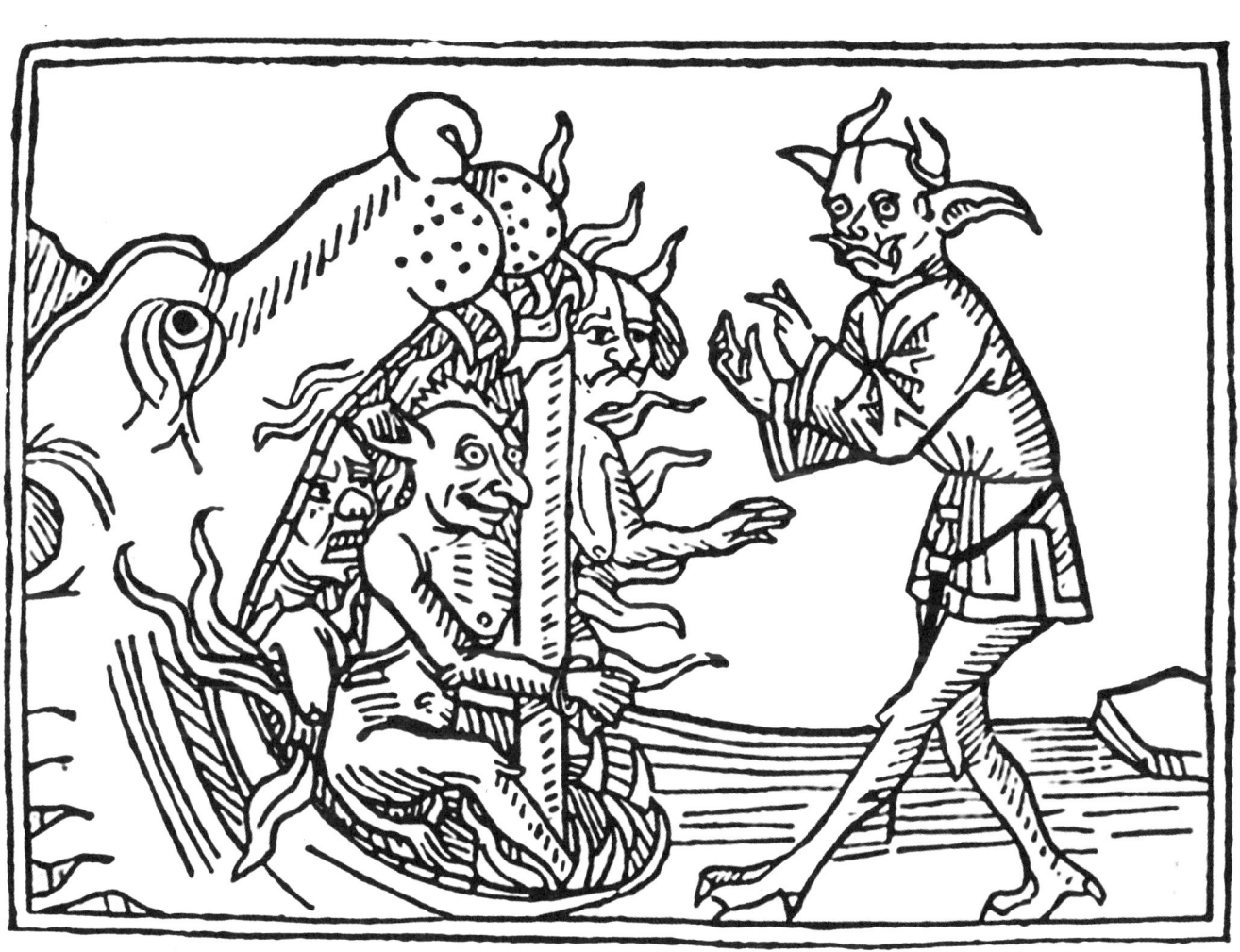

Luke 10:25–37

THE GOOD SAMARITAN

And behold, a lawyer stood up to put him to the test, saying, "Teacher, what shall I do to inherit eternal life?" He said to him, "What is written in the Law? How do you read it?" And he answered, "You shall love the Lord your God with all your heart and with all your soul and with all your strength and with all your mind, and your neighbor as yourself." And he said to him, "You have answered correctly; do this, and you will live."

But he, desiring to justify himself, said to Jesus, "And who is my neighbor?" Jesus replied, "A man was going down from Jerusalem to Jericho, and he fell among robbers, who stripped him and beat him and departed, leaving him half dead. Now by chance a priest was going down that road, and when he saw him he passed by on the other side. So likewise a Levite, when he came to the place and saw him, passed by on the other side. But a Samaritan, as he journeyed, came to where he was, and when he saw him, he had compassion. He went to him and bound up his wounds, pouring on oil and wine. Then he set him on his own animal and brought him to an inn and took care of him. And the next day he took out two denarii and gave them to the innkeeper, saying, 'Take care of him, and whatever more you spend, I will repay you when I come back.' Which of these three, do you think, proved to be a neighbor to the man who fell among the robbers?" He said, "The one who showed him mercy." And Jesus said to him, "You go, and do likewise."

The Good Samaritan

EDWARD KNIPPERS | WOODCUT

Tim Keller wrote, "Jesus' parable of the Good Samaritan teaches that we are not only to love our brothers and sisters in Christ but also our neighbors . . . Paul follows up with the command to 'Do good to all men, especially the household of faith' (Galatians 6:10). Here Paul clearly tells believers to serve the interests of their non-Christian neighbors. The word 'good' includes giving material benefits (as in the parable of the Good Samaritan) out of love and desire for a person's well being in every way. Thus Paul calls Christians to consider and work for the 'common good' of their neighborhood and city. It is no wonder that Christians seeking to obey Christ and Paul have over the centuries worked to abolish slavery, repeal child labor laws, and open voting rights to all citizens, as well as to begin thousands of programs and ministries that help the poor and needy."

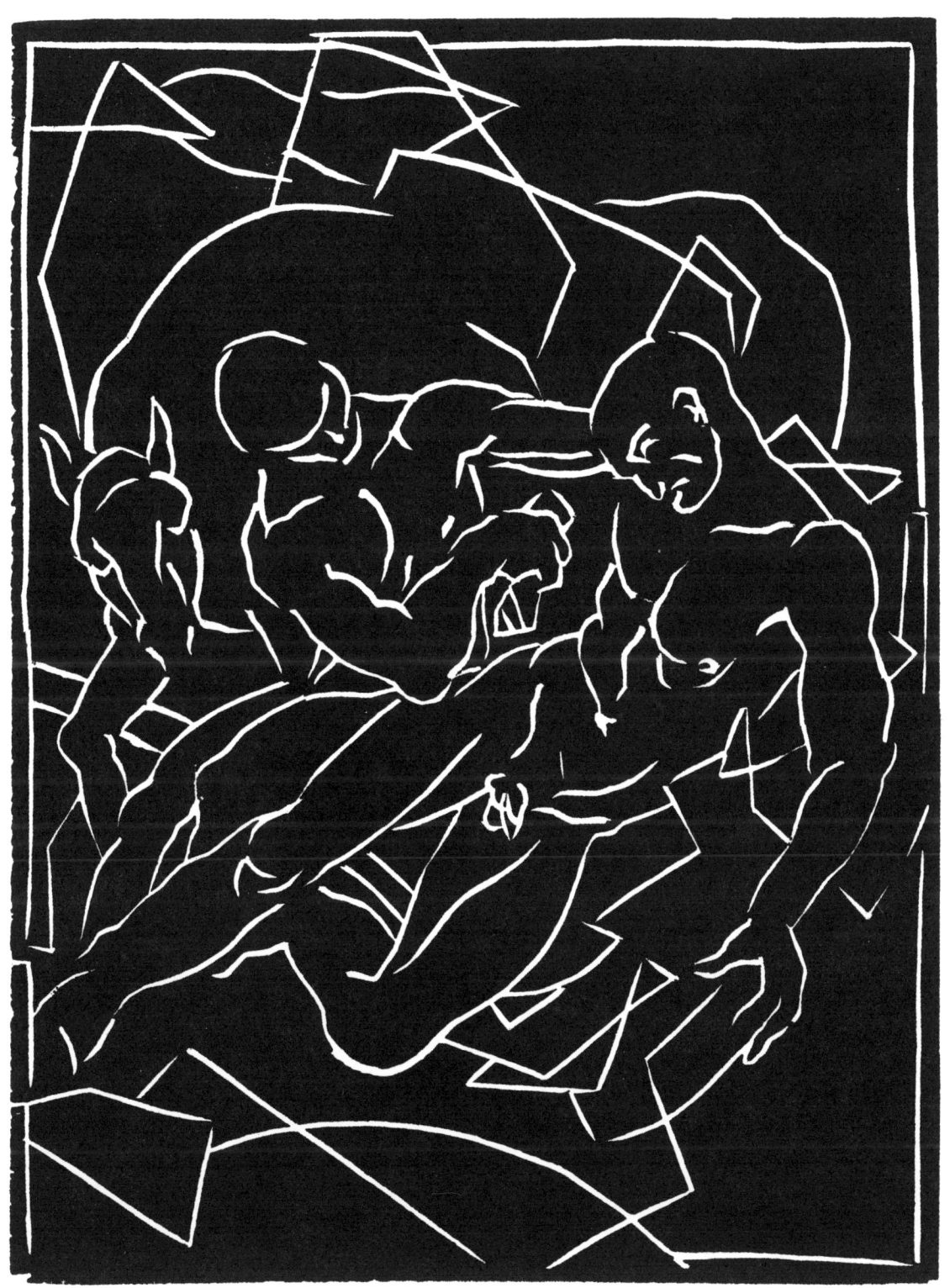

Luke 15:11–24

THE PRODIGAL SON

And he said, "There was a man who had two sons. And the younger of them said to his father, 'Father, give me the share of property that is coming to me.' And he divided his property between them. Not many days later, the younger son gathered all he had and took a journey into a far country, and there he squandered his property in reckless living. And when he had spent everything, a severe famine arose in that country, and he began to be in need. So he went and hired himself out to one of the citizens of that country, who sent him into his fields to feed pigs. And he was longing to be fed with the pods that the pigs ate, and no one gave him anything.

But when he came to himself, he said, 'How many of my father's hired servants have more than enough bread, but I perish here with hunger! I will arise and go to my father, and I will say to him, "Father, I have sinned against heaven and before you. I am no longer worthy to be called your son. Treat me as one of your hired servants."' And he arose and came to his father. But while he was still a long way off, his father saw him and felt compassion, and ran and embraced him and kissed him. And the son said to him, 'Father, I have sinned against heaven and before you. I am no longer worthy to be called your son.' But the father said to his servants, 'Bring quickly the best robe, and put it on him, and put a ring on his hand, and shoes on his feet. And bring the fattened calf and kill it, and let us eat and celebrate. For this my son was dead, and is alive again; he was lost, and is found.' And they began to celebrate.

The Prodigal Son

CHRIS KOELLE | ETCHING

"Do you realize, then, what Jesus is teaching? Neither son loved the father for himself. They both were using the father for their own self-centered ends rather than loving, enjoying, and serving him for his own sake," writes Tim Keller in *The Prodigal God: Recovering the Heart of the Christian Faith.* He then continues, "This means that you can rebel against God and be alienated from him either by breaking his rules or by keeping all of them diligently." The border details of this etching/aquatint/drypoint include modern song lyrics and lines from the Old and New Testaments. Koelle explains that these elements "give context to the central image of the father embracing his long-lost son, tattered and torn, lifted up and finally at one with his father in a union of steadfast love."

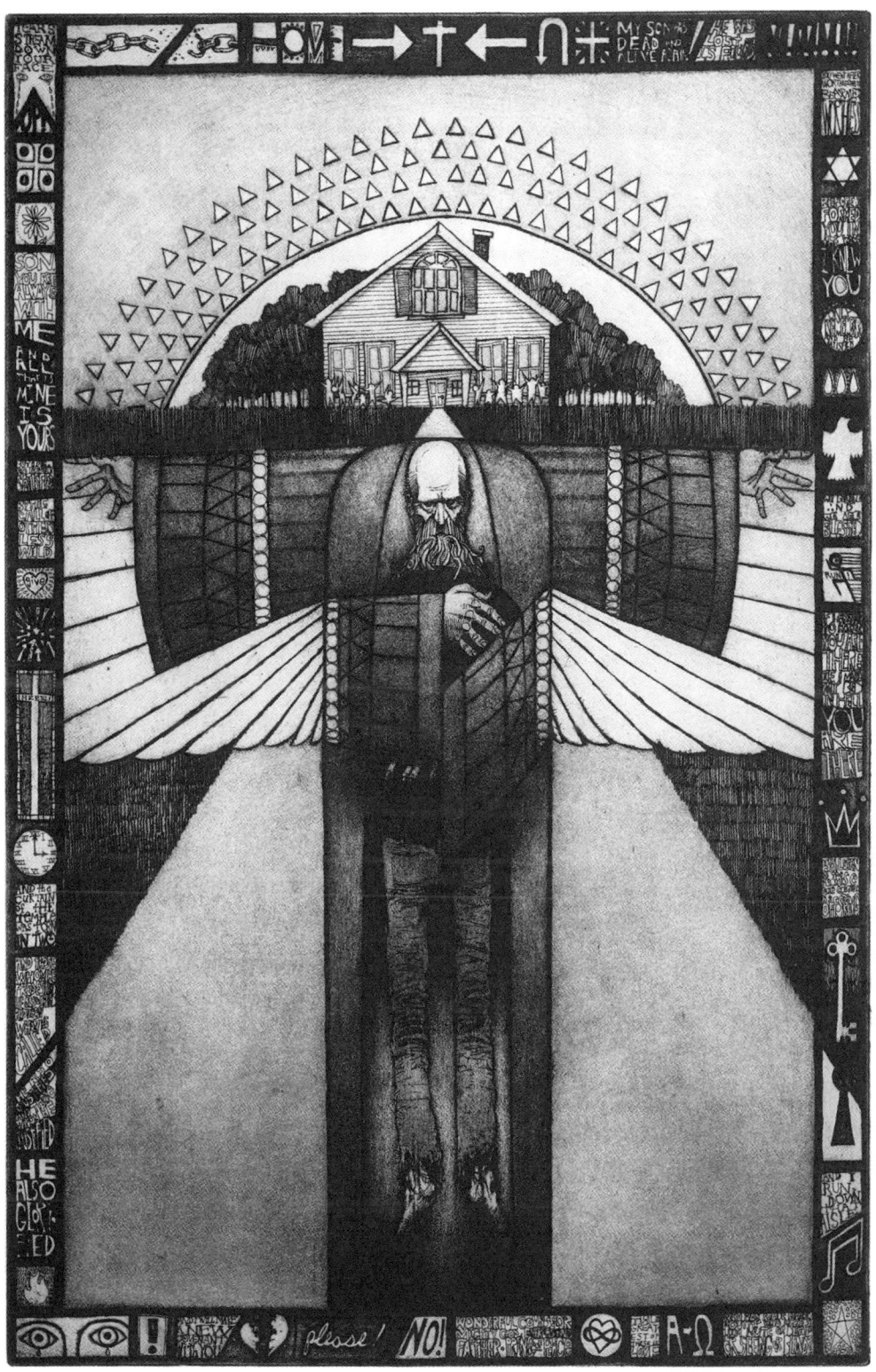

John 11:32–46

THE RAISING OF LAZARUS

Now when Mary came to where Jesus was and saw him, she fell at his feet, saying to him, "Lord, if you had been here, my brother would not have died." When Jesus saw her weeping, and the Jews who had come with her also weeping, he was deeply moved in his spirit and greatly troubled. And he said, "Where have you laid him?" They said to him, "Lord, come and see." Jesus wept. So the Jews said, "See how he loved him!" But some of them said, "Could not he who opened the eyes of the blind man also have kept this man from dying?"

Then Jesus, deeply moved again, came to the tomb. It was a cave, and a stone lay against it. Jesus said, "Take away the stone." Martha, the sister of the dead man, said to him, "Lord, by this time there will be an odor, for he has been dead four days." Jesus said to her, "Did I not tell you that if you believed you would see the glory of God?" So they took away the stone. And Jesus lifted up his eyes and said, "Father, I thank you that you have heard me. I knew that you always hear me, but I said this on account of the people standing around, that they may believe that you sent me." When he had said these things, he cried out with a loud voice, "Lazarus, come out." The man who had died came out, his hands and feet bound with linen strips, and his face wrapped with a cloth. Jesus said to them, "Unbind him, and let him go."

Many of the Jews therefore, who had come with Mary and had seen what he did, believed in him, but some of them went to the Pharisees and told them what Jesus had done.

Take Off the Grave Clothes
KEVIN LINDHOLM | LINOCUT

Historically, Jews believed that the spirit of the deceased remained around the body for three days after death. Jesus delays going to Lazarus and when he arrives Lazarus has been dead four days. The text describes Jesus as deeply moved and greatly troubled in spirit. But Jesus told his disciples he would raise Lazarus from the dead. In spite of knowing Lazarus would be raised, Jesus is devastated by the death of his friend. The very presence of death disturbs Jesus because it is the harshest imprint of the Fall. It is interesting how people respond to the resurrection. Some respond to the raising of Lazarus with faith. Others stand in opposition to God and run to the Pharisees. Yet there is always hope for those who trust the God who raises the dead.

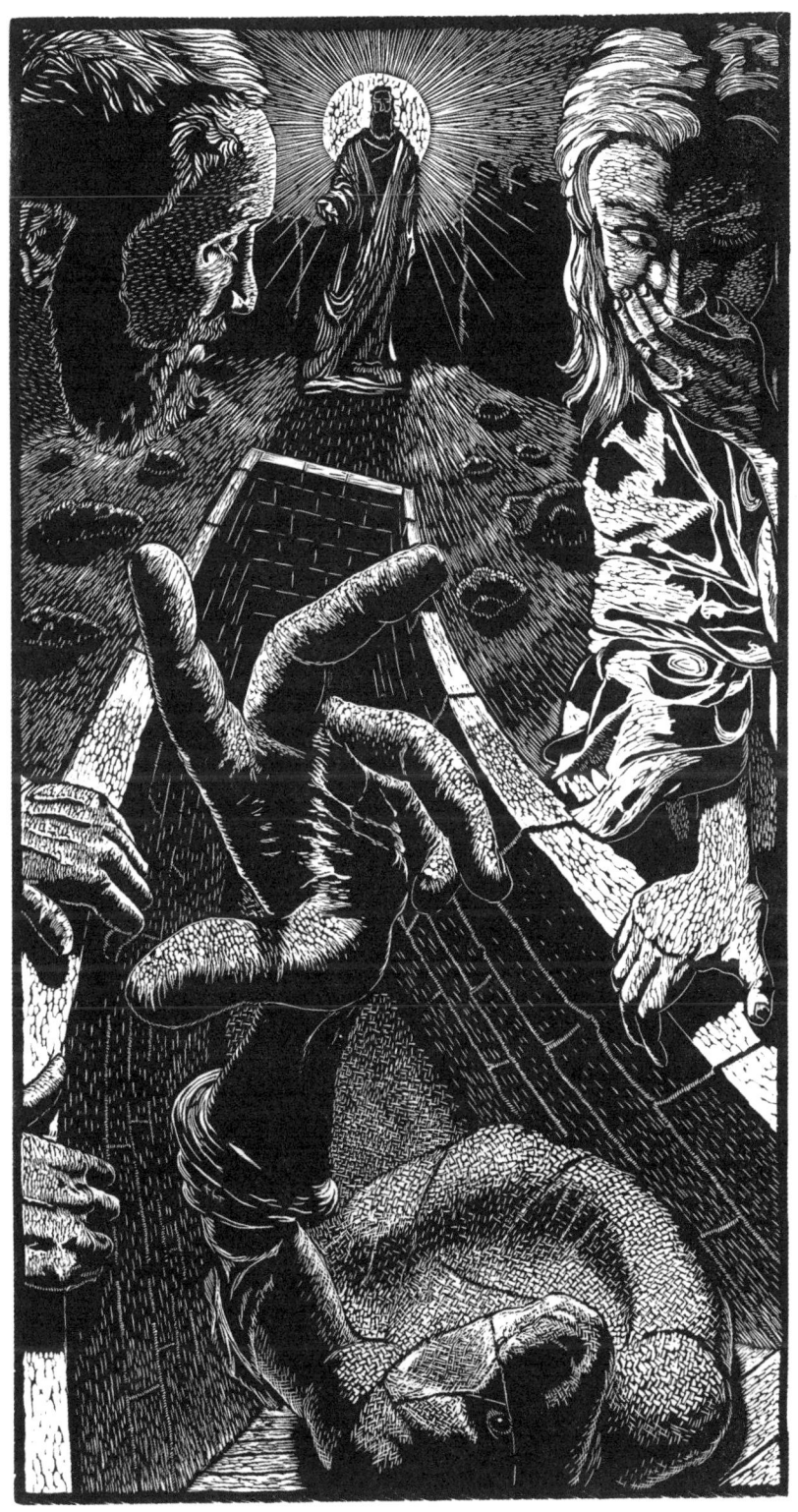

Matthew 21:1–11

THE TRIUMPHAL ENTRY

Now when they drew near to Jerusalem and came to Bethphage, to the Mount of Olives, then Jesus sent two disciples, saying to them, "Go into the village in front of you, and immediately you will find a donkey tied, and a colt with her. Untie them and bring them to me. If anyone says anything to you, you shall say, 'The Lord needs them,' and he will send them at once." This took place to fulfill what was spoken by the prophet, saying,

> "Say to the daughter of Zion,
> 'Behold, your king is coming to you,
>   humble, and mounted on a donkey,
>   on a colt, the foal of a beast of burden.'"

The disciples went and did as Jesus had directed them. They brought the donkey and the colt and put on them their cloaks, and he sat on them. Most of the crowd spread their cloaks on the road, and others cut branches from the trees and spread them on the road. And the crowds that went before him and that followed him were shouting, "Hosanna to the Son of David! Blessed is he who comes in the name of the Lord! Hosanna in the highest!" And when he entered Jerusalem, the whole city was stirred up, saying, "Who is this?" And the crowds said, "This is the prophet Jesus, from Nazareth of Galilee."

The Triumphal Entry

DIEGO JOURDAN PEREIRA | WOODCUT

According to Jewish tradition the glory of God appeared through the Beautiful Gate and will appear again when the Messiah comes (Ezekiel 44:1–3). And it is said that Jesus entered through this gate on Palm Sunday. But the gate, disciples, crowds, cloaks, palm branches, and hosannas are all missing from this depiction of the Triumphal Entry. All that remains is a downcast donkey and a sorrowful Jesus. The artist explains, "The more I thought about it, the more it seemed to me that while everyone else was celebrating around him, Christ's mind was elsewhere. He was thinking about the destruction of Jerusalem and his own impending fate on the Cross. His tears were internal as well as external." But Jesus would not turn aside from the path. Luke 9:51 says, "When the days drew near for him to be taken up, he set his face to go to Jerusalem."

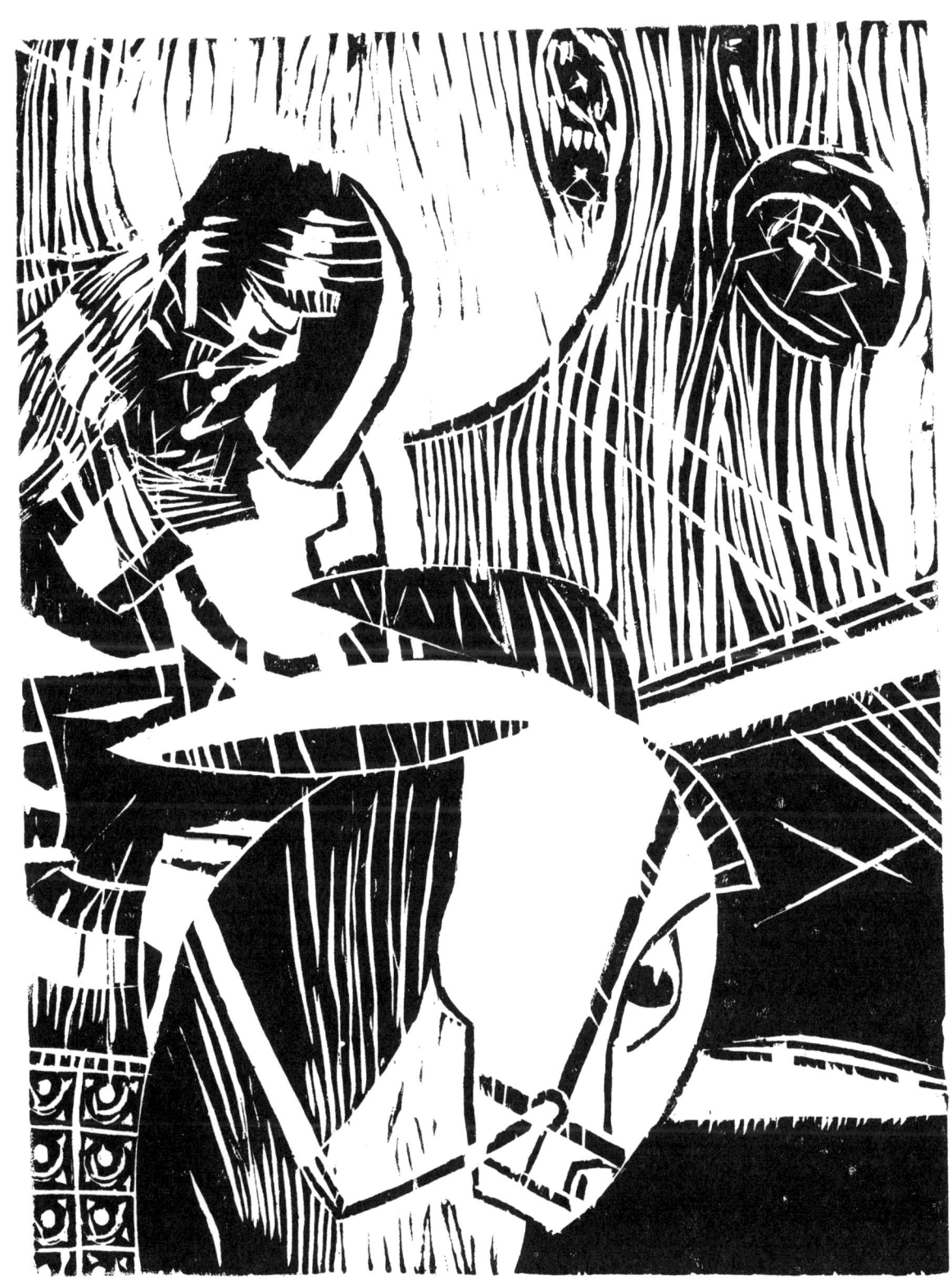

Matthew 21:12–17

CLEANSING THE TEMPLE

And Jesus entered the temple and drove out all who sold and bought in the temple, and he overturned the tables of the money-changers and the seats of those who sold pigeons. He said to them, "It is written, 'My house shall be called a house of prayer,' but you make it a den of robbers."

And the blind and the lame came to him in the temple, and he healed them. But when the chief priests and the scribes saw the wonderful things that he did, and the children crying out in the temple, "Hosanna to the Son of David!" they were indignant, and they said to him, "Do you hear what these are saying?" And Jesus said to them, "Yes; have you never read,

> "'Out of the mouth of infants and nursing babies
> you have prepared praise'?"

And leaving them, he went out of the city to Bethany and lodged there.

Christ Driving the Moneylenders from the Temple
ALBRECHT DÜRER | WOODCUT

In contrast to Late Gothic depictions of a delicate or fragile Christ, in this piece Dürer created an intense, militant, and manly Christ. A modern Jesus would politely ask the money changers to leave. But that is not the Jesus of Scripture. He forcefully drives the moneychangers out, overturning tables and throwing seats. Jesus acts in this audacious manner because he knows he owns the temple. He is defending his place in the same way a home owner would defend his own house. Jesus is violent, defiant and takes into his own hands the removal of those who desecrate the temple. This work was part of a larger series of prints called *The Small Passion*, and was quite relevant to the time. A Christ who was fighting for holiness rang true with young Reformers.

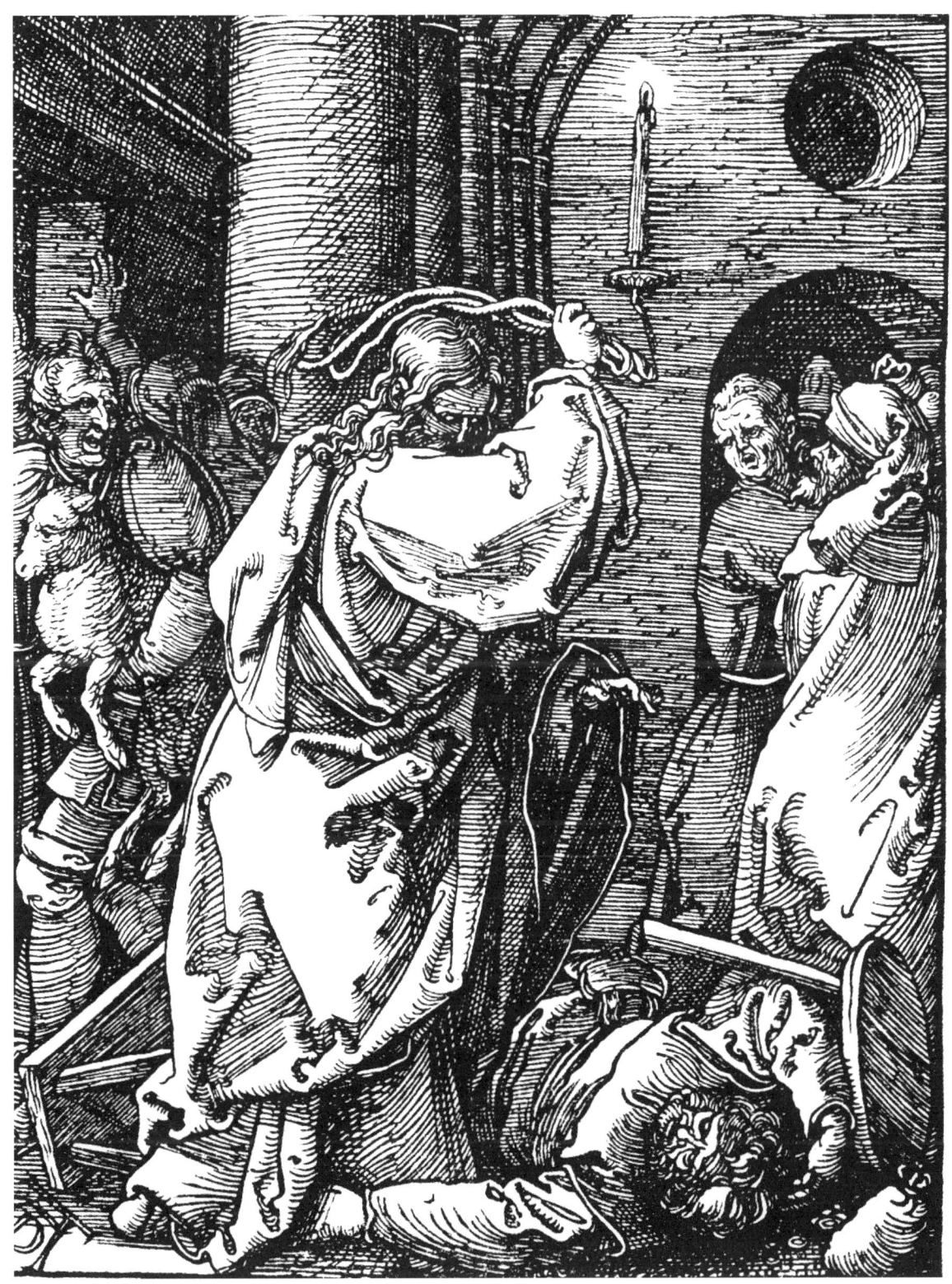

Matthew 21:33–41

KILLING THE MASTER'S SON

"Hear another parable. There was a master of a house who planted a vineyard and put a fence around it and dug a winepress in it and built a tower and leased it to tenants, and went into another country. When the season for fruit drew near, he sent his servants to the tenants to get his fruit. And the tenants took his servants and beat one, killed another, and stoned another. Again he sent other servants, more than the first. And they did the same to them. Finally he sent his son to them, saying, 'They will respect my son.' But when the tenants saw the son, they said to themselves, 'This is the heir. Come, let us kill him and have his inheritance.' And they took him and threw him out of the vineyard and killed him. When therefore the owner of the vineyard comes, what will he do to those tenants?" They said to him, "He will put those wretches to a miserable death and let out the vineyard to other tenants who will give him the fruits in their seasons."

Parable of the Vineyard
ANONYMOUS | WOODCUT

C.H. Spurgeon wrote, "The rejection of God's prophets is the sin of our common humanity; and the murder of the Son of God was the crime, not of the Jews only, 'but of the whole human race. We, too, have a share in it, for we have rejected the Son of the Highest. . . . [T]he Son of God himself has come to you in the preaching of the gospel. You have heard of his death, and of his atoning sacrifice, but you have rejected them; and, in acting thus, you have done, as far as you could, the same as they did who crucified the Saviour. You still refuse to have him for your Saviour; you disown him as your King; you strive against his righteous sway. You tell me that you do not. Well, then, you have yielded to him, and you are saved. But if that be not the case, you still remain such an adversary of God that you reject his Son."

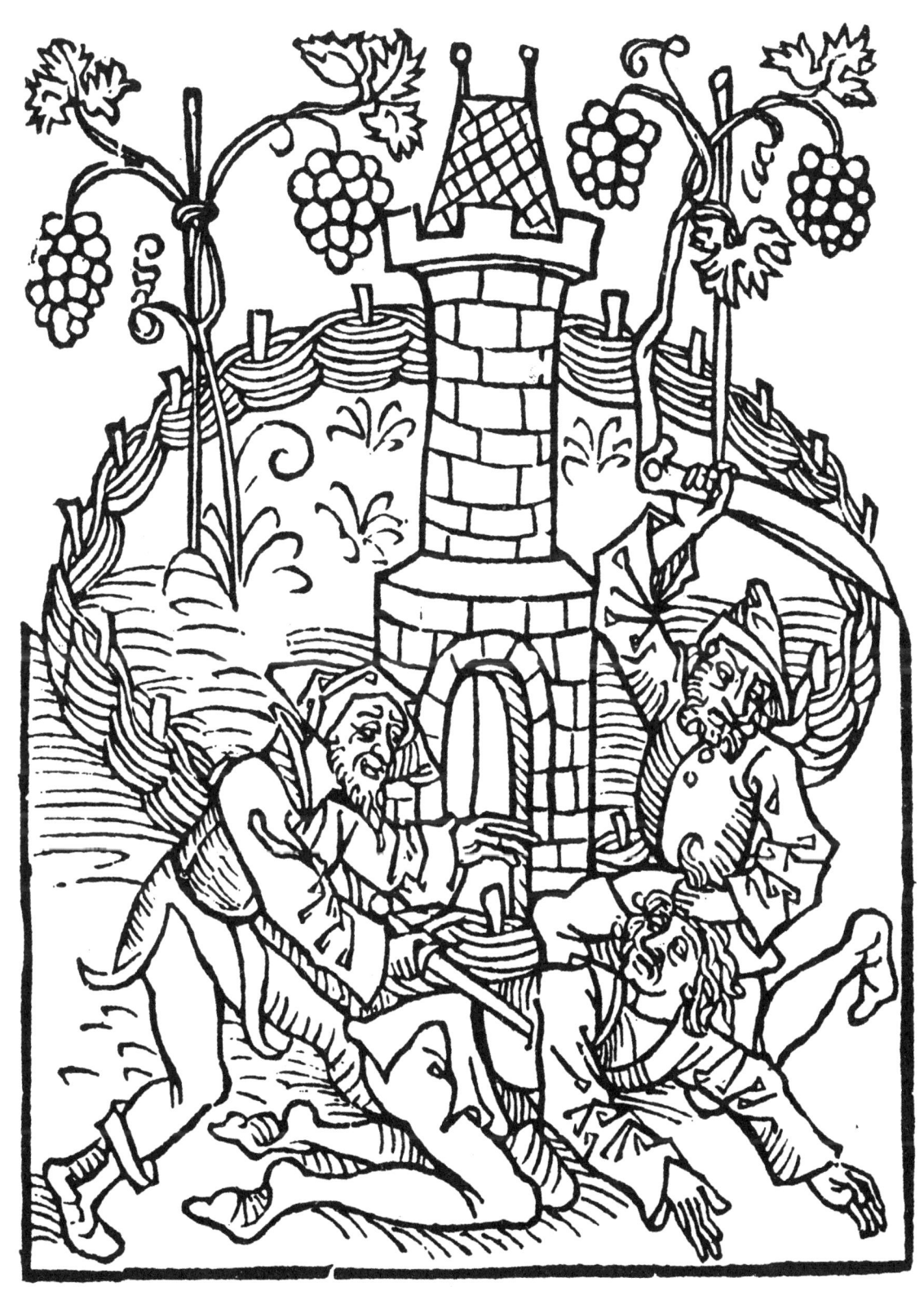

Matthew 26:17–30

THE LAST SUPPER

Now on the first day of Unleavened Bread the disciples came to Jesus, saying, "Where will you have us prepare for you to eat the Passover?" He said, "Go into the city to a certain man and say to him, 'The Teacher says, My time is at hand. I will keep the Passover at your house with my disciples.'" And the disciples did as Jesus had directed them, and they prepared the Passover.

When it was evening, he reclined at table with the twelve. And as they were eating, he said, "Truly, I say to you, one of you will betray me." And they were very sorrowful and began to say to him one after another, "Is it I, Lord?" He answered, "He who has dipped his hand in the dish with me will betray me. The Son of Man goes as it is written of him, but woe to that man by whom the Son of Man is betrayed! It would have been better for that man if he had not been born." Judas, who would betray him, answered, "Is it I, Rabbi?" He said to him, "You have said so."

Now as they were eating, Jesus took bread, and after blessing it broke it and gave it to the disciples, and said, "Take, eat; this is my body." And he took a cup, and when he had given thanks he gave it to them, saying, "Drink of it, all of you, for this is my blood of the covenant, which is poured out for many for the forgiveness of sins. I tell you I will not drink again of this fruit of the vine until that day when I drink it new with you in my Father's kingdom."

And when they had sung a hymn, they went out to the Mount of Olives.

Bitter Herbs

TANJA BUTLER | LINOCUT

Scottish pastor Robert Bruce wrote in the sixteenth century, "When you are at the Lord's Table, watching what the minister does outwardly, in breaking and distributing the bread, in pouring out and distributing the wine, think of this: Christ is as busy doing all these things spiritually to your soul. He is busy giving to you his own body, with his own hand; He is as busy giving to you his own blood, with its power and efficacy." In this print, Christ offers Judas bread with his own hand, a gift the defecting disciple receives with a distracted mind and heart. On the table lie the bitter herbs and salt water required for the Passover, reminders of the bitter tears shed by the people of God in bondage and foreshadows of the tears Christ would soon shed in the Garden as he approached the *Cross* to free his people from the bondage to sin and death.

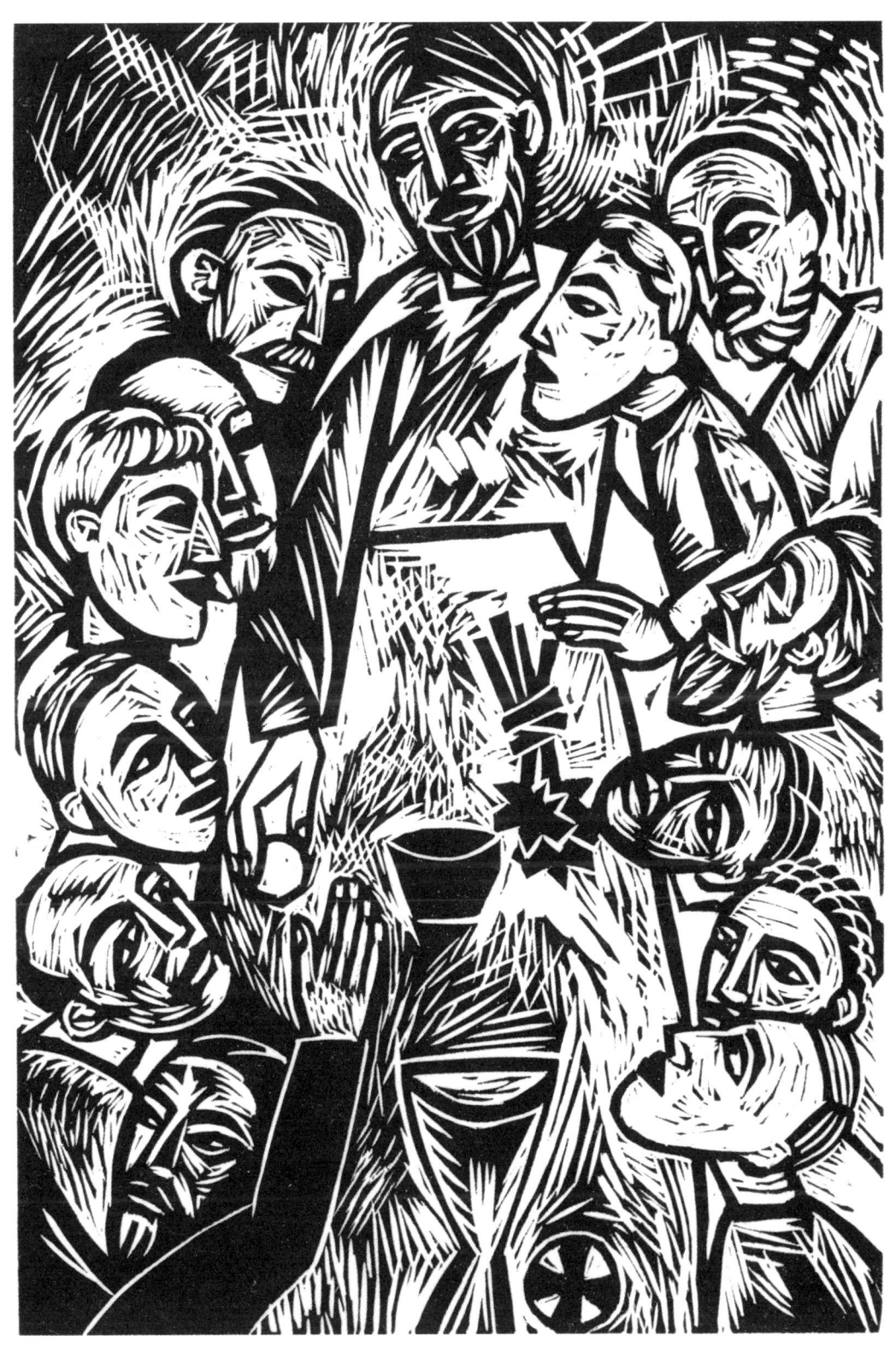

Matthew 26:36–46

THE GARDEN OF GETHSEMANE

Then Jesus went with them to a place called Gethsemane, and he said to his disciples, "Sit here, while I go over there and pray." And taking with him Peter and the two sons of Zebedee, he began to be sorrowful and troubled. Then he said to them, "My soul is very sorrowful, even to death; remain here, and watch with me." And going a little farther he fell on his face and prayed, saying, "My Father, if it be possible, let this cup pass from me; nevertheless, not as I will, but as you will." And he came to the disciples and found them sleeping. And he said to Peter, "So, could you not watch with me one hour? Watch and pray that you may not enter into temptation. The spirit indeed is willing, but the flesh is weak." Again, for the second time, he went away and prayed, "My Father, if this cannot pass unless I drink it, your will be done." And again he came and found them sleeping, for their eyes were heavy. So, leaving them again, he went away and prayed for the third time, saying the same words again. Then he came to the disciples and said to them, "Sleep and take your rest later on. See, the hour is at hand, and the Son of Man is betrayed into the hands of sinners. Rise, let us be going; see, my betrayer is at hand."

Christ on the Mount of Olives

ERNST BARLACH | WOODCUT

In this piece Barlach beautifully captures the writhing agony of Christ in the garden. In the twenty-second chapter of Luke's record of this event it says, "being in an agony he prayed more earnestly; and his sweat became like great drops of blood falling down to the ground." The obedience of Jesus to go to the Cross was not without cost. This swirling image of the Son of Man is full of sadness, angst, and suffering. The agony of obedience was crucial for the salvation of his followers. As John Newton wrote, "Our righteousness is in him, and our hope depends, not upon the exercise of grace in us, but upon the fullness of grace and love in him, and upon his obedience unto death."

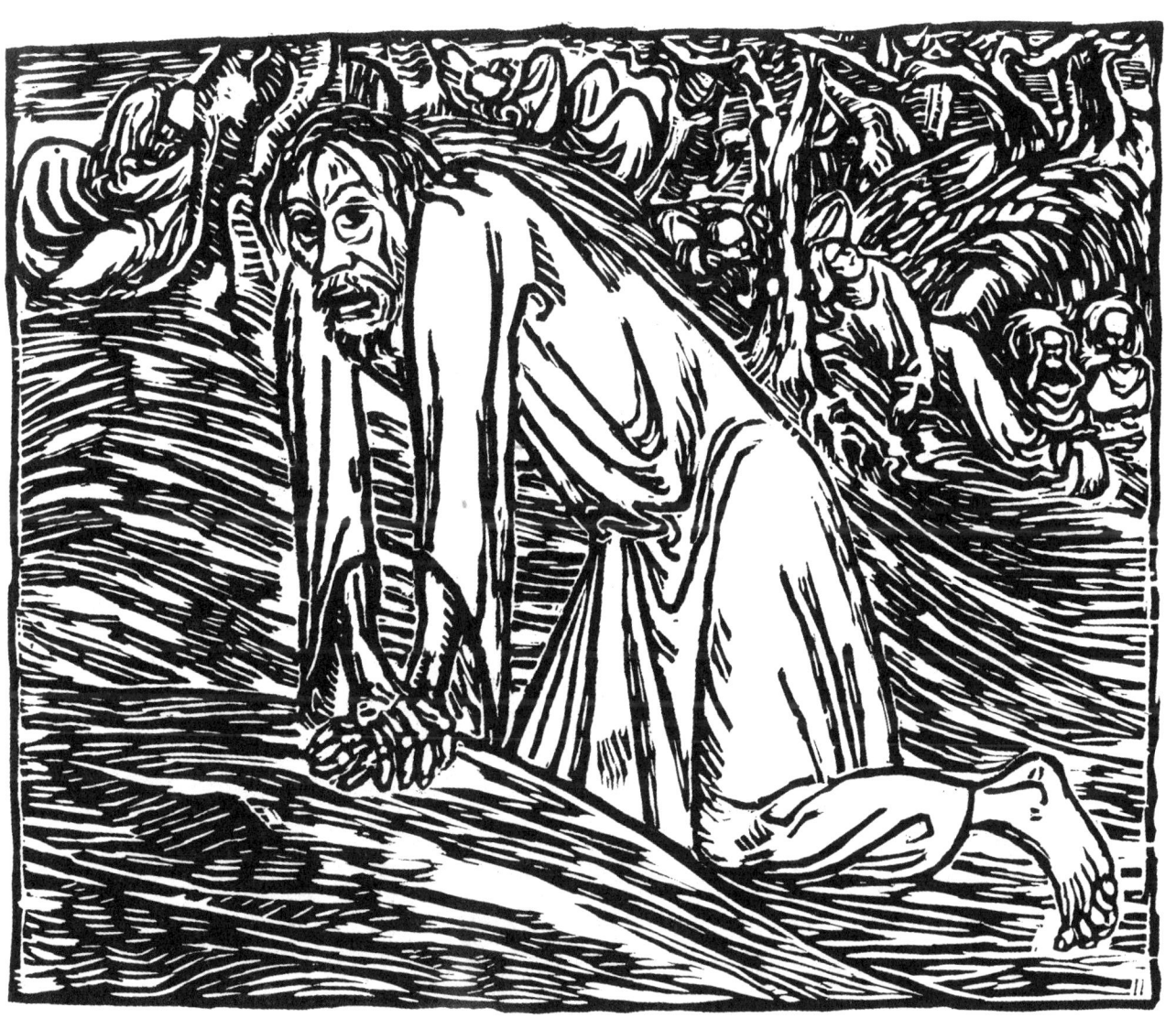

Matthew 26:47–56

JUDAS' KISS

While he was still speaking, Judas came, one of the twelve, and with him a great crowd with swords and clubs, from the chief priests and the elders of the people. Now the betrayer had given them a sign, saying, "The one I will kiss is the man; seize him." And he came up to Jesus at once and said, "Greetings, Rabbi!" And he kissed him. Jesus said to him, "Friend, do what you came to do." Then they came up and laid hands on Jesus and seized him. And behold, one of those who were with Jesus stretched out his hand and drew his sword and struck the servant of the high priest and cut off his ear. Then Jesus said to him, "Put your sword back into its place. For all who take the sword will perish by the sword. Do you think that I cannot appeal to my Father, and he will at once send me more than twelve legions of angels? But how then should the Scriptures be fulfilled, that it must be so?" At that hour Jesus said to the crowds, "Have you come out as against a robber, with swords and clubs to capture me? Day after day I sat in the temple teaching, and you did not seize me. But all this has taken place that the Scriptures of the prophets might be fulfilled." Then all the disciples left him and fled.

The Betrayal of Christ (Small Passion)
ALBRECHT DÜRER | WOODCUT

It was only a little kiss—what's the big deal? U2 sings on behalf of Judas: *"In the garden I was playing the tart / I kissed your lips and broke your heart / You . . . you were acting like it was / The end of the world."* A kiss is an act that is as meaningful as the heart that makes it. Jesus was kissed by the woman who washed his feet with her hair and it was a true expression of deep love. Yet for Judas, the kiss was merely a marker, an external act with no true connection to the heart. The irony that a kiss was the symbol of Judas' betrayal—a gesture of love for an act of historic evil—was not lost on Jesus. He points out the hypocrisy of it all (as it is recorded in Luke's account of the event) saying, "Judas, would you betray the Son of Man with a kiss?"

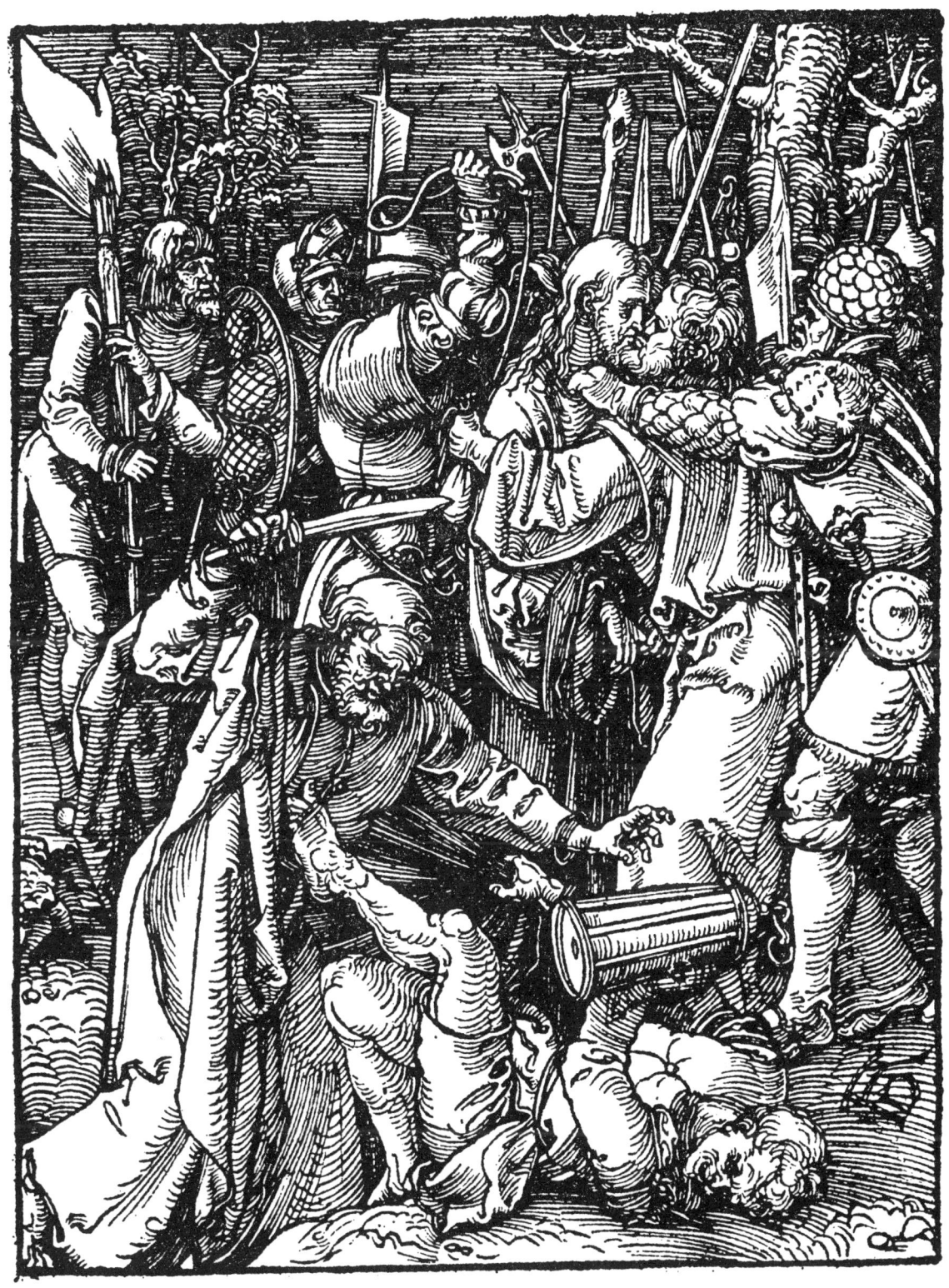

John 19:1–11

PILATE AND CHRIST

Then Pilate took Jesus and flogged him. And the soldiers twisted together a crown of thorns and put it on his head and arrayed him in a purple robe. They came up to him, saying, "Hail, King of the Jews!" and struck him with their hands. Pilate went out again and said to them, "See, I am bringing him out to you that you may know that I find no guilt in him." So Jesus came out, wearing the crown of thorns and the purple robe. Pilate said to them, "Behold the man!" When the chief priests and the officers saw him, they cried out, "Crucify him, crucify him!" Pilate said to them, "Take him yourselves and crucify him, for I find no guilt in him." The Jews answered him, "We have a law, and according to that law he ought to die because he has made himself the Son of God." When Pilate heard this statement, he was even more afraid. He entered his headquarters again and said to Jesus, "Where are you from?" But Jesus gave him no answer. So Pilate said to him, "You will not speak to me? Do you not know that I have authority to release you and authority to crucify you?" Jesus answered him, "You would have no authority over me at all unless it had been given you from above. Therefore he who delivered me over to you has the greater sin."

The Mocking of Christ

EDWARD KNIPPERS | LINOCUT

If God was promising the forgiveness of sin through the death of Christ since the cursing in the Garden (the "Protoevangelium"), are Pilate, the Jewish religious leaders, and the soldiers held accountable for killing Jesus? D.A. Carson responds, "God's sovereignty over the death of Christ does not mitigate the guilt of the human conspirators. On the other hand, the malice of their conspiracy has not caught God flat-footed, as if he had not foreseen the Cross, much less planned it. The text plainly insists that God's sovereignty is not mitigated by human actions, and human guilt is not exculpated by appeal to divine sovereignty. This duality is sometimes called *compatibilism:* God's utter sovereignty and human moral responsibility are compatible."

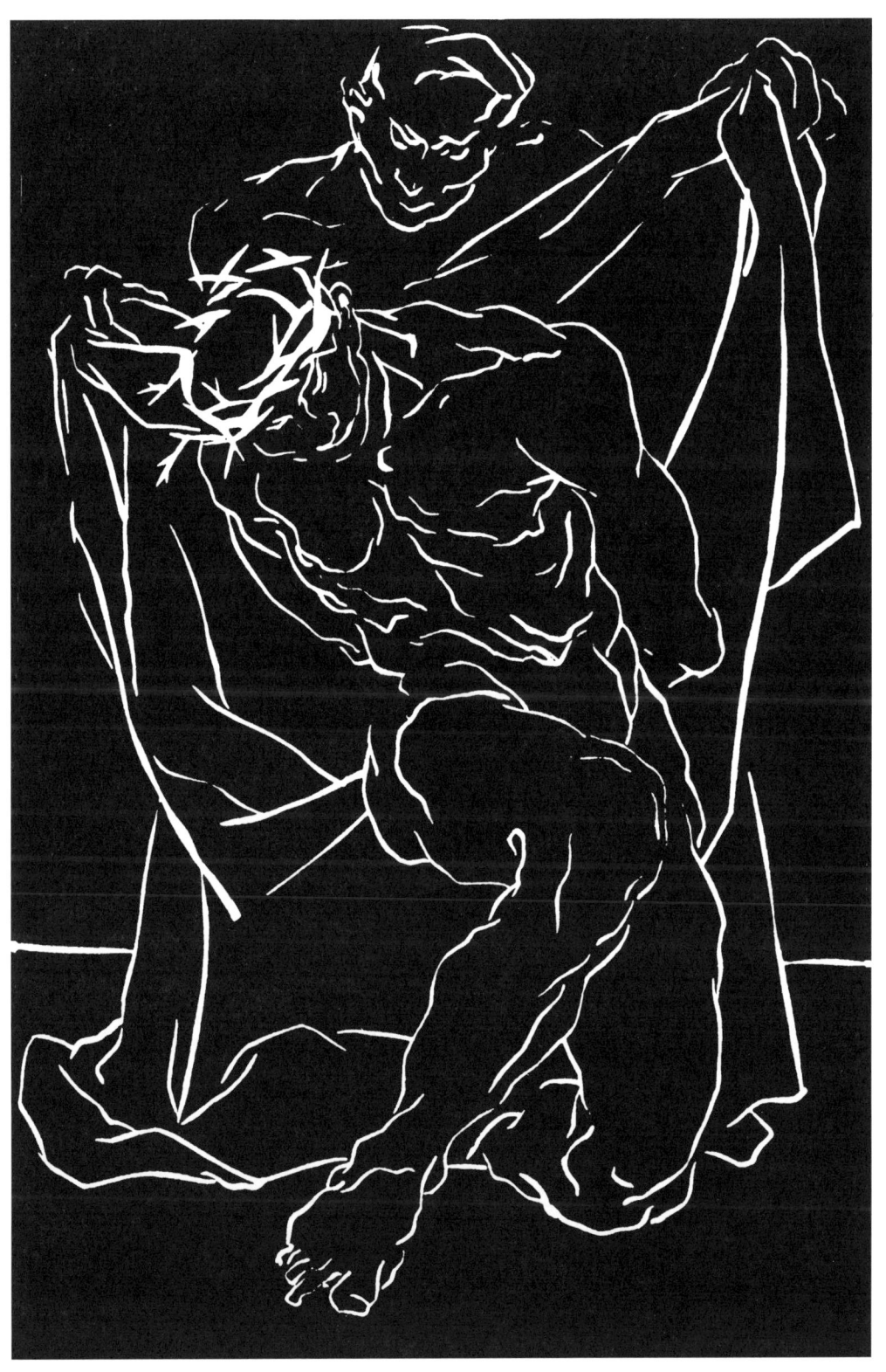

Luke 23:20–34a
SIMON OF CYRENE

Pilate addressed them once more, desiring to release Jesus, but they kept shouting, "Crucify, crucify him!" A third time he said to them, "Why, what evil has he done? I have found in him no guilt deserving death. I will therefore punish and release him." But they were urgent, demanding with loud cries that he should be crucified. And their voices prevailed. So Pilate decided that their demand should be granted. He released the man who had been thrown into prison for insurrection and murder, for whom they asked, but he delivered Jesus over to their will.

And as they led him away, they seized one Simon of Cyrene, who was coming in from the country, and laid on him the cross, to carry it behind Jesus. And there followed him a great multitude of the people and of women who were mourning and lamenting for him. But turning to them Jesus said, "Daughters of Jerusalem, do not weep for me, but weep for yourselves and for your children. For behold, the days are coming when they will say, 'Blessed are the barren and the wombs that never bore and the breasts that never nursed!' Then they will begin to say to the mountains, 'Fall on us,' and to the hills, 'Cover us.' For if they do these things when the wood is green, what will happen when it is dry?"

Two others, who were criminals, were led away to be put to death with him. And when they came to the place that is called The Skull, there they crucified him, and the criminals, one on his right and one on his left. And Jesus said, "Father, forgive them, for they know not what they do."

Christ Falls Under His Cross
LOVIS CORINTH | DRYPOINT

As Isaac carried the wood on his back for the sacrifice so many years before, so too Jesus the Son of God carried the wood on his back for the sacrifice. But as God provided a substitution for Isaac through the ram caught in the thicket, he also provided a substitution for us in providing Jesus incarnated into time and space. Sinclair Ferguson wrote, "Christ's death was substitutionary . . . Jesus was taking our place. That is why the charges brought against him were blasphemy and treason, for these are the very charges we face before the judgment seat of God. We have made ourselves into gods, and thus blasphemed his holy Name; we have rebelled against His rightful rule over our lives, and we are guilty of high treason against his gracious majesty."

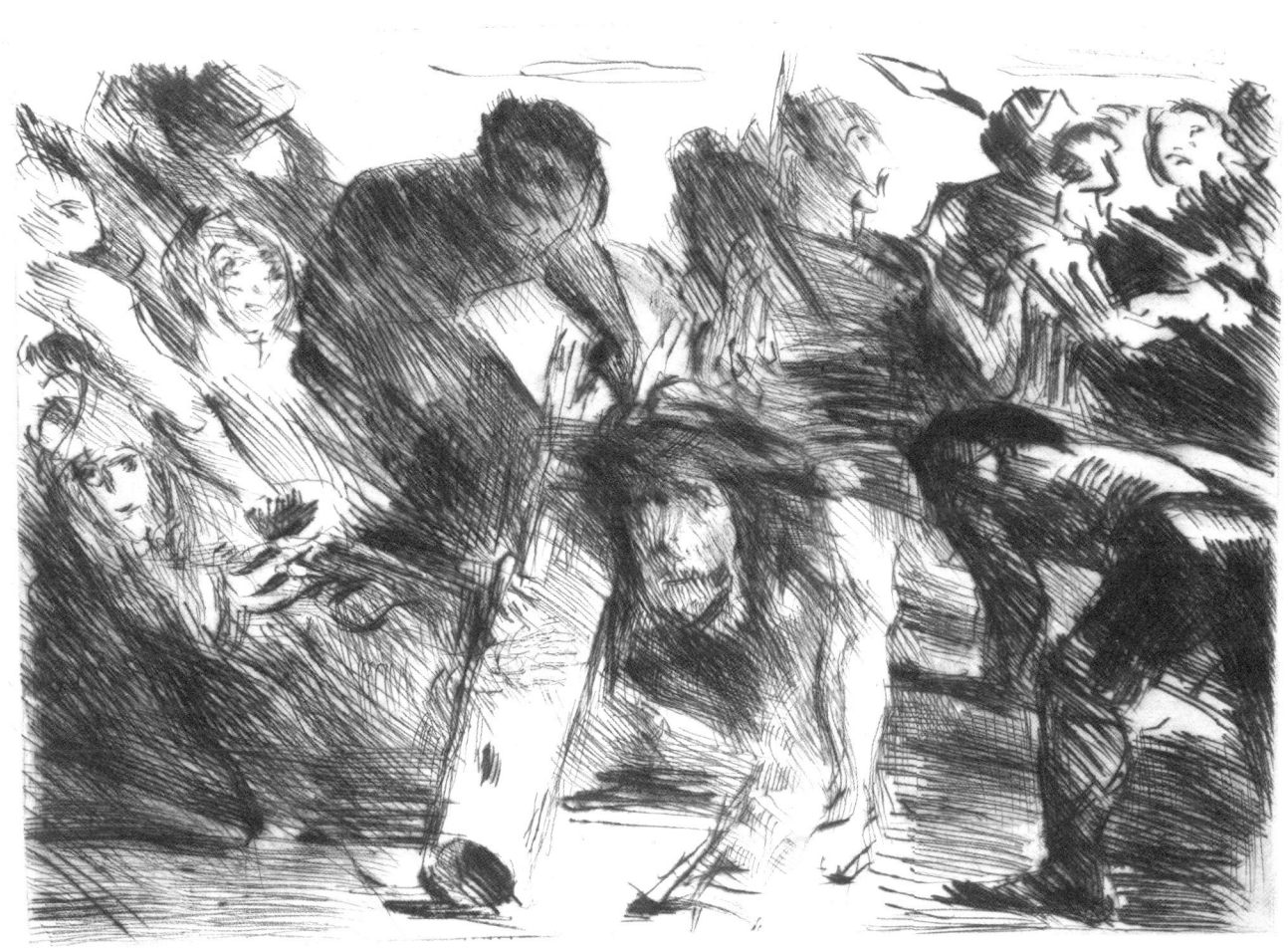

John 19:23–30
THE CRUCIFIXION

When the soldiers had crucified Jesus, they took his garments and divided them into four parts, one part for each soldier; also his tunic. But the tunic was seamless, woven in one piece from top to bottom, so they said to one another, "Let us not tear it, but cast lots for it to see whose it shall be." This was to fulfill the Scripture which says,

> "They divided my garments among them,
> and for my clothing they cast lots."

So the soldiers did these things, but standing by the cross of Jesus were his mother and his mother's sister, Mary the wife of Clopas, and Mary Magdalene. When Jesus saw his mother and the disciple whom he loved standing nearby, he said to his mother, "Woman, behold, your son!" Then he said to the disciple, "Behold, your mother!" And from that hour the disciple took her to his own home.

After this, Jesus, knowing that all was now finished, said (to fulfill the Scripture), "I thirst." A jar full of sour wine stood there, so they put a sponge full of the sour wine on a hyssop branch and held it to his mouth. When Jesus had received the sour wine, he said, "It is finished," and he bowed his head and gave up his spirit.

The Crucifixion
ERIC GILL | WOODCUT

Eric Gill said that the Crucifixion was "the image of God spent utterly for love." But the Cross is not merely an image, an idea, or a theological distinction. It is a man tortured and humiliated, dying a slow and painful death in front of his mother, his aunt and others who love him. It is a man, filled with love for others, dying for us, as the only solution to our sinful, evil, corruption. It is a sort of spiritual rape as our sins weigh down and violate the one who never committed a sin. He carried that burden as he suffered and died. And yet, in spite of the horror of the Crucifixion, according to St. John Chrysostom the Cross is also "the will of the Father, the glory of the only-begotten, the joy of the Holy Spirit, the ornament of angels, the protection of the church, [and] the lamp of all the world."

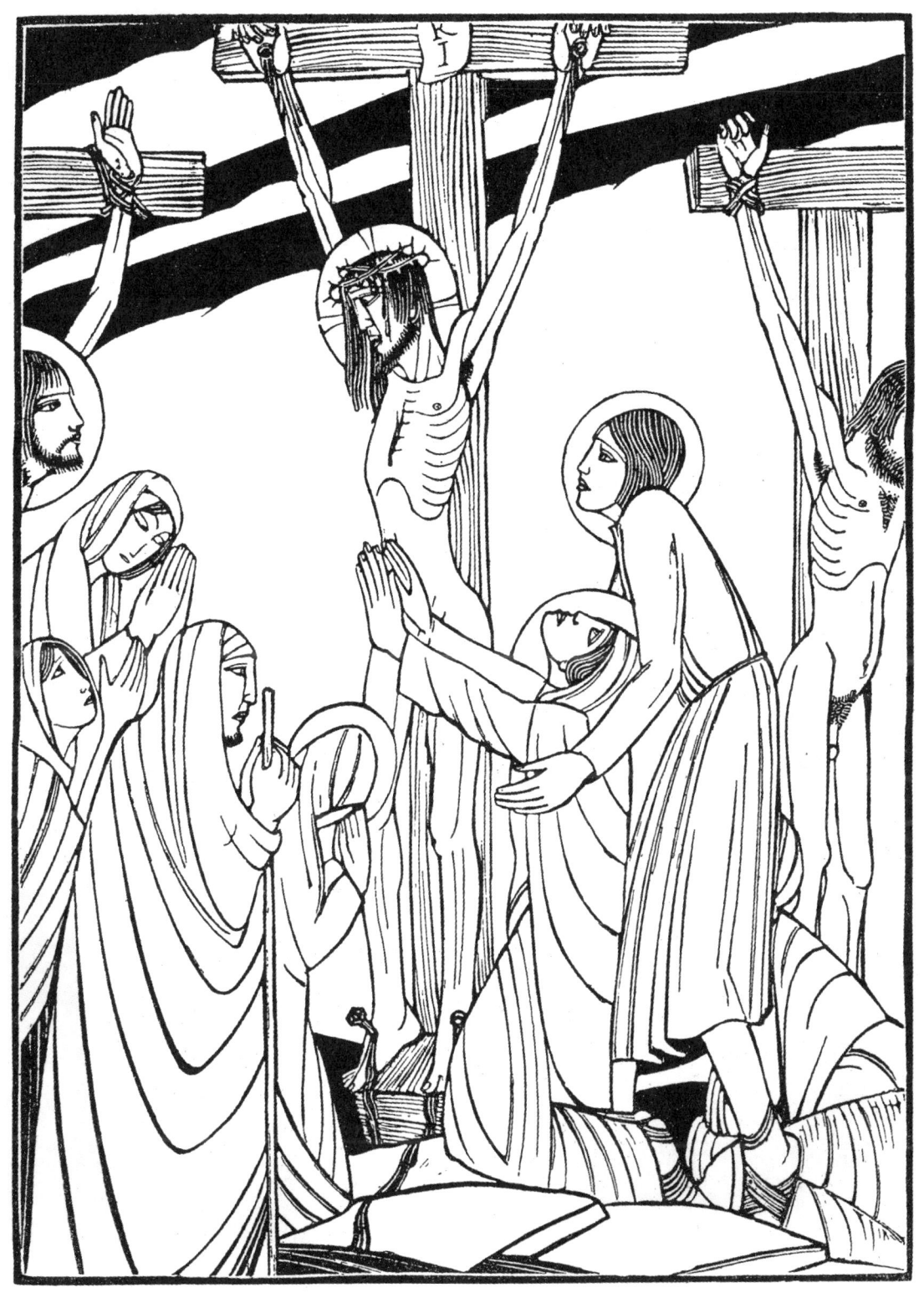

Mark 15:37–47

THE DESCENT FROM THE CROSS

And Jesus uttered a loud cry and breathed his last. And the curtain of the temple was torn in two, from top to bottom. And when the centurion, who stood facing him, saw that in this way he breathed his last, he said, "Truly this man was the Son of God!"

There were also women looking on from a distance, among whom were Mary Magdalene, and Mary the mother of James the younger and of Joses, and Salome. When he was in Galilee, they followed him and ministered to him, and there were also many other women who came up with him to Jerusalem.

And when evening had come, since it was the day of Preparation, that is, the day before the Sabbath, Joseph of Arimathea, a respected member of the council, who was also himself looking for the kingdom of God, took courage and went to Pilate and asked for the body of Jesus. Pilate was surprised to hear that he should have already died. And summoning the centurion, he asked him whether he was already dead. And when he learned from the centurion that he was dead, he granted the corpse to Joseph. And Joseph bought a linen shroud, and taking him down, wrapped him in the linen shroud and laid him in a tomb that had been cut out of the rock. And he rolled a stone against the entrance of the tomb. Mary Magdalene and Mary the mother of Joses saw where he was laid.

Descent from the Cross by Torchlight

REMBRANDT HARMENSZOON VAN RIJN | ETCHING

One single torch illuminates the extinguished Light of the World. Joseph of Arimathea lays out a white shroud as others struggle to remove Christ's broken body from the Cross, while one figure still reaches out towards the Savior. But he is not alone. What at first seems to be a very lonely scene upon further inspection fills with a crowd of onlookers and mourners. All their hope is lost for the present, but joy will come on Sunday morning. "We are told that Christ was killed for us, that his death has washed out our sins, and that by dying he disabled death itself. That is the formula. That is Christianity. That is what has to be believed."—C.S. Lewis

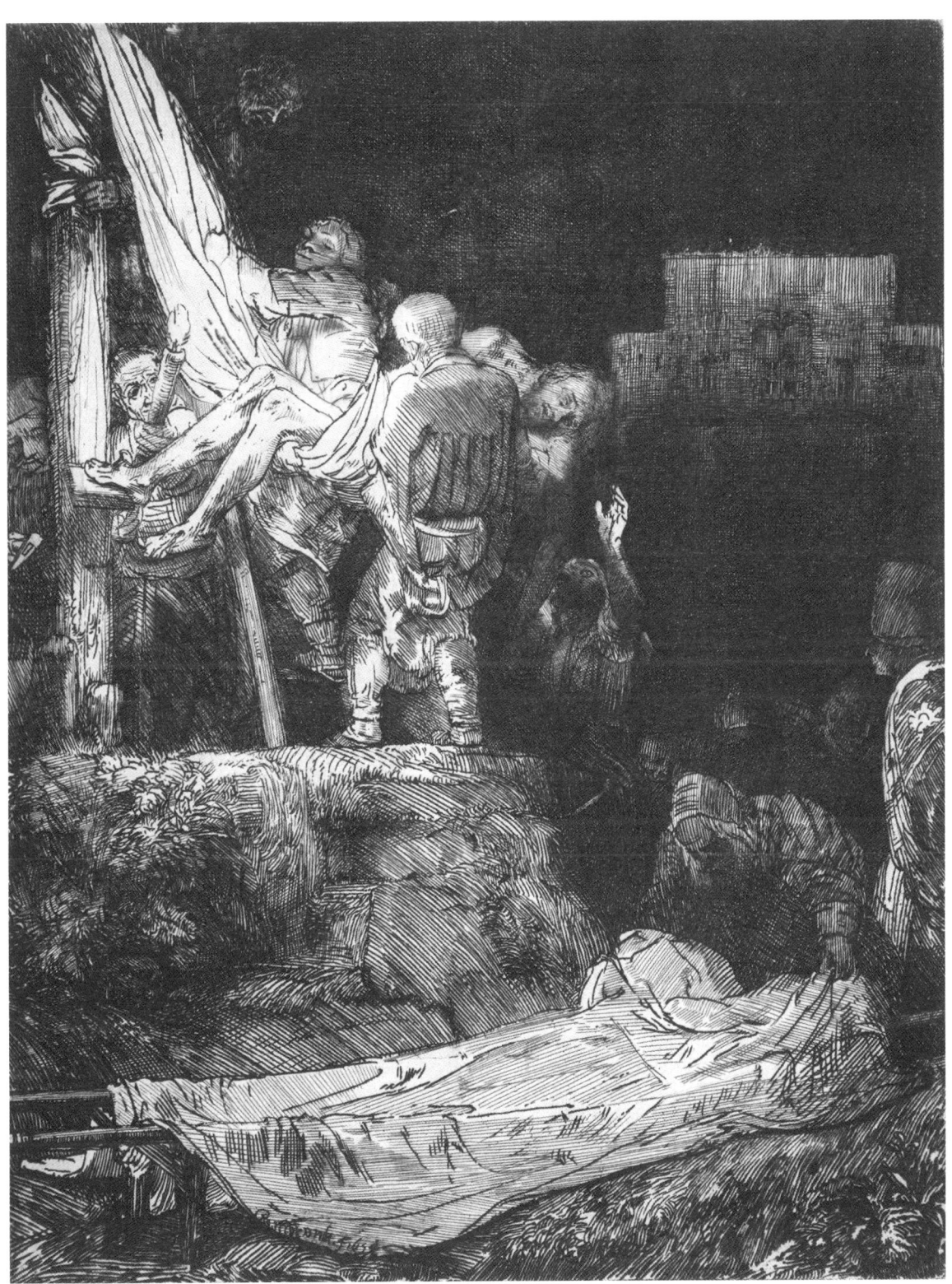

Matthew 27:51–54, 57–66

THE ENTOMBMENT OF CHRIST

And behold, the curtain of the temple was torn in two, from top to bottom. And the earth shook, and the rocks were split. The tombs also were opened. And many bodies of the saints who had fallen asleep were raised, and coming out of the tombs after his resurrection they went into the holy city and appeared to many. When the centurion and those who were with him, keeping watch over Jesus, saw the earthquake and what took place, they were filled with awe and said, "Truly this was the Son of God!"

. . .

When it was evening, there came a rich man from Arimathea, named Joseph, who also was a disciple of Jesus. He went to Pilate and asked for the body of Jesus. Then Pilate ordered it to be given to him. And Joseph took the body and wrapped it in a clean linen shroud and laid it in his own new tomb, which he had cut in the rock. And he rolled a great stone to the entrance of the tomb and went away. Mary Magdalene and the other Mary were there, sitting opposite the tomb.

The next day, that is, after the day of Preparation, the chief priests and the Pharisees gathered before Pilate and said, "Sir, we remember how that impostor said, while he was still alive, 'After three days I will rise.' Therefore order the tomb to be made secure until the third day, lest his disciples go and steal him away and tell the people, 'He has risen from the dead,' and the last fraud will be worse than the first." Pilate said to them, "You have a guard of soldiers. Go, make it as secure as you can." So they went and made the tomb secure by sealing the stone and setting a guard.

Christ Carried to the Tomb

REMBRANDT HARMENSZOON VAN RIJN | ETCHING

In the book *Rembrandt's Faith: Church and Temple in the Dutch Golden Age*, Shelley Perlove observes, "Through this vignette in *Christ Carried*, Rembrandt contrasts the new converts to Christianity, who are bearing Christ's actual body to the tomb, with the Jews of the Old Dispensation [on the hill], who expressly turn their backs on the entire event." The Jews were returning to the familliar comfort and weight of the Law. Sinclair Ferguson reminds Christians of the hope that comes by following Christ into the tomb: "We are adopted into God's family through the resurrection of Christ from the dead in which he paid all our obligations to sin, the law, and the devil, in whose family we once lived. Our old status lies in his tomb. A new status is ours through his resurrection."

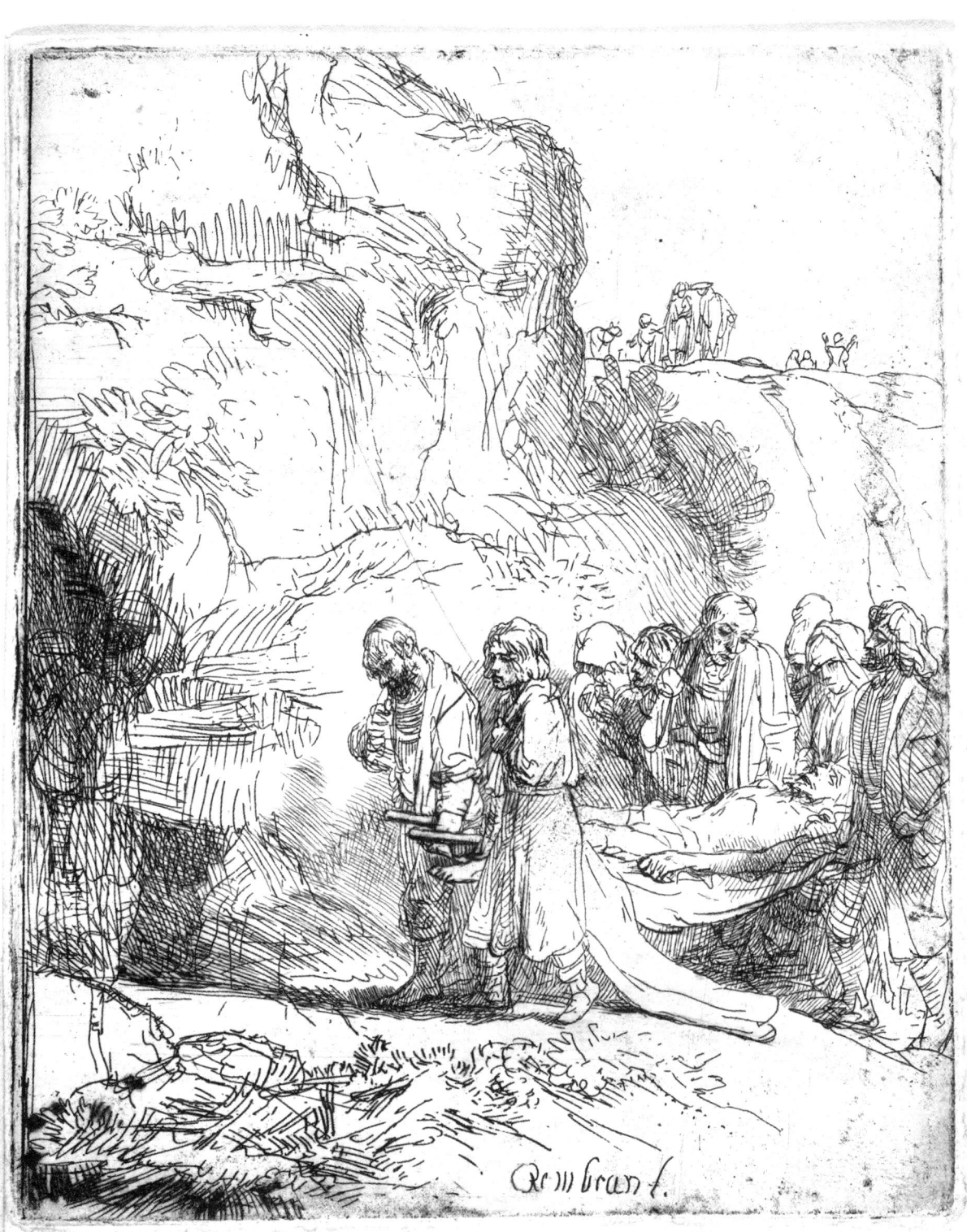

Matthew 28:1–15

THE RESURRECTION OF CHRIST

Now after the Sabbath, toward the dawn of the first day of the week, Mary Magdalene and the other Mary went to see the tomb. And behold, there was a great earthquake, for an angel of the Lord descended from heaven and came and rolled back the stone and sat on it. His appearance was like lightning, and his clothing white as snow. And for fear of him the guards trembled and became like dead men. But the angel said to the women, "Do not be afraid, for I know that you seek Jesus who was crucified. He is not here, for he has risen, as he said. Come, see the place where he lay. Then go quickly and tell his disciples that he has risen from the dead, and behold, he is going before you to Galilee; there you will see him. See, I have told you." So they departed quickly from the tomb with fear and great joy, and ran to tell his disciples. And behold, Jesus met them and said, "Greetings!" And they came up and took hold of his feet and worshiped him. Then Jesus said to them, "Do not be afraid; go and tell my brothers to go to Galilee, and there they will see me."

While they were going, behold, some of the guard went into the city and told the chief priests all that had taken place. And when they had assembled with the elders and taken counsel, they gave a sufficient sum of money to the soldiers and said, "Tell people, 'His disciples came by night and stole him away while we were asleep.' And if this comes to the governor's ears, we will satisfy him and keep you out of trouble." So they took the money and did as they were directed. And this story has been spread among the Jews to this day.

Christ Risen

EDWARD KNIPPERS | LINOCUT

Andrew Murray wrote, "A dead Christ I must do everything for; a living Christ does everything for me." The Jewish religious leaders knew of the importance of the resurrection of the body, so they asked Pilate for the tomb to be sealed and soldiers set guard. Then after the resurrection emptied that tomb, the religious leaders bribed the soldiers: "Tell people, 'His disciples came by night and stole him away while we were asleep.'" But news of the miracle spread throughout the entire world. In this print Knippers' Christ explodes from the grave, the Second Adam conquering Death. The ground shatters, falling away from the body of Jesus, the wounds of his mocking and crucifixion now tracing all over him in power like lightning—marks of sin and shame now glowing and glorified like gold.

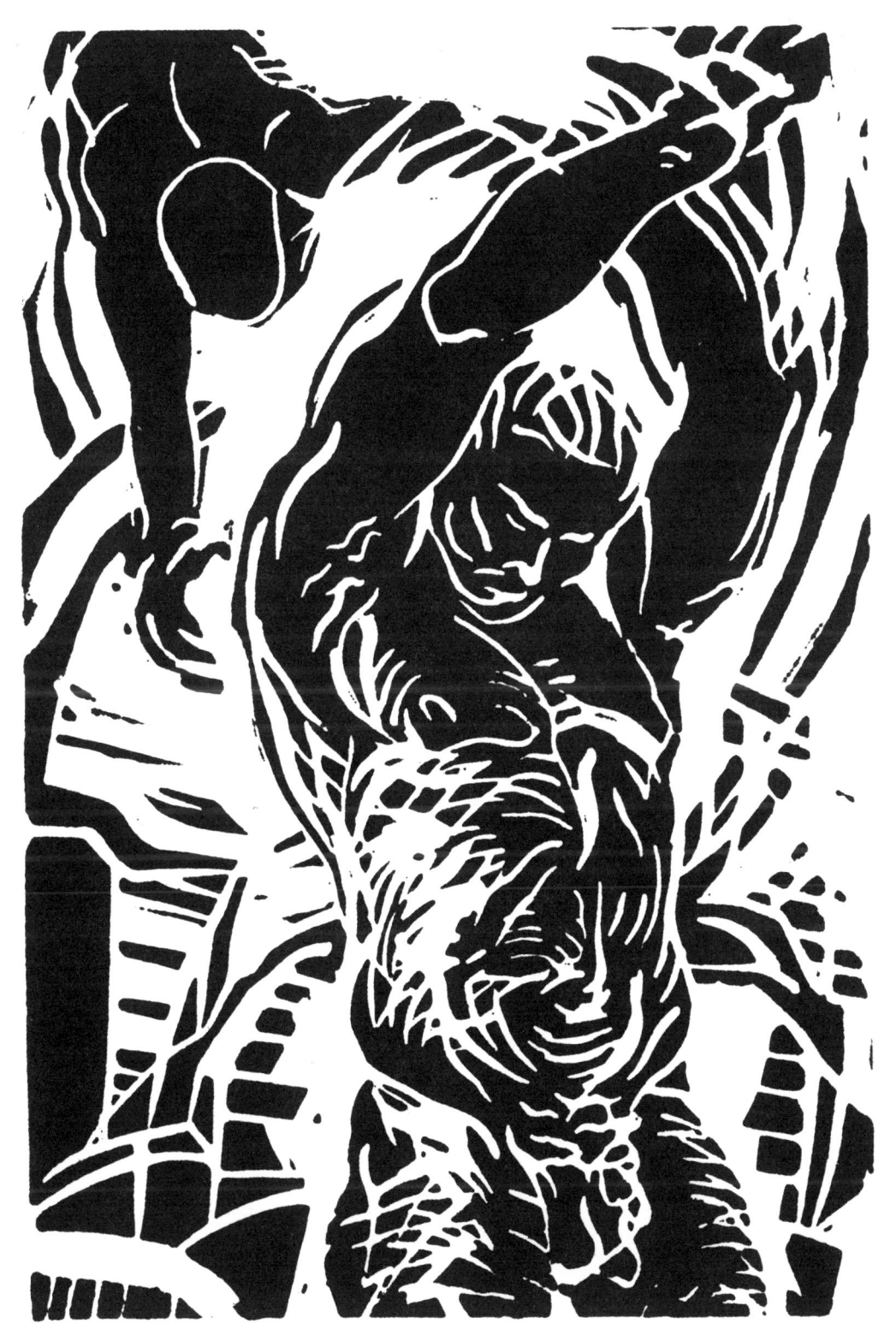

John 20:11–18

JESUS APPEARS TO MARY

But Mary stood weeping outside the tomb, and as she wept she stooped to look into the tomb. And she saw two angels in white, sitting where the body of Jesus had lain, one at the head and one at the feet. They said to her, "Woman, why are you weeping?" She said to them, "They have taken away my Lord, and I do not know where they have laid him." Having said this, she turned around and saw Jesus standing, but she did not know that it was Jesus. Jesus said to her, "Woman, why are you weeping? Whom are you seeking?" Supposing him to be the gardener, she said to him, "Sir, if you have carried him away, tell me where you have laid him, and I will take him away." Jesus said to her, "Mary." She turned and said to him in Aramaic, "Rabboni!" (which means Teacher). Jesus said to her, "Do not cling to me, for I have not yet ascended to the Father; but go to my brothers and say to them, 'I am ascending to my Father and your Father, to my God and your God.'" Mary Magdalene went and announced to the disciples, "I have seen the Lord"—and that he had said these things to her.

Second Eve

NED BUSTARD | LINOCUT

The original title for this piece was going to be *Noli Me Tangere*, which in Latin means "touch me not." In the Greek it is better translated as "stop clinging to me." The title has been used for countless works of art from late antiquity to the present. In this print (inspired by Matisse's linocuts) the garden scene is shown through the eyes of Jesus. The rock is rolled away from the tomb and Mary—a second Eve—extends her hand toward the second Adam. It is interesting that the emphasis of Jesus' message to Mary is that he is going to ascend. The ascension is a gift to believers. By itself, the Cross is sufficient to forgive sins. But without the resurrection and ascension who would know what the Cross accomplished? The disciples could point to the resurrected Lord who ascended as one who overcame sin and death.

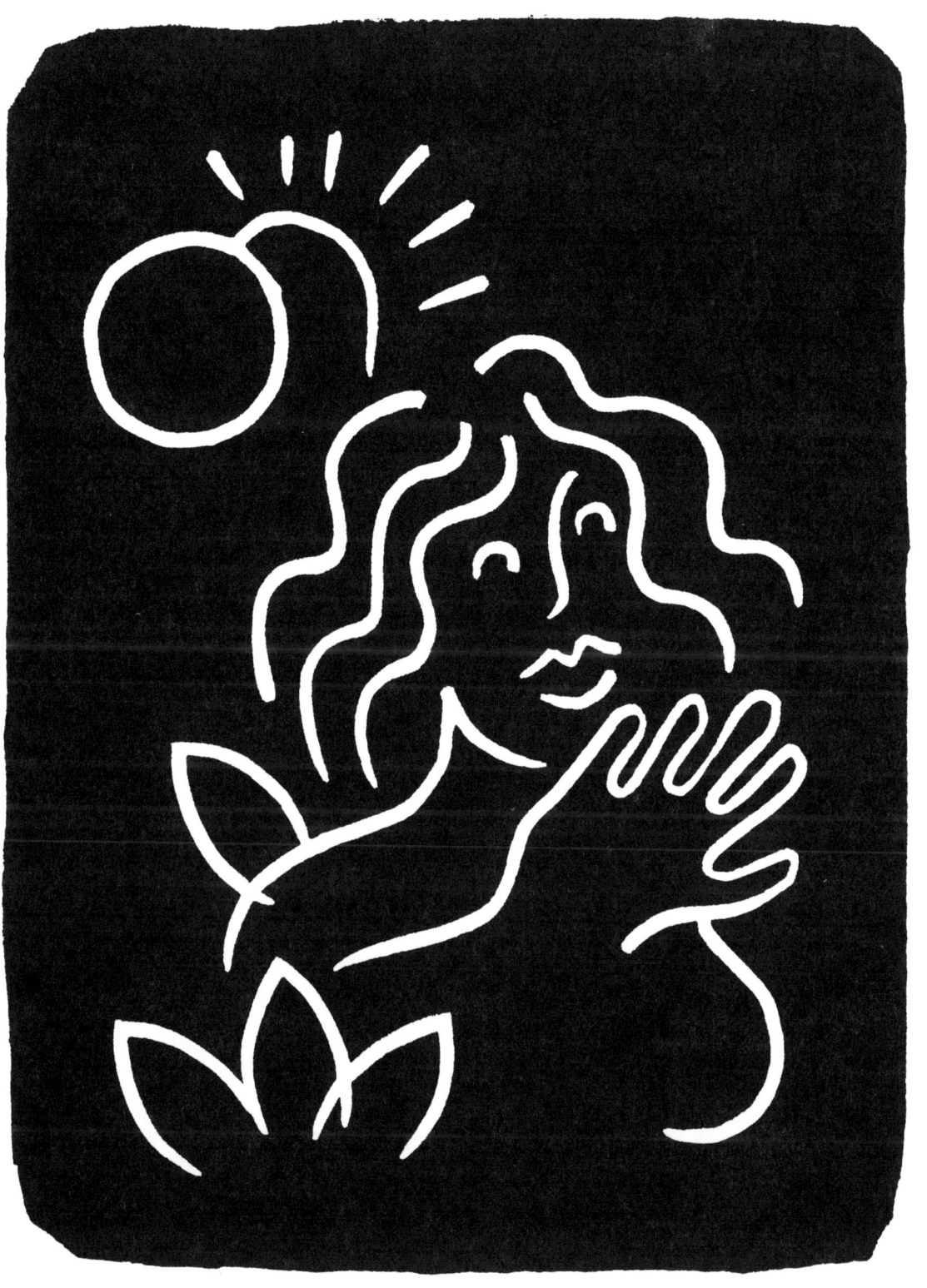

Luke 24:13–16, 25–32

ROAD TO EMMAUS

That very day two of them were going to a village named Emmaus, about seven miles from Jerusalem, and they were talking with each other about all these things that had happened. While they were talking and discussing together, Jesus himself drew near and went with them. But their eyes were kept from recognizing him.

And he said to them, "O foolish ones, and slow of heart to believe all that the prophets have spoken! Was it not necessary that the Christ should suffer these things and enter into his glory?" And beginning with Moses and all the Prophets, he interpreted to them in all the Scriptures the things concerning himself.

So they drew near to the village to which they were going. He acted as if he were going farther, but they urged him strongly, saying, "Stay with us, for it is toward evening and the day is now far spent." So he went in to stay with them. When he was at table with them, he took the bread and blessed and broke it and gave it to them. And their eyes were opened, and they recognized him. And he vanished from their sight. They said to each other, "Did not our hearts burn within us while he talked to us on the road, while he opened to us the Scriptures?"

Shroud 2

WAYNE ADAMS | SILKSCREEN

Blinded by their grief and loss, Cleopas and his companion were veiled from seeing Christ as they walked towards Emmaus. But as they journeyed together Jesus lifted one veil so they could see him in the Old Testament. Then He broke bread with them and the final veil was lifted. Another famous veil connected with Christ is the Shroud of Turin. It was once believed to hold a mysterious impression of the face of Jesus, a reflection burned into the cloth. The idea of the Shroud being a copy of the original that was not *actually* accurate appealed to the artist. Adams writes, "I like the image because of its supposed authority as a proof of Jesus—both his existence and what he looked like. This plays with a thread of my work that focuses on what we believe and how we conceive of Jesus." Is seeing believing or believing seeing?

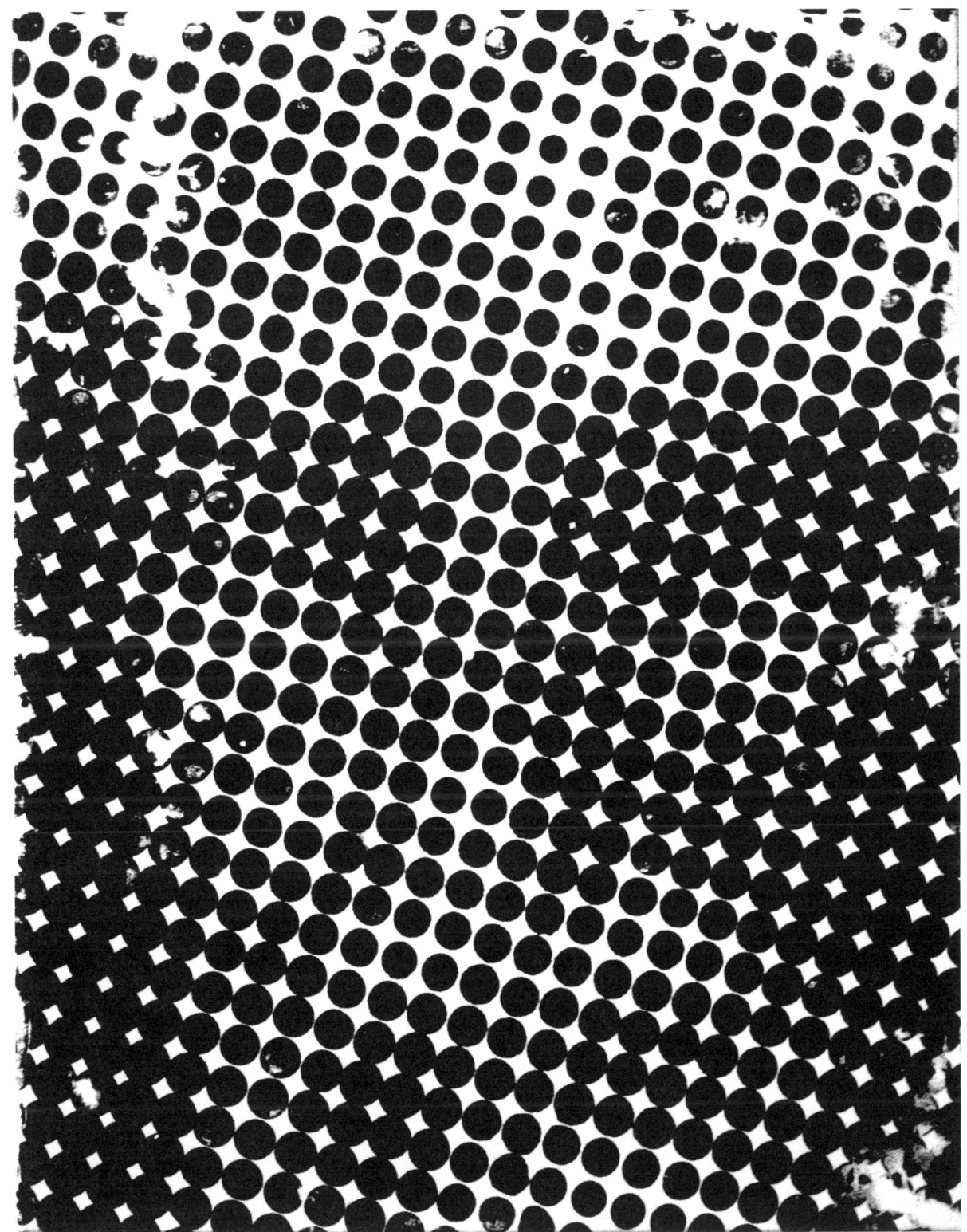

John 20:24–29

THOMAS BELIEVES

Now Thomas, one of the Twelve, called the Twin, was not with them when Jesus came. So the other disciples told him, "We have seen the Lord." But he said to them, "Unless I see in his hands the mark of the nails, and place my finger into the mark of the nails, and place my hand into his side, I will never believe."

Eight days later, his disciples were inside again, and Thomas was with them. Although the doors were locked, Jesus came and stood among them and said, "Peace be with you." Then he said to Thomas, "Put your finger here, and see my hands; and put out your hand, and place it in my side. Do not disbelieve, but believe." Thomas answered him, "My Lord and my God!" Jesus said to him, "Have you believed because you have seen me? Blessed are those who have not seen and yet have believed."

Doubting Thomas (Small Passion)

ALBRECHT DÜRER | WOODCUT

C.S. Lewis wrote, "When you are asked for trust you may give it or withhold it; it is senseless to say that you will trust if you are given demonstrative certainty. There would be no room for trust if demonstration were given. When demonstration is given what will be left will be simply the sort of relation which results from having trusted, or not having trusted, before it was given." The Bible does not act as though there is no reason to be sceptical. Incredible things are claimed here and the text shows that even insiders doubted. But Jesus encourages those who question by not condemning or rejecting Thomas. Rather, he gives Thomas the absolute evidence he demanded. This shows the weak in faith can ask good questions of the biblical text, examine the historical record, and have hope in the answers they get.

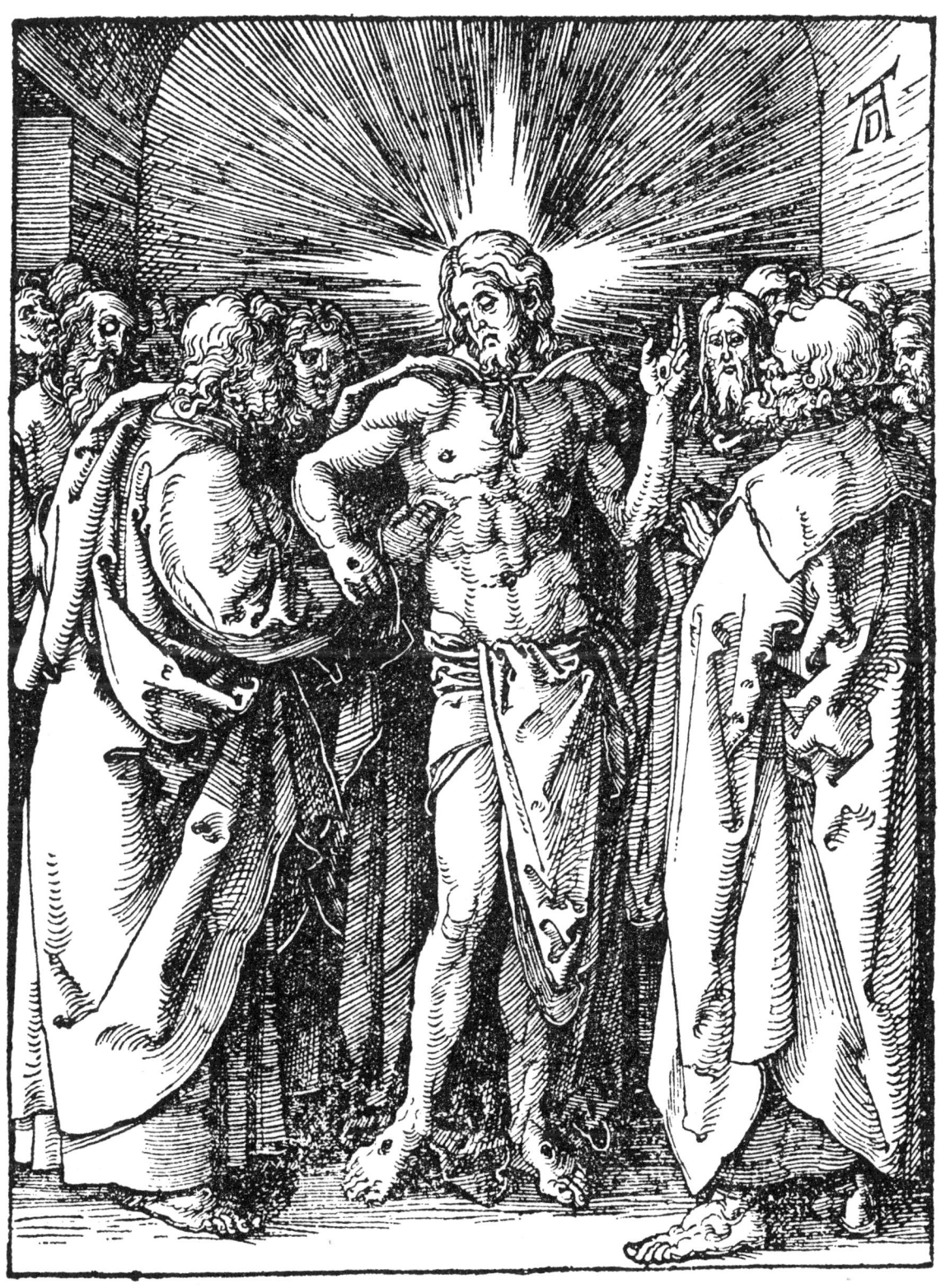

John 21:9–19

THE RESTORATION OF PETER

When they got out on land, they saw a charcoal fire in place, with fish laid out on it, and bread. Jesus said to them, "Bring some of the fish that you have just caught." So Simon Peter went aboard and hauled the net ashore, full of large fish, 153 of them. And although there were so many, the net was not torn. Jesus said to them, "Come and have breakfast." Now none of the disciples dared ask him, "Who are you?" They knew it was the Lord. Jesus came and took the bread and gave it to them, and so with the fish. This was now the third time that Jesus was revealed to the disciples after he was raised from the dead.

When they had finished breakfast, Jesus said to Simon Peter, "Simon, son of John, do you love me more than these?" He said to him, "Yes, Lord; you know that I love you." He said to him, "Feed my lambs." He said to him a second time, "Simon, son of John, do you love me?" He said to him, "Yes, Lord; you know that I love you." He said to him, "Tend my sheep." He said to him the third time, "Simon, son of John, do you love me?" Peter was grieved because he said to him the third time, "Do you love me?" and he said to him, "Lord, you know everything; you know that I love you." Jesus said to him, "Feed my sheep. Truly, truly, I say to you, when you were young, you used to dress yourself and walk wherever you wanted, but when you are old, you will stretch out your hands, and another will dress you and carry you where you do not want to go." (This he said to show by what kind of death he was to glorify God.) And after saying this he said to him, "Follow me."

Peter, Do You Love Me?
STEVE HALLA | WOODCUT

In this print the artist focused on the phrase "feed my sheep." Two hands are shown making a gesture of the church as in the children's rhyme "Here is the church, Here is the steeple, Open the doors . . ." The gesture serves a symbol of the childlike faith needed to follow Jesus' call, while the hands themselves are a reminder that the church is ultimately the people of God and that feeding sheep is hard, dirty work that requires humility and self-sacrifice. The wedding ring on the left hand is an allusion to the church as the bride of Christ, while the three ropes allude to the Roman Catholic, Orthodox, and Protestant traditions. The three ropes wrapped tightly around the wrists also serve as a symbol of the church's history of suffering persecution and martyrdom as the church follows Jesus' call to feed his sheep regardless of the cost.

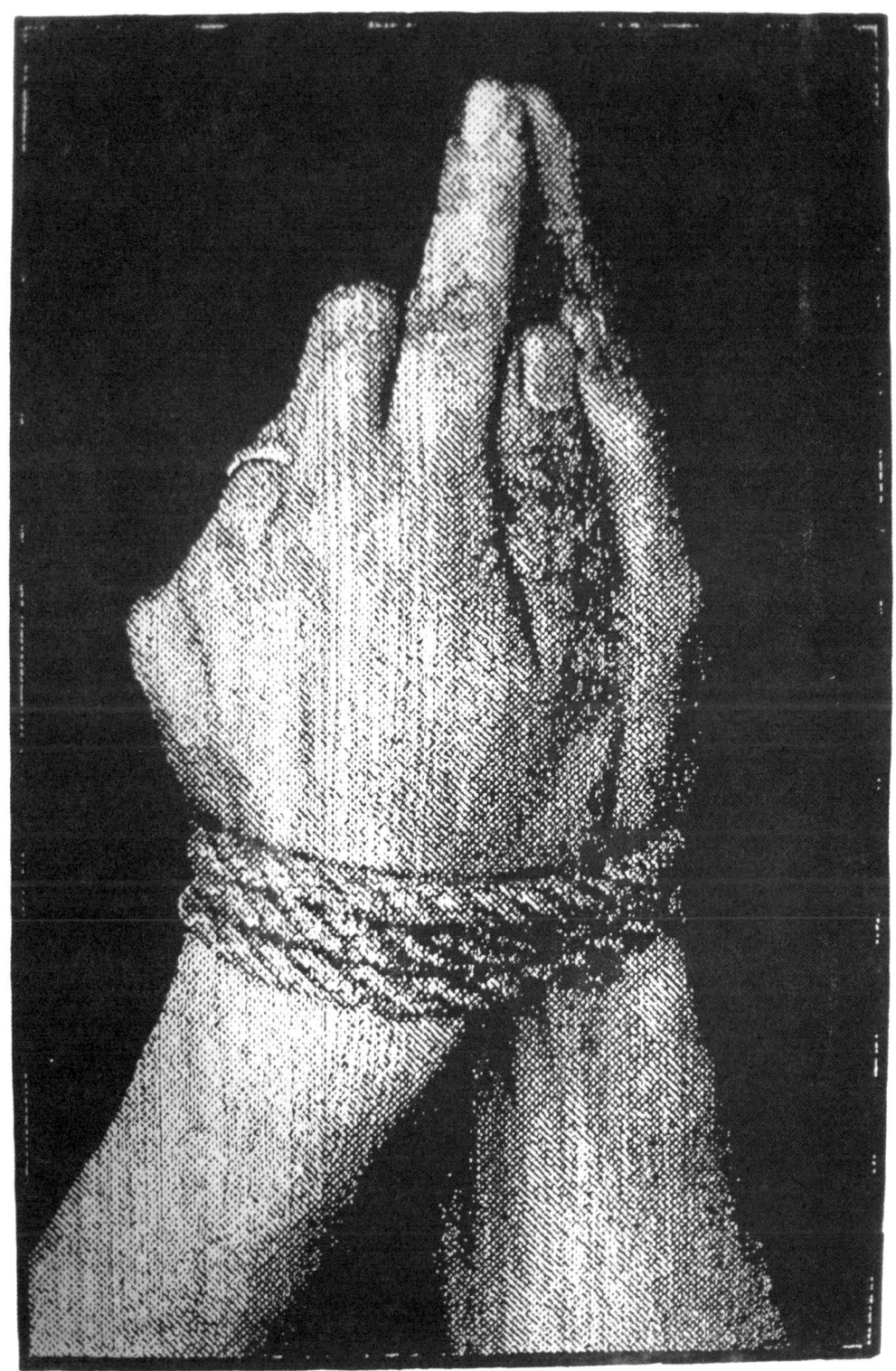

Acts 1:6–18

THE ASCENSION OF CHRIST

So when they had come together, they asked him, "Lord, will you at this time restore the kingdom to Israel?" He said to them, "It is not for you to know times or seasons that the Father has fixed by his own authority. But you will receive power when the Holy Spirit has come upon you, and you will be my witnesses in Jerusalem and in all Judea and Samaria, and to the end of the earth." And when he had said these things, as they were looking on, he was lifted up, and a cloud took him out of their sight. And while they were gazing into heaven as he went, behold, two men stood by them in white robes, and said, "Men of Galilee, why do you stand looking into heaven? This Jesus, who was taken up from you into heaven, will come in the same way as you saw him go into heaven."

Then they returned to Jerusalem from the mount called Olivet, which is near Jerusalem, a Sabbath day's journey away. And when they had entered, they went up to the upper room, where they were staying, Peter and John and James and Andrew, Philip and Thomas, Bartholomew and Matthew, James the son of Alphaeus and Simon the Zealot and Judas the son of James. All these with one accord were devoting themselves to prayer, together with the women and Mary the mother of Jesus, and his brothers.

Ascension (after "It Is Well with My Soul")
WAYNE FORTE | LINOCUT

The angels told the disciples that Jesus would return as they saw him go. This print about the departure of Christ alludes to his return: the dove descending from heaven (as he did at the baptism of Christ), the angels blowing trumpets of judgment, and "the clouds be rolled back as a scroll," as it says in the old hymn (referencing Revelation 6:14). Jesus spoke of the preparation required for the coming of the kingdom of heaven. In this text what is interesting is that Jesus does not answer the question regarding the timing of his actions. Instead, he promises something better—they will receive the Holy Spirit who will equip them to be witnesses and energize them to take the good news of Christ to the end of the world.

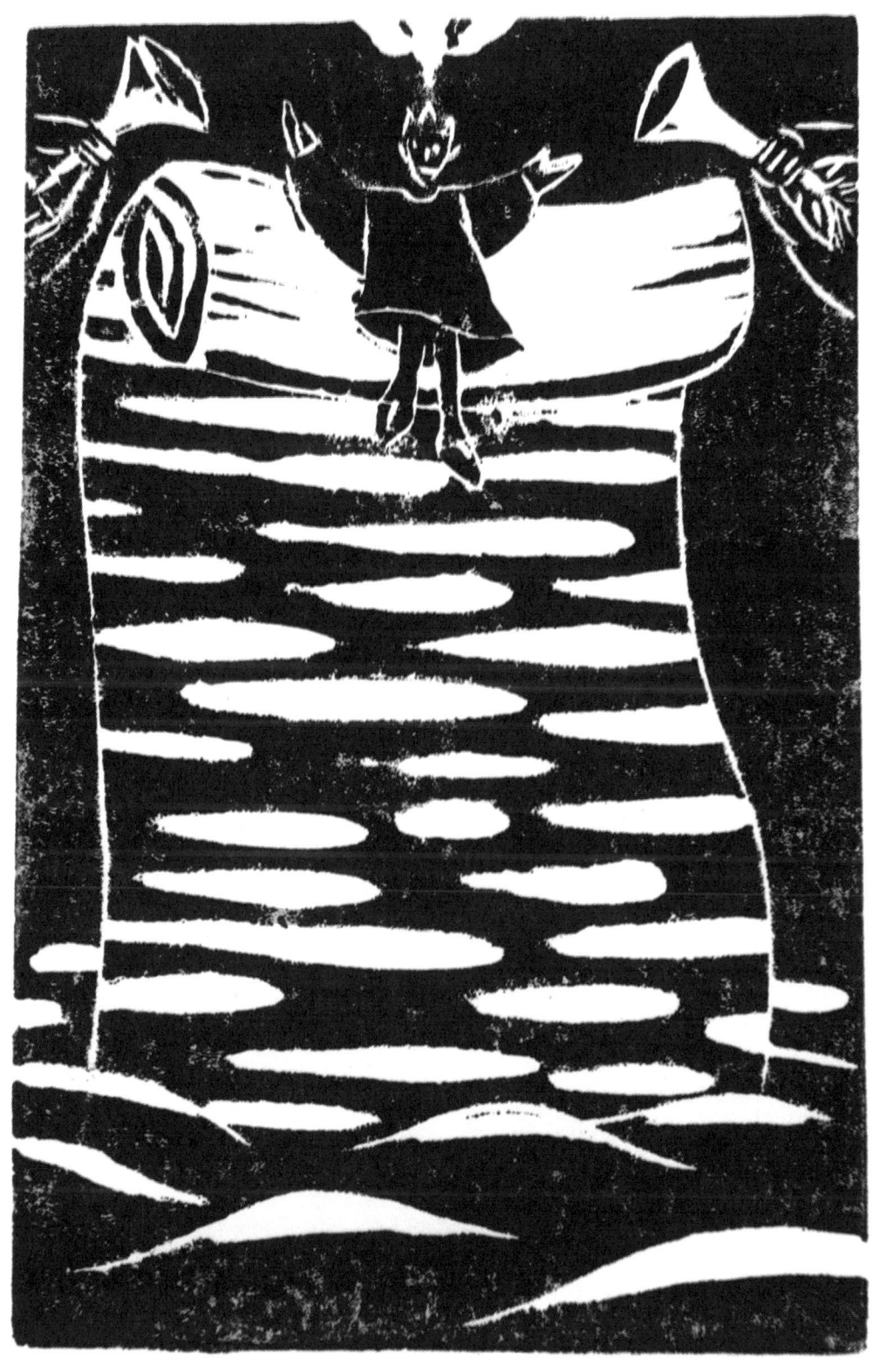

Acts 2:1–12

PENTECOST

When the day of Pentecost arrived, they were all together in one place. And suddenly there came from heaven a sound like a mighty rushing wind, and it filled the entire house where they were sitting. And divided tongues as of fire appeared to them and rested on each one of them. And they were all filled with the Holy Spirit and began to speak in other tongues as the Spirit gave them utterance.

Now there were dwelling in Jerusalem Jews, devout men from every nation under heaven. And at this sound the multitude came together, and they were bewildered, because each one was hearing them speak in his own language. And they were amazed and astonished, saying, "Are not all these who are speaking Galileans? And how is it that we hear, each of us in his own native language? Parthians and Medes and Elamites and residents of Mesopotamia, Judea and Cappadocia, Pontus and Asia, Phrygia and Pamphylia, Egypt and the parts of Libya belonging to Cyrene, and visitors from Rome, both Jews and proselytes, Cretans and Arabians—we hear them telling in our own tongues the mighty works of God." And all were amazed and perplexed, saying to one another, "What does this mean?"

Communion/Pentecost

CHRIS STOFFEL OVERVOORDE | WOODCUT

Gregg Strawbridge writes, "The Great Table is about joy and not mourning. It is about feasting and not fasting. It is about a completed sacrifice and not a re-sacrifice. It is about a completed work and not working our way to the Table. It is about grace and not about merit. We come to a Table and we cannot buy or earn the bread or the wine." The disciples of Christ are gathered together in an upper room just before Pentecost. There is expectation and fear in the various expressions around the table. The Spirit was promised by Jesus when he ascended, but for now they must simply wait and hope. They are in communion with each other and sharing in the Eucharist. The interplay of light and dark created by their bodies close together forms the shape of the Cross, symbolizing that together they are the body of Christ.

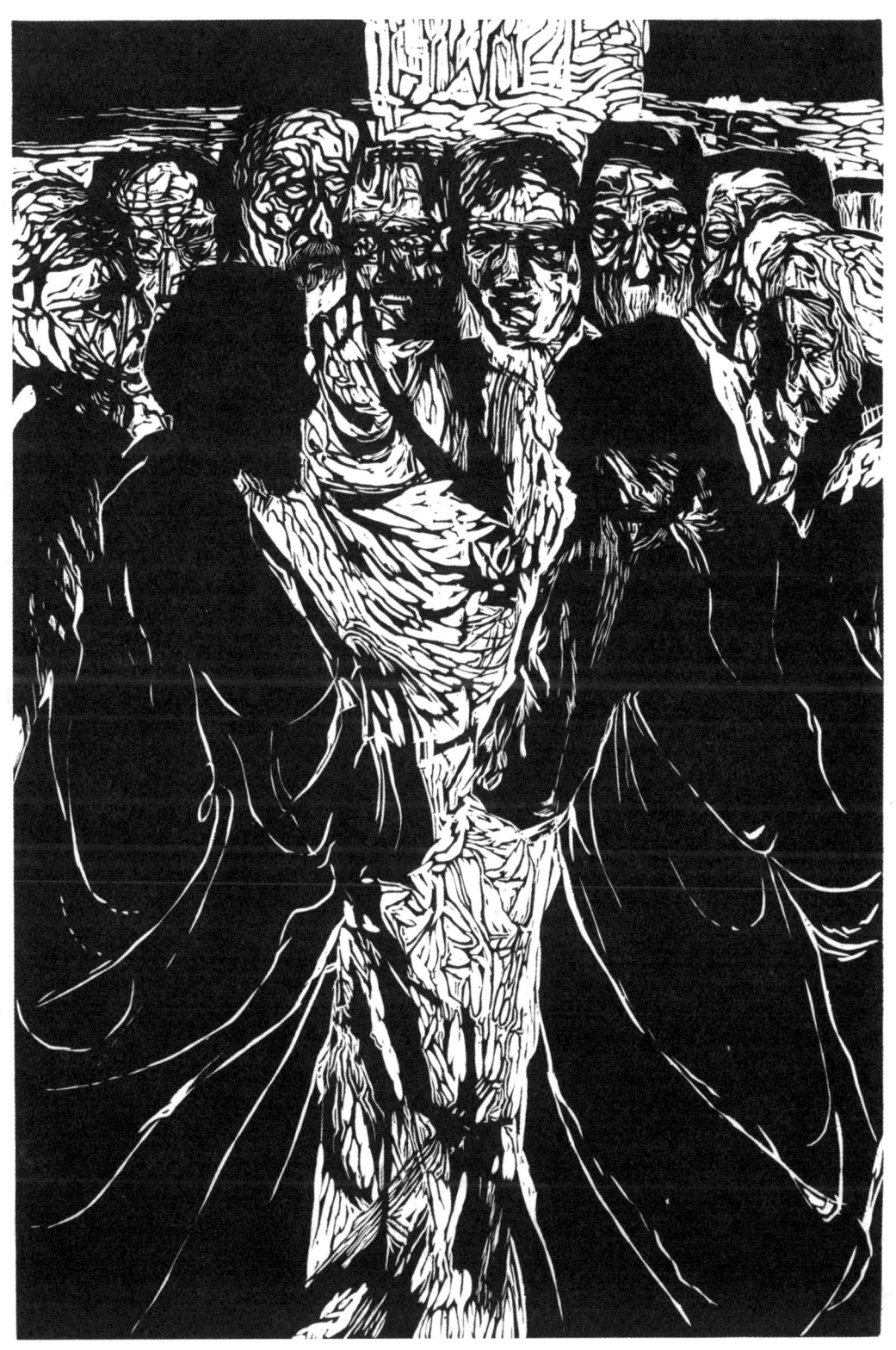

Acts 2:29–39

PETER'S SERMON

"Brothers, I may say to you with confidence about the patriarch David that he both died and was buried, and his tomb is with us to this day. Being therefore a prophet, and knowing that God had sworn with an oath to him that he would set one of his descendants on his throne, he foresaw and spoke about the resurrection of the Christ, that he was not abandoned to Hades, nor did his flesh see corruption. This Jesus God raised up, and of that we all are witnesses. Being therefore exalted at the right hand of God, and having received from the Father the promise of the Holy Spirit, he has poured out this that you yourselves are seeing and hearing. For David did not ascend into the heavens, but he himself says,

"'The Lord said to my Lord,
"Sit at my right hand,
until I make your enemies your footstool."'

Let all the house of Israel therefore know for certain that God has made him both Lord and Christ, this Jesus whom you crucified."

Now when they heard this they were cut to the heart, and said to Peter and the rest of the apostles, "Brothers, what shall we do?" And Peter said to them, "Repent and be baptized every one of you in the name of Jesus Christ for the forgiveness of your sins, and you will receive the gift of the Holy Spirit. For the promise is for you and for your children and for all who are far off, everyone whom the Lord our God calls to himself."

We Got Spirit, Yes We Do . . .

RYAN STANDER | LITHOGRAPH

On the first Sunday of Pentecost there were no red liturgical vestments to alert the worshipers to the season. Instead, they had Peter, loudly preaching and making people think he was drunk—at nine in the morning! But rather than being filled with beer, he was filled with the Holy Spirit. In tongues like flame the Spirit had descended upon the disciples with the sound of a rushing wind. In his sermon, Peter called for people to turn from their sin and be baptized. The inverted hearts in this piece represent repentance, and the shell is a historical sign for baptism (a shell was used to pour the water over the baptismal candidates). The genealogy diagram at the bottom is a reference to the promise that, like the sign of the covenant in the Old Testament, this new sign of the covenant was both for Peter's listeners and their children.

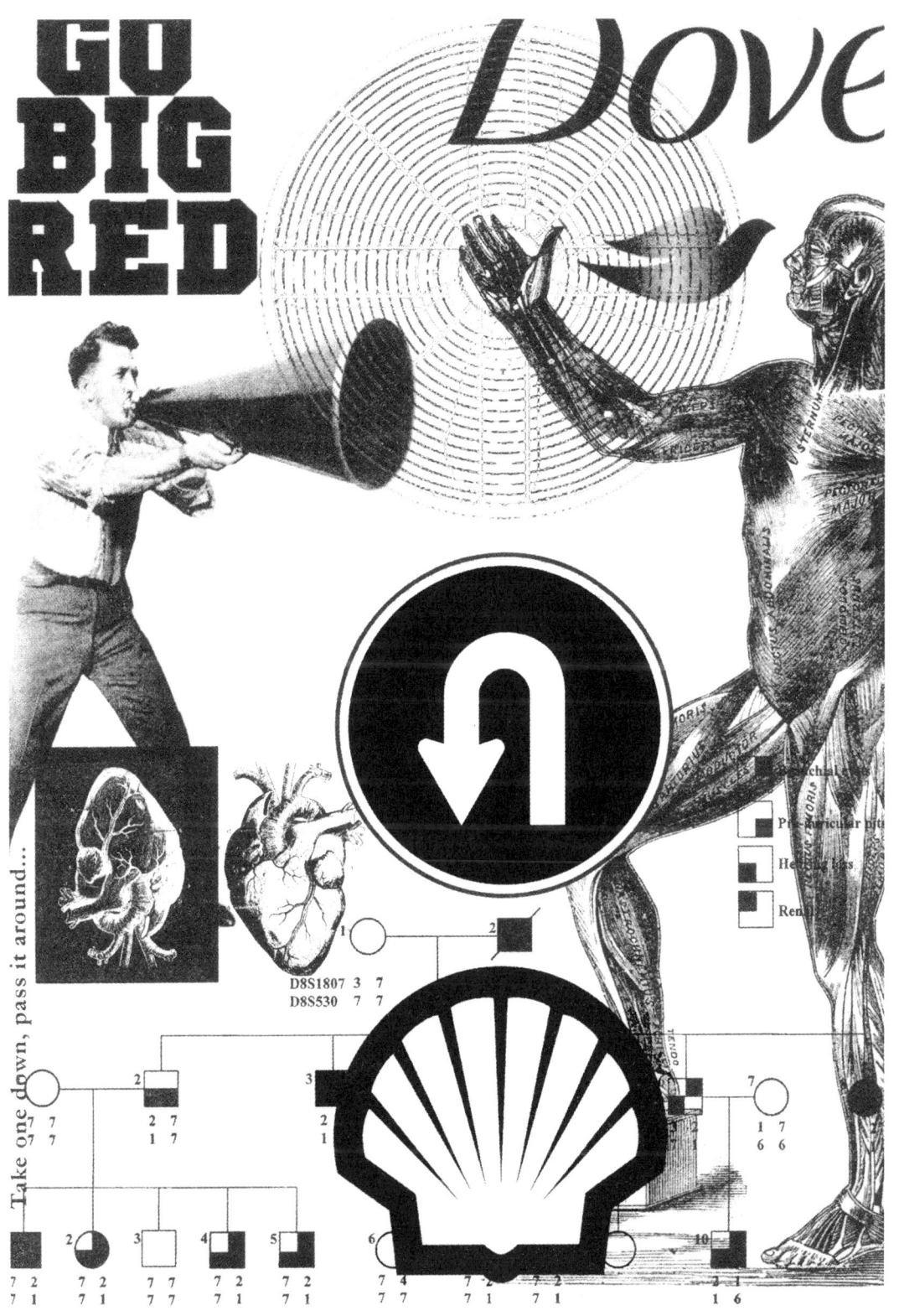

Acts 5:1–11

ANANIAS AND SAPPHIRA

But a man named Ananias, with his wife Sapphira, sold a piece of property, and with his wife's knowledge he kept back for himself some of the proceeds and brought only a part of it and laid it at the apostles' feet. But Peter said, "Ananias, why has Satan filled your heart to lie to the Holy Spirit and to keep back for yourself part of the proceeds of the land? While it remained unsold, did it not remain your own? And after it was sold, was it not at your disposal? Why is it that you have contrived this deed in your heart? You have not lied to man but to God." When Ananias heard these words, he fell down and breathed his last. And great fear came upon all who heard of it. The young men rose and wrapped him up and carried him out and buried him.

After an interval of about three hours his wife came in, not knowing what had happened. And Peter said to her, "Tell me whether you sold the land for so much." And she said, "Yes, for so much." But Peter said to her, "How is it that you have agreed together to test the Spirit of the Lord? Behold, the feet of those who have buried your husband are at the door, and they will carry you out." Immediately she fell down at his feet and breathed her last. When the young men came in they found her dead, and they carried her out and buried her beside her husband. And great fear came upon the whole church and upon all who heard of these things.

Ananias and Sapphira

MICAH BLOOM | LITHOGRAPH

As in Joshua 7 when Achan stole and lied, the guilty parties in this account also had to be immediately disciplined for the good of God's people and the growth of the Kingdom. "The nearer we come to God the more truly shall we find that he is a jealous God who will not wink at sin. It was not Peter's word, but the judgement of God, which slew Ananias," wrote C.H. Spurgeon about this first act of divine church discipline. "[Sapphira] had time for reflection, yet she stuck to the falsehood. It is a sad thing when husband and wife go hand in hand to hell, and most of all so when they make a profession of religion . . . The chaff was driven out, and kept out, but the true saints were all the more ready to join the church. Holy discipline does not diminish the church, it is the sure means of increasing it with the right people."

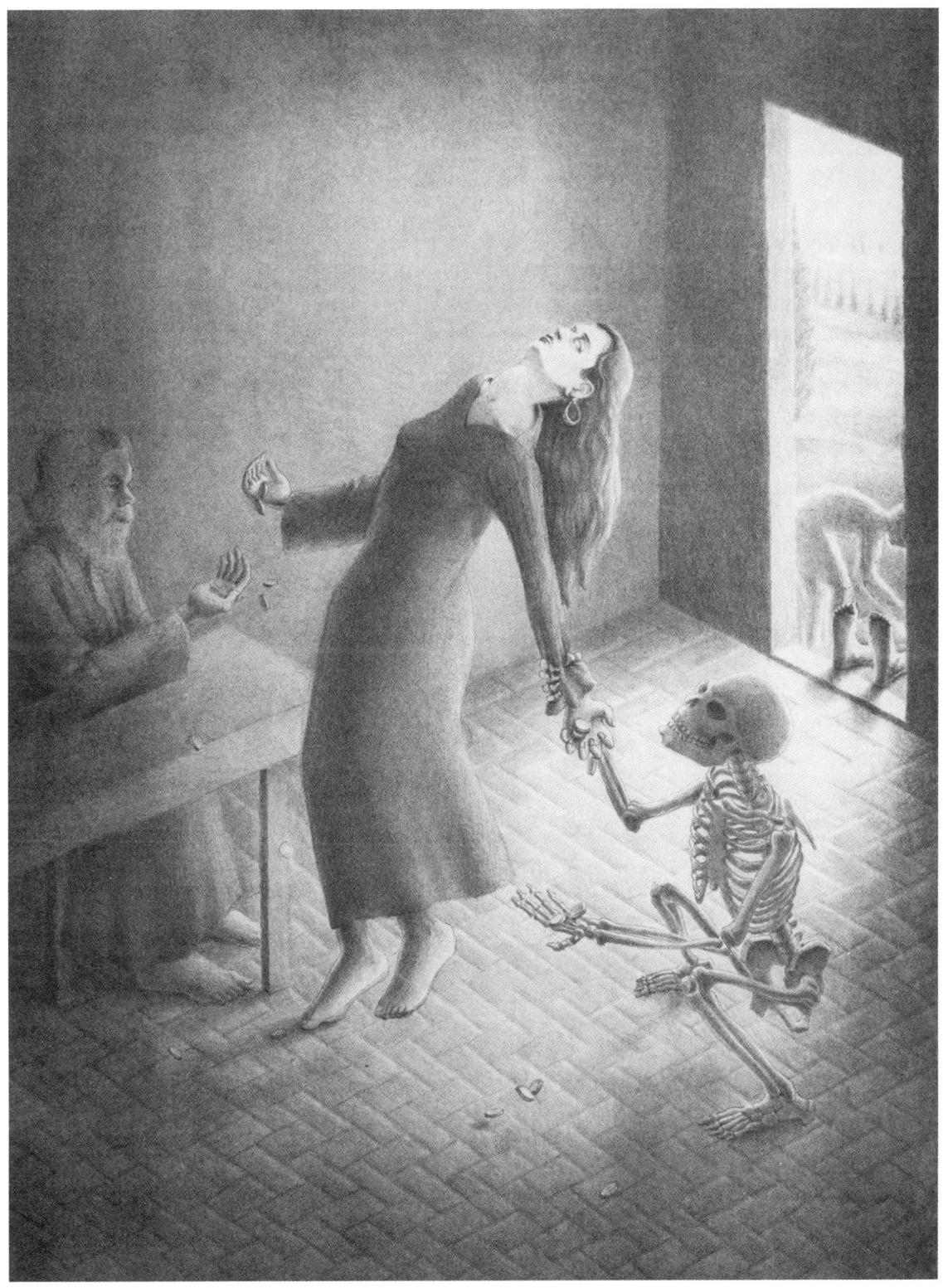

Acts 7:54–8:3
THE CHURCH'S FIRST MARTYR

Now when they heard these things they were enraged, and they ground their teeth at him. But he, full of the Holy Spirit, gazed into heaven and saw the glory of God, and Jesus standing at the right hand of God. And he said, "Behold, I see the heavens opened, and the Son of Man standing at the right hand of God." But they cried out with a loud voice and stopped their ears and rushed together at him. Then they cast him out of the city and stoned him. And the witnesses laid down their garments at the feet of a young man named Saul. And as they were stoning Stephen, he called out, "Lord Jesus, receive my spirit." And falling to his knees he cried out with a loud voice, "Lord, do not hold this sin against them." And when he had said this, he fell asleep.

And Saul approved of his execution.

And there arose on that day a great persecution against the church in Jerusalem, and they were all scattered throughout the regions of Judea and Samaria, except the apostles. Devout men buried Stephen and made great lamentation over him. But Saul was ravaging the church, and entering house after house, he dragged off men and women and committed them to prison.

Stoning of Stephen (Peril)
EDWARD KNIPPERS | WOODCUT

This piece comes from a portfolio of prints which includes both the image of Lot and Jacob from earlier in this book. It is interesting to compare this composition to that of *Jacob's Ladder*. Both have similar prone figures and use cubist elements to represent another realm of existence. Here the physical world and the spiritual world are crashing together, and Stephen can see them both at once. To some extent Stephen shows us a glimpse of heaven where Jesus stands at the right hand of God. The passage records that Saul approved of this execution and participated in great persecution against the church. Later Saul would meet Christ and be converted. His name was changed to Paul and he went on to evangelize throughout most of the Mediterranean region, as well as write most of the New Testament.

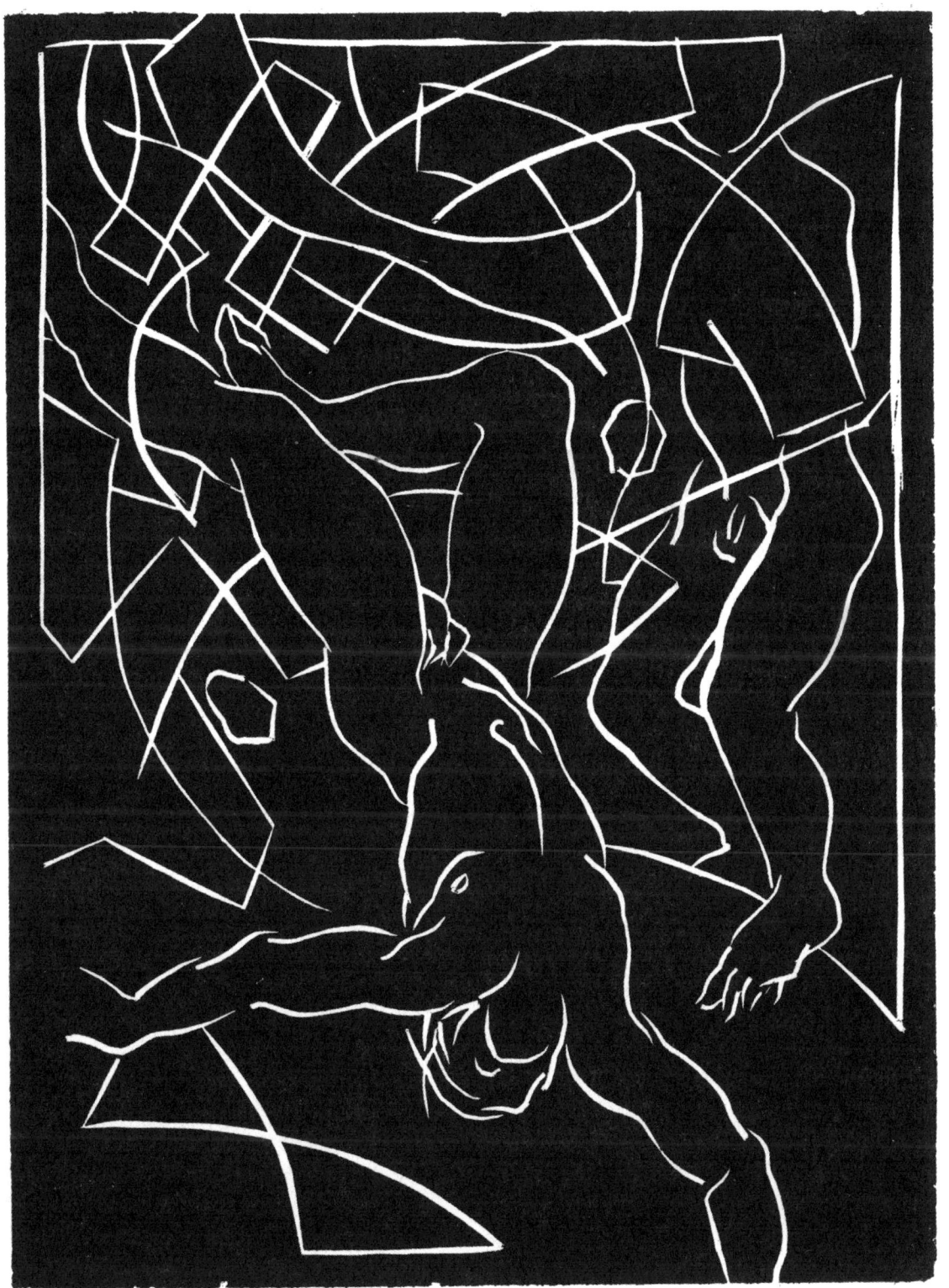

Romans 6:3–13

DEAD TO SIN, ALIVE TO GOD

Do you not know that all of us who have been baptized into Christ Jesus were baptized into his death? We were buried therefore with him by baptism into death, in order that, just as Christ was raised from the dead by the glory of the Father, we too might walk in newness of life. For if we have been united with him in a death like his, we shall certainly be united with him in a resurrection like his. We know that our old self was crucified with him in order that the body of sin might be brought to nothing, so that we would no longer be enslaved to sin. For one who has died has been set free from sin. Now if we have died with Christ, we believe that we will also live with him. We know that Christ, being raised from the dead, will never die again; death no longer has dominion over him. For the death he died he died to sin, once for all, but the life he lives he lives to God. So you also must consider yourselves dead to sin and alive to God in Christ Jesus. Let not sin therefore reign in your mortal body, to make you obey its passions. Do not present your members to sin as instruments for unrighteousness, but present yourselves to God as those who have been brought from death to life, and your members to God as instruments for righteousness.

Blessing/Sacrifice/Restoration

DAVID JOHNSON | WOODCUT

In William Tyndale's 1526 prologue to Romans he wrote about the impact that the sacrifice of Christ should have on lifestyle of believers. He urges the reader to "Remember that Christ made not this atonement, that thou shouldest anger God again; neither died he for thy sins, that thou shouldest live still in them; neither cleansed he thee, that thou shouldest return (as a swine) unto thine old puddle again; but that thou shouldest be a new creature and live a new life after the will of God and not of the flesh." This rather large woodcut combines the baptism of Christ (on the right) with his burial (on the left) to frame the crucifixion of in the middle, while at the top of the print Christ ascends to glory in Heaven.

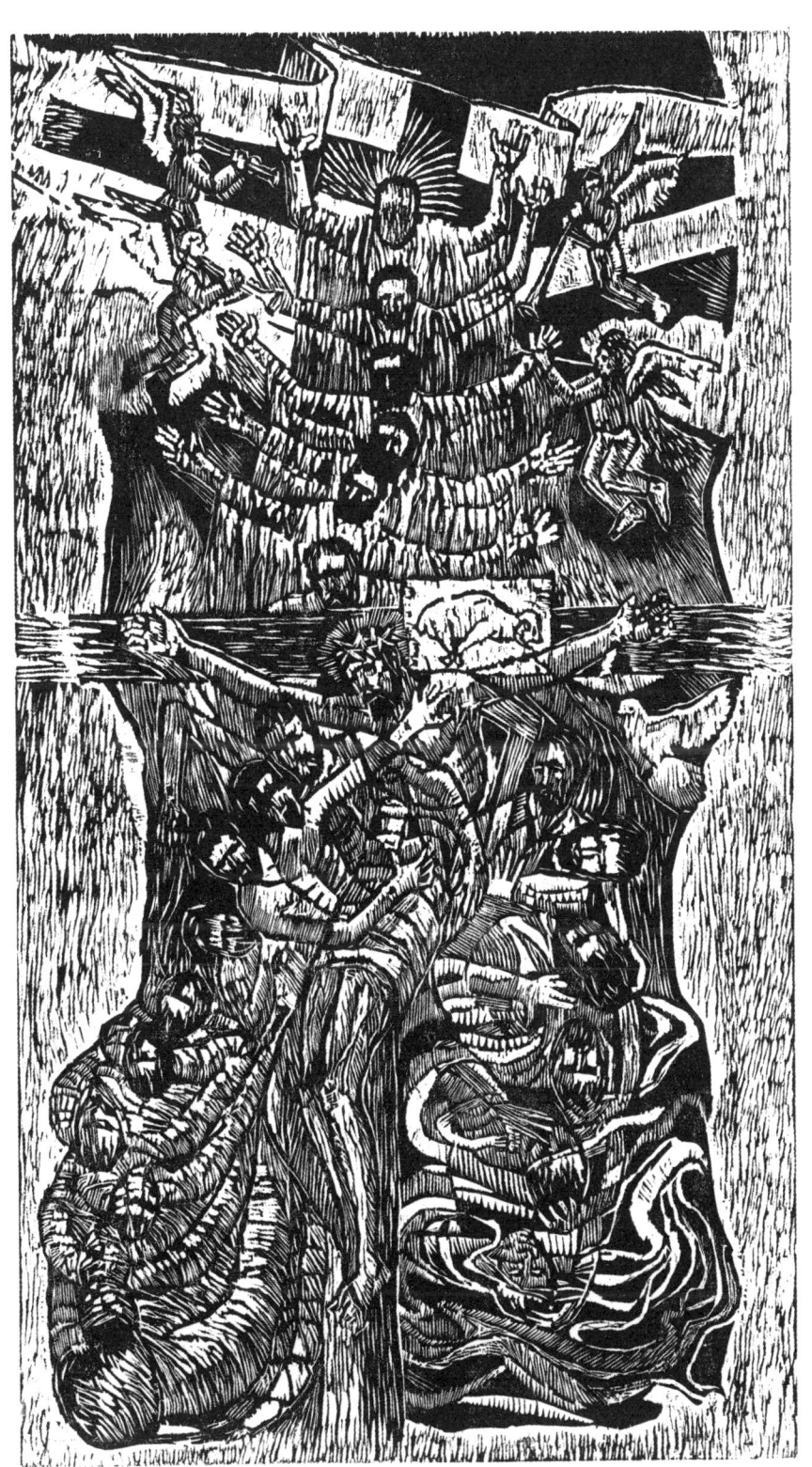

Romans 7:21–8:2, 35–39

NO CONDEMNATION

So I find it to be a law that when I want to do right, evil lies close at hand. For I delight in the law of God, in my inner being, but I see in my members another law waging war against the law of my mind and making me captive to the law of sin that dwells in my members. Wretched man that I am! Who will deliver me from this body of death? Thanks be to God through Jesus Christ our Lord! So then, I myself serve the law of God with my mind, but with my flesh I serve the law of sin.

There is therefore now no condemnation for those who are in Christ Jesus. For the law of the Spirit of life has set you free in Christ Jesus from the law of sin and death.

. . .

Who shall separate us from the love of Christ? Shall tribulation, or distress, or persecution, or famine, or nakedness, or danger, or sword? As it is written,

> "For your sake we are being killed all the day long;
> we are regarded as sheep to be slaughtered."

No, in all these things we are more than conquerors through him who loved us. For I am sure that neither death nor life, nor angels nor rulers, nor things present nor things to come, nor powers, nor height nor depth, nor anything else in all creation, will be able to separate us from the love of God in Christ Jesus our Lord.

Simul Justus et Peccator
NED BUSTARD | LINOCUT

This passage declares that nothing can separate us from the love of God, even if we still feel like slaves to sin. *Simul justus et peccator* is Latin for "at the same time just (or righteous) and a sinner." R.C. Sproul explains that "under the analysis of God's scrutiny, we still have sin; we're still sinners. But, by imputation and by faith in Jesus Christ, whose righteousness is now transferred to our account, then we are considered just or righteous." This print conveys the idea of being both sinful *and* righteous through symbols from Christian art. The black bird, the Adam's apple, and the thirty pieces of silver represent sin. The candle and mirror are God's Word. The man is clothed in Christ's righteousness—in the form of the robe and sash ubiquitous in Sunday school pictures of Jesus. The square halo indicates that he is a living saint.

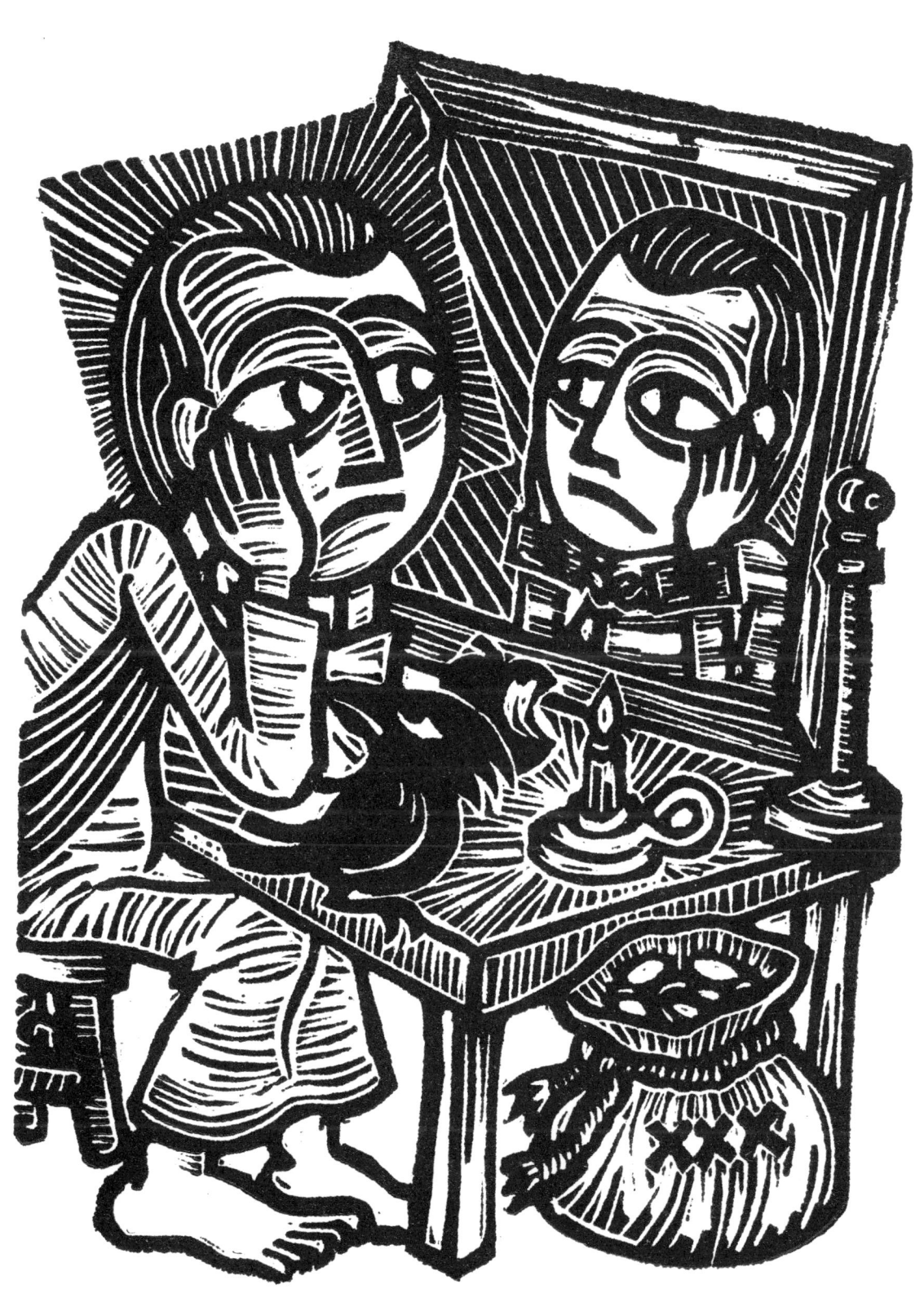

1 Corinthians 5:9–11, 6:9–11
THE BODY IS FOR THE LORD

I wrote to you in my letter not to associate with sexually immoral people—not at all meaning the sexually immoral of this world, or the greedy and swindlers, or idolaters, since then you would need to go out of the world. But now I am writing to you not to associate with anyone who bears the name of brother if he is guilty of sexual immorality or greed, or is an idolater, reviler, drunkard, or swindler—not even to eat with such a one.

. . .

Or do you not know that the unrighteous will not inherit the kingdom of God? Do not be deceived: neither the sexually immoral, nor idolaters, nor adulterers, nor men who practice homosexuality, nor thieves, nor the greedy, nor drunkards, nor revilers, nor swindlers will inherit the kingdom of God. And such were some of you. But you were washed, you were sanctified, you were justified in the name of the Lord Jesus Christ and by the Spirit of our God.

The Monkey and the Bride
NED BUSTARD | LINOCUT

The woman in this print is bruised and battered by the ravaging effects of sin. The Holy Spirit offers her the crown of heaven, but the monkey on her back must be cast away for her to enter the Kingdom of God. It is true that any sin will keep us out of the presence of a holy God, not simply the ones Paul references. But the church in Corinth struggled particularly with sexual immorality and the rest this list. So Paul warns the Corinthians that they must get out from under the control of these particular sins. Yet he also encourages them that they have been justified in Christ. The good news of the gospel is Jesus *will* save his bride. Through the Cross her body will be washed and purified. And Jesus will clothe her in his righteousness.

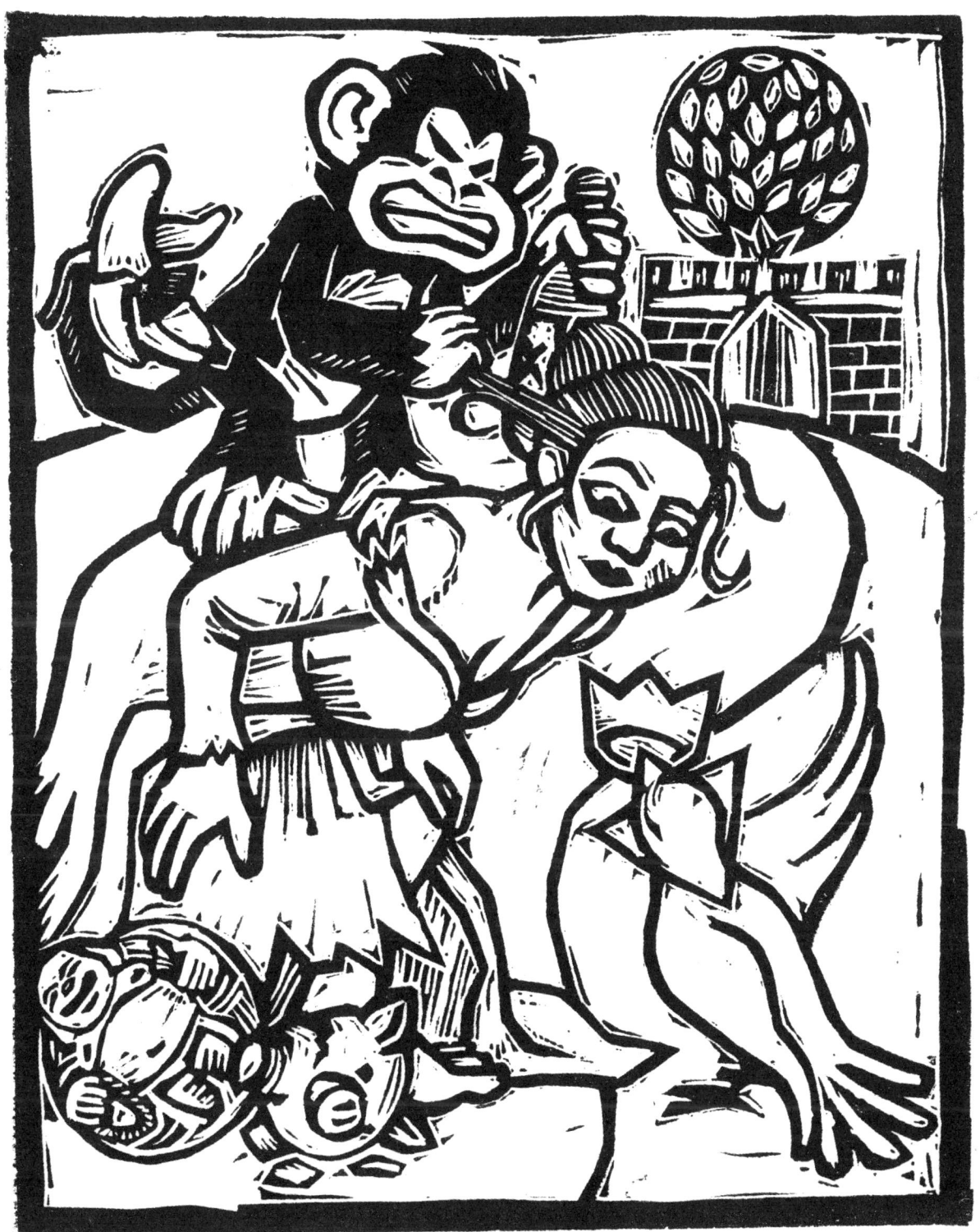

1 Corinthians 6:15–7:6

GLORIFY GOD IN YOUR BODY

Do you not know that your bodies are members of Christ? Shall I then take the members of Christ and make them members of a prostitute? Never! Or do you not know that he who is joined to a prostitute becomes one body with her? For, as it is written, "The two will become one flesh." But he who is joined to the Lord becomes one spirit with him. Flee from sexual immorality. Every other sin a person commits is outside the body, but the sexually immoral person sins against his own body. Or do you not know that your body is a temple of the Holy Spirit within you, whom you have from God? You are not your own, for you were bought with a price. So glorify God in your body.

Now concerning the matters about which you wrote: "It is good for a man not to have sexual relations with a woman." But because of the temptation to sexual immorality, each man should have his own wife and each woman her own husband. The husband should give to his wife her conjugal rights, and likewise the wife to her husband. For the wife does not have authority over her own body, but the husband does. Likewise the husband does not have authority over his own body, but the wife does. Do not deprive one another, except perhaps by agreement for a limited time, that you may devote yourselves to prayer; but then come together again, so that Satan may not tempt you because of your lack of self-control.

Psalm 1: Slow Dance
STEVE PRINCE | LINOCUT

A married couple is dancing in their bedroom to a love song that is playing on their old stereo phonograph. In the next room a television is blaring, but separating them from the noise of the world is a wall bearing a symbol of their covenant vows and a symbol of the faith that covers their marriage. A sliver of the ceiling shows two intersecting barrel vaults forming a "groin vault." The groin vault in this print symbolizes the pelvis regions of the couple's bodies: the two complimentary vaults stabilize the building as the two complimentary pelvises stabilize the marriage. The wife is wearing a translucent negligee for their time of coming together. A runaway slave motif can be seen on the husband's pajamas, symbolically alluding to the fact that—in spite of the great pain and separation African Americans have endured from generation to generation—these two have still found love.

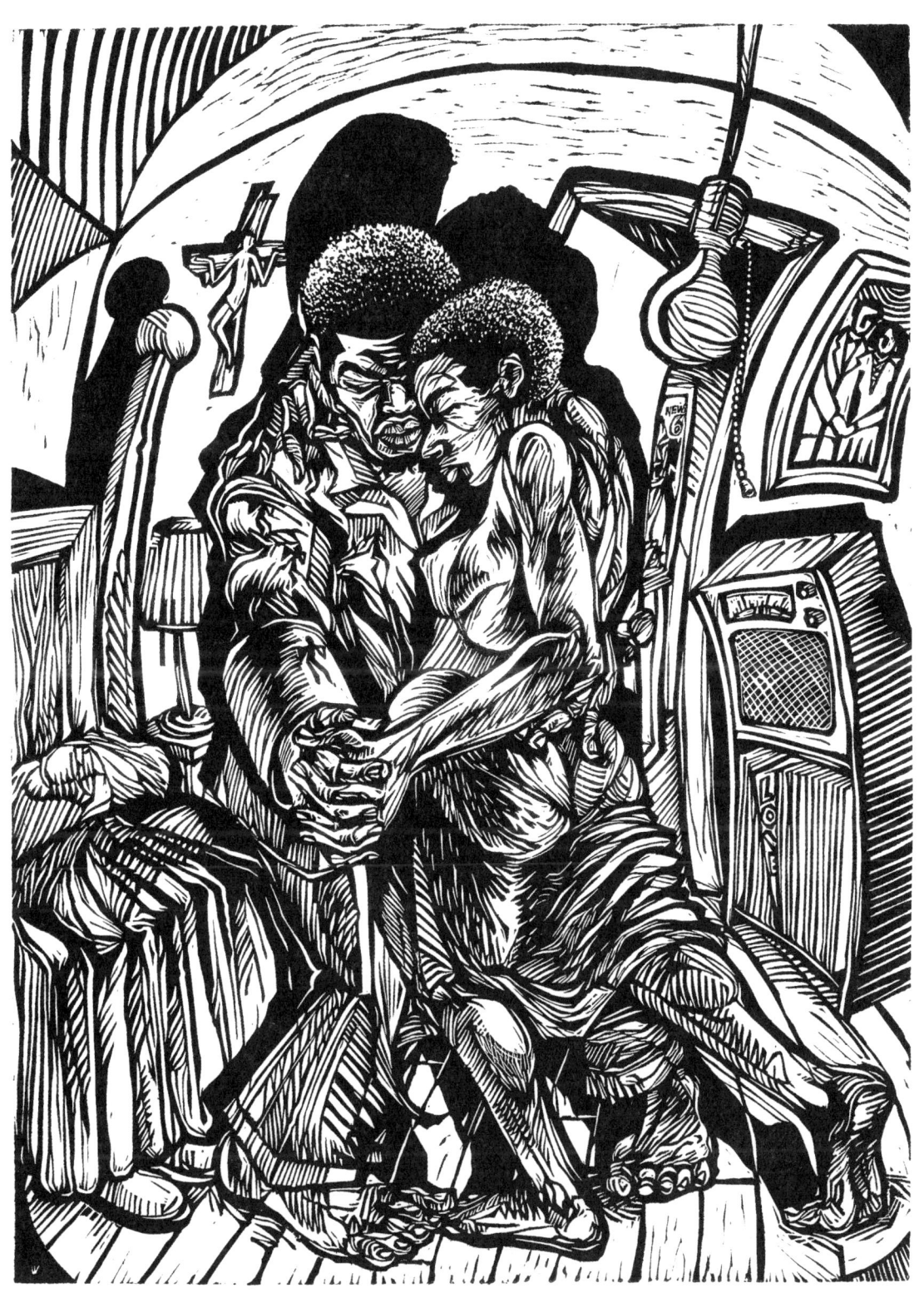

1 Corinthians 15:42–44, 51–58

RESURRECTION OF THE BODY

So is it with the resurrection of the dead. What is sown is perishable; what is raised is imperishable. It is sown in dishonor; it is raised in glory. It is sown in weakness; it is raised in power. It is sown a natural body; it is raised a spiritual body. If there is a natural body, there is also a spiritual body.

. . .

Behold! I tell you a mystery. We shall not all sleep, but we shall all be changed, in a moment, in the twinkling of an eye, at the last trumpet. For the trumpet will sound, and the dead will be raised imperishable, and we shall be changed. For this perishable body must put on the imperishable, and this mortal body must put on immortality. When the perishable puts on the imperishable, and the mortal puts on immortality, then shall come to pass the saying that is written:

> "Death is swallowed up in victory."
> "O death, where is your victory?
> O death, where is your sting?"

The sting of death is sin, and the power of sin is the law. But thanks be to God, who gives us the victory through our Lord Jesus Christ.

Therefore, my beloved brothers, be steadfast, immovable, always abounding in the work of the Lord, knowing that in the Lord your labor is not in vain.

Sown in Corruption, Raised in Incorruption
MATTHEW L. CLARK | LINOCUT

In A.D. 80 Saint Clement of Rome wrote to the church in Corinth, "Let us consider, beloved, how the Master is continually proving to us that there will be a future resurrection, of which he has made the Lord Jesus Christ the firstling, by raising him from the dead. Let us look, beloved, at the resurrection which is taking place seasonally. Day and night make known the resurrection to us. The night sleeps, the day arises. Consider the plants that grow. How and in what manner does the sowing take place? The sower went forth and cast each of the seeds onto the ground; and they fall to the ground, parched and bare, where they decay. Then from their decay the greatness of the Master's providence raises them up, and from the one grain more grow and bring forth fruit."

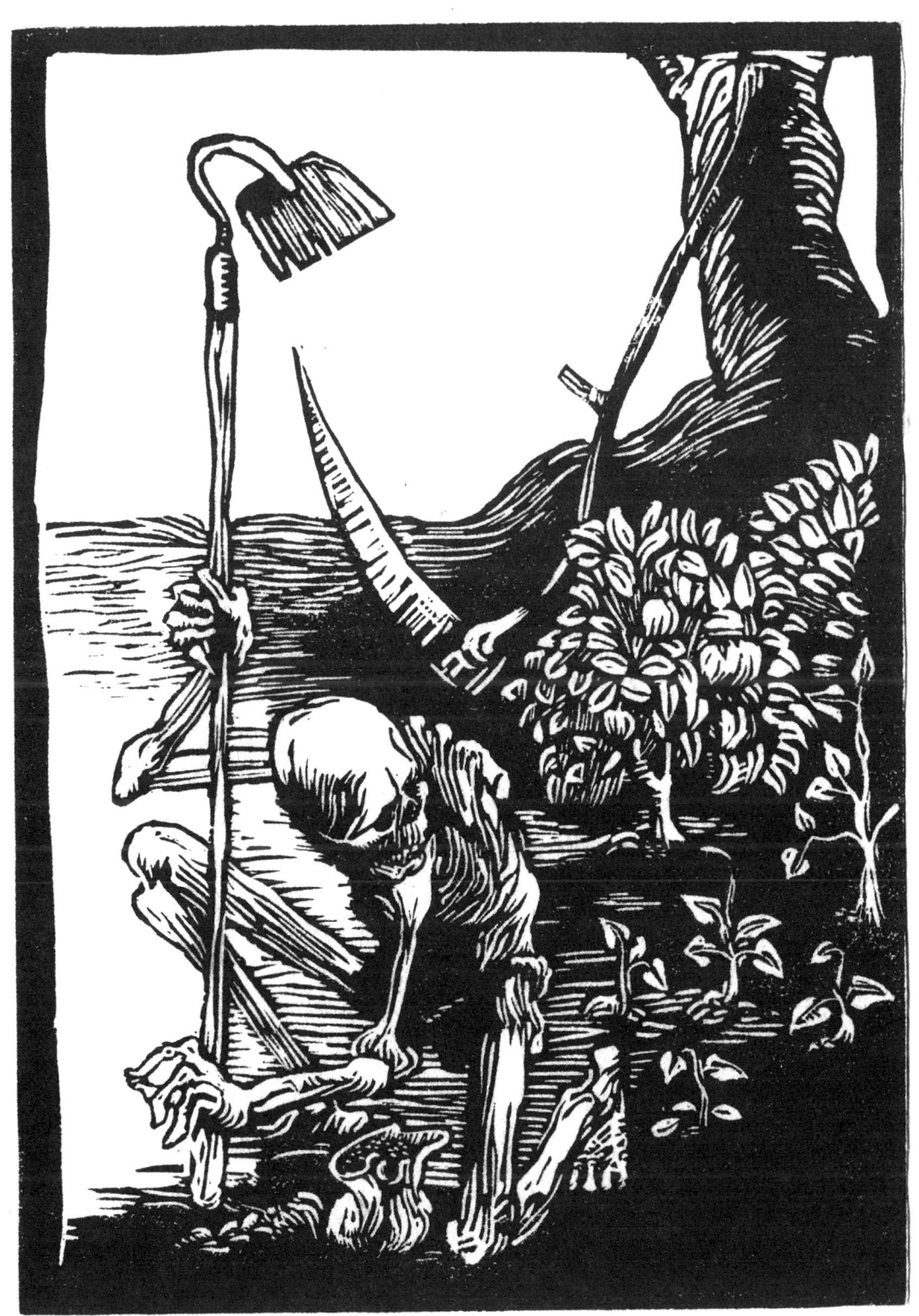

Galatians 5:1–15

FREEDOM IN CHRIST

For freedom Christ has set us free; stand firm therefore, and do not submit again to a yoke of slavery.

Look: I, Paul, say to you that if you accept circumcision, Christ will be of no advantage to you. I testify again to every man who accepts circumcision that he is obligated to keep the whole law. You are severed from Christ, you who would be justified by the law; you have fallen away from grace. For through the Spirit, by faith, we ourselves eagerly wait for the hope of righteousness. For in Christ Jesus neither circumcision nor uncircumcision counts for anything, but only faith working through love.

You were running well. Who hindered you from obeying the truth? This persuasion is not from him who calls you. A little leaven leavens the whole lump. I have confidence in the Lord that you will take no other view, and the one who is troubling you will bear the penalty, whoever he is. But if I, brothers, still preach circumcision, why am I still being persecuted? In that case the offense of the cross has been removed. I wish those who unsettle you would emasculate themselves!

For you were called to freedom, brothers. Only do not use your freedom as an opportunity for the flesh, but through love serve one another. For the whole law is fulfilled in one word: "You shall love your neighbor as yourself." But if you bite and devour one another, watch out that you are not consumed by one another.

Severed

NED BUSTARD | LINOCUT

Martin Luther wrote that what this passage means is that those who submit to circumcision must submit to the whole Law: "To obey Moses in one point requires obedience to him in all points . . . Thus to acknowledge the Law is tantamount to declaring that Christ is not yet come. And if Christ is not yet come, then all the Jewish ceremonies and laws concerning meats, places, and times are still in force, and Christ must be awaited as one who is still to come . . . The Galatians were hindered in the Christian life when they turned from faith and grace to the Law." In this image a Jewish man is considering the implications of Paul's wish to see the Judaizers emasculate themselves. His shirt metamorphizes into a pair of scissors, and perhaps he begins to understand the seriousness of adding anything to the gospel.

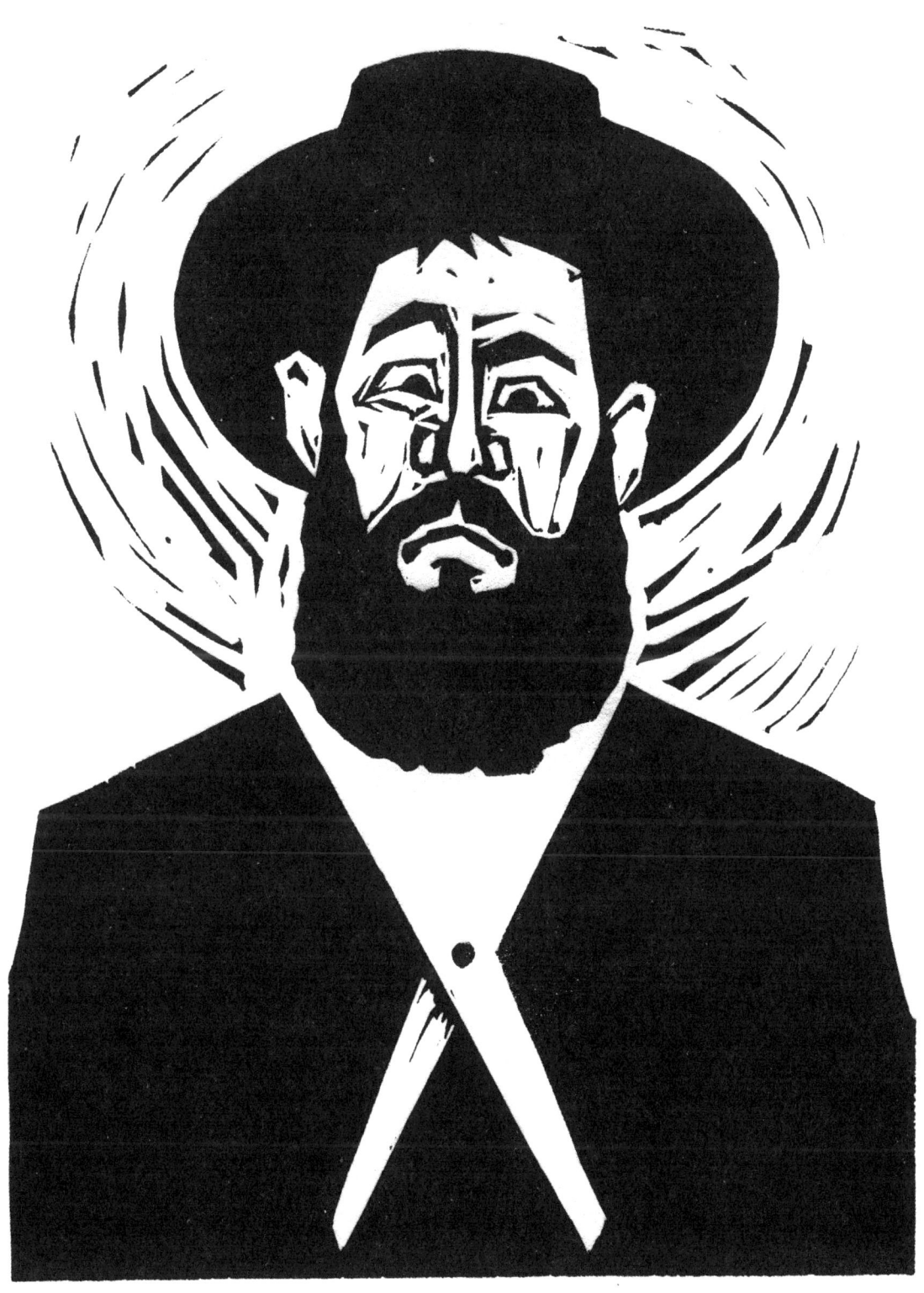

Galatians 5:16–26

THE FRUIT OF THE SPIRIT

But I say, walk by the Spirit, and you will not gratify the desires of the flesh. For the desires of the flesh are against the Spirit, and the desires of the Spirit are against the flesh, for these are opposed to each other, to keep you from doing the things you want to do. But if you are led by the Spirit, you are not under the law. Now the works of the flesh are evident: sexual immorality, impurity, sensuality, idolatry, sorcery, enmity, strife, jealousy, fits of anger, rivalries, dissensions, divisions, envy, drunkenness, orgies, and things like these. I warn you, as I warned you before, that those who do such things will not inherit the kingdom of God. But the fruit of the Spirit is love, joy, peace, patience, kindness, goodness, faithfulness, gentleness, self-control; against such things there is no law. And those who belong to Christ Jesus have crucified the flesh with its passions and desires.

If we live by the Spirit, let us also keep in step with the Spirit. Let us not become conceited, provoking one another, envying one another.

Still Life with Fruit

KREG YINGST | LINOCUT

Followers of God do not pick one fruit over another to exhibit in their lives. For example, a person may want to say they have faithfulness and joy but simply can't muster forbearance and self-control. For the Christian, such selectivness is unacceptable. The fruit of the Spirit is a unified process. Over time, a life truly lived in the Spirit *will* produce the fruit. Speaking of fruit, a title such as the one for this print generally refers to a picture like the one hanging over the man's left shoulder. But this still life incorporates a man, a Bible, an apple, a cup of coffee, and a descending dove. These symbols (along with the words protruding from the man's fingers) suggest that a life of prayer, study, and waiting on the Spirit—that is, *a still life*—leads to a person becoming transformed into the Fruit that God desires.

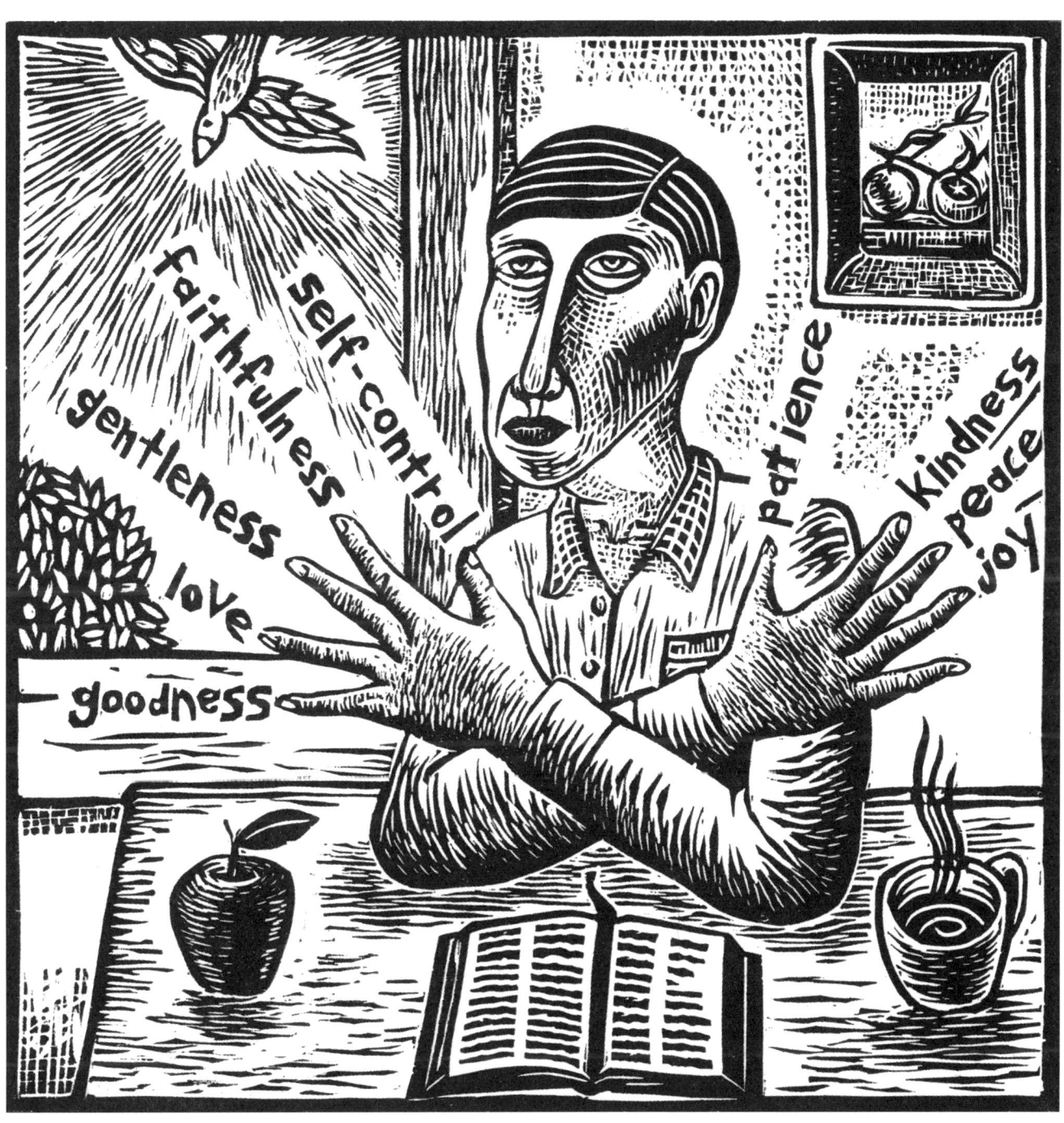

Ephesians 2:1–10
BUT GOD

And you were dead in the trespasses and sins in which you once walked, following the course of this world, following the prince of the power of the air, the spirit that is now at work in the sons of disobedience—among whom we all once lived in the passions of our flesh, carrying out the desires of the body and the mind, and were by nature children of wrath, like the rest of mankind. But God, being rich in mercy, because of the great love with which he loved us, even when we were dead in our trespasses, made us alive together with Christ—by grace you have been saved—and raised us up with him and seated us with him in the heavenly places in Christ Jesus, so that in the coming ages he might show the immeasurable riches of his grace in kindness toward us in Christ Jesus. For by grace you have been saved through faith. And this is not your own doing; it is the gift of God, not a result of works, so that no one may boast. For we are his workmanship, created in Christ Jesus for good works, which God prepared beforehand, that we should walk in them.

Praying Skeleton
ANONYMOUS | WOODCUT

But God. Martyn Lloyd-Jones said these two words "contain the whole of the gospel. The gospel tells of what God has done, God's intervention; it is something that comes entirely from outside us and displays to us that wondrous and amazing and astonishing work of God." This print illustrates the degree of dependence people find themselves in when relating to God. Even to be able to assume a posture of prayer would require the bones to be thus positioned by an outside agent. The skeleton is not searching for God and in no way can it make a decision to follow him. To live for God it must be made alive. And the only way sinews shall come upon the skeleton, and flesh cover it, is if the breath of God blows upon it. As R.C. Sproul wrote, "The grace that brings us life comes to us at the very time we are dead in sin and trespasses. It is the act of God."

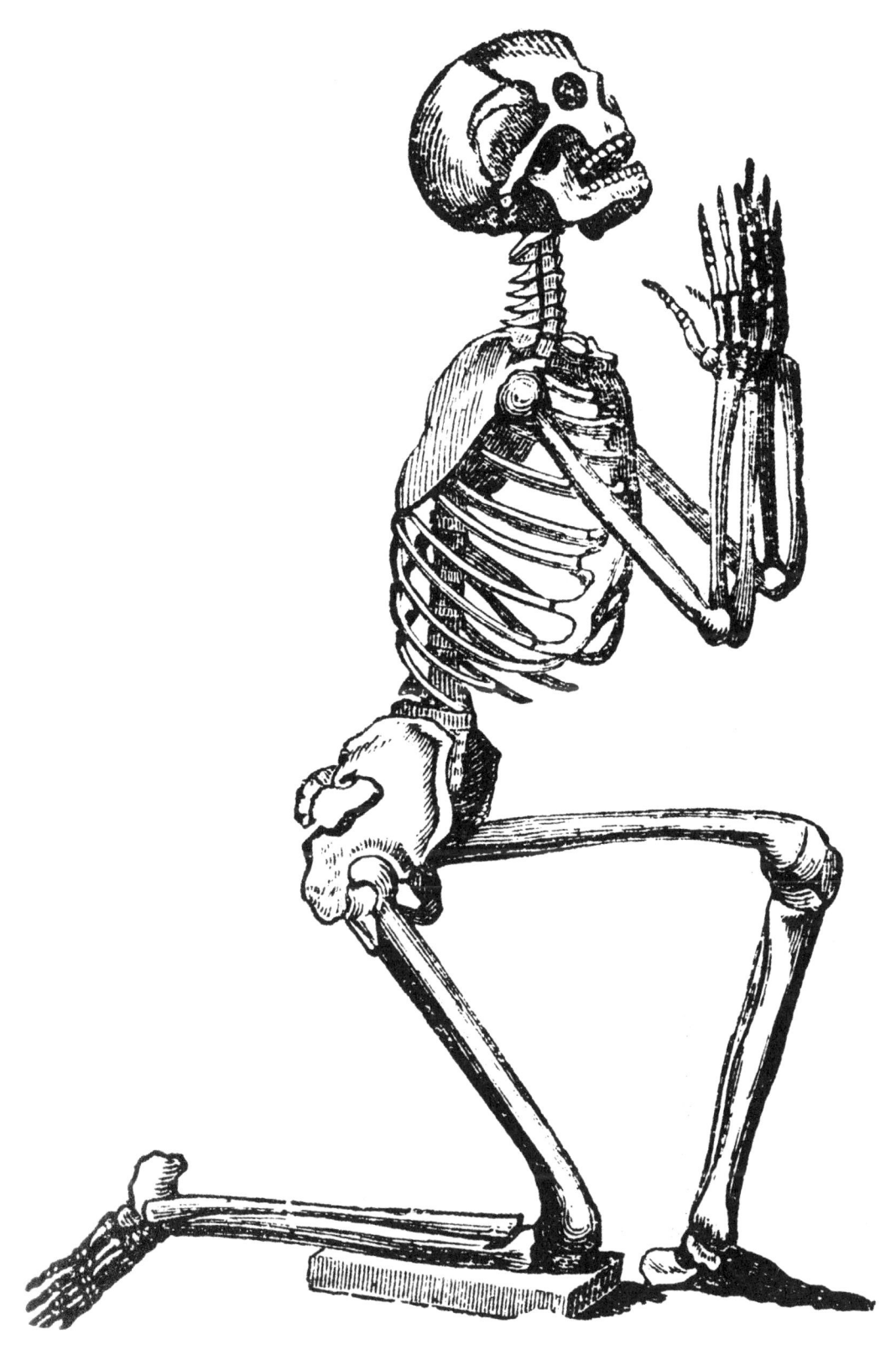

Philippians 2:1–13

THE HUMILITY OF CHRIST

So if there is any encouragement in Christ, any comfort from love, any participation in the Spirit, any affection and sympathy, complete my joy by being of the same mind, having the same love, being in full accord and of one mind. Do nothing from selfish ambition or conceit, but in humility count others more significant than yourselves. Let each of you look not only to his own interests, but also to the interests of others. Have this mind among yourselves, which is yours in Christ Jesus, who, though he was in the form of God, did not count equality with God a thing to be grasped, but emptied himself, by taking the form of a servant, being born in the likeness of men. And being found in human form, he humbled himself by becoming obedient to the point of death, even death on a cross. Therefore God has highly exalted him and bestowed on him the name that is above every name, so that at the name of Jesus every knee should bow, in heaven and on earth and under the earth, and every tongue confess that Jesus Christ is Lord, to the glory of God the Father.

Therefore, my beloved, as you have always obeyed, so now, not only as in my presence but much more in my absence, work out your own salvation with fear and trembling, for it is God who works in you, both to will and to work for his good pleasure.

Kenosis (After Sadao Watanabe)

NED BUSTARD | LINOCUT

We are called to have the mind of Christ. This works itself out as we exhibit humility, look to the interests of others, and take on the role of a servant. Sadao Watanabe (1913–1996) converted from Buddhism to Christianity at the age of 17. He combined his new faith with the traditional Japanese folk art of stencil dyeing (or *katazome*) and made colorful representations of the events recorded in the Bible. He said, "I owe my life to Christ and the gospel. My way of expressing my gratitude is to witness to my faith through the medium of biblical scenes." This print combines elements from three of Watanabe's prints: *A Modern Madonna*, Christ from *Descent from the Cross*, and an angel from *Christ is Risen* to illustrate this passage—particularly verses 7–9.

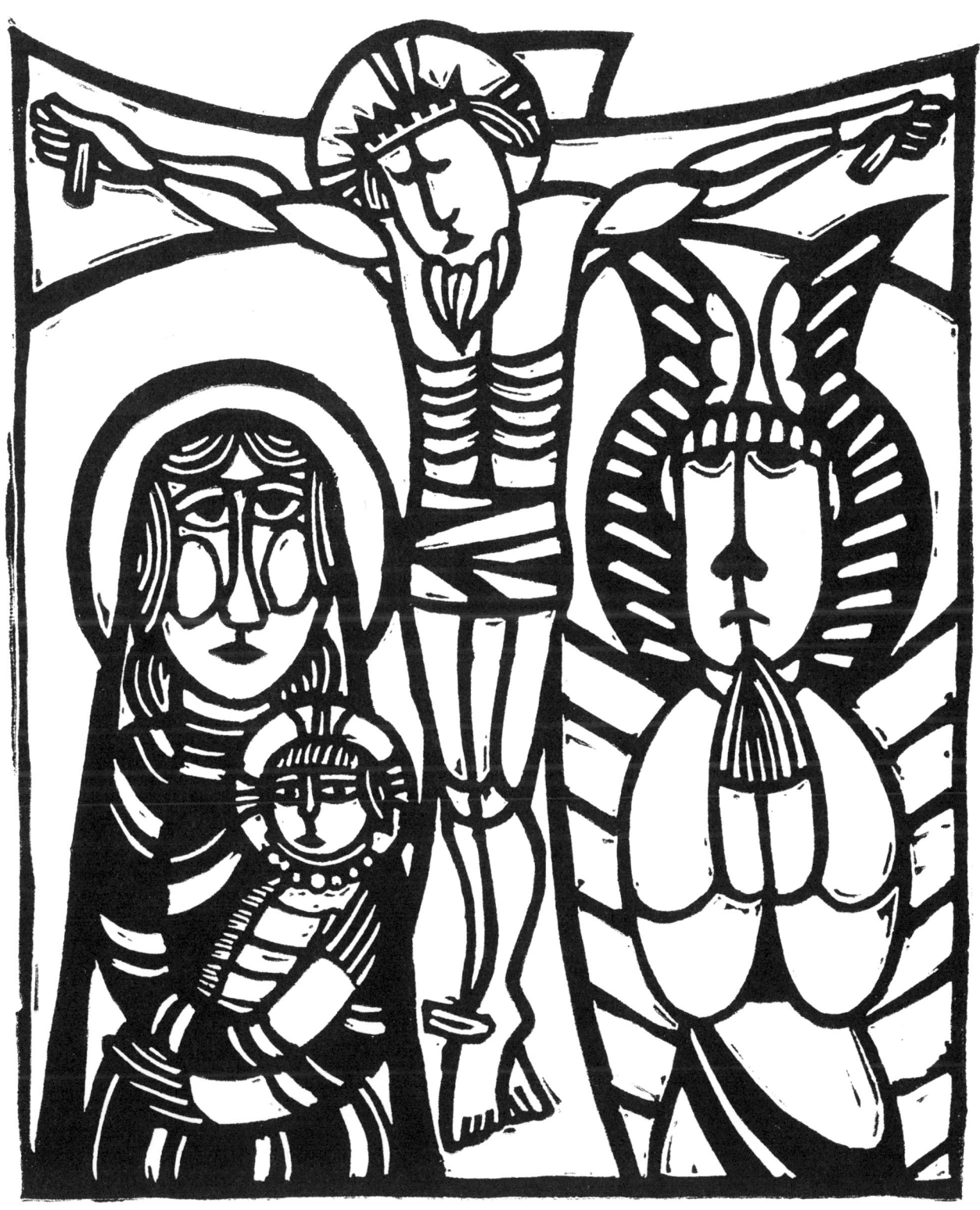

Colossians 2:8–14

LIFE IN CHRIST

Therefore, as you received Christ Jesus the Lord, so walk in him, rooted and built up in him and established in the faith, just as you were taught, abounding in thanksgiving.

See to it that no one takes you captive by philosophy and empty deceit, according to human tradition, according to the elemental spirits of the world, and not according to Christ. For in him the whole fullness of deity dwells bodily, and you have been filled in him, who is the head of all rule and authority. In him also you were circumcised with a circumcision made without hands, by putting off the body of the flesh, by the circumcision of Christ, having been buried with him in baptism, in which you were also raised with him through faith in the powerful working of God, who raised him from the dead. And you, who were dead in your trespasses and the uncircumcision of your flesh, God made alive together with him, having forgiven us all our trespasses, by canceling the record of debt that stood against us with its legal demands. This he set aside, nailing it to the cross.

Sacrament

RICHARD GASTON | MONOTYPE

It is a glorious mystery that in Jesus the spiritual reality of God became physical. A sacrament is also a mystery. It is a physical symbol that transmits a spiritual reality. In the sacraments God mysteriously but also truly gives grace to his people through the means of water, bread, and wine. In this passage Paul uses the Greek words *eucharistia* (meaning "thanksgiving," from which comes the word "eucharist") and *baptismo* (meaning "I wash," which was used in Jewish texts for ritual purification washings). During his earthly ministry Jesus instituted baptism—replacing the gender-based covenantal membership rite of circumcision—and the Eucharist. In this print either of these two sacraments seem to appear. The artist is either depicting the Spirit descending on the water, the minister raising his hands over the wine in consecration, or both.

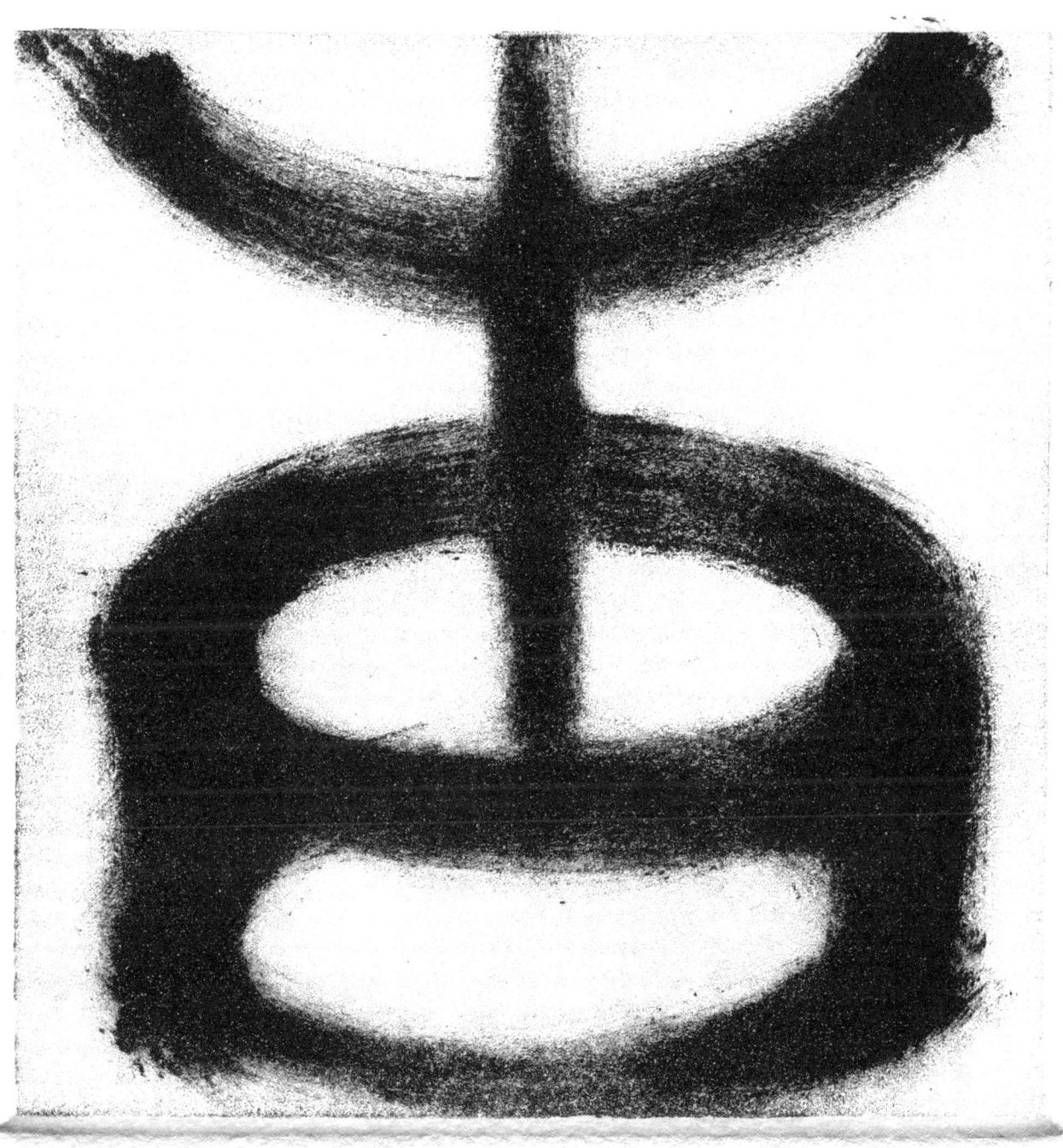

2 Thessalonians 2:1–12

THE MAN OF LAWLESSNESS

Now concerning the coming of our Lord Jesus Christ and our being gathered together to him, we ask you, brothers, not to be quickly shaken in mind or alarmed, either by a spirit or a spoken word, or a letter seeming to be from us, to the effect that the day of the Lord has come. Let no one deceive you in any way. For that day will not come, unless the rebellion comes first, and the man of lawlessness is revealed, the son of destruction, who opposes and exalts himself against every so-called god or object of worship, so that he takes his seat in the temple of God, proclaiming himself to be God. Do you not remember that when I was still with you I told you these things? And you know what is restraining him now so that he may be revealed in his time. For the mystery of lawlessness is already at work. Only he who now restrains it will do so until he is out of the way. And then the lawless one will be revealed, whom the Lord Jesus will kill with the breath of his mouth and bring to nothing by the appearance of his coming. The coming of the lawless one is by the activity of Satan with all power and false signs and wonders, and with all wicked deception for those who are perishing, because they refused to love the truth and so be saved. Therefore God sends them a strong delusion, so that they may believe what is false, in order that all may be condemned who did not believe the truth but had pleasure in unrighteousness.

Parable

MARK T. SMITH | LINOCUT

Across a wasteland littered with signs of sin and evil (a pitchfork, skull dice, flames, and XXX) marches the Man of Lawlessness . . . in a pair of cowboy boots. He clearly sees the scales, knows what justice is, and does not do it. He is a man of power and authority—respresented in his flaming crown and Caesar-like wreath encircling his head. He is also a man of evil—shown in his devil tail, horns, and pointed beard. But the people are deceived because he is a man who can conjure up "false signs and wonders" and has a pair of angel wings tacked on his back along with a symbol for Jesus painted on his skull. The Man of Lawlessness likely tosses out a few earnest "God bless America"s, and that is all it takes for his followers to be deluded into thinking good is bad and bad is good. God will kill this anti-Christ figure with the breath of his mouth.

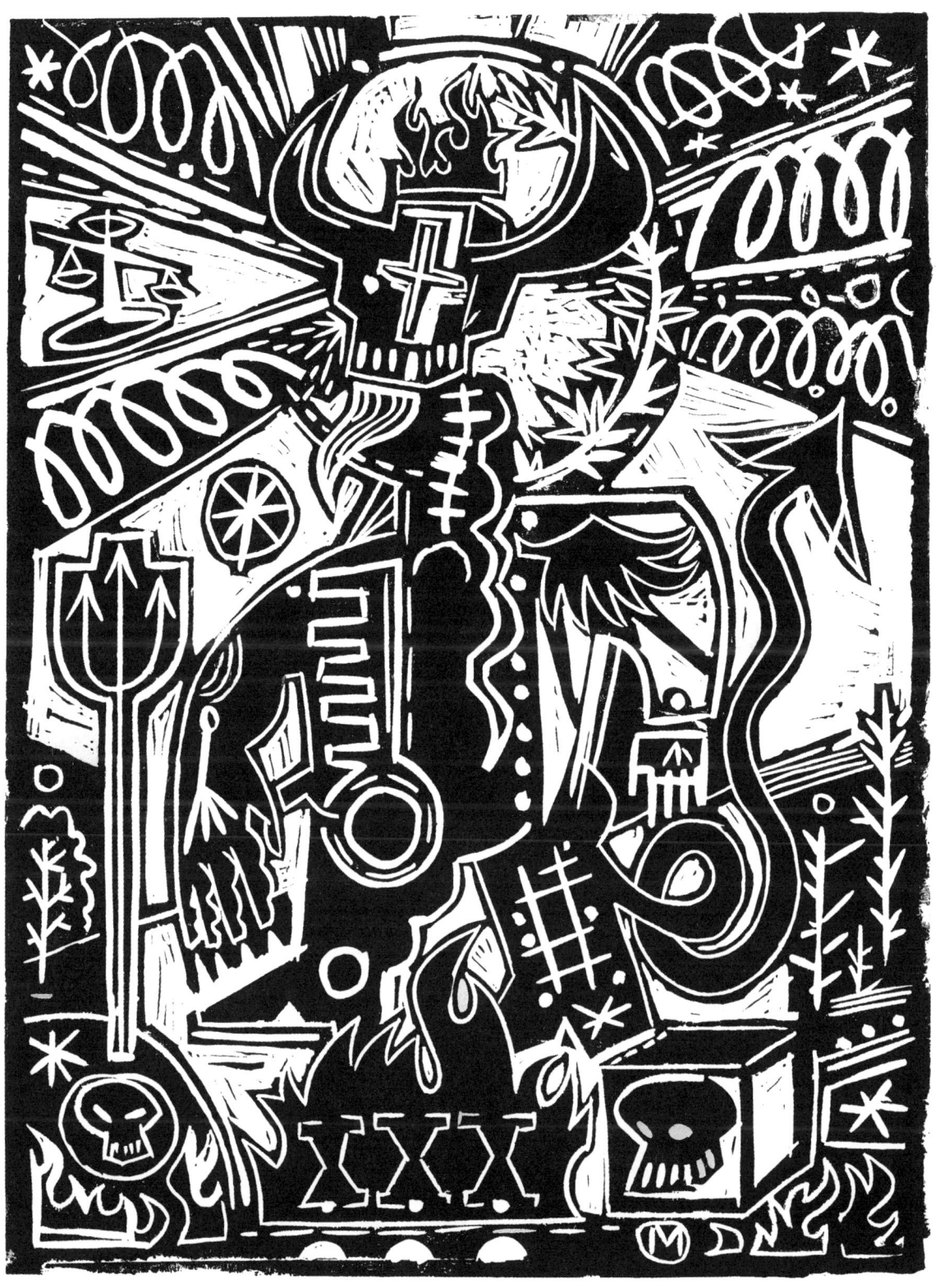

1 Timothy 2

PRAYER . . . AND THE FALL

First of all, then, I urge that supplications, prayers, intercessions, and thanksgivings be made for all people, for kings and all who are in high positions, that we may lead a peaceful and quiet life, godly and dignified in every way. This is good, and it is pleasing in the sight of God our Savior, who desires all people to be saved and to come to the knowledge of the truth. For there is one God, and there is one mediator between God and men, the man Christ Jesus, who gave himself as a ransom for all, which is the testimony given at the proper time. For this I was appointed a preacher and an apostle (I am telling the truth, I am not lying), a teacher of the Gentiles in faith and truth.

   I desire then that in every place the men should pray, lifting holy hands without anger or quarreling; likewise also that women should adorn themselves in respectable apparel, with modesty and self-control, not with braided hair and gold or pearls or costly attire, but with what is proper for women who profess godliness—with good works. Let a woman learn quietly with all submissiveness. I do not permit a woman to teach or to exercise authority over a man; rather, she is to remain quiet. For Adam was formed first, then Eve; and Adam was not deceived, but the woman was deceived and became a transgressor. Yet she will be saved through childbearing—if they continue in faith and love and holiness, with self-control.

Eve with Fruit

TANJA BUTLER | LINOCUT

In a perfect world the only perfect and sinless woman that ever lived was fed the first lie . . . and she bit. In the Garden of Eden, while sitting under the Tree of the Knowledge of Good and Evil, Eve was tricked. On the other hand, her husband was not taken in. Adam broke the Law knowingly. And he was punished for his disobedience. But that was not the end of it. Since Adam was the representative for all of humanity, his wife and all of their children were also punished for his sin in perpetuity. Part of the punishment was that both Adam's labor and Eve's labor were saddled with pain. As men and women have complementary gifts, they also have complimentary cursings. Yet there is hope. Paul says that even in spite of the conditions of the curse (like the dangers of childbirth), the descendants of Eve and Adam will be saved—if they continue on in the faith.

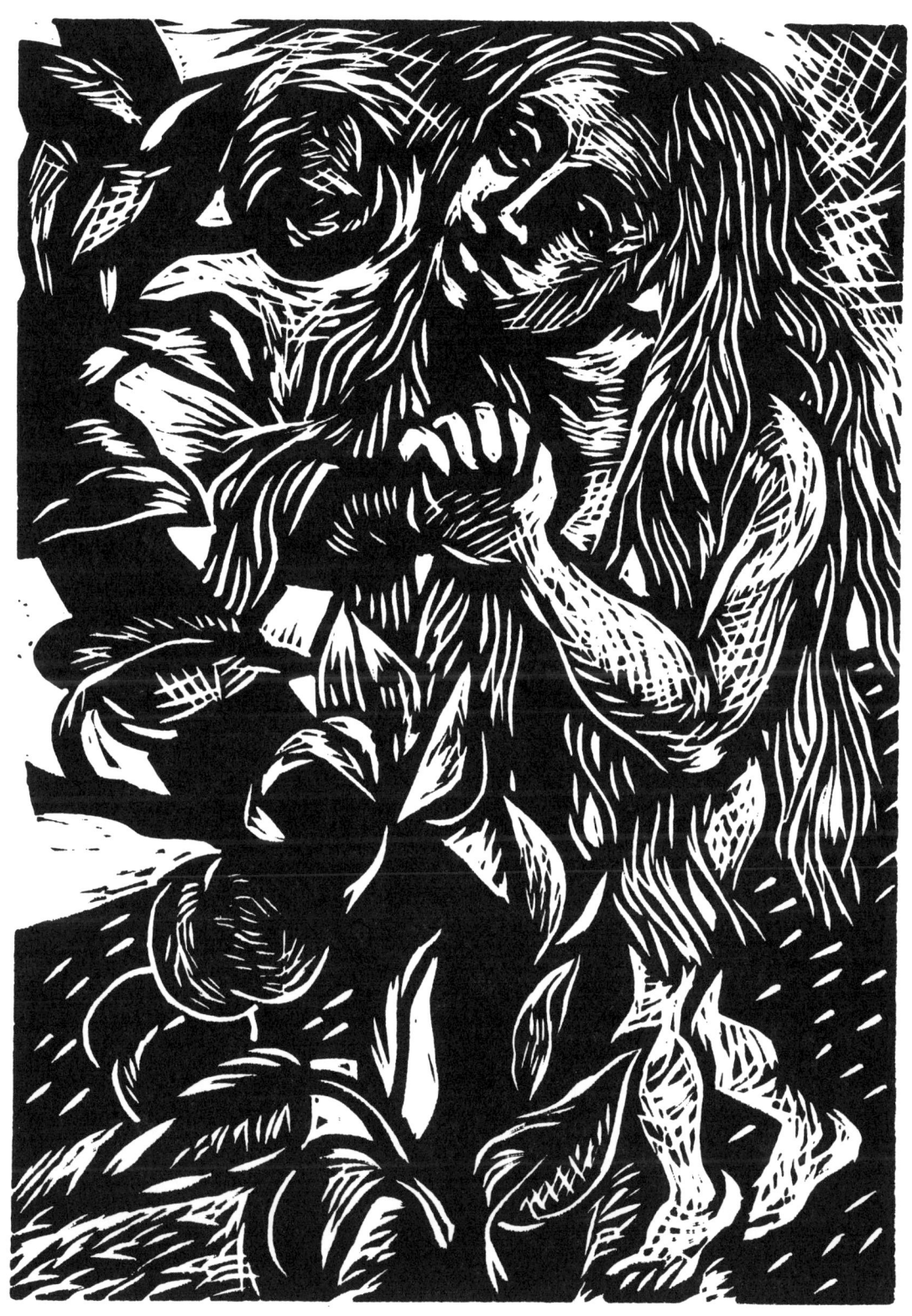

Hebrews 9:12–22

THE BLOOD OF CHRIST

[Christ] entered once for all into the holy places, not by means of the blood of goats and calves but by means of his own blood, thus securing an eternal redemption. For if the blood of goats and bulls, and the sprinkling of defiled persons with the ashes of a heifer, sanctify for the purification of the flesh, how much more will the blood of Christ, who through the eternal Spirit offered himself without blemish to God, purify our conscience from dead works to serve the living God.

Therefore he is the mediator of a new covenant, so that those who are called may receive the promised eternal inheritance, since a death has occurred that redeems them from the transgressions committed under the first covenant. For where a will is involved, the death of the one who made it must be established. For a will takes effect only at death, since it is not in force as long as the one who made it is alive. Therefore not even the first covenant was inaugurated without blood. For when every commandment of the law had been declared by Moses to all the people, he took the blood of calves and goats, with water and scarlet wool and hyssop, and sprinkled both the book itself and all the people, saying, "This is the blood of the covenant that God commanded for you." And in the same way he sprinkled with the blood both the tent and all the vessels used in worship. Indeed, under the law almost everything is purified with blood, and without the shedding of blood there is no forgiveness of sins.

Kruisweg

HENRI VAN STRATEN | LINOCUT

This print is by the same artist whose work was used to illustrate Ezekiel 23. In that piece, the worshiping of other gods was depicted as unfaithful women in a disreputable part of the city chasing after finely dressed men. The buildings and the pavement tiles in this print seem to indicate that the Crucifixion is happening in the same city. Now the ultimate result of the whoring discussed in Ezekiel 23 is seen as finely dressed men nail Christ to the Cross to rid themselves of the nuisance of God. Yet what they meant for evil, God intended for good. The death of Christ would pay for the past sins of Israel and the future sins of her adopted sister, the church. But this sacrifice is only effectual through faith. John Newton says faith is "a renouncing of everything we are apt to call our own and relying wholly upon the blood, righteousness and intercession of Jesus."

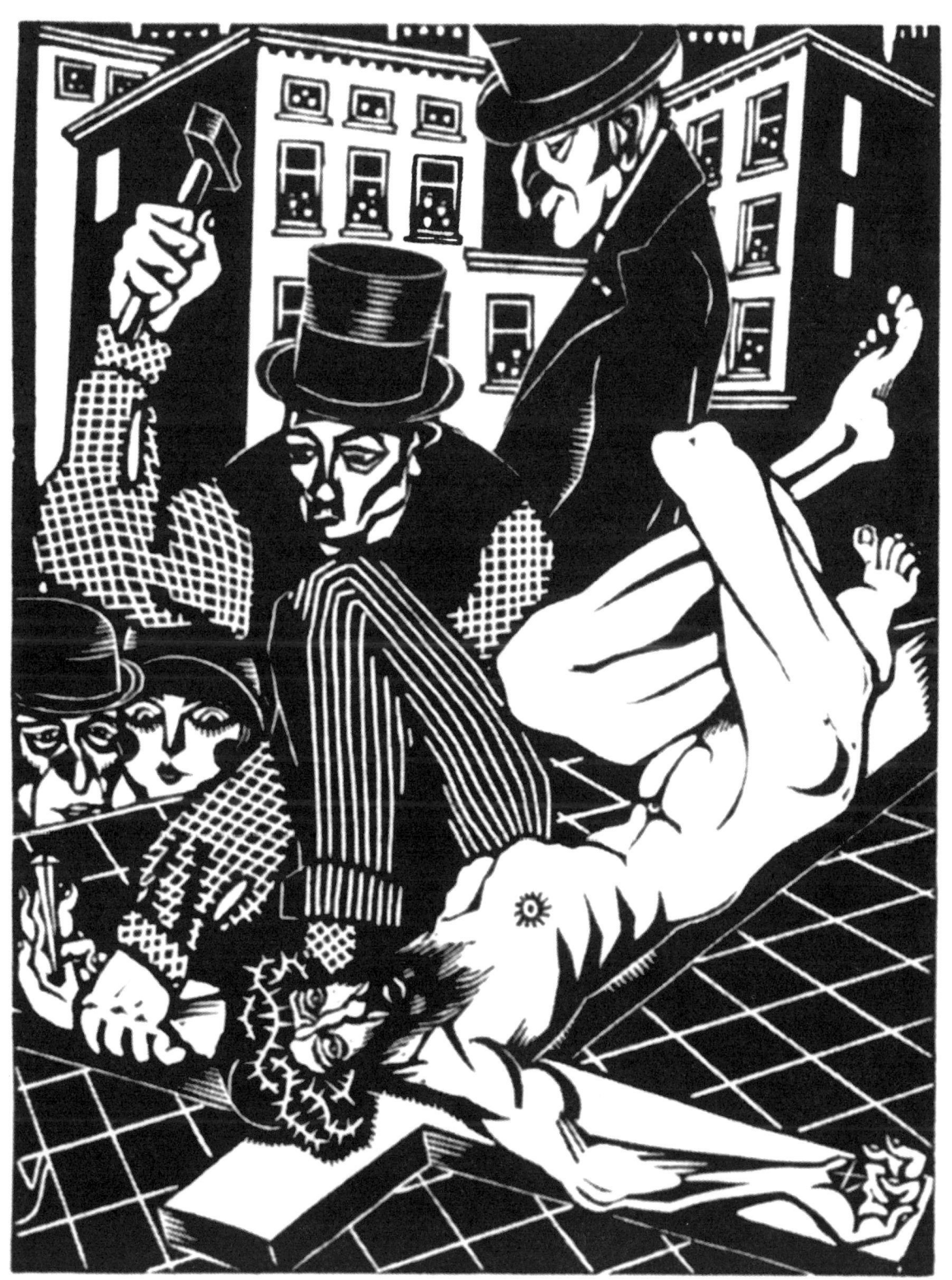

James 1:2–4, 12–22
LIVE HOLY LIVES

Count it all joy, my brothers, when you meet trials of various kinds, for you know that the testing of your faith produces steadfastness. And let steadfastness have its full effect, that you may be perfect and complete, lacking in nothing.

. . .

Blessed is the man who remains steadfast under trial, for when he has stood the test he will receive the crown of life, which God has promised to those who love him. Let no one say when he is tempted, "I am being tempted by God," for God cannot be tempted with evil, and he himself tempts no one. But each person is tempted when he is lured and enticed by his own desire. Then desire when it has conceived gives birth to sin, and sin when it is fully grown brings forth death.

Do not be deceived, my beloved brothers. Every good gift and every perfect gift is from above, coming down from the Father of lights with whom there is no variation or shadow due to change. Of his own will he brought us forth by the word of truth, that we should be a kind of firstfruits of his creatures.

Know this, my beloved brothers: let every person be quick to hear, slow to speak, slow to anger; for the anger of man does not produce the righteousness of God. Therefore put away all filthiness and rampant wickedness and receive with meekness the implanted word, which is able to save your souls.

But be doers of the word, and not hearers only, deceiving yourselves.

Crucifixion
WAYNE FORTE | ETCHING

The zephyr from a butterfly's wings and the devastation from a hurricane are both divinely ordained elements in God's great story. Trials are used by God for his glory and the greatest good for his chosen people. In this print Jesus is shown experiencing the ultimate trial—death on the Cross. Jesus' agony exemplifies the blessed man from Psalm 1, who by the power of the Holy Spirit and in love and obedience to God remains steadfast under trials. The blessed man believes that trials and delights are both gifts from the hand of a loving and generous Father. Knowing that allows God's children to grow in maturity as they learn to live patiently in the difficult tensions that trials bring them. Like James, the writer of Hebrews encourages God's adopted sons and daughters to live holy lives, "looking to Jesus, the founder and perfecter of our faith, who for the joy that was set before him endured the cross…"

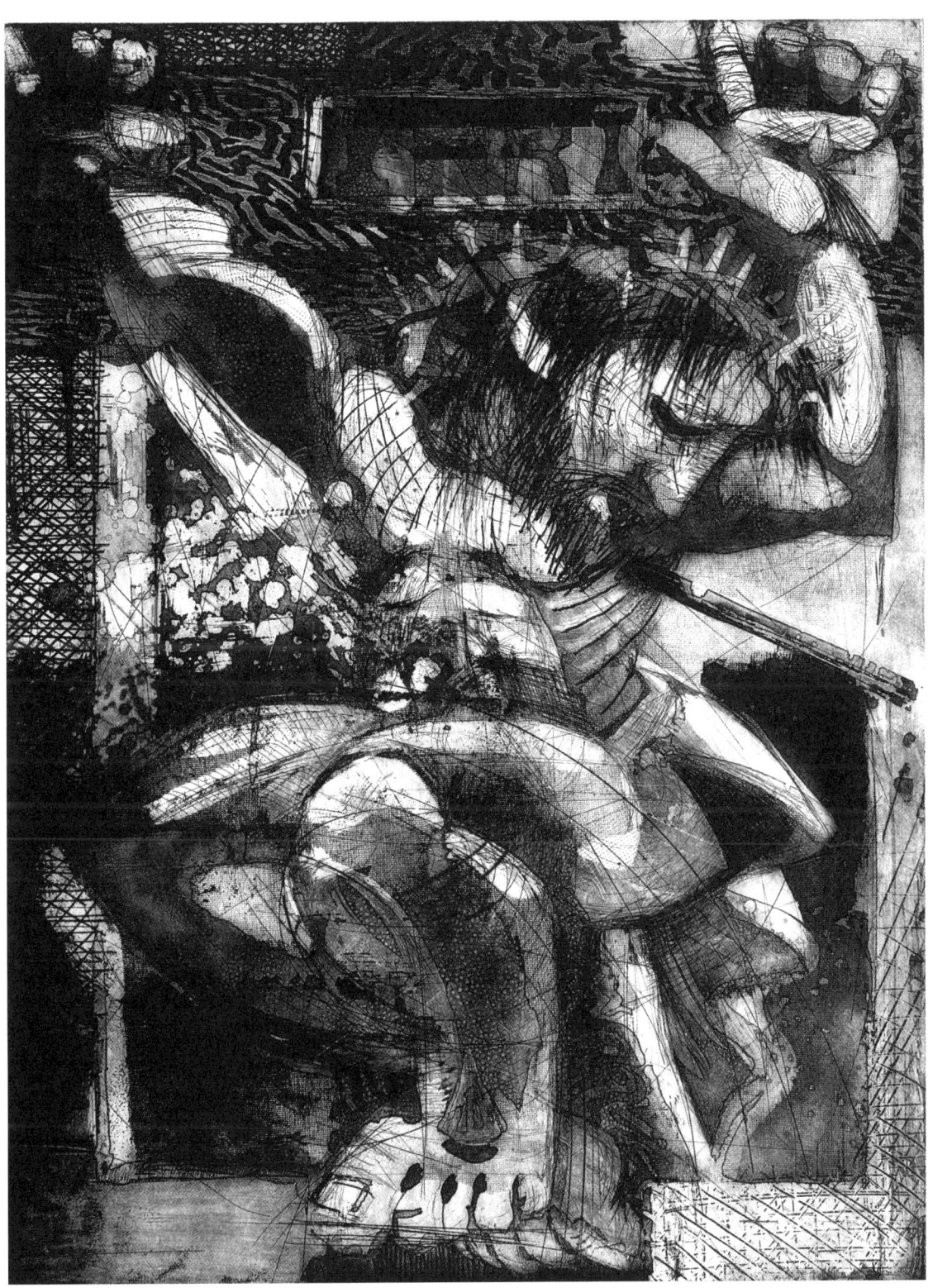

1 Peter 1:3–12

SALVATION REVEALED

Blessed be the God and Father of our Lord Jesus Christ! According to his great mercy, he has caused us to be born again to a living hope through the resurrection of Jesus Christ from the dead, to an inheritance that is imperishable, undefiled, and unfading, kept in heaven for you, who by God's power are being guarded through faith for a salvation ready to be revealed in the last time. In this you rejoice, though now for a little while, if necessary, you have been grieved by various trials, so that the tested genuineness of your faith—more precious than gold that perishes though it is tested by fire—may be found to result in praise and glory and honor at the revelation of Jesus Christ. Though you have not seen him, you love him. Though you do not now see him, you believe in him and rejoice with joy that is inexpressible and filled with glory, obtaining the outcome of your faith, the salvation of your souls.

Concerning this salvation, the prophets who prophesied about the grace that was to be yours searched and inquired carefully, inquiring what person or time the Spirit of Christ in them was indicating when he predicted the sufferings of Christ and the subsequent glories. It was revealed to them that they were serving not themselves but you, in the things that have now been announced to you through those who preached the good news to you by the Holy Spirit sent from heaven, things into which angels long to look.

Christ's Return

EDWARD KNIPPERS | MONOPRINT

Peter is bursting out with praise for God and the work of the Trinity. He reminds his readers that they share in an incorruptible inheritance. Salvation was revealed at the resurrection of Jesus Christ, but like the prophets of old, we do not see him. We wait along with the angels to see the full glory of Christ revealed to the whole universe at the end of time. In this monoprint the victorious Christ is revealed, crackling with life as he bursts out of the tomb on Easter morning. Lesslie Newbigin writes, "The resurrection is the revelation to chosen witnesses of the fact that Jesus who died on the Cross is indeed king—conqueror of death and sin, Lord and Savior of all. The resurrection is not the reversal of a defeat but the proclamation of a victory. The King reigns from the tree. The reign of God has indeed come upon us, and its sign is not a golden throne but a wooden cross."

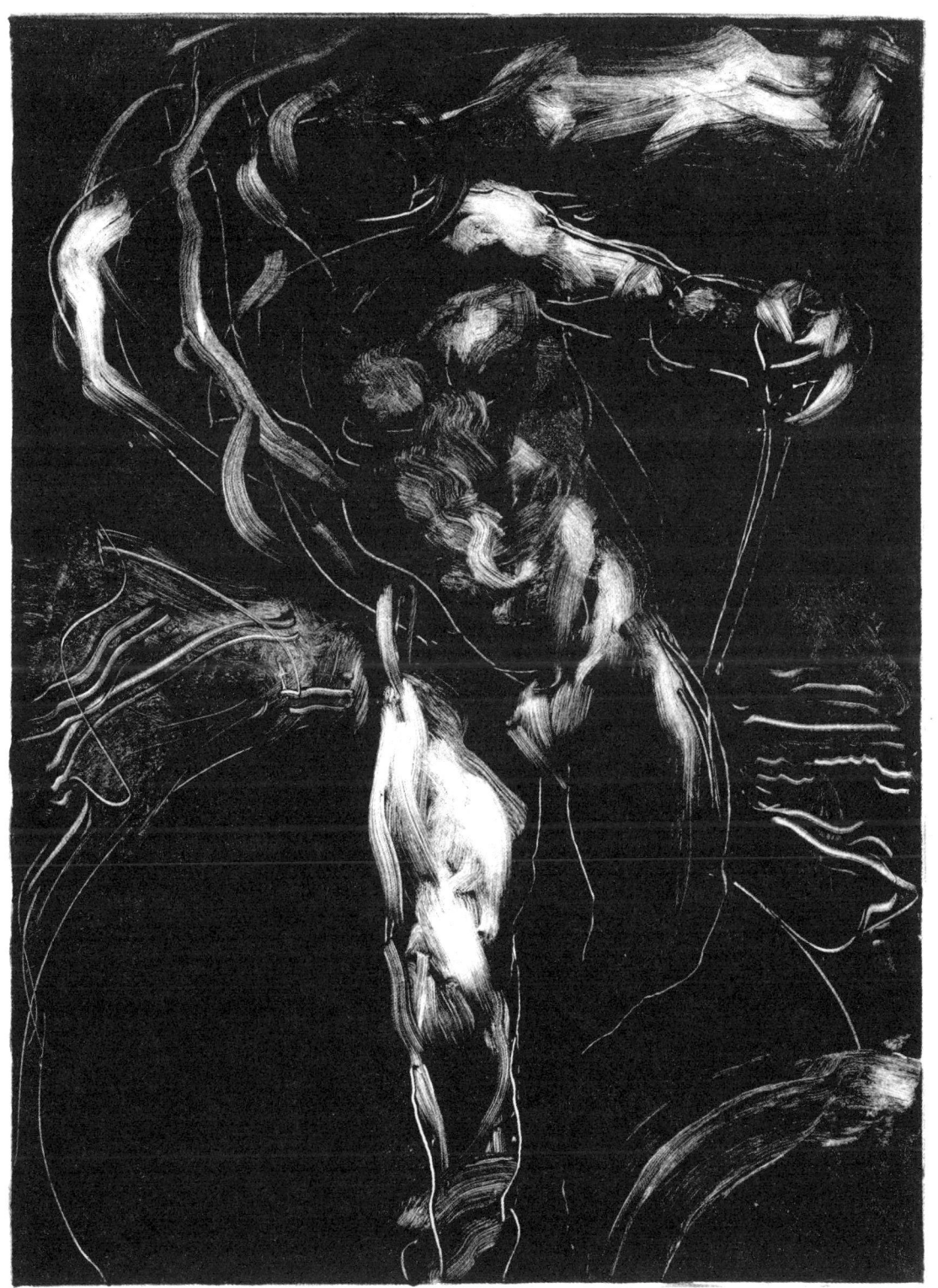

1 John 5:1–12

THE THREE WHO TESTIFY

Everyone who believes that Jesus is the Christ has been born of God, and everyone who loves the Father loves whoever has been born of him. By this we know that we love the children of God, when we love God and obey his commandments. For this is the love of God, that we keep his commandments. And his commandments are not burdensome. For everyone who has been born of God overcomes the world. And this is the victory that has overcome the world—our faith. Who is it that overcomes the world except the one who believes that Jesus is the Son of God?

This is he who came by water and blood—Jesus Christ; not by the water only but by the water and the blood. And the Spirit is the one who testifies, because the Spirit is the truth. For there are three that testify: the Spirit and the water and the blood; and these three agree. If we receive the testimony of men, the testimony of God is greater, for this is the testimony of God that he has borne concerning his Son. Whoever believes in the Son of God has the testimony in himself. Whoever does not believe God has made him a liar, because he has not believed in the testimony that God has borne concerning his Son. And this is the testimony, that God gave us eternal life, and this life is in his Son. Whoever has the Son has life; whoever does not have the Son of God does not have life.

The Trinity with Chalice

ERIC GILL | WOODCUT

The artist attempts here to visually represent the Trinity. Although mysterious, the Trinity is a theological concept that offers sweet assurance of God's commitment to those he has saved. Before time began, the Father chose his people, then the Son died for his people, and now the Spirit sanctifies his people. Sinclair Ferguson wrote, "Woven into the warp and woof of the New Testament's exposition of what it means for us to be holy is the great groundwork that the self-existent, thrice holy, triune God has—in himself, by himself and for himself—committed himself and all three Persons of his being to bringing about the holiness of his own people. This is the Father's purpose, the Son's purchase and the Spirit's ministry."

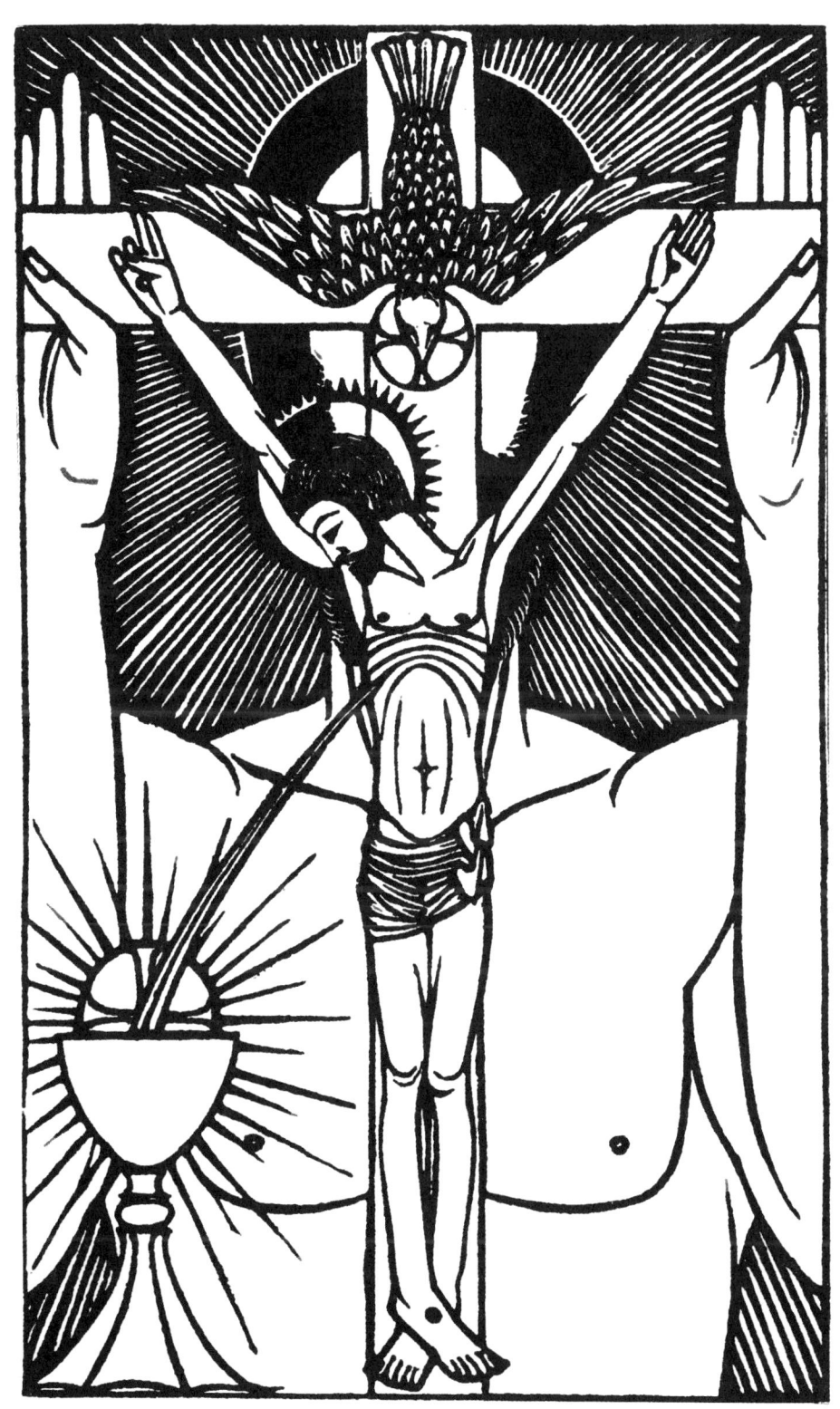

Jude 5–10

DESTRUCTION OF UNBELIEVERS

Now I want to remind you, although you once fully knew it, that Jesus, who saved a people out of the land of Egypt, afterward destroyed those who did not believe. And the angels who did not stay within their own position of authority, but left their proper dwelling, he has kept in eternal chains under gloomy darkness until the judgment of the great day—just as Sodom and Gomorrah and the surrounding cities, which likewise indulged in sexual immorality and pursued unnatural desire, serve as an example by undergoing a punishment of eternal fire.

Yet in like manner these people also, relying on their dreams, defile the flesh, reject authority, and blaspheme the glorious ones. But when the archangel Michael, contending with the devil, was disputing about the body of Moses, he did not presume to pronounce a blasphemous judgment, but said, "The Lord rebuke you." But these people blaspheme all that they do not understand, and they are destroyed by all that they, like unreasoning animals, understand instinctively.

The Lord Rebuke You
TANJA BUTLER | LINOCUT

In Ephesians it says to put on the whole armor of God, "that you may be able to withstand in the evil day, and having done all, to stand firm." Armor is for war, and there is a Great War going on in the spiritual realms between the forces of heaven and hell. One of those battles is described here, when Satan tried to take the body of Moses. Matthew Henry suggests that Satan wanted to tempt the Israelites to worship the grave of Moses in a similar way as the Bronze Serpent had been twisted for idol worship. Good is always in danger of being bent towards evil. In this passage Jude reminds the reader of the fiery ends decreed for those who twist good to evil ends: the freed Israelite slaves who put on the chains of idolatry; the once-glorious angels who attempted a coup d'état; and the Sodomites who embraced immoral sexual activity.

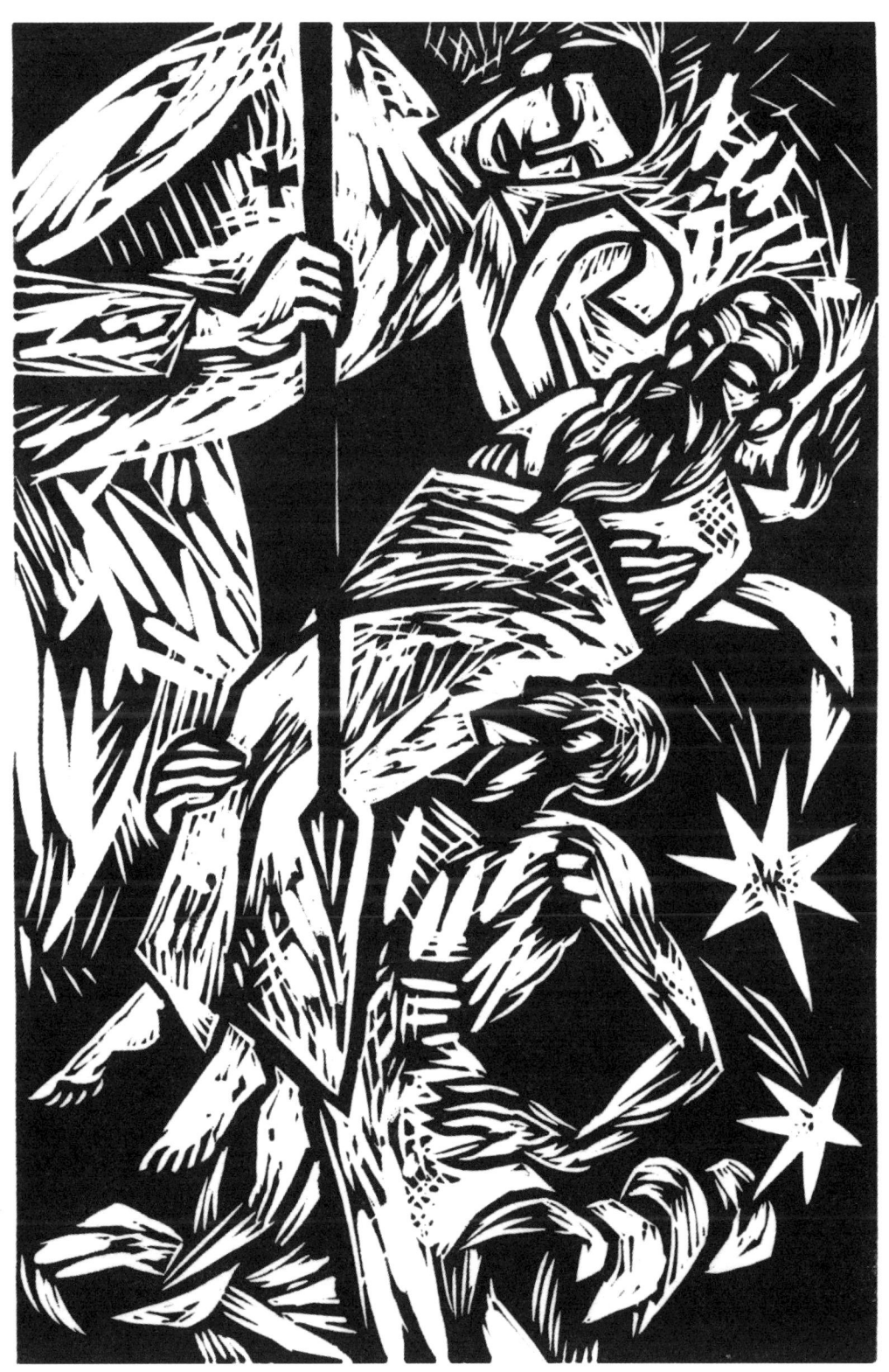

Revelation 9:13–21

PLAGUES AND UNREPENTANCE

Then the sixth angel blew his trumpet, and I heard a voice from the four horns of the golden altar before God, saying to the sixth angel who had the trumpet, "Release the four angels who are bound at the great river Euphrates." So the four angels, who had been prepared for the hour, the day, the month, and the year, were released to kill a third of mankind. The number of mounted troops was twice ten thousand times ten thousand; I heard their number. And this is how I saw the horses in my vision and those who rode them: they wore breastplates the color of fire and of sapphire and of sulfur, and the heads of the horses were like lions' heads, and fire and smoke and sulfur came out of their mouths. By these three plagues a third of mankind was killed, by the fire and smoke and sulfur coming out of their mouths. For the power of the horses is in their mouths and in their tails, for their tails are like serpents with heads, and by means of them they wound.

The rest of mankind, who were not killed by these plagues, did not repent of the works of their hands nor give up worshiping demons and idols of gold and silver and bronze and stone and wood, which cannot see or hear or walk, nor did they repent of their murders or their sorceries or their sexual immorality or their thefts.

The Warring Angels

ALBRECHT DÜRER | WOODCUT

The *Apocalypse* is a series of fifteen magnificent woodcuts based on the book of Revelation that was published 1498, a time when there were great anxieties of the end of the world—believed to be coming in two years. Fortunately, the end of the world did *not* come in 1500, and therefore Dürer was able to benefit from the great deal of fame that the series brought to him. It is interesting to notice the "third of mankind" that Dürer chose to represent in this piece: in the lower right-hand corner the pope and the emperor are about to be killed while in the lower left-hand corner an armored knight is also about to perish. It appears that the Reformation-era artist wanted his viewers to understand that religion, power, and wealth were no protection from the wrath of God. Only Grace alone through Faith in Christ alone will save a person at The End.

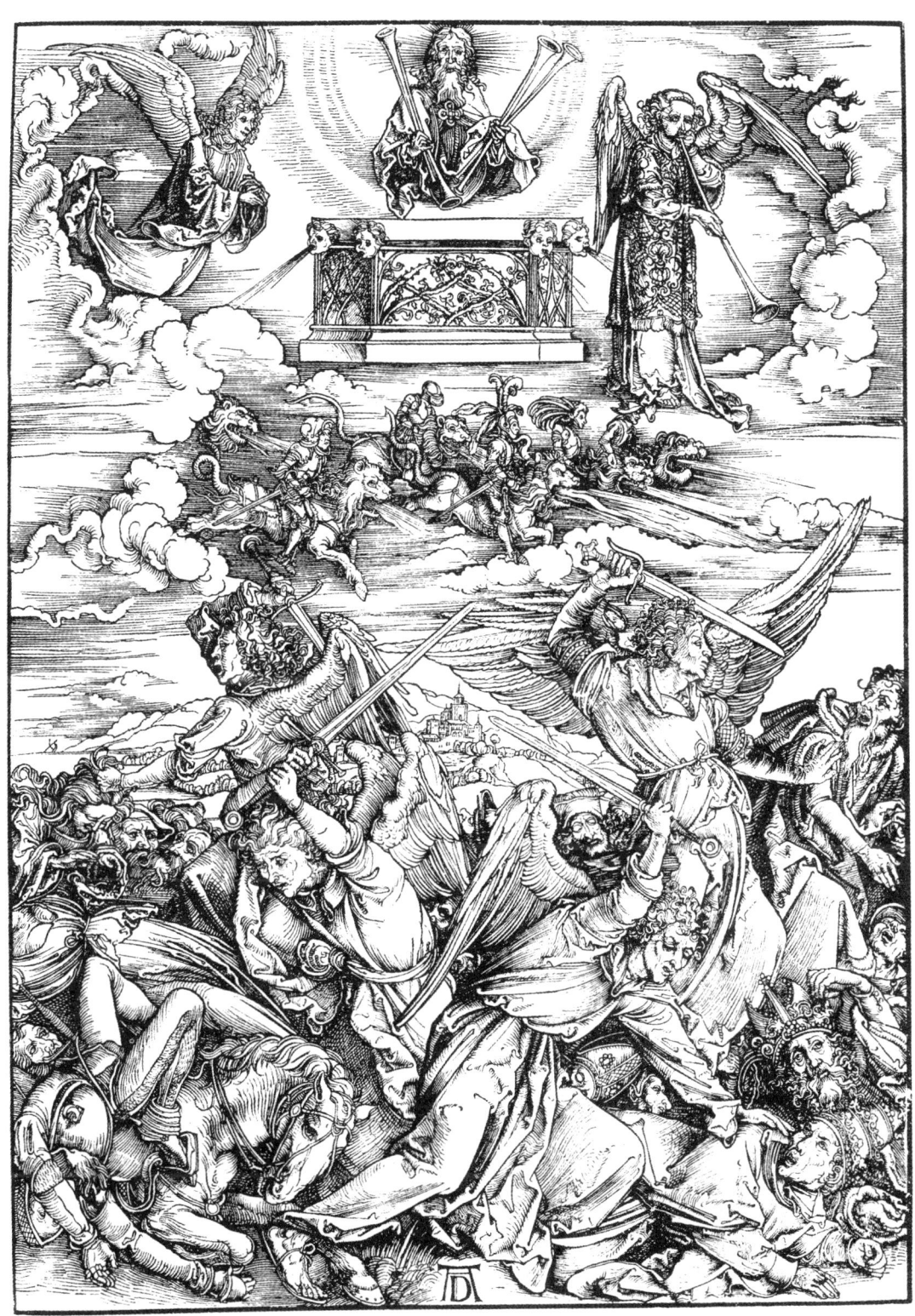

Revelation 18:20–24

THE FALL OF BABYLON

    Rejoice over her, O heaven,
        and you saints and apostles and prophets,
    for God has given judgment for you against her!"

Then a mighty angel took up a stone like a great millstone and threw it into the sea, saying,

    "So will Babylon the great city be thrown down with violence,
        and will be found no more;
    and the sound of harpists and musicians, of flute players
        and trumpeters, will be heard in you no more,
    and a craftsman of any craft
        will be found in you no more,
    and the sound of the mill
        will be heard in you no more,
    and the light of a lamp
        will shine in you no more,
    and the voice of bridegroom and bride
        will be heard in you no more,
    for your merchants were the great ones of the earth,
        and all nations were deceived by your sorcery.
    And in her was found the blood of prophets and of saints,
        and of all who have been slain on earth."

Apocalypse

ERIC GILL | WOODCUT

"At the end of history there will be no division between faithful Israel and Gentile Christians. All will honor Jesus together as the Messiah who saves us from our sins," writes theologian A.D. Bauer in *The End: A Readers' Guide to Revelation*. "In Revelation 18, the church celebrates the fall of unfaithful Jerusalem (vs. 20) because of her crimes and because in her was found the blood of the prophets and the saints." Some commentaries suggest that Babylon represents Rome. But Revelation 11:8 describes Babylon as the place "where their Lord was crucified." This, combined with the statement in verse 24 that "in her was found the blood of the prophets and the saints," requires Jerusalem, rather than Rome, to be Babylon because no prophet was killed in Rome. This woodcut was made in 1936 and comes from *The Aldine Bible*, Vol. IV.

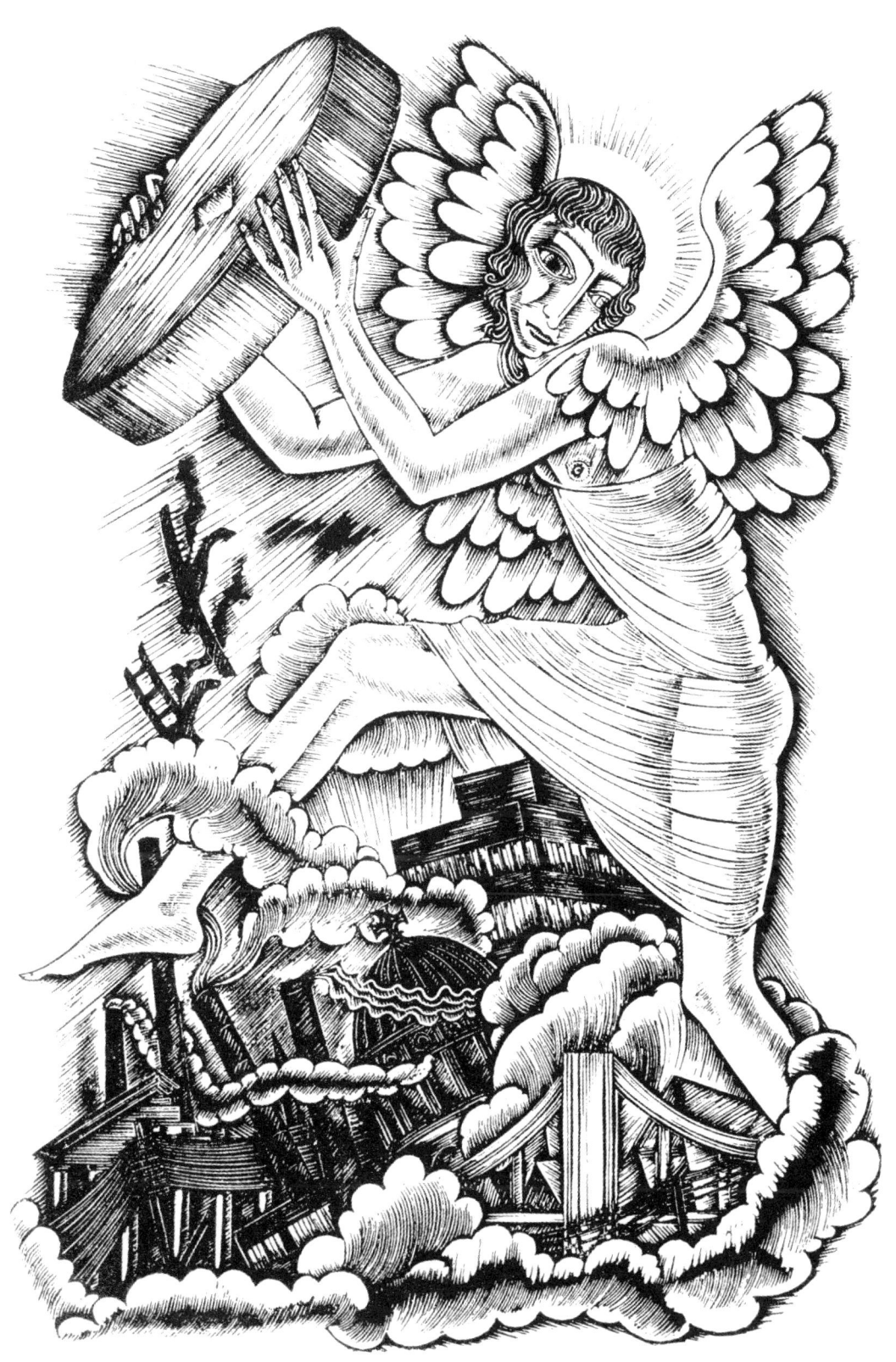

Revelation 21:1–10

NEW JERUSALEM

Then I saw a new heaven and a new earth, for the first heaven and the first earth had passed away, and the sea was no more. And I saw the holy city, new Jerusalem, coming down out of heaven from God, prepared as a bride adorned for her husband. And I heard a loud voice from the throne saying, "Behold, the dwelling place of God is with man. He will dwell with them, and they will be his people, and God himself will be with them as their God. He will wipe away every tear from their eyes, and death shall be no more, neither shall there be mourning, nor crying, nor pain anymore, for the former things have passed away."

And he who was seated on the throne said, "Behold, I am making all things new." Also he said, "Write this down, for these words are trustworthy and true." And he said to me, "It is done! I am the Alpha and the Omega, the beginning and the end. To the thirsty I will give from the spring of the water of life without payment. The one who conquers will have this heritage, and I will be his God and he will be my son. But as for the cowardly, the faithless, the detestable, as for murderers, the sexually immoral, sorcerers, idolaters, and all liars, their portion will be in the lake that burns with fire and sulfur, which is the second death."

Then came one of the seven angels who had the seven bowls full of the seven last plagues and spoke to me, saying, "Come, I will show you the Bride, the wife of the Lamb." And he carried me away in the Spirit to a great, high mountain, and showed me the holy city Jerusalem coming down out of heaven from God, having the glory of God . . .

New Creation

NED BUSTARD | LINOCUT

N. T. Wright writes, "The last scene in the Bible is the new heaven and the new earth, and the symbol for that is the marriage of Christ and his church. It's not just one or two verses here and there which say this or that. It's an entire narrative which works with this complementarity so that a male-plus-female marriage is a signpost or a signal about the goodness of the original creation and God's intention for the eventual new heavens and new earth." In this piece the woodcut from the beginning of *Revealed* is remade: the four winds are now the four winged beasts, the heavenly beings are now the twenty-four elders (represented by the symbols for the twelve tribes and the twelve apostles), and the Garden is now a City with the Tree of Life growing out of it. The ships of Tarshish from Isaiah 60 have arrived, and the Bride stands next to the Bridegroom in joyful anticipation of the great Wedding Feast.

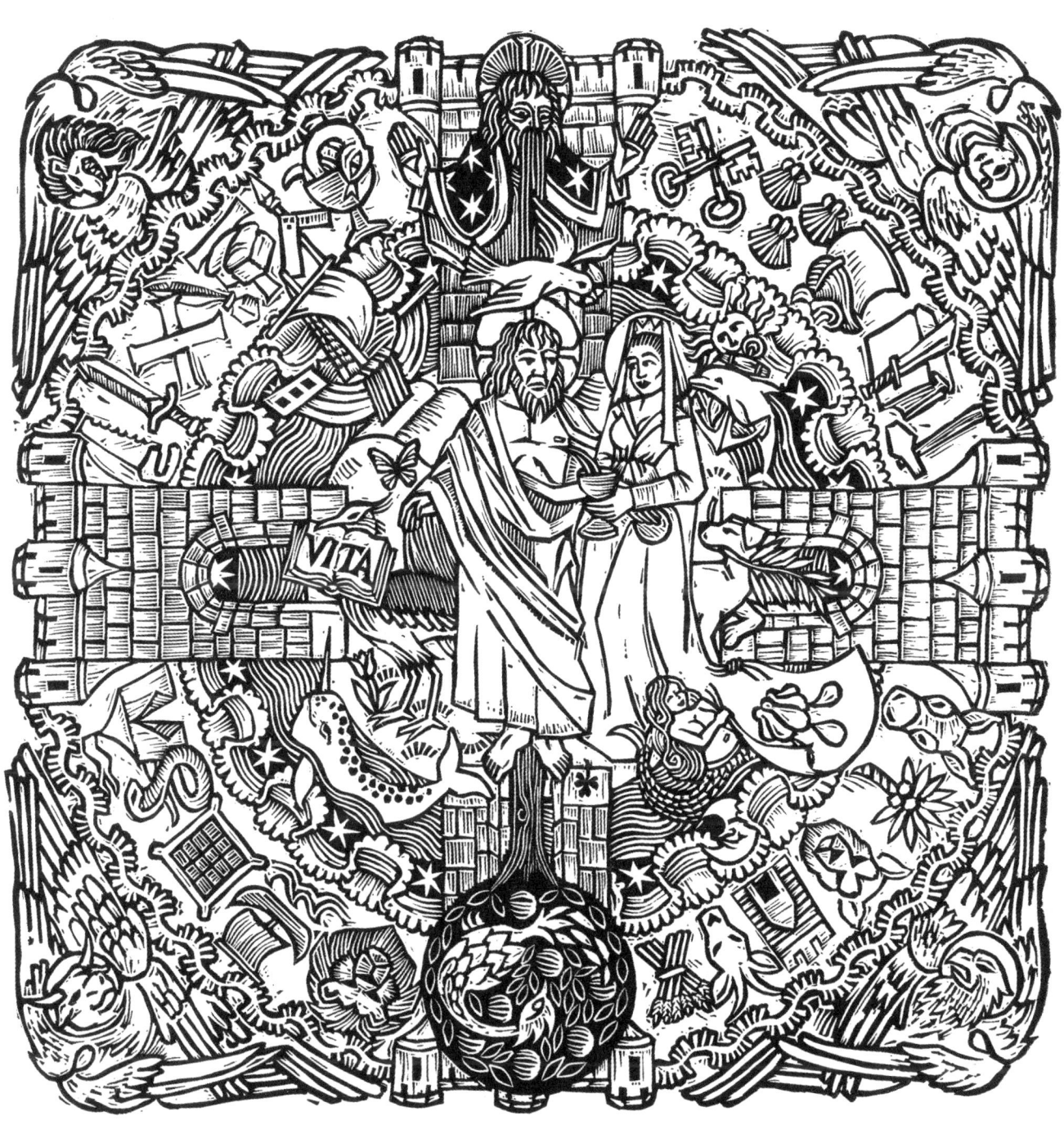

Artist Bios

Wayne Adams (b. 1974)
Adams is a Brooklyn-based artist who received his B.F.A. from Calvin College and M.F.A. from Washington University in St. Louis. He has exhibited throughout the Midwest, New York, and Vienna, Austria. Adams currently serves as president of the board of Christians in the Visual Arts.
wayneadamsstudio.com

Ernst Barlach (1870–1938)
Barlach was a German expressionist sculptor, printmaker and writer. Although he was a supporter of the war in the years leading to World War I, his participation in the war made him change his position, and he is mostly known for his sculptures protesting against the war. This created many conflicts during the rise of the Nazi Party, when most of his works were confiscated as degenerate art.

Rick Beerhorst (b. 1960)
Beerhorst is a narrative figure painter and printmaker. He is a recipient of an NEA artist grant and two Pollock/Krasner awards. His art is featured in prominent collections around the world. The Beerhorst family has been the subject of an Etsy.com artist profile film. Rick and his family currently live and work in Grand Rapids, Michigan, on an micro urban farm downtown.
studiobeerhorst.com

William Blake (1757–1827)
Blake was an English painter, poet, and printmaker. His writings have influenced countless writers and artists through the ages, and he has been hailed as both a major poet and an original thinker. It is said that Blake's relief etching technique was the most innovative aspect of his art.

Micah Bloom (b. 1975)
Bloom is an artist and educator who lives in North Dakota. He holds an M.F.A. in painting and drawing from the University of Iowa and has been selected for numerous artist-in-residence fellowships. His works have been published in literary and art journals, and he has shown work nationally and internationally, including private galleries in China and the Museum of Contemporary Art Shanghai.
micahbloom.com

Katherine Brimberry (b. 1947)
Brimberry is a printmaker and serves as senior Master Printer for Flatbed Press. Brimberry founded Flatbed Press, a collaborative publishing fine print studio, in 1989. Her own work is represented by Flatbed Press and Gallery and is in many collections including the Modern Art Museum of Fort Worth, Texas Tech University Library and the 3M Permanent Collection. Her work was included in the *CIVA Silver 2005* portfolio.

Hans Burgkmair (1473–1531)
Burgkmair was a German painter and woodcut printmaker. His work is known for its striking compositions and blend of Italian Renaissance forms and German style. He was responsible for nearly half of the 135 prints in *The Triumphs of Maximilian* and appears to be the first printmaker to create a print that was designed to be printed only in color.

Margaret Bustard (b. 1999)
Maggie was introduced to printmaking while homeschooling. In collaboration with her father she developed a body of work based on the animals on Noah's Ark. Together they presented a show of their work called *The Flood* in the Square Halo Gallery.

Ned Bustard (b. 1967)
Bustard is a graphic designer, children's book illustrator, author, and printmaker. Books he has worked on include the *Legends & Leagues* series, *The Sailing Saint, Ella Sings Jazz, Squalls Before War: His Majesty's Schooner* Sultana, *It Was Good: Making Art to the Glory of God, The Church History ABC's,* and *Bigger on the Inside: Christianity and Doctor Who.*
nedbustard.com

Tanja Butler (b. 1955)
Butler is a painter, printmaker, liturgical artist, and illustrator. Her collection of 600 graphic images, *Icon: Visual Images for Every Sunday,* was published by

Augsburg Fortress Publishers. Her work is represented in the Vatican Museum of Contemporary Art; the Billy Graham Center Museum at Wheaton, Illinois; the Portland (Maine) Museum of Art; the DeCordova Museum in Lincoln, Massachusetts; and the Boston Public Library.
tanjabutler.com

Matthew L. Clark (b. 1976)
Clark received a B.F.A. from the University of Central Florida with a drawing specialization and earned an M.F.A. in the area of printmaking at the University of Florida. He currently teaches art at The Geneva School.
drawingmatthewclark.com

Lovis Corinth (1858–1925)
Corinth was a painter and printmaker whose work brought together Impressionism and Expressionism. His early work was naturalistic, but after a stroke it loosened and took on expressionistic qualities. Corinth explored nearly every printmaking technique, but favored drypoint and lithography.

Erin Cross (b.1980)
Cross received her M.F.A. in visual studies with a focus in printmaking. Her work has been published and exhibited nationally and internationally and resides in numerous private and public collections. She is currently an adjunct professor in drawing and design methods.
erinmcross.com

Albrecht Dürer (1471–1528)
Dürer was a German painter, engraver, printmaker, mathematician, and theorist. Dürer revolutionized printmaking, raising it to the level of an independent art form and is considered to be one of the greatest artists of the Northern Renaissance. His body of work includes altarpieces, religious works, numerous portraits and self-portraits, copper engravings, and watercolour landscapes.

Jean Duvet (1485–c. 1570)
Duvet was a French goldsmith and engraver, now best known for his engravings. His most famous works are a series of twenty-three engravings on the Apocalypse that borrow heavily from Dürer's famous series of the same name. His other noted work is his series of six prints on the unicorn.

Wayne Lacson Forte (b. 1950)
Forte has an M.F.A. from the University of California, Irvine. He is a full-time painter and occasional teacher who resides in Laguna Niguel, California. Forte specializes in contemporary interpretations of biblical subjects.
wayneforte.com

Richard Gaston (b. 1967)
Richard Gaston received his art degree from Wheaton College in 1989. While concentrating in drawing and printmaking for years, Richard has also worked as a sculptor and photographer. His photo book *Lancaster City* was exhibited at the Griffin Museum of Photography in 2015.
richardgastonimages.com

Eric Gill (1882–1940)
Gill was an English sculptor, typeface designer, stonecutter, and printmaker who was associated with the Arts and Crafts movement. He is a controversial figure, with his well-known religious views and subject matter being seen as at odds with his erotic art. The typeface you are now reading was designed by Gill, based on sans serif lettering originally intended for the London Underground.

Steve Halla (b. 1972)
Halla is a printmaker and assistant professor of art at Union University in Jackson, Tennessee. He received a Th.M. in historical theology from Dallas Theological Seminary and a Ph.D. in aesthetic studies from the University of Texas. He learned the art of woodblock printmaking at the Carving Arts Center in Plano, Texas, under the tutelage of artist Carl Bindhammer.

Craig Hawkins (b. 1978)
Hawkins earned an M.F.A. in drawing and painting from the Lamar Dodd School of Art. He works as a professional studio artist and teaches at Valdosta State University. His work has been included in such publications as

Artists *continued*

New American Paintings, Juxtapose Magazine, and Manifest Gallery's *International Drawing Annual.* Mason Fine Art gallery and Anne Neilson Fine Art gallery currently represent his work.
craighawkinsart.com

David Busch Johnson (b. 1934)
Johnson is a retired college art professor, calligrapher, printmaker, and sculptor. Exhibits include two solo shows and numerous other exhibits in the Kansas City area. His works are included in many private collections.

Diego Jourdan Pereira (b. 1977)
Jourdan is a professional artist specializing in comics, illustration, restoration, and printmaking. Mainly known for his work on Teenage Mutant Ninja Turtles, Transformers, Toy Story, the Smurfs, and Lego. Diego's clients list includes publishers DC Thomson & Co. Ltd., Topps, Immediate Media, Dover Publications, ACK Media, El Mercurio S.A.P., and Grupo Expansion.
diegojourdanpro.strikingly.com

Edward Knippers (b. 1946)
Knippers is a painter and printmaker. His work has been exhibited widely in the United States as well as abroad in Italy, England, and Greece. His work is included in numerous public and private collections, including the Vatican Museum of Contemporary Religious Art, Rome; the Grunewald Print Collection at the Armand Hammer Museum; and the Billy Graham Museum. His work has been featured in many publications including *Life Magazine, Christianity Today, New American Paintings,* and the *New Art Examiner.*
edwardknippers.com

Chris Koelle (b. 1982)
Koelle is an illustrator and designer with a deep love of printmaking. He is a resident member of The Printshop in Greenville, South Carolina. His illustrated works include *The Book of Revelation* graphic novel, *The History of Redemption, JŌB* (a retelling by John Piper), and *Men in Black,* an animated segment in the Oscar-nominated documentary *Operation Homecoming: Writing the Wartime Experience.*
chriskoelle.com

Kevin Lindholm (b.1981)
Lindholm is a teacher, illustrator, and printmaker. He currently teaches art, design, history, and worldview at Sequitur Classical Academy in Baton Rouge, Louisiana. Originally from California, Kevin studied traditional, printmaking techniques at the University of Louisiana Lafayette and Ohio State University.

Franz Marc (1880–1916)
Marc was a one of the key figures of the German Expressionist movement. In 1936 and 1937, the Nazis condemned the late Marc as an *entarteter Künstler* (degenerate artist) and ordered approximately 130 of his works removed from exhibition in German museums.

Chris Stoffel Overvoorde (b. 1934)
Overvoorde, a trained diesel mechanic, is a printmaker, painter, graphic designer and a worship environmentalist. He joined the art faculty at Calvin College in 1966 and currently is professor of art emeritus. He is the author of *Passing the Colors.*
calvin.edu/~over

Steve Prince (b. 1968)
Prince received his B.F.A. from Xavier University of Louisiana and his M.F.A. in printmaking and sculpture from Michigan State University. He is currently an Assistant Professor of Printmaking and Drawing at Allegheny College. He has taught with the Art League since 1995, and has shown his art in various exhibitions and has lectured internationally.
eyekons.com/steve_prince

Mark T. Smith (b. 1968)
Smith's work is has been displayed in the U.S. and abroad, including all the major contemporary art fairs. Corporate patronage helped Smith become an increasingly recognizable figure in the crowded New York City art world, and his patrons included MTV, Pepsi, Taco Bell, AT&T, Budweiser, VH1, Walt Disney, Absolut Vodka, the United States Olympic Team, and more.
marktsmith.com

Justin Sorensen (b. 1986)
Sorensen is an artist working in performance, printmaking, sculpture, photography, and drawing. He received his M.F.A. from the Rhode Island School of Design. His work has been exhibited throughout the United States, most notably at David Krut Projects, the Granoff Center, and the Heuser Art Center.
justinsorensen.us

Ryan Stander (b. 1975)
Stander is a photographer and printmaker currently serving as an assistant professor of art at Minot State University, where he also directs Flat Tail Press. His work has been exhibited internationally in Canada, South Africa, China, Central and South America; nationally in New York, Massachusetts, New Jersey, and Texas; and across the Upper Midwest.
ryanstander.com

Rembrandt van Rijn (1606–1669)
Rembrandt is one of the greatest artists of all time. His ability to translate the stark visual contrast of black and white, which is inherent to the print medium, into dynamic compositions that realize spiritual contention made him a printmaker with few equals. He achieved early success as a portrait painter, taught many important Dutch painters, and saw both his etchings and paintings receive high praise during his lifetime.

Henri Van Straten (1892–1944)
Van Straten was one of "The Five," who were part of the renewal of the woodcut as an artistic medium in Belgium after the First World War. He was a wood cutter, painter, lithographer, etcher, and illustrator. He had several gallery and museum exhibitions, including showing his work at the Museum Dhondt-Dhaenens.

Kreg Yingst (b. 1959)
Yingst is a painter and printmaker. He has illustrated and self-published *Psalms in Block Prints and Light from Darkness: Portraits and Prayers*, among a handful of others. His works can be found in numerous collections including at Purdue University, Pensacola State College, and the Halsey Institute of Contemporary Art.
kregyingst.com

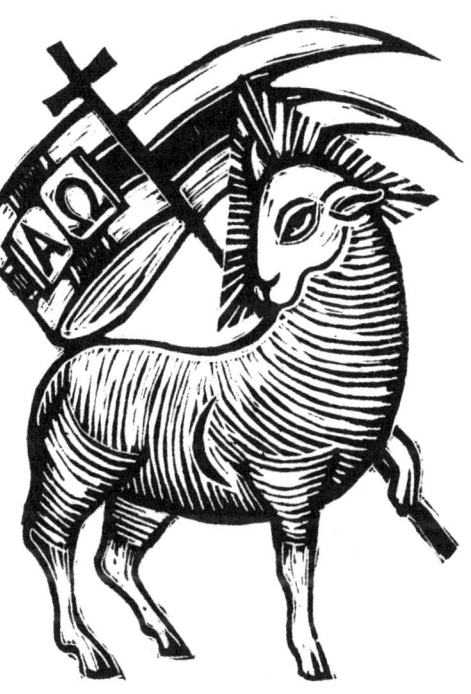

Thank you to all of the artists who gave of their gifts to fill these pages. Your talents are incredible, your insights into God's Word are invigorating, and your generousity is inspiring. Also, a very special word of thanks to my dear friend Matthew L. Clark (a master printmaker and a godly man), for giving me a love of making prints. —*Ned Bustard*

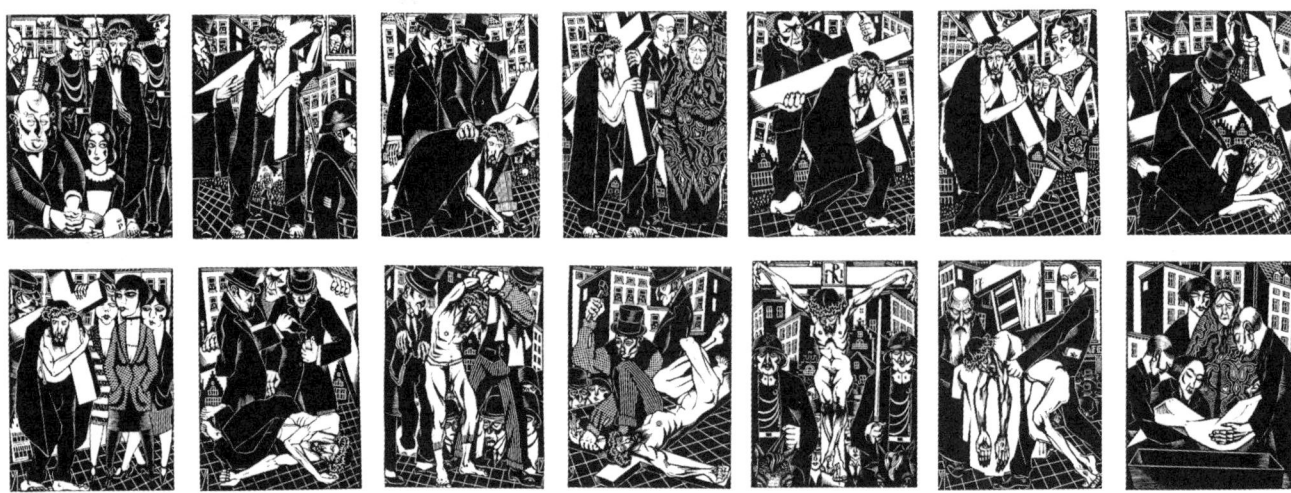

SQUARE HALO BOOKS
EXTRAORDINARY BOOKS FOR ORDINARY SAINTS

C.S. LEWIS AND THE ARTS: CREATIVITY IN THE SHADOWLANDS

"We need more books like this: books that not only celebrate and decipher Lewis's defense of the arts and of the ineradicable links between the Good, the True, and the Beautiful, but that wrestle alongside Lewis, extending and nuancing his arguments so that they will speak with direct and prophetic power to our modern and postmodern colleges and universities."

—Dr. Louis Markos, author of *Restoring Beauty: The Good, the True, and the Beautiful in the Writings of C.S. Lewis*

IT WAS GOOD: MAKING ART TO THE GLORY OF GOD

"*It Was Good* is one of the best examples I know of the new day that is dawning in Christian conversation on the arts. What we have needed is a thick description both of Christianity and of art making. And both are here in abundance, along with generous displays of great art motivated by faith both from the present and the past."

—William Dyrness, author of *Visual Faith: Art, Theology, and Worship in Dialogue*

OBJECTS OF GRACE: CONVERSATIONS ON CREATIVITY AND FAITH

"A colorful and concise collection of interviews and art from some of America's most intriguing Christian artists. [James] Romaine interviews ten artists, presenting color reproductions of the artists' work along with the text of the interviews. Each artist dialogues on what it means for a Christian to engage in the creating process."

— Gregory Wolfe, editor of *Image: A Journal of the Arts and Religion*

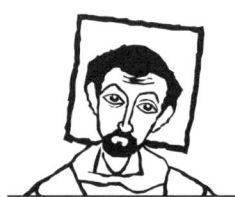

In Christian art, the square halo identified a living person presumed to be a saint. Square Halo Books is devoted to publishing works that present contextually sensitive biblical studies, and practical instruction consistent with the Doctrines of the Reformation. The goal of Square Halo Books is to provide materials useful for encouraging and equipping the saints. To see all the titles from Square Halo books, visit: www.SquareHaloBooks.com.